Making Sense of Heidegger

NEW HEIDEGGER RESEARCH

Series Editors

The New Heidegger Research series promotes informed and critical dialogue that breaks new philosophical ground by taking into account the full range of Heidegger's thought, as well as the enduring questions raised by his work.

Making Sense of Heidegger: A Paradigm Shift, Thomas Sheehan
After the Greeks, Laurence Paul Hemming (forthcoming)
Heidegger and the Environment, Casey Rentmeester (forthcoming)

Making Sense of Heidegger

A Paradigm Shift

Thomas Sheehan

ROWMAN &
LITTLEFIELD
INTERNATIONAL

London • New York

Published by Rowman & Littlefield International Ltd.
Unit A, Whitacre Mews, 26-34 Stannary Street, London SE11 4AB
www.rowmaninternational.com

Rowman & Littlefield International Ltd. is an affiliate
of Rowman & Littlefield
4501 Forbes Boulevard, Suite 200, Lanham, Maryland 20706, USA
With additional offices in Boulder, New York, Toronto (Canada),
and Plymouth (UK)
www.rowman.com

British Library Cataloguing in Publication Data
A catalogue record for this book is available from the British Library

ISBN: HB 978-1-78348-118-7
PB 978-1-78348-119-4

Library of Congress Cataloging-in-Publication Data
Sheehan, Thomas.
Making sense of Heidegger : a paradigm shift / Thomas Sheehan.
pages cm. — (New Heidegger research)
Includes bibliographical references.
ISBN 978-1-78348-118-7 (cloth : alk. paper) — ISBN 978-1-78348-119-4 (pbk. : alk. paper) — ISBN 978-1-78348-120-0 (electronic)
1. Heidegger, Martin, 1889–1976. I. Title.
B3279.H49S426 2015
193—dc23 2014021462

∞™ The paper used in this publication meets the minimum requirements of American National Standard for Information Sciences—Permanence of Paper for Printed Library Materials, ANSI/NISO Z39.48-1992.

Printed in the United States of America

FOR
WILLIAM J. RICHARDSON, S.J.
Gentleman and scholar *sans pareil*

In respect and gratitude

ἀπὸ τῆς ἀληθινῆς σοφίας,
ἣν φιλοσόφως τε καὶ ὑγιῶς ἐπήσκησεν

Contents

Frequently Cited German Texts and Their Abbreviated English Translations

(For a complete list, see “Bibliographies: Heidegger’s German Texts and Their English Translations”)

SZ = *Being and Time* (Macquarrie-Robinson)
GA 2 = *Being and Time* (Stambaugh)
GA 3 = *Kant and the Problem of Metaphysics*
GA 4 = *Elucidations of Hölderlin’s Poetry*
GA 5 = *Off the Beaten Track*
GA 6 = *Pathmarks*
GA 8 = *What Is Called Thinking?*
GA 9 = *Pathmarks*
GA 10 = *The Principle of Reason*
GA 11 = *Identity and Difference*
GA 12 = *On the Way to Language*
GA 14 = *On Time and Being*
GA 15 = *Heraclitus Seminar 1966/67* and *Four Seminars*
GA 17 = *Introduction to Phenomenological Research*
GA 18 = *Basic Concepts of Aristotelian Philosophy*
GA 19 = *Plato’s Sophist*
GA 20 = *History of the Concept of Time*
GA 21 = *Logic: The Question of Truth*
GA 22 = *Basic Concepts of Ancient Philosophy*
GA 24 = *The Basic Problems of Phenomenology*
GA 25 = *Phenomenological Interpretation of Kant’s Critique of Pure Reason*
GA 26 = *The Metaphysical Foundations of Logic*
GA 27 = *Introduction to Philosophy*
GA 29/30 = *The Fundamental Concepts of Metaphysics*
GA 31 = *The Essence of Human Freedom*
GA 32 = *Hegel’s Phenomenology of Spirit*
GA 33 = *Aristotle’s Metaphysics Θ 1–3*
GA 34 = *The Essence of Truth: On Plato’s Cave Allegory and the Theaetetus*
GA 36/37 = *Being and Truth*

GA 38 = *Logic as the Question Concerning the Essence of Language*
GA 39 = *Hölderlin's Hymn "Germanien" and "Der Rhein"*
GA 40 = *Introduction to Metaphysics*
GA 41 = *What Is a Thing?*
GA 42 = *Schelling's Treatise on the Essence of Human Freedom*
GA 45 = *Basic Questions of Philosophy: Selected "Problems" of "Logic"*
GA 50 = *Introduction to Philosophy—Thinking and Poetizing*
GA 51 = *Basic Concepts*
GA 53 = *Hölderlin's Hymn "The Ister*
GA 54 = *Parmenides*
GA 56/57 = *Towards the Definition of Philosophy*
GA 58 = *Basic Problems of Phenomenology: Winter Semester 1919/20*
GA 59 = *Phenomenology of Intuition and Expression*
GA 60 = *Phenomenology of Religious Life*
GA 61 = *Phenomenological Interpretations of Aristotle*
GA 63 = *Ontology: Hermeneutics of Facticity*
GA 64 = *The Concept of Time: The First Draft of Being and Time*
GA 65 = *Contributions to Philosophy: Of the Event*
GA 66 = *Mindfulness*
GA 71 = *The Event*
GA 77 = *Country Path Conversations*
GA 79 = *Bremen and Freiburg Lectures*
GA 85 = *On the Essence of Language*

Foreword

The following effort at a paradigm shift in interpreting Heidegger is deeply indebted to the work and guidance of my lifelong teacher, mentor, and friend, William J. Richardson, S.J., whose monumental achievement, *Heidegger: Through Phenomenology to Thought*, first opened my eyes to the significance of Heidegger some fifty years ago. I still remember the effect of reading, as a fourth-year philosophy undergraduate, his first article on Heidegger, which appeared in 1963 in the *Revue Philosophique de Louvain* under the title "Heidegger and the Problem of Thought." This was a separate publication of what would appear later that year as the introduction to his book. I had wrestled for two years with the few Heidegger texts available at the time, including the new translation of *Being and Time* (1962) and all the English and French secondary sources I could get my hands on. It was all very exciting—and very dark. Then suddenly, with this article the clouds parted. To adapt Alexander Pope:

> Heidegger and all his works lay hid in night.
> God said "Let Richardson be!" and all was light.

A thorough reading of his book in the summer of 1964 set my path to Fordham University, where he was then teaching, and to the extraordinary experience of studying under him. For that, and for the years of friendship, support, and collegial exchange since then, I am forever grateful.

The present effort would not be possible without Fr. Richardson's lucid, incisive, and richly documented masterwork, the first text to make sense of the whole of Heidegger as it was then known and to render that accessible to non-German readers. Drawing on his vast erudition and critical penetration while coming to Heidegger at a later date and from a different starting point, I conceive of the present effort as building on his immense accomplishments. That said, I make no claim that he agrees with what I have written here. The dedication of this book to him is simply an expression of how much I owe him by way of philosophical insight and wholehearted encouragement in the execution of a project about which he has expressed occasional—and serious—reservations.

As regards the title of the book: I try to make sense of Heidegger by showing that his work, both early and late, was not about "being" as Western philosophy has understood that term for over twenty-five hundred years, but rather about sense itself: meaningfulness and its source. In schematic form:

1. I read his work strictly as what he himself declared it to be—namely, *phenomenology*, which means that it is about one thing only: sense or meaning (I take them as the same), both in itself and in terms of its source.
2. Heidegger understands both “beingness” (*Seiendheit*) in traditional metaphysics and “being” (*Sein*) in his own work as formally the same.[1] Both of these terms are formal indications of the “realness” of things, however that realness might be read.[2] But as a phenomenologist Heidegger argues that both of these co-equal expressions, whether implicitly (in metaphysics) or explicitly (in Heidegger’s own work) bespeak the *Anwesen* of things—that is, their meaningful presence within the worlds of human interests and concerns, whether those be theoretical, practical, aesthetic, religious, or whatever.
3. However, Heidegger’s project finally makes sense only when we realize that he was after the *source* of such meaningful presence, whatever that source might turn out to be. To put it in formally indicative terms, that source would be whatever makes it necessary and possible for us to understand things only discursively—that is, only in terms of their meaningful presence, whatever form that presence might take. Heidegger argued that this source turns out to be what he called “the appropriated clearing” (*die ereignete Lichtung*),[3] which is the same as thrown-open/appropriated human ex-sistence (*das geworfene/ereignete Da-sein*).

I argue that the “being” discourse, the *Sein*-ology that has dominated Heidegger research for the last half-century, has hit the wall. Since 1989, when Heidegger’s *Beiträge zur Philosophie* was published (English translation, *Contributions to Philosophy*), it has become increasingly clear that what I call “the classical paradigm”—the various ways mainstream Heidegger scholarship has understood his work over the last fifty years—is no longer able to accommodate the full range of his lectures and writings as they are now published in his virtually complete *Gesamtausgabe*. As my late colleague Richard Rorty once advised me, “When your argument hits the wall, start making some distinctions.” The present work takes that advice seriously. In the spirit of Aristotle’s διορίσωμεν,[4] it is all about distinctions, and especially the dis-

---

1. See chapter 2, note 11.

2. I use the word “realness” in what Heidegger calls its “traditional” (and still formally indicative) sense of “being”: SZ 211.26 = 254.32–33. See also below, chapter 2, note 6.

3. GA 71: 211.9 = 180.1–2.

4. *Metaphysics* X 6, 1048a26: “Let us make some distinctions.” All citations from Aristotle in Greek are taken from *Aristotelis opera*, ed. Immanuel Bekker.

tinctions that we must make now that the Heideggerian "being"-discourse has exhausted its explanatory power.

Some of my philosophy colleagues (not to mention my three sons) have suggested that it is about time that I move on beyond the narrow confines of Heidegger scholarship into the wider world of philosophical discourse and into the arguably more pressing issues—economic, social, and political—that call for one's attention. I agree. But I want to be sure that when I move beyond Heidegger, it is *Heidegger* that I am moving beyond, and not a caricature of his philosophy. It may be finally impossible (and it is certainly not my life's goal) to find out what he "really" was driving at throughout those 102 volumes of his *Collected Works*, but I thought it was at least worth a try. So over the last few years I have closely read or reread as many of those volumes as I could in an effort to ferret out and perhaps understand what was the "single thought" that he said guided him through the six decades of his philosophical career. This volume presents what I argue is that single thought, as well as some of its philosophical ramifications.

Does what follows constitute a "paradigm shift"? And if so, does this paradigm explain more of Heidegger than do the alternatives? The reader will have to decide. Given many of the readings of Heidegger that are currently in vogue, I think the answer to both questions is yes, and the course of the argument will attempt to show as much.

The text is heavily annotated with references to Heidegger's texts, but with few references to the secondary literature in any language. There are two reasons for this. First, many scholars will take this reading of Heidegger to be quite controversial if not downright wrong—and they may well be right. So I wanted to show, as thoroughly as I can, how my reading is grounded in Heidegger's own texts and not in the work, as excellent as it might be, of others. (The footnotes may also provide, as William J. Richardson once put it, "a few friendly spots of blood that would show how someone else made his way over the rocks.")[5] Secondly, my own understandings are heavily indebted—and gratefully so—to the superb interpretations of Heidegger that have been generated by scholars throughout the world (with a special shout-out to my colleagues in the Heidegger Circle). Nonetheless, I want to assume full and sole responsibility for what I write, especially for any eventual errors.

As regards references, I cite Heidegger's texts by page and line (the line number follows the period) in both the *Gesamtausgabe* and the current English translations. The bibliography at the end of this book lists the titles of the German sources and the corresponding translations. An exception to the rule: I cite the German pagination of Heidegger's *Sein und Zeit* not in the *Gesamtausgabe*

5. Richardson, *Heidegger*, xxviii.9–10; also 707.2.

edition (GA 2) but in the eleventh, unchanged edition published by Max Niemeyer Verlag in 1967, which is more readily available to readers. I abbreviate the parts and divisions of *Being and Time*, both as published and as promised, as follows: SZ I.1, I.2, I.3 and II.1, II.2, and II.3. (See chapter 5 for a diagram of the book.) I often use my own translations from the German or else change and adapt the published English translations without notice. All Greek and Latin terms and phrases are explained either within the text or in the footnotes. I cite Aristotle's works sometimes by their English titles, sometimes by their traditional Latin titles. For example, I refer to Aristotle's *De anima* and to his *De interpretatione* rather than use their English titles because I think that "soul" is not a proper translation of ψυχή and that "interpretation" is not what Aristotle meant by ἑρμηνεία. The Latin *anima* and *interpretatio* may be little better, but they might help de-familiarize the usual titles and point to the Greek terms that underlie them.

SOME REMARKS ON TERMINOLOGY AND TRANSLATIONS

Heidegger's technical lexicon can be quite confusing, not just because he gives common words uncommon meanings but more importantly because he was notoriously sloppy in how he used his key term, *Sein* (being). Chapter 1 provides the rationale for how I translate that word, but some brief indications may be helpful at this point.

Throughout his fifty-year career Heidegger was scandalously inconsistent in how he employed the word *Sein*, and that has thrown off the scholarship for over eighty years. Nonetheless, he does insist that whatever form the word "being" takes in a given philosopher (for example, as εἶδος in Plato, or ἐνέργεια in Aristotle, or *esse* in Aquinas), the term always bespeaks what that philosopher thinks constitutes the "realness" of things, or what Heidegger calls the *Sein* or *Seiendheit* of entities. In his clearer moments Heidegger reads *das Sein* ("being") and *die Seiendheit* ("beingness") as the same: co-equal, formally indicative names for whatever a given philosopher thinks the realness of things consists in. But in his less clear moments he also uses *das Sein* to name the thrown-open clearing. To avoid the confusion generated by these two very different uses of *Sein*, I will reserve the word *Sein* exclusively for the *being of things*.

That brings us to the next step. As a phenomenologist, Heidegger understands *Sein* in all its historical incarnations as the *meaningful presence* (*Anwesen*) of things to human beings—that is, as the changing *significance* of things within various contexts of human interests and concerns. *Sein* as the meaningful presence of things holds both for metaphysics, which generally was unaware of this fact, and for Heidegger's own philosophical work. Hence throughout this book the terms "being," "beingness," "meaningful presence," "significance," and "intelligibility" (*Sein, Seiendheit, Anwesen, Bedeutsamkeit, Verständlichkeit*) will be used interchangeably to refer to the same thing—namely, the "realness" of things in the way Heidegger the *phenomenologist* understands that heuristic term. For him things are real to the extent that they are meaningfully present (*anwesend*) to human beings. (See chapter 2: Heidegger's interpretation of *Metaphysics* IX 10.) Even though this position—being = realness = meaningfulness—is Heidegger's own, it may not make all Heideggerians happy. But at least it will obviate the hair-pulling confusion caused by Heidegger's extraordinary carelessness in his use of the word *Sein*.

But this phenomenological interpretation of *Sein* as *Anwesen* is only the first step. The single issue that drove Heidegger's work was not being-as-meaningful-presence but rather the *source or origin* of such meaningful presence—what he called *die Herkunft von Anwesen*. He called that source the clearing (*die Lichtung*), or more precisely, the thrown-open or appropriated clearing (*die ereignete Lichtung*). By contrast, many Heideggerians think that "being itself (*das Sein selbst*) is "the thing itself" of Heidegger's philosophy. However, as Heidegger uses that phrase in its primary and proper sense, "being itself" is not any kind of *Sein* at all. It is not even a phenomenon, much less the Final Phenomenon, the "Super-*Sein*" that it has morphed into in the secondary literature. "Being itself" or "being as such" is a way of saying "the *essence* of being," and all three of those terms are simply *formal indications* and heuristic stand-ins that point toward the sought-for answer to Heidegger's question—namely, whatever will turn out to be the "essence" of being, that which accounts for and is the source or origin of meaningful presence at all. And that turns out to be the appropriated clearing, or in shorthand, appropriation (*Ereignis*)—which is simply the later Heidegger's re-inscription of what he had earlier called "thrownness" (*Geworfenheit*) or "thrown-openness" (*der geworfener Entwurf*). Metaphorically speaking, as thrown-open (i.e., appropriated), human being is the "open space" or clearing within which the meaningful presence of things can occur. (The previous sentence is Heidegger's philosophy in a nutshell.) In Heidegger's lexicon the following terms (and there are yet others) are simply different names for the same phenomenon:

appropriation	*Ereignis*
thrownness	*Geworfenheit*
thrown-openness	*der geworfene Entwurf*
the thrown-open realm	*der Entwurfbereich*
the essence of human being	*Existenz* or *Da-sein*
the clearing	*die Lichtung*
the appropriated clearing	*die ereignete Lichtung*
the open	*das Offene*

They all name *ex aequo* what the formally indicative phrases "being itself," "being as such," or "the essence of being" formally indicate: that which accounts for the "being"/meaningful presence of things in the human world. Therefore, after chapter 1, I will avoid as much as possible the phrase "being itself." Instead, I will represent the heuristic term *das Sein selbst* (or likewise *Sein* or *Seyn* when Heidegger carelessly uses them as equivalent to *Sein selbst*) by some of the terms listed above. I will do this without notice, even in the English translations of Heidegger's texts.

To concretize the previous paragraphs: We may restate Heidegger's main question (*Grundfrage*) in phenomenological rather than ontological terms:

1. the *Befragtes*: The subject matter—but not the goal—of his question is the intelligibility (the *Anwesen*, significance, or meaningful presence) of things.
2. the *Gefragtes*: The question Heidegger puts to that subject matter is this: "What is the source of such meaningful presence?"
3. the *Erfragtes*: The sought-for answer to that question turns out to be the appropriated clearing (or other synonyms).

❖ ❖ ❖

Heidegger often (but not always) distinguished between *Dasein* on the one hand and *Da-sein* or *Existenz* on the other. Strictly speaking, the first word refers to any concrete, existentiel person, whereas the other two refer equally to the "essence" or existential structure of any human being. (I use the adjectives "existent*iel*" as referring to any specific person, and "existent*ial*" as referring to the essential structure of human being.) However, Heidegger frequently obscures this important distinction by writing simply "*Dasein*" (unhyphenated) when he actually means *Da-sein/Existenz*. In order to emphasize the unique characteristic that Heidegger intends to bring out by both *Dasein* (existentiel) and *Da-sein/Existenz* (existential), I will translate all three of those terms as "ex-sistence," hyphenated to stress its etymology. In each of these three terms Heidegger would have us hear the Latin *ex* + *sistere*, where the "ex-" or "out-and-beyond" dimension of human being forms an openness or clearing that he called "the *Da*."[6] (In chapter 5 we shall see that this "*Da*" should never be translated as "there," "here," or "t/here.") But ex-sistence does not mean "*standing* out and beyond," as if we ourselves took the initiative to "take a stand." Rather, *sistere* is a causative verb: "to *make* someone or something stand out and beyond." Therefore, as Heidegger uses *ex-sistere* of human be-

---

6. See GA 83: 72.23–24: "Das *sistere*—ex: Wesen der Existenz des Menchen." See ibid., 69.4: "*Exsistentia*, ἔκστασις—distentia."

ing, it means "*to be made* to stand out and beyond." Thus the term *Existenz* is already a pre-indication of what gets expressed in Heidegger's early work as *Geworfenheit* and *der geworfene Entwurf* (both of which I will interpret as "thrown-openness") and in his later work as *Ereignis*.[7]

I translate Heidegger's "*Mensch*" as "a human being," "human beings," or "man," where "man" refers to human being (the Greek ἄνθρωπος) rather than to the male of the species. *Das Seiende* is translated mostly as "things" or "a thing," sometimes as "entities" or "an entity," occasionally as "beings" or "a being," and very occasionally as "the real." *Ereignis* is always translated as "appropriation" and (following Heidegger's clear instructions on the matter) never as "event" or "the event of appropriation." *Vorhanden* is translated as "objectively present," and *zuhanden* as "useful" or "usable." As the argument of the book will show, "a priori" means "always already operative." I eschew as much as possible the word "ecstatic" (*ekstatisch*). Sometimes I misspell it as "ex-static," but mostly I use the word "thrown-open."

I translate all German terms that refer to ἀλήθεια (for example, *Wahrheit*, *Entbergung*, *Entborgenheit*, *Unverborgenheit*, *Unverdecktsein*, and so on, along with their cognates) by variations on the word "disclosedness," sometimes hyphenated as dis-closedness; or by "openness," sometimes written awkwardly as "open*ed*ness" in order to stress that openness (the clearing) is *thrown* open. Likewise I interpret *Unwahrheit*, *Verborgenheit*, and cognate terms by "hiddenness" in the sense of inaccessibility to cognition, whether theoretical or practical. Some may argue that subtle nuances are blurred by this practice, and they are right. However, the clarity achieved by highlighting the dis-closed-ness (i.e., open-ness) that underlies each of those German terms far outweighs whatever marginal advantages that more nuanced English translations might offer.

In *Being and Time* Heidegger blurs—and thereafter rarely observes—the distinction between *Entdecktheit* (the dis-coveredness of things) and *Erschlossenheit* (the dis-closedness or openedness of the clearing).[8] I choose to translate both terms by "disclosedness" or "openness," or sometimes, when it is a matter of things, as "availability." All of these terms refer to *intelligibility*. I use "intellect" in the broad sense of νοῦς as well as in the specific sense of λόγος understood as discursive intellect in correlation with worlds of significance and their contents. I use "intelligible" to mean "accessible to intellect" whether in theory, practice, enjoyment, or whatever.

Heidegger's use of *Sinn* and *Bedeutung* evolves over time and is not always consistent, but in any case he does not use these terms the way either Frege or

7. See GA 65: 239.5 = 188.25.

8. For example, at SZ 226.28 = 269.21–2: "entdeckt . . . erschlossen."

Husserl do. *Sinn* does not refer to an ideal unity of sense, a pure, unchanged ideality that is unaffected by the psychological acts that grasp it, nor is it the noema of a Husserlian noesis. Likewise *Bedeutung* does not mean “reference” (or “referent”), as in Frege, and it does not refer merely to a linguistic expression, as in Husserl’s *Logical Investigations*. In *Being and Time*, *Sinn* and *Bedeutung* are closely related, although *Sinn* is broader than *Bedeutung*, and they are usually translated interchangeably as “sense” and “meaning.” *Bedeutung* always refers to the sense or meaning of a *particular thing*. But when it comes to *Sinn*, we must make some distinctions:

1. When *Sinn* is used in conjunction with *things* (as in fact it rarely is), it refers to their sense, meaningfulness, or intelligibility.[9]
2. When it is used in conjunction with *Sein* (*der Sinn vom Sein*), *Sinn* is a formal indication of the clearing that accounts for intelligibility at all.[10] Other such formal indications include the “essence” or “place” or “truth” (*Wesen*, *Ort*/*Ortschaft*/τόπος, *Wahrheit*) of the being of things.
3. *Being and Time*, Division 2, does in fact argue to the *content* of the formally indicative word *Sinn*, which turns out to be the thrown-open *horizon* within which being appears as itself intelligible.
4. In his middle and later work, Heidegger abandons the transcendental-horizonal approach of *Being and Time*, and the word *Sinn* gets replaced by a number of co-equal terms, some of which I indicated above: the “open” (*Offene*) or the “thrown-open domain” (*Entwurfbereich*)[11] or especially “the clearing” (*Lichtung*) for meaningful presence at all.

Heidegger’s search for the *der Sinn von Sein* was not a search for a definition or a concept of being. As far as he was concerned, such a concept was already available throughout Western philosophy, at least implicitly, since the Greeks: *Sein* has always meant *Anwesen*, “presence,” and in Heidegger’s phenomenological interpretation, it means specifically the *meaningful* presence of things to man. And so, again, “*der Sinn von Sein*” is merely a formally indicative phrase that points towards the eventual outcome of Heidegger’s search: whatever will turn out to be responsible for the fact that things can and must be

9. For example, at GA 19: 205.13–14 = 141.33–34; SZ 151.22–4 = 192.35–37; and ibid., 12.14–15 = 32.23–24.

10. The intelligibility of *Sein* is what accounts for the fact that any particular thing can have a *Bedeutung*, a meaning. For example, SZ 151.29–31 = 193.6–8: We take a thing *in terms of* its intelligibility [Sinn = Woraufhin des Entwurfs], such that the thing is able to have a meaning—that is, can be understood *as* this-or-that (“etwas als etwas verständlich wird”).

11. See, for example, GA 9: 201.31 = 154.13; GA 14: 35.23–24 = 27.31–33; and Heidegger, *Schellings Abhandlung*, 229.4 = 188.38.

discursively intelligible (= must "have being") if we are to encounter them at all. And that answer eventually will be this: the ever-operative yet intrinsically hidden thrown-openness that is the appropriated clearing.

These innovations in translating Heidegger are not made lightly or arbitrarily but rather in an effort to break with Heideggerian fundamentalism and make Heidegger speak English in what Milton called an "answerable style."[12] All too often Anglophone scholars leave Heidegger's technical terms untranslated (e.g., *Dasein, Ereignis*, *Geschick*), or else resort to a Deutschlish discourse—half German, half English—that sounds like a German-American Bund in the 1920s. (As these chapters will show, I am a prime offender in that regard.) Other scholars insist on repeating Heidegger's technical language over and over again—pristine, unchanged, and very under-interpreted—almost as an atropaic mantra against the dangers of analytic philosophy or, for that matter, against the risks of original thinking. The upshot is that Heideggerians tend to paint themselves into a corner, warbling to each other like

> Lovers whose bodies smell of each other
> Who think the same thoughts without need of speech
> And babble the same speech without need of meaning.[13]

Whether successful or not, what follows is an effort to break out of such narcissistic babbling, to avoid what Karl Jaspers called *Heideggergegacker* ("Heidegger cackling"),[14] and to offer a straightforward and finally critical account of what Heidegger was getting at.

I attempt all of this by laying out the elements of a paradigm shift that I argue is necessary in order to understand his whole corpus, to take on board its positive contributions to philosophy, and to throw overboard what may be of no help. I may not have gotten any of that right, but it's the best I can do at this point. As has been said of Hegel, so too here: when it comes to Heidegger, there are no experts, only varying degrees of ignorance. In that spirit I welcome any and all criticisms of this effort, suggestions on how it might be improved, and alternate interpretations that will make better sense of Heidegger's work as a whole and show a clearer way beyond him.

12. Milton, *Paradise Lost*, X, 20.

13. T. S. Eliot, "Dedication to My Wife," *The Complete Poems*, 206.

14. Jaspers, *Notizien zu Martin Heidegger*, 207.35.

I want to thank my nephew and dear friend Michael Vargas for his indispensible help in solving a major computer problem within this text. Without his skill the manuscript would have never made it to the publisher. Finally, I want to thank Mr. Scott Wales for his supererogatory generosity and dedication in creating the website "Heidegger at Stanford."

Tom Sheehan
Oakwood Street, the Mission
San Francisco
15 July 2014

Introduction

1

Getting to the Topic

διορίσωμεν

What, after all, was Heidegger's philosophy about? The usual answer has been "being" (*das Sein*), at least since the early 1960s when William J. Richardson and Otto Pöggeler crafted their brilliant and still dominant paradigms for understanding Heidegger. But the uncertainty of Heidegger scholarship is nowhere more evident than with that key term. What, in fact, does Martin Heidegger mean by "being"? This is the first question we must take up.

To show that the problem of being has troubled Western philosophers from ancient times, Heidegger opens his major work, *Being and Time*, by citing a passage from Plato's *Sophist*, where the Eleatic Stranger asks his dialogue partners Theaetetus and Theodorus:

> How are we to understand this being (τὸ εἶναι) of yours? . . . We are at an impasse, so explain to us what you mean when you say "being" (ὄν). It's obvious that *you* have long known what you mean by these things, whereas we who formerly imagined we knew are now baffled.[1]

Much the same thing might be said about Heidegger. *He* may have known what he meant by "*Sein*," but he did not always make that clear to the rest of us. In fact, we might well make our own the plea that the Eleatic Stranger expresses in the next sentence of *The Sophist*: "So first teach us this very thing so that we won't *seem* to know what you told us when in fact we do not."[2] Heidegger's remark on Heraclitus' fragment 72 articulates that same problem in yet other terms. Without naming who the "they" might be, he says, "They say '*is*' without knowing what '*is*' really means."[3]

1. *Sophist* 243e2, 244a4–8. All citations from Plato in Greek are taken from *Platonis opera*, ed. John Burnet.

2. *Sophist* 244a8–b1.

3. GA 15: 277.17–18 = 5.7–8.

This puzzlement goes to the heart of Heidegger's project. So, as Aristotle advises, "Let us make some distinctions." Was Heidegger's central and final topic "being"? In his later years he said it was not. When it comes down to "the thing itself" (*die Sache selbst*) of his work, he declared "there is no longer room *even for the word* 'being.'"[4] Then was his topic something "being-er than being" (*wesender als das Sein*)?[5] And could that perhaps be "being itself," *das Sein selbst*, understood as "something that exists for itself, whose independence is the true essence of 'being'"?[6] And if so, how exactly does "being itself" differ (if it differs at all) from "being" as the being-of-beings (*das Sein des Seienden*) or being as the beingness-of-beings (*die Seiendheit des Seienden*)? Or was his topic not *Sein* but perhaps *Seyn*? Or was it rather *Seyn qua* ~~Seyn~~[7]—and if so, what might that mean?

Or was his topic not "being" in any of its instances or spellings but rather the *meaning* of being (*der Sinn vom Sein*)? But according to Heidegger we already know what the meaning of being is. From the ancient Greeks onward, the terms εἶναι, οὐσία, *esse*, *das Sein* (and so on) have all meant the "constant, steadfast presence" of things.[8] And whereas the theme of presence occupies much of Heidegger's thought, it was not his final focus. In that case, was he after the *essence* of being (*das Wesen des Seins*)? Or was it, rather, the essencing of the truth of being, *die Wesung der Wahrheit des Seins*?[9] Or was it the truth of the essencing of being, *die Wahrheit der Wesung des Seyns*?[10] Or was Heidegger's topic none of the above but, instead, the clearing (*die Lichtung*)? Or "appropriation" (*Ereignis*)? Or ἀλήθεια? Or perhaps the Λήθη that lurks within ἀλήθεια? Or was it the ontological difference?[11]

4. GA 15: 365.17–18 = 60.9–10, my emphasis: "ist sogar für den Namen Sein kein Raum mehr." For "the thing itself" as τὸ πράγμα αὐτό: Plato, "Seventh Letter" (ἐπιστολή Z), 341c7; *Protagoras*, 330d5, cited at GA 14: 76.1–2 = 61.9. Husserl always used the plural: for example, *Logische Untersuchungen, Husserliana* XIX/1,10.13–14 = I, 252.11, where a "thing" is what is given in direct intuition.

5. GA 73, 2: 1319.23.

6. GA 33: 31.9–10 = 25.12–13: "etwas für sich Bestehendes und in dieser Eigenständlichkeit das wahre Wesen des Seins?" See also GA 66: 340.13–14 = 303.18–19.

7. GA 73, 2: 997.20: "Seyn ist nicht ~~Seyn~~." Further on ~~Seyn~~: ibid., 968.7; 1033.10; 1039.10; 1122.7; etc.; also GA 9: 306 (g) = 374 (a): "~~Seyn~~ ist . . . das Ereignis." But cf. loc. cit., "Sein qua Ereignis." At GA 81: 76.18, Sein and Seyn are equated, but at GA 76: 49.15–19 they are contrasted.

8. GA 31: 113.22–23 = 79.18: "Anwesenheit und Beständigkeit."

9. GA 65: 73.21 = 58.35–36.

10. GA 65: 78.26 = 63.4–5.

11. The ontological difference is "the central thought of Heideggerian philosophy" according to John Haugland, "Truth and Finitude," I, 47. Compare that with GA 15: 366.27–28 = 60.44–61.1: "Mit dem Sein verschwindet auch die ontologische Differenz" and GA 73, 2: 1344.13–14: "'Ontologische Differenz' . . . von Seiendem und Sein, was *der Onto-Logie* das Thema gibt" (my emphasis). On the two senses of the ontological difference, see chapter 7.

There is, in fact, considerable confusion at the heart of the Heideggerian enterprise, and it may not be the fault of Heidegger scholars. Heidegger himself said that "it remains unclear *what* we are supposed to think under the name 'being.'"[12] In the partly fictitious "Dialogue on Language," based on a 1953–1954 conversation, Heidegger's interlocutor, Professor Tomio Tezuka of the Imperial University of Tokyo, lays most of the blame for the muddle at Heidegger's own doorstep.

> *Tezuka*: [The problem is due] mainly to the confusion that was created by your ambiguous use of the word "*Sein*."
>
> *Heidegger*: You are right. [Nonetheless, my thinking] knows clearly the distinction between "*Sein*" as the "*Sein des Seienden*" and "*Sein*" as "*Sein*" with regard to its own proper sense, which is dis-closedness (clearing).
>
> *Tezuka*: Then why didn't you immediately and decisively hand back the word "*Sein*" exclusively to the language of metaphysics? Why didn't you immediately give your own name to what you were seeking as the "meaning of *Sein*" on your path through the essence of time?
>
> *Heidegger*: How can I give a name to what I'm still searching for? Finding it would depend on assigning to it the word that would name it.
>
> *Tezuka*: Then we have to endure the confusion that has arisen.[13]

And indeed, for some eighty years Heidegger's readers have had to endure an avalanche of confusion (needless confusion, as I hope to show) in trying to sort out exactly what Heidegger meant by *Sein* and its cognates. Consider the number of German terms that Heidegger himself gathers around the term "being." How are we to distinguish (*if* we are to distinguish) one from the other?

seiend[14]
"das Seiend" when it is equivalent to "das Sein"[15]
"Seiend und seiend ist nicht ohne weiteres dasselbe."[16]
das Seiende[17]
das Seyende[18]

---

12. GA 40: 34.34–35 = 35.23–24.
13. GA 12: 104.16–105.3 = 20.14–32.
14. Heidegger's translation of ὄν in the passage above from the *Sophist*.
15. GA 83: 155.14 and 162.12; GA 15: 333.30 = 40.9.
16. GA 34: 33.17–18 = 26.5.
17. GA 34: 33.31–40.10 = 26.15–27.
18. GA 73, 2: 1046.18.

das Nichtseiende[19]
seiender[20]
das Seiendere[21]
"Seienderes" in scare quotes in the phrase "es gibt 'Seienderes'"[22]
das Seiendste[23]
"Wassein als das Seiendste"[24]
"Das Seyn ist das Seiendste"[25]
"Gott ist . . . das Seiendste"[26]
das Seiend-seiende[27]
das seiende Sein[28]
das seiend-Sein[29]
das Seiendsein[30]
das Seiend-*sein*[31]
die Seiendheit
"Seiendheit ist das Sein"[32]
das Sein (four different meanings)[33]
das Sein des Seienden
das Sein selbst

---

19. GA 15: 349.3 = 49.40.

20. GA 5: 40.2 = 30.3–4: "Sie [die Lichtung] ist, vom Seienden her gedacht, seiender als das Seiende." But in a different sense at ibid., 43.15 = 32.22: "alles Seiende seiender"; see also GA 34: 33.16 = 26.4.

21. GA 34: 33.22 = 26.9 (italicized).

22. GA 34: 33.35–34.1 = 26.19.

23. GA 45: 85.25 = 76.28; GA 40: 193.2–3 = 205.6; GA 34: 66.32 = 49.30. See GA 6.1: 454.12 = 29.6–7: das Seiendste am Seienden.

24. GA 45: 85.25 = 76.28.

25. GA 74: 22.1.

26. GA 73, 2: 997.11, with "Seiendste" in italics.

27. GA 31: 46.17 = 33.2

28. GA 40: 168.28 = 178.2.

29. GA 11: 26.18 = 97.11.

30. GA 40: 34.7 = 34.28, where it is translated as "to be in being." See GA 15: 344.16 = 46.39, where it is translated "being a thing." Heidegger first encountered this term in Carl Braig, *Die Grundzüge der Philosophie,* 43.5.

31. GA 29/30: 432.34 = 299. 7, where it is translated "*being* a thing." The Moser Nachschrift of "Grundbegriffe der Metaphysik" at 575.34 has simply "Seiendsein," without the emphasis. The Nachschrift is available at the Simon Silverman Phenomenology Center (see bibliography).

32. GA 74: 6.3.

33. See GA 73, 2: 1041.1–9.

das Sein als solches
"Sein" in the line-up "Sein, Wahrheit, ~~Sein~~, Ereignis"[34]
"Sein" in scare quotes in the phrase "'das Sein' (Austrag)"[35]
"Sein" without scare quotes in the phrase "Sein disappears in Ereignis"[36]
"Sein" in scare quotes in the phrase "'Sein' disappears in Wahrheit"[37]
"Sein" in scare quotes in the phrase "'Sein' als Wahrheit des Seins"[38]
das ~~Sein~~[39]
"Sein" in the phrase "Das Sein 'ist'—(*nicht* hat Sein)"[40]
"Sein" and "ist" when written as: "~~Sein~~ | ~~ist~~"[41]
"Seinen" as a verbal noun[42]
das Seyn[43]
das Seyn as das Seyende[44]
das Seyn as "das Seyende" in scare quotes[45]
"sey" and "sei," both in the subjunctive[46]
"Seyn—: Seiendes als Seiendes"[47]
das Seyn selbst[48]
das Seyn des Seyns[49]
"Seyn—ein Vorname seiner selbst"[50]
"Sein (Seyn) als Ereignis"[51]

34. GA 9: 369 note d = 280 note d.
35. GA 9: 306 note f = 233 note f.
36. GA 14: 27.8 = 22.3–4.
37. GA 9: 366, note a = 278 note a.
38. Heidegger, "Die 'Seinsfrage' in *Sein und Zeit*," 10.22–23.
39. GA 9: 385.6 = 291.7.
40. GA 86: 480.7.
41. GA 86: 482.7.
42. GA 81: 176.4.
43. GA 81: 209.8: "die Er-eignung . . . was vormals Sein geheißen"; ibid., 76.18: "Sein ist Seyn." But contrast GA 76: 49.15–19. At GA 83: 155.7 Seyn is equivalent to "das Seiende im allgemeinen vorgestellt, ens rationis" (!). (Compare passim: Freyheit/Freiheit, Daseyn/Dasein, Seynsgeschichte/ Seinsgeschichte.)
44. GA 73, 1: 780.17.
45. GA 73, 1: 732.5.
46. GA 73, 1: 788.7 and .8.
47. GA 72, 2: 957.14.
48. GA 45: 5.31 = 7.2.
49. GA 73, 2: 922.19.
50. GA 73, 2: 997.21.
51. GA 73, 2: 943.9.

"Seyn" in the phrase "Das Seyn des Da—aber *transitiv*!"[52]

das ~~Seyn~~[53]

das Wesen des ~~Seyns~~[54]

"~~Seyn~~ ist . . . das Ereignis"[55]

"Seyn *qua* Ereignis"[56]

"Sein ist Seyn"[57]

Sein ≠ Seyn[58]

"'Sein' als 'Seyn'" with both nouns in scare quotes[59]

"Seyn als Seyn"[60] both without scare quotes

"Seyn *qua* ~~Seyn~~"[61]

"Seyn ist nicht ~~Seyn~~"[62]

"Seyn und Sein"[63]

"das Seyn als die Wahrheit des Seyns"[64]

"das Seyn" in the phrase "die Wesung der Wahrheit des Seyns"[65]

"das Seyn" in the phrase "die Wahrheit der Wesung des Seyns"[66]

"Das Was-sein ist das Daß-sein"[67]

Erseyn[68]

erseyn in italics in the phrase "Das Da—*erseyn*"[69]

das Isten[70]

---

52. GA 73, 1: 472.4.
53. GA 9: 306, note g = 374, note a. GA 73, 2: 968.18; 1033.10; 1037.2; 1122.7.
54. GA 73, 2: 1137.1–2.
55. GA 9: 306 note g = 374 note a.
56. GA 9: 306 note 5 = 374 note a.
57. GA 81:76.19.
58. GA 76: 49.15–19.
59. GA 73, 2: 972.4.
60. GA 73, 1: 687.25.
61. GA 9: 306 note g = 374 note a.
62. GA 73, 2: 997.20.
63. GA 73,1: 687.30.
64. GA 73, 1: 788.10.
65. GA 65: 73.21 = 58.35–36.
66. GA 65: 78.26 = 63.4–5. For lists of the kinds of Sein and Seiendes, see, for example, GA 27: 71.26–72.1 and GA 29/30: 398.24–25 = 275.9–10.
67. GA 74: 6.5–6.
68. GA 73, 1: 472.5.
69. GA 73, 1: 472.4.
70. GA 73, 1: 896.13.

When it comes to "being," Heidegger, like Mao, seems to have let a hundred flowers bloom.[71] Or perhaps in the spirit of Walt Whitman: "Do I contradict myself? / Very well then I contradict myself, / (I am large, I contain multitudes.)"[72] Long ago Aristotle famously declared that "being" (the Greek word he used was the participle ὄν in the sense of "the real") is an analogical term that accommodates many diverse meanings, all of which, however, refer to one principal meaning that anchors the rest. Such an analogical view may well apply to Heidegger's work. But we shall see that even when Heidegger establishes—correctly as far as it goes—that the word *Sein* refers to the disclosedness of something to human understanding, he still had not arrived at his goal—because *Sein* was not his final topic.[73]

❖ ❖ ❖

So we repeat the sentence with which we began: What, after all, was Heidegger's philosophy about? In his *Four Seminars* we read at 6 September 1973, "The only question that has ever moved Heidegger is the question of *Sein*: what does *Sein* mean?"[74] But right there we run into a major problem. The word *Sein* or "being" comes from the lexicon of traditional realist metaphysics, where it usually refers to the "substance"—the essence and/or existence—of anything insofar as it is understood to be real. However, Heidegger's own work takes two major steps away from metaphysics and its traditional concern with "being."

In the first place, Heidegger's philosophy was not in pursuit of *Sein* at all. Rather, he was after *das Woher des Seins*, the "whence" of being, "that from which and through which . . . being occurs."[75] (We note the frustrating ambiguity in the meaning of "*Sein*" in this case. It could refer either to the clearing or to the being of things. Here I take it in the second sense.) Originally Heidegger called this "whence" the *intelligibility* of being (= *der Sinn von Sein*). Over the years he reformulated that as the "disclosedness" or "place" or "clearing" or "openness" or "thrown-open realm" for the being of things, all *ex aequo*.[76] His

71. Mao Zedong, "百花齐放" "On the Correct Handling of Contradictions among the People" (speech at the enlarged Eleventh Session of the Supreme State Conference, 27 February 1957), section VIII.1.

72. Whitman, *Song of Myself*, 51.

73. See GA 14: 27.8 = 22.3–4: "Sein verschwindet im Ereignis."

74. GA 15: 377.18–20 = 67.13–14.

75. GA 73, 1: 82.15–16: "das von woher und wodurch . . . das Sein west."

76. GA 15: 335.11–16 = 41.5–9, and 344.29 = 47.7: Sinn, Wahrheit, Ortschaft/Ortlichkeit/τόπος. Also ibid., 345.15–16 = 47.24–25; 403.32–404.1 = 94.28–29 and SZ 170.23–25 = 214.23–26. GA 16: 424.21 = 5.14–15: "Unverborgenheit oder Lichtung (Verstehbarkeit)."

endeavors were to bring to light this intrinsically hidden "whence" that classical ontology had overlooked and forgotten. Being (*Sein*) in *all* its incarnations is the topic of metaphysics. Heidegger, on the other hand, is after the essence or source of being and thus the ground of metaphysics.

In the second place, long before *Being and Time*, Heidegger had carried out a Copernican Revolution under the banner of phenomenology. He took a decisive step away from the naïve realism of the Aristotelian-Thomistic ontology in which he had been steeped as a young man, in order to focus instead on the *correlativity* of man and being in what he would eventually call a "*phenomenological* ontology."[77] This means that the only entrance into Heidegger's work is through the phenomenological reduction. Over the door of his Academy is engraved ἀφαινομενολέγητος μηδεὶς εἰσίτω, which translates roughly as follows: "No phenomenological reduction? Don't even *try* to get in."[78]

The material object of traditional metaphysics is the real insofar as it lies ἔξω ὂν καὶ χωριστόν: "outside of thinking and separated from it [= independent of it]."[79] Phenomenology, on the other hand, regards things only insofar as they are meaningfully present to us within our concerns and performances—that is, insofar as they are "present to mind" in the broadest sense.[80] Years ago Professor Aron Gurwitsch pointed out that once one has carried out the phenomenological reduction (the *sine qua non* of phenomenological work) "there are no other philosophical problems except those of sense, meaning, and signification."[81] To the degree that Heidegger's work is phenomenological (and to the end of his life he insisted it was),[82] it was solely and exclusively about *meaningfulness and its source*. Heidegger interprets the essence of "mind" in terms

---

GA 65: 295.3 = 232.30: "das Offen für das Sein." Entwurfbereich as the thrown-open domain: GA 9: 201.31 = 154.13 and GA 14: 35.23–24 = 27.31–33 with GA 49: 41.25–28: "Ent-wurf besagt: "Er-öffnung und Offenhalten des Offenen, Lichten der Lichtung, in der das, was wir Sein (nicht das Seiende) nennen und somit unter diesem Namen auch kennen, eben als *Sein offenkundig* ist."

77. SZ 38.21 = 62.32, my emphasis.

78. On the legendary inscription over the entrance to Plato's Academy ("No one who is ignorant of geometry may enter"), see Henri-Dominique Saffrey, "Ἀγεωμέτρητος μηδεὶς εἰσίτω." See also Johannes Philoponus, *In Aristotelis de anima* in *Commentaria in Aristotelem Graeca*, XV, 117.16–17.

79. *Metaphysics* XI 8, 1065a24. See ibid., ἔξω [τὴς διανοίας]: *Metaphysics*, VI 4, 1028a 2, taken with 1027b34–1028a1: "outside" [i.e., independent] of thinking. See GA 6, 2: 380.2–13 = 16.17–26.

80. GA 83: 80.8: "Anwesung für das Verstehen." See Aquinas, *Scriptum super sententiis*, I, distinctio 3, quaestio 4, articulum 5, corpus: "id quod est praesens intelligibile."

81. Gurwitsch, 652.8–9 (italicized in the original).

82. See GA 14: 147.15–16 = 201.1: "die weitere Frage [re das Wesen des Seins], die ich als phänomenologische beanspruche." Ibid. 54.2–3 = 44.32–33: "Dieses Vorgehen [in 'Zeit und Sein'] kann als phänomenologisch bezeichnet werden."

of what he calls "being-in-the-world," where "world" means the meaning-giving context opened up by and as ex-sistence. Why, then, as Professor Tezuka asked, did Heidegger continue to employ, in his own phenomenological work, the ontological vocabulary of a surpassed metaphysics? For example, when Heidegger declares that "*das Sein* lets things be present,"[83] is he claiming that *Sein* "presences" amoebas during the Proterozoic era, two billion years before Homo sapiens?[84] Or is he referring to the arrival of things in the realm of human apprehension—that is, "insofar as things can be encountered [by human beings] at all"?[85] Clearly it is the latter.

> It is with us human beings that *Sein* comes into play.[86]
>
> *Das Sein*: that which appears only and specifically in man.[87]
>
> There can be no *Sein des Seienden* without man.[88]

Or again: When Heidegger claims that in the modern world "things, to be sure, are still given . . . but *Sein* has deserted them," this "desertion" does not mean the disappearance of the "out-there-ness" of things (their *existentia* or *Vorhandensein*) but refers, rather, to the loss of the understanding of how things become meaningfully present at all: "Where struggle [πόλεμος] ceases, things certainly do not disappear, but world [i.e., the meaning-giving clearing] disappears."[89]

On both accounts, therefore—(1) that *Sein* was not his focal topic and (2) that what he *did* mean by *Sein* was the intelligibility of things—why didn't Heidegger obviate the problem at the outset (and steal a march on the obscurity and incomprehension that still haunts his philosophy) by simply surrendering the word "being" to the metaphysics that owns the term, and then go on

83. GA 15: 363.24–26 = 59.3–4: "das Sein läßt das Seiende anwesen."

84. Against the position that das Sein "presences" amoebas, note that "aller ontisch-kausale Beiklang ausgeschlossen ist" ["all ontic-causal overtones are excluded"] from Heidegger's understanding of Anwesen: GA 15: 363.23–24 = 59.2. See also ibid., 363.30–31 = 59.7–8: "Dies 'Lassen' ist etwas von 'Machen' grundlegend Verschiedenes." Also GA 34: 27.9–12 = 21.22–24: Human beings always comport themselves to what is in Sein, whereas animals never do. What is "in Sein" is meaningful-to-human-beings-alone.

85. GA 19: 205.7–10 = 141.27–30: "*sofern das Seiende da* ist, wie wir sagen, sofern das Seiende überhaupt *begegen* kann" (Heidegger's emphasis). Note the meaning of "da": not just "in the universe" but rather able to be *meaningfully* encountered.

86. GA 73, 1: 90.28: "Bei uns—den Menschen—kommt das Sein ins Spiel."

87. GA 73, 1: 337: "Das Sein jenes—was nur im Menschen eigens erscheint."

88. *Zollikon Seminare* 221.27–29 = 176.17–18: "Also kann es Sein von Seienden *ohne* den Menschen gar nicht geben."

89. For the last two sentences: GA 40: 67.26–28 = 69.13–15 and 67.3–4 = 68.15–16.

to articulate in *phenomenological* terms what he was after? But for whatever reason, he did not, and he thereby opened a Pandora's Box of misclues and misunderstandings that still hamstrings his work to this day. Professor Tezuka was quite right: when it comes to the needless confusion that dogs Heidegger's philosophy (not only among analytical philosophers but among Heideggerians as well), much of the blame must be laid at Heidegger's own doorstep.

As an example, we may note how Heidegger reads Greek philosophy. Most commentators might offer Aristotle, Heidegger's favorite philosopher, as an example of traditional objectivist ontology. But when Heidegger reads Aristotle, he in fact interprets him not as a naïve realist but as a phenomenologist *avant la lettre*. We note that this interpretation is not yet Heidegger's "retrieval of the unsaid" (*die Wiederholung des Ungesagten*) in Aristotle, which would be the articulation of the *ground* of being that metaphysics had overlooked. Rather, this phenomenological reading is based on Heidegger's conviction, from the winter semester of 1921–1922 onward, that Aristotle's metaphysical texts are replete with unthematized examples of the proto-phenomenological correlation between things and the apprehension of them. In his famous 1939 text on φύσις in Aristotle's *Physics* II 1, Heidegger argues that Aristotle always understands things as phenomena—that is, as what shows up *within the field of human comportment and interpretation*. Aristotle's phrase τὸ ὂν λεγόμενον (things insofar as they are taken up in λόγος) refers to things insofar as we apprehend them as intelligible in this way or that.[90] In other words, Aristotle always, if implicitly, understands things as situated in a phenomenological relation with human beings and thus—since man is the living thing that has λόγος—in correlation with human intelligence. We do not merely bump up against things with our bodily senses and then add meanings to them. Rather, we always have an a priori relation *not* to the specific meaning of the thing but to its general intelligibility, its *ability* to have a specific meaning within a specific context. Thus Heidegger boldly declares that Aristotle was as much an idealist as was Kant.

> If the meaning of "idealism" amounts to understanding that being [i.e., the meaningful presence of entities] can never be explained by way of those entities but is already "transcendental" with regard to each of those entities, then idealism affords the only correct possibility for a philosophical problematic. If so, Aristotle was no less an idealist than Kant.[91]

90. Aristotle, *Metaphysics* VI 2, 1026a33. GA 19: 207.22–23 = 143.21–22. GA 22: 59.14 = 50.8: "das Enthüllte, λεγόμενον." GA 6, 2: 317.8–9 = 212.23–24: "Im 'als solches' wird gesagt: das Seiende ist unverborgen."

91. SZ 208.3–7 = 251.35–39.

Heidegger's interpretations of Aristotle are always imbued with the phenomenological way of seeing that he had learned in the 1920s from his mentor Edmund Husserl. The keystone of that phenomenological vision is the ineluctable fact of meaningfulness. Yes, Heidegger does use the language of Aristotelian ontology, but he uses it with a phenomenological valence that has not been sufficiently thematized in the scholarship. Heidegger always philosophizes within a phenomenological view of things as *ad hominem* (κατὰ τὸν λόγον)[92]—that is, in correlation with human concerns and interests. This entails that whatever we encounter is a priori meaningful.[93] In fact, when it comes to useful things in the world of everyday practice, Heidegger holds to the strictly phenomenological position that the "in-itself-ness" of such things is not located somehow "within" those things when taken as separate from human interests. Rather, the in-itselfness of a tool is precisely its status as usable *in relation to* the intentions of the person who is using it.[94] For Heidegger, *Sein* in all its forms is always written under phenomenological erasure—that is, under the aegis of a phenomenological reduction of things to their meaningfulness to man.

❖ ❖ ❖

So, again, what was Heidegger's philosophy about? In what sense is Heidegger's basic question, in its traditional ontological formulation, concerned with "being itself" (*das Sein selbst*), and in what sense is it not? This question has bedeviled Heidegger scholarship from the start; and so we must proceed cautiously, step-by-step. Let us begin by asking about the general structure of any question and then go on to apply it to the "guiding question" (*Leitfrage*) of metaphysics and the "basic question" (*Grundfrage*) of Heidegger's own work.

Heidegger designates the three moments of any question as the *Befragtes*, the *Gefragtes*, and the *Erfragtes*. These terms stand for, respectively, the "object," the "optic," and the "heuristic outcome" of the inquiry.[95]

1. The *Befragtes* or *object* of a question refers to the thing under investigation, what medieval Scholasticism called the *obiectum materiale quod* or material object.

---

92. *Physics* II 1, 193a31. Heidegger translates: "[das Seiende,] das sich für die Ansprechung zeigt": GA 9: 273.9 = 208.36, a thesis that he explains in the next three pages of the German text.

93. See GA 56/57: 73.1–8 = 61.24–29: "In einer Umwelt lebend, bedeutet es mir überall und immer."

94. SZ 71.37–38 = 101.27–28: "Zuhandenheit ist die ontologisch-kategoriale Bestimmung von Seiendem, wie es 'an sich' ist" (all italicized in the original). Also ibid., 74.31–34 = 105.1–6.

95. SZ 5.13–17 = 24.19–27. Also GA 88: 12.17–20; 20.12–15; and 23.25–26.

2. The *Gefragtes* or *optic* refers to the formal focus the inquirer adopts in investigating the material object, and the question that follows from that.[96]
3. Finally, the *Erfragtes* or *outcome* is a formal indication of the answer the inquirer hopes to obtain by bringing the formal focus to bear on the material object.

With this in mind, we can distinguish metaphysics' question from Heidegger's meta-metaphysical question. Metaphysics takes *things* (whatever is real, whatever "has being")[97] as its material object; and then asks about what it is that makes them be real. In the traditional reading of Aristotle's metaphysics (and here I focus on its ontological moment and prescind from its theological moment), that inquiry unfolds as follows.

1. The material object that metaphysics takes up is things, whatever is real, whatever "has being" (τὸ ὄν).
2. The formal focus on those things is then articulated by the proviso: insofar as they are real (ᾗ ὄν); and the question becomes: What accounts for their realness?
3. Finally, the sought-for outcome of that question is formally indicated as: whatever it is that makes those things be real. Depending on the metaphysician, the *content* that fills out that formal indication will vary: for Plato it will be εἶδος, for Aristotle, ἐνέργεια, for Aquinas *esse* or *actus essendi*; and so on.[98]

METAPHYSICS' *LEITFRAGE*

das Befragte:	things that are real—that "have being"
das Gefragte:	What accounts for them *as real*?
das Erfragte:	their realness/being *qua* εἶδος, ἐνέργεια, *esse*, etc.

As these formulations show, the metaphysical question is focused decidedly on things, specifically from the viewpoint of why, how, and to what extent they are real. That is, the question that metaphysics puts to things is this: What

96. Cf. GA 20: 423.8–11 = 306.33–35: "die Hinsicht; woraufhin es gesehen wird und gesehen werden soll."

97. GA 22: 7.14–15 = 5.36: "Es ist, es *hat* Sein" (Heidegger's italics).

98. At GA 22: 60.3 = 50.21–22 metaphysics' Erfragtes is formally indicated as follows: "[Das,] was allein das Seiende selbst in seinem Sein zugänglich macht." Cf. GA 73, 2: 997.2: "*esse* = quo est." On ἰδέα as Seiendheit: GA 94: 424.6–7.

is their "essence" (i.e., their *esse*-ness, being-ness, real-ness), in the broad sense of whatever it is that lets them be real? Metaphysics begins with things, then "steps beyond" them to discover their realness in a variety of historically changing forms.[99] But finally metaphysics *returns* to those things with that news. As Aristotle puts it, metaphysics announces "whatever belongs to things in and of themselves" and specifically their "first principles and highest causes."[100] Heidegger indicates that all three of the following questions name *ex aequo* the concern of Aristotelian metaphysics:

> What is "a thing insofar as it is in being"?
> What is a thing in its being?
> What is the being of a thing?[101]

Metaphysics is clearly a matter of *onto*-logy insofar as the operations of questioning and answering (-logy) all bear ultimately on *things* (onto-).

❖ ❖ ❖

Heidegger's *meta*-metaphysical inquiry, on the other hand, takes up where metaphysics leaves off. It turns the outcome of the *Leitfrage* into the material object of the *Grundfrage* by taking the very realness of things (whatever its historical form: εἶδος, ἐνέργεια, etc.) and puts *that* under the microscope as the subject matter of a radically new question. What about this realness *itself*, this οὐσία that things "have"? This is the question not about ὂν ᾗ ὄν but about οὐσία ᾗ οὐσία, *Sein als Sein*, and specifically the question about *what accounts for* the fact that there is *Sein* at all (which things are said to "have.") Heidegger was concerned with

> *Sein* as *Sein*, that is, the question about how there can be meaningful presence as such.[102]
> Where and how does the meaningful presence [of a thing] become present?[103]

---

99. GA 14: 70.10–12 = 56.18–20: "daß es [= metaphysisches Denken], ausgehend vom Anwesenden, dieses in seiner Anwesenheit vorstellt."

100. *Metaphysics* IV 1, 1003a21–22 and 26–27. ἀρχαί, ἀκροτάται αἰτίαι.

101. GA 49: 169.16–18. Also in *Schellings Abhandlung*, 213.21–23 = 175.37–39.

102. GA 14: 86.24–87.1 = 70.9–10: "Sein als Sein, d.h. die Frage, inwiefern es Anwesenheit als solche geben kann."

103. GA 15: 405.30 = 96.12: "Wo und wie west anwesen an?"

The basic question: *How does the being* [of anything] *become present*?[104]
How does *Sein* come about?[105]

But herein lies a problem: Much of the scholarship fails to see that Heidegger's goal was not *Sein* at all, but rather what *accounts* for *Sein*:

> that which grounds the inner possibility and necessity of being and its openness to us.[106]

> What does the openness of being and its relation to man consist of, and *what is it grounded in*?[107]

Being/realness is always the being or realness *of things*, that which allows *them* to be present,[108] and metaphysics had already covered that topic. Heidegger, on the other hand, is asking, "Why *Sein* at all?" and "How and why does *it* become present?" We may state Heidegger's question in traditional ontological language as follows. (Later I will express it in a more appropriate phenomenological form.)

HEIDEGGER'S *GRUNDFRAGE* IN TRADITIONAL ONTOLOGICAL TERMS

das Befragte:	the very being [of things], whatever form it takes
das Gefragte:	How is such being possible and necessary at all?
das Erfragte:	[Let X formally indicate the sought-for outcome.]

If we postpone for a moment what the heuristic X will turn out to be, I am arguing that *Sein* or being in *any and all* of its incarnations is definitely not the heuristic goal of Heidegger's question, only its subject matter, the *Befragtes*. And the *Erfragtes*—which as yet remains undecided and is only formally indicated by the X—is whatever will turn out to answer the question about why there is *Sein* at all, and what makes it necessary for human comportment. Consider the following analogy, which, for all its limitations, may nonetheless get us into the ballpark of Heidegger's question:

---

104. GA 65: 78.22 = 62.30: "Die Grundfrage: *wie west das Seyn?*"

105. GA 88: 9.7: "Wie west das Sein?"

106. GA 16: 66.15–16: "worin gründet die innere Möglichkeit und Notwendigkeit der Offenbarkeit des Seins."

107. GA 16: 423.3–15 = 4.3–14: "worin gründet und besteht die Offenbarkeit des Seins und seines Verhältnis zum Menschen." My emphasis.

108. SZ 9.7 = 29.13: "Sein ist jeweils das Sein eines Seienden."

	ASKING ABOUT THE KIDS	ASKING ABOUT THEIR MOTHER
das Befragte:	the Smith children	Ms. Smith
das Gefragte:	How did they get here?	How did she get here?
das Erfragte:	their mother [= X]	her mother [= X]

Beginning with the left side of the text box: Metaphysics is a bit like asking the question "Who are these children?" and trying to answer it by finding out who their *mother* is. The children are the subject matter of the question, and the inquiry reaches back behind them in the direction of the heuristic *Erfragtes*, or X, which is "the mother of these kids, whoever she might be." This latter phrase is the *formal indication* of the sought-for answer; and inasmuch as it is merely formal, it does not yet have concrete material content. Eventually the actual content of that formal indication will turn out to be: Jane Smith. We can see, therefore, the very important distinction between, on the one hand, a mere *formal indication* and, on the other, the *actual content* that will eventually cash out that formal indication.

1. the mere formal indication: "the mother of the Smith children" (whoever she might turn out to be)
2. the material content that will eventually fill out that formal indication: Jane Smith

Fine. But the question is nonetheless geared entirely to *defining the children* in light of Ms. Smith.

But on the other hand (and moving to the right side of the text box), Heidegger's *meta*-metaphysical question is a bit like starting with Jane Smith *herself* and considering her not as the mother of the little Smiths (which, of course, she never ceases to be, even if we bracket that out for a moment) but rather querying her about her own background. Ms. Smith herself now becomes the subject matter of a new question, and that inquiry reaches back behind her in the direction of a new heuristic *Erfragtes*: "the mother of Jane Smith." Heidegger's *Grundfrage* is analogous to Ms. Smith's night out, without the kids. The *Befragtes* is now Jane Smith seen for herself, quite apart from her relation to the children. And the question reaches "behind" Ms. Smith to her own origins, formally indicated as "the mother of Jane Smith—whoever that person may turn out to be." And the material content that fills out that formal indication will finally turn out to be: Ms. Jones.

This is analogous to what Heidegger means when he says that his effort is "to think *Sein* without regard to its being grounded in terms of *Seiendes*"[109]—that is: to think being (which is always the being of *things*) *in and of itself*, prescinding from its relation to things. And "to think it" means "to discover what makes it possible." The problem, however, lies with the intensifier "itself" (*das Sein selbst*). This potentially misleading modifier might make us think that Heidegger is searching for The-Really-Real-Form-of-Being—say, the way one might look around a cocktail party for the host, and say to one's partner, "No, not him, nor him, nor him"—and then, "There he is: that's the host *himself*." This is definitely not what Heidegger has in mind when he speaks of "being itself."

Here we run into a major problem that has confused Heidegger scholarship from the very beginning: the damnable fact that Heidegger uses "*das Sein selbst*" in two very distinct senses—namely, as both the *Befragtes* and as the *Erfragtes* of his meta-metaphysical question.

THE TWO MEANINGS OF "*DAS SEIN SELBST*"

As the *Befragtes* it means:	the very being [of a thing] as the subject matter of Heidegger's question.
As the *Erfragtes* it is:	a *formal indication* of whatever will answer the question about what accounts for such being.

In the first case above, "being itself" names the *Befragtes* or subject matter of Heidegger's question; and there it means the being of things, but now taken in and of itself, analogous to the way Jane Smith as *Befragtes* was queried for herself and not as the mother of the little Smiths.[110] However, in the second case above (and with almost inevitable confusion) the phrase "being itself" names the *Erfragtes* or sought-for outcome of the question. Here "being itself" is merely a heuristic device, a formal indicator, like the X that stands in for the as-yet-unknown-to-be-known of any question. In this latter capacity, "being itself" is a way of saying "the *essence* of being,"[111] where "essence" means "that-which-allows-for-being," the *Lassen von Anwesen*.[112] Thus the phrase "being itself" points *beyond* being (cf. ἐπέκεινα τῆς οὐσίας)[113] toward

109. GA 14: 5.32–33 = 2.12–14.

110. "Being itself" has this sense, for example, at SZ 152.11 = 193.31: "nach ihm [= das Sein] selbst"; at GA 40: 183.22 = 194.23; GA 73, 1: 82.11–17; etc.

111. GA 73, 1: 108.14: "das *Wesen* des Seins," my emphasis. GA 14: 141.3–4: "Grundfrage nach dem Wesen und der Wahrheit des Seins."

112. GA 14: 46.18 = 37.26.

113. *Republic*, VI 509b9.

das Woher or "whence" of being: "that from which and through which being [which is always the being *of things*] comes to pass at all."[114] This "whence" will turn out to be *Ereignis*: the structural ap-*propri*-ation of ex-sistence to its *proper* state as the thrown-open clearing.[115] The point of all this is not to confuse (1) "being itself" as the *Befragtes* or subject matter of Heidegger's question with (2) "being itself" as a formal indication of the *Erfragtes*, the sought-for answer to that question. To do so would be a bit like confusing Jane Smith with "the mother of Jane Smith"—who, as we have seen, turns out to be Ms. Jones. You wouldn't want to mix up mother and daughter. That could be quite embarrassing—not to mention a major category mistake.

"Being in and of itself" is the subject matter that Heidegger is interrogating (*befragen*) in order to discover what lets it come about; and that will turn out to be the clearing that is opened up by and as the appropriation of ex-sistence. "Appropriation yields the openness, the clearing, within which meaningful things can perdure."[116] Therefore, "being itself" as the sought-for X of Heidegger's question is not at all something in and for itself, a Super-*Sein* as some Higher Form of Being that is different from and superior to the plain ol' being of things. Rather, it stands for whatever makes possible the being of things. Heidegger's goal was to think meaningful presence itself back to its origin in the appropriation of ex-sistence ("*auf das Ereignis zu . . . gedacht*")[117] as the indefinable "it" (*es*) that "gives" all configurations of the clearing-for-being: *das Ereignis gibt die Lichtung*. This move back to the origin is what Heidegger calls "the return from meaningful presence to appropriation."[118] And once one gets there, he says, "there is no more room *even for the word* 'being.'"[119]

As Heidegger conceded in speaking with Tezuka, confusion is virtually inevitable. We can see such confusion very much at work when Heidegger defines his central topic as "*das Sein selbst in dessen Wesen*"—"being itself in its own essence."[120] This German phrase brings together *both* senses of "being itself." The first three words refer to the *Befragtes* of Heidegger's question, whereas the last three words refer to the *Erfragtes*.

114. GA 73, 1: 82.15–16: "das von woher und wodurch . . . das Sein west." GA 94: 249.5 and .19: "[die] Wesung des Seins."

115. See note 129 in this chapter.

116. GA 12: 247.2–4 = 127.18–19: " das Ereignen . . . er-gibt das Freie der Lichtung, in die Anwesendes anwahren . . . kann."

117. GA 14: 45.29–30 = 37.5–6. See GA 12: 249.30–31 = 129.38–40: "Dagegen läßt das Sein hinsichtlich seiner Wesensherkunft aus dem Ereignis denken."

118. GA 14: 55.8 = 45.32: "Rückgang vom Anwesen zum Ereignen."

119. GA 15: 365.17–18 = 60.9–10. My emphasis.

120. GA 40: 183.22 = 194.23.

(1) *DAS SEIN SELBST* (2) *IN DESSEN WESEN*

In ontological terms:

Befragtes = das Sein selbst.	The very being [of things] is under investigation.
Erfragtes = in dessen Wesen.	We seek the *essence*, i.e., the *whence* of such being.

In more appropriate phenomenological terms:

Befragtes = das Anwesen selbst.	The very intelligibility of things is under investigation.
Erfragtes = in dessen Woher.	We seek what accounts for such intelligibility at all.

Heidegger's way of expressing this matter is certainly confusing, and at this point one is tempted to mutter *Lasciate ogni speranza voi ch'entrate qui.* Or to switch from Dante to Dodgson, Heidegger often sounds like Humpty-Dumpty: "When I use a word, it means just what I choose it to mean—neither more nor less."[121] But lest one despair, there is a way out of this Alice-in-Wonderland world.

❖ ❖ ❖

In his later work, especially from 1960 until his death in 1976, Heidegger expressed himself a bit more clearly. He declared that the merely formal indication "*das Sein selbst*" finally turns out to be *die Lichtung*, the thrown-open clearing, which he designated as the *Urphänomen* of all his work.[122] The clearing is the always-already opened-up "space" that makes the being of things (phenomenologically: the intelligibility of things) possible and necessary. Heidegger calls it "the open region of understanding" and "the realm of disclosedness or clearing (understandability)"[123]—that is, that *whereby* the understandability of things occurs in the first place. The heuristic X now has actual, real content; and what previously was only *formally* indicated now has *material content* and is properly named. How so?

121. Carroll/Dodgson, *Through the Looking-Glass*, chapter 6, 66.21–24.

122. GA 14: 81.13–14 = 65.30–32: Urphänomen, Ur-sache.

123. Respectively, GA 9: 199.21 = 152.24: "[das] Offene des Begreifens" (E.T. by John Sallis) and GA 16: 424.20–21 = 5.19–20 "der Bereich der Unverborgenheit oder Lichtung (Verstehbarkeit)." Verstehbarkeit is a philosophical neologism that does not appear in the Grimm brothers' *Deutsches Wörterbuch.*

For us, the *Sein* of something shows up only in discursive thinking and acting—that is, only when we take a thing *as* such-and-so, or *in terms of* this or that possibility. When I take something *as*, whether in theory or praxis, I understand the *Sein* of the thing, whether correctly or incorrectly. For Heidegger, "Understanding the *Sein* of a thing = understanding the what-it-is and how-it-is of that thing."[124] This whatness and howness is what Plato, Aristotle, and all metaphysics mean by the realness of the thing, its οὐσία, *das Sein des Seienden*. If we translate those ontological terms into a phenomenological framework, the argument comes out as follows:

1. To think or act dis-cursively entails "running back and forth" (*dis-currere*) between the thing and its meaning, or the tool and the task, as we check out whether this thing actually does have that meaning or whether in fact this tool is suitable for that task.
2. Whenever we take something *as* this-or-that or *as suitable for* a task, we (rightly or wrongly) understand the current meaning that the thing has for us—ontologically, we understand *das jeweilige Sein des Seienden*, the current being of the thing.
3. But we *can* think and act discursively only by metaphorically "traversing the open space"[125] between the tool and the task, or the thing and its possible meaning.
4. But that space (the clearing) must be already open and functioning in order for there to be an "as" or an "as-suitable-for" at all. That is, if we are to see the current meaning of some thing, there must be already operative a *possible relation* between the relata (between the thing and its meaning, or the tool and the task).
5. Hence, this already-operative possibility—the always-already thrown-open clearing—is what allows for all cases of meaningfulness (ontologically: all instances of the being of things).[126]
6. Therefore, the always-already-operative thrown-open clearing is the "thing itself" of all Heidegger's work.[127]

---

124. GA 9: 131.21–22 = 103.33–35: "Verständnis des Seins (Seinsverfassung: Was- und Wie-sein) des Seienden."

125. GA 15: 380.6 = 68.43. See GA 14: 81.35 and 84.3–4 = 66.19 and 68.9 (durchmißt, duchmeßbaren) and GA 7: 19.12 = 18.32 (durchgeht).

126. Why "thrown-*openness*"? Answer: What Da-sein is thrown into is its own ex-sistence as the open clearing: SZ 276.16–17 = 321.11 with SZ 133.5 = 171.22.

127. Below we shall see that the thrown-open/appropriated-open *clearing* is the same as thrown-open/appropriated *ex-sistence*. See GA 73, 1: 585.19: "Er-eignet uns dem Da," in italics; also 585.27: "in dem es [das Ereignis] uns dem Da er-eignet."

Given this chain of argument (which is Heidegger's), we may clarify his Alice-in-Wonderland use of *das Sein* and *das Sein selbst* by simply substituting for those ambiguous ontological terms what Heidegger actually meant by them in his phenomenology.

1. As regards the subject matter or *Befragtes* of his question: We should always understand the misleading ontological terms "the being" or "be-ingness" of things as the intelligibility of things: their meaningful presence to man.
2. As regards the sought-for answer or *Erfragtes* of his question: Instead of the merely formally indicative term "*das Sein selbst*" (which is only Heidegger's lorem ipsum for the goal of his thought), we should speak of "thrown-openness" or "the thrown-open clearing"; or, in his later terminology: the appropriation of ex-sistence, or the appropriated clearing. All of these terms name *ex aequo* what "being itself" only provisionally stands in for. All those terms name "the thing itself" that Heidegger was ultimately after.

Hence the solution to the Humpty-Dumpty-ism of *das Sein selbst*: Heidegger's basic question breaks down as follows:

1. Field: the intelligibility of things, taken for itself.
2. Focus: What accounts for it, what makes it possible and necessary?
3. Final answer: thrown-open or appropriated ex-sistence as the clearing for intelligibility.

Of course (ὃ μὴ γένοιτο), one *could* use the surpassed language of *Sein* in speaking of Heidegger's phenomenological work (as is unfortunately the fashion in the scholarship today). But even if one were to do so, it is clear that *Sein* is not at all what Heidegger was after, for again: Once one gets to the thing itself, there is no longer room even for the word "being."[128] Instead, what one finds at the core of Heidegger's thought is what he called either appropriated ex-sistence[129] or the appropriated clearing.[130] His earlier work stressed *ex-sistence* insofar as its thrownness has always already opened up the clearing and holds it open (*Da-sein*), whereas his later work stressed the *clearing as held open* by thrown-open ex-sistence (*Da-sein*). But as he declared to

128. GA 73, 2: 1319.21 and .23: The clearing as appropriated-open is "wesender als das Sein."

129. See GA 12: 249.4–6 = 129.11–13: "Die Vereignung des Menschen . . . [entläßt] das Menschenwesen in sein Eigenes"—that is, ex-sistence as appropriated into its proper state of thrown-openness as the clearing; also ibid., 247.2–4 = 127.18–19; and 249.1–2 = 129.9; GA 14: 28.18–19 = 23.15–17; GA 65: 407, note = 322 note 1; GA 94: 448.31.

130. GA 71: 211.9 = 180.1–2: "die ereignete Lichtung."

William J. Richardson in April of 1962, this change of emphasis in no way implies "a change in the standpoint, much less an abandoning of the fundamental issue, of *Being and Time*."[131]

Some have tried to argue that ex-sistence is not the clearing *tout court*, by alleging that, yes, ex-sistence *is* the clearing but *not all* of the clearing—presumably on the premise that the clearing is divvied up between ex-sistence and "being itself." (There is absolutely no textual evidence for this claim). Others invoke Heidegger's statement that man stands "in relation to" the clearing as "that which man is not."[132] However, Heidegger immediately explains what he means by that phrase when he continues, "insofar as human being *receives its determination from the clearing*."[133] That is, the clearing is human being's raison d'être or οὗ ἕνεκα or *Worumwillen*.[134] The clearing is the very reason why ex-sistence ex-sists at all: it is nothing more or less than the determination and definition of human being. As the τέλος of ex-sistence, the clearing *structurally determines* what and why ex-sistence is at all. But the clearing is not different from ex-sistence.

Heidegger's thematization of the thrown-open clearing is the basis of his claim to have overcome (*überwinden*) or gotten free of (*verwinden*) metaphysics. The last two chapters of this book offer a critique of this claim. Meanwhile the text argues three theses:

1. Heidegger's work was phenomenological from beginning to end.
2. What Heidegger means by *das Sein* is the intelligibility of things, their meaningful presence (*Anwesen*) to human intelligence taken in the broad sense of νοῦς and λόγος, whether practical or theoretical.
3. Heidegger's final goal, the so-called "thing itself," was not intelligibility but what makes intelligibility possible, which, stated formally, is *das Ermöglichende*; and materially is ex-sistence as the thrown-open clearing.[135]

131. GA 11: 149.23–24 = xvi.27–28.

132. GA 15: 390.9–11 = 75.4–5: "zu dem . . . was nicht der Mensch ist."

133. GA 15: 390.10–11 = 75.4–5: "indem er doch von dort seine Bestimmung empfängt." My emphasis in the English.

134. At *Metaphysics* XII 7, 1072b1–3 Aristotle distinguishes between τὸ οὗ ἕνεκα τινί (the for-the-sake-of-the-good-for-*something*-or-*someone-else*) and τὸ οὗ ἕνεκα τινός (the for-the-sake-of-one's-*own*-good). It is the latter meaning that is operative here.

135. Analogous—but only analogous—to τὸ ἀγαθόν in *Republic* VI, 505a2 and VII, 517b8: das Tauglichmachende = das Ermöglichende: GA 6, 2: 379.16–18 = 15.34–16.1.

The book begins where Heidegger did: with the Greeks. The goal of chapters 2 and 3 is to lay out Heidegger's view of what Greek metaphysics, and in particular Aristotle, did and did not accomplish. Some readers may find these chapters a bit thick, and for that I offer my apologies in advance. Nonetheless, this path is essential to a proper understanding of Heidegger's problematic in general and of how he formulated and answered his own basic question. We must insist that the advice Heidegger gave his students about studying Nietzsche applies as well to reading his own works: "First study Aristotle for ten or fifteen years."[136]

Some might find it easier to start directly with chapter 4, even though it is arguably quite difficult (I would say: impossible) to adequately understand Heidegger without understanding how he read the Greeks in general and Aristotle in particular. I argue that many of the needless quandaries in contemporary Heidegger scholarship stem from inadequate understandings of how he made his way through Aristotle to his own question. To take only one example: The key to Heidegger's own phenomenology and specifically to how he understands *Sein* in *Being and Time* lies in his embrace of Aristotle's dictum that any given thing "has as much disclosedness [ἀλήθεια] about it as it has being [εἶναι]."[137] Heidegger anchored that thesis in his brilliant interpretation of *Metaphysics* IX 10, which establishes that in the highest sense (κυριώτατα)[138] *Sein* means the disclosedness-to-understanding of whatever is in question.[139] Heidegger thus argued that, within the limitations of metaphysics, Aristotle had established the proto-phenomenological fact that the analogical unity of all modes of being is disclosedness-to-understanding. Only on this basis was Heidegger able to step beyond Husserl's extraordinary discovery of the categorial intuition (*Logical Investigations* VI/6) into his own question about what makes such categorial intuitions possible. The confluence of these two culminating moments—*Metaphysics* IX 10 as the apex of the whole of the *Metaphysics*, and Investigation VI/6 as the highpoint of *Logical Investigations*—started Heidegger on his lifelong search for the appropriation of ex-sistence as the clearing.

Heidegger's formative insight was that neither Aristotle nor the early Husserl had gone far enough. Neither of these two greats, at the beginning and at the end of metaphysics, asked *how and why* the intelligible disclosure of things to understanding is possible and necessary. Neither of them raised the question: How does a thing's meaningful-presence-as come about? Heideg-

136. GA 8: 78.9 = 73.33: "studieren zuvor zehn oder fünfzehn Jahre hindurch Aristoteles" (as it seems Heidegger himself did).

137. *Metaphysics* II 1, 993b30–31.

138. *Metaphysics* IX 10, 1051b1.

139. GA 73, 2: 975.24: "Sein ist nie ohne Offenbarkeit von Seienden zu Denken."

ger claims that this question—which is his own *Grundfrage*—was not posed either by the pre-Socratics or in any philosophical thinking since then. To be sure, metaphysics, structured as onto-theology, does trace the being of things (whether as εἶδος, ἐνέργεια, *esse*, or whatever) back to a highest exemplar of such being, usually called "God."[140] But that still does not answer—in fact, does not even ask—the question "Why being *at all*?"

To raise that question, Heidegger first abandoned realist metaphysics for phenomenology and thus shifted the subject matter of philosophy from things-in-their-*being* to things-in-their-*intelligibility*. That entailed working out how we make sense of things at all: the task of much of *Being and Time*. But that was only the first step. The second and crucial step consisted in tracing meaningful presence as such (*Anwesen als solches*) back to *Ereignis* as the *Lassen* of *Anwesen*, the letting-be of intelligibility. It was only by grappling with metaphysics in Aristotle that Heidegger arrived at this twofold task. Therefore, because the point is so important, one has to say that even the reader who is not terribly interested in Heidegger's interpretations of Aristotle should at least peruse chapters 2 and 3 in order to see how and where Heidegger positioned his own question vis-à-vis Aristotle's metaphysics.

❖ ❖ ❖

Part One of the book reviews how Heidegger re-read classical Greek philosophy and hit upon the question that guided his own work for over a half century. Chapter 2 probes Heidegger's interpretation of Aristotle as a proto-phenomenologist who implicitly understood that οὐσία is the intelligible appearance or meaningful presence (ἀλήθεια and παρουσία) of things in λόγος, and thus that οὐσία is the openness and availability of things to human beings. For Heidegger this insight, grounded in his reading of *Metaphysics* IX 10, freed being from its confinement to the copula, an achievement that he also found in Husserl's *Logical Investigations*. This allowed Heidegger to set his focus on intelligible disclosedness *itself* and to raise the question, unasked by the Greeks, about its source and necessity.

Chapter 3 shows how Heidegger stepped beyond Aristotelian οὐσία as παρουσία to his own question about the source of παρουσία at all. This chapter spells out the difference between (1) the "guiding question" of metaphysics, which is about the various forms of realness that account for things as real, and (2) Heidegger's own "basic question," which is about what accounts for all forms of realness-as-intelligibility. Heidegger's phenomenological re-reading of Aristotle pushed to their limits three central terms in the *Metaphysics*:

---

140. GA 72, 2: 991.13: "Das Seiendste des Seienden ist der Gott."

ἀλήθεια, εἶδος, and οὐσία. All of them, Heidegger argues, bespeak a relatedness to human intelligence; but unthematized in these phenomena is the prior openedness—ex-sistence as the appropriated clearing—that makes that correlation possible and necessary. One of Heidegger's ur-terms for that open*ed*ness is ἀ-λήθεια (dis-closedness, hence open*ed*ness) in its primary sense. This primary sense is what I call ἀλήθεια-1, which in his early work Heidegger dubbed (misleadingly) "ontological truth." It is ex-sistence itself as the appropriated clearing. Ἀλήθεια-1 is what makes possible the intelligibility of the things we encounter in our pre-theoretical, pre-propositional activities. Such derivative dis-closedness I designate as ἀλήθεια-2 (early Heidegger: "ontic truth").[141] In turn, this pre-propositional intelligibility of a given state of affairs is a necessary condition for the correct correspondence of one's intellect and that state of affairs (ἀλήθεια-3). Only at this third level, where it properly belongs, should we use the word "truth."

Part Two discusses *Being and Time* in three chapters. Chapter 4 spells out Heidegger's phenomenological interpretation of the being of things as their meaningful presence to human beings, without denying the existence of things "out there" in the universe apart from the human disclosure of them. The chapter then lays out Heidegger's interpretation of ex-sistence (*Da-sein*) as *In-der-Welt-sein*—that is, being-and-sustaining the clearing for discursive

intelligibility.[142]

Chapter 5 discusses the sustaining of the clearing-for-intelligibility in terms of *der geworfene Entwurf* or *Ereignis*—thrown-openness or ap-*propri*-ation: ex-sistence as "being made to stand out" (*ex* + *sistere*) *as* possibility *among* possibilities. Such ex-sistence can be glimpsed *in ovo* by comparing and contrasting it with life in general, and especially animal life, under the four headings of: possibility and self-disclosure; having-to-be; bivalent movement; and openness. For Heidegger, the movement of ex-sistence—the fact that it structurally *transcends* things and *returns* to them—is what existentially holds open the clearing and makes possible the particular meanings (*Bedeutungen*) of things. As a whole, this kinetic structure of transcendence-and-return is called *Rede* (λόγος), which is yet another term for *In-der-Welt-sein*.

---

141. Heidegger states the relation of ἀλήθεια-1 and ἀλήθεια-2 at GA 9: 131.22–23 = 103.35: "Enthülltheit des Seins ermöglicht erst Offenbarkeit von Seienden." Italicized in the original.

142. Re "sustaining": *Zollikoner Seminare*, 273.31–274.1 = 218.14–15: "'existieren' mit 'aus-stehen eines Offenheitsbereiches' zu übersetzen." "Ausstehen" should not be translated as "to withstand" as in the ET of GA 9: 374.7 and .10–11 = 284.1 and .4. Heidegger also expresses man's "sustaining" of the clearing in terms of "standing in" it: for example, GA 9: 377.21–22 = 286.29: "der ekstatische, d.h. im Bereich des Offenen innestehende geworfene Entwurf."

Chapter 6 discusses how we can become our "whole" self in what Heidegger calls the resolute anticipation of death: the effective acknowledgement and embrace of the finitude and mortality of our thrown-openness. Experiencing the rare and momentary collapse of all our meaning-giving worlds lets us see the utter groundlessness—the "absurdity"—of ex-sistence as the clearing-for-intelligibility. This experience throws us back (cf. *abweisen*) into our ineluctable engagement with things in their intelligibility, but now with an awareness of what is at stake and with the possibility of assuming authorship of our own groundless and mortal lives. Authentic assumption of our absurd thrown-openness entails personally becoming the finitude and mortality that we are, as we live with and make sense of whomever and whatever we encounter. To make such a choice, Heidegger says, is to become "authentically temporal." This in turn makes possible "authentic historicity." We shall have to redefine these two terms in the course of this chapter.

Part Three focuses on Heidegger after *Being and Time* and shows the unity and continuity of the earlier and later formulations of his project. Chapter 7 discusses some of the obstacles that Heidegger faced in moving from the first moment of his project (the structure of ex-sistence as sustaining the clearing-for-meaning: SZ I.1–2) to the second moment (the thrown-open clearing as the source of all forms of meaningful presence: SZ I.3). For Heidegger to have finished *Being and Time* as it was originally planned would have meant completing his "fundamental ontology" within a transcendental framework; and this was to have provided the groundwork for elaborating certain regional ontologies under the rubric of "metontology." However, by December of 1930 Heidegger's momentous discovery of the *intrinsic hiddenness* of the appropriated clearing rendered the transcendental approach of *Being and Time* inadequate for completing the project. Thus he began the famous change (*Wandel*) of the 1930s from transcendentalism to what he called a *seinsgeschichtlich* approach, where "*seinsgeschichtlich*" in its proper and restricted sense is not about "history" at all, but has to do with how appropriation makes possible ("gives," "sends," "dispenses") the various configurations of the clearing-for-meaning throughout Western metaphysics.

Chapter 8 discusses appropriation and the much-misunderstood term *die Kehre* (usually "the turn"). This chapter shows the sameness of thrownness in *Being and Time* and appropriation in the later work and argues that appropriation bespeaks the ur-fact that ex-sistence is thrown open as the clearing. The chapter also lays out the various meanings of the "turn," and shows that the usual meaning (the apparent reversal from *Dasein* to *Sein* in the 1930s) is not the primary and proper meaning of *die Kehre*.

Chapter 9 investigates Heidegger's so-called "history of being" (*Seinsgeschichte*), which in fact is four distinct things. First of all, it is a straightforward historical (*historisch*) account about what being is and how it functions in a dozen or so philosophers from the pre-Socratics through Nietzsche. Secondly, it argues that these philosophers either did not question (in the case of the pre-Socratics) or overlooked and forgot (from Plato to Husserl) the appropriation of ex-sistence. As such, the *Seinsgeschichte* is also a *Vergessenheitsgeschichte*, a history of the forgetting *not* of "being" but of "appropriation." Thirdly, the so-called *Seinsgeschichte* is an argument that appropriation "gives" or "sends" the various historical configurations of the clearing-for-meaning "to" the philosophers who comprise Heidegger's history, even as those philosophers overlook the source of such "sendings." Fourthly, this history of (a) the overlooking of *Ereignis* coupled with (b) the "sending" of configurations of the clearing-for-meaning—becomes a narrative of the devolution of Western culture, a downfall that is due precisely to the overlooking of appropriation. This alleged concatenation of ever-increasing stages of obliviousness culminates, in Heidegger's story, in the contemporary global modus vivendi that is characterized by such widespread techno-think and techno-do that any inkling of appropriation is obliterated, with disastrous consequences.

The Conclusion, comprised of Chapter 10, offers critical reflections on Heidegger's 1953 lecture "The Question of Technology." I argue that the lecture exposes the severe limitations of Heidegger's later philosophy, especially regarding history in general and modernity in particular.

PART ONE

Aristotelian Beginnings

2

Being in Aristotle

"Philosophy," Heidegger says, "is knowledge of the essence of things."[1] It searches for the causes and principles of things in order to get at the ultimate reasons that explain what, why, and how things are. With Socrates and Plato the philosophical question formally emerges in the West as the dialectical inquiry beyond, for example, virtues to virtue-ness (the *Meno*) or beyond pious acts to pious-ness (the *Euthyphro*). In general terms the philosophical question asks for the X-ness of any X. We may designate this "-ness" dimension as the *essence* of X, if we may use the word "essence" broadly and prescind for now from the distinction of essence/existence.

But the highest form of philosophy—what Aristotle called "first philosophy"[2]—asks not about the essence of particular things or regions of things (the X-ness of all Xs, the Y-ness of all Ys). It asks instead about the very "is-ness" of all-that-is, the realness that makes anything be real. It is "justified speech about the whole and the first," or in Heidegger's terms, about "the whole with regard to its origins."[3] It encompasses everything that exists, and inquires into it from the most universal viewpoint, that of its realness as such. In that sense, this question does not belong to any of the "partial" or "regional" sciences.[4] Such sciences cut off one or another attribute of things (motion, for example, in Aristotle's *Physics*) and study things under that aspect. By contrast, the question of first philosophy becomes: What is a thing, any particular thing, insofar as it is real? For Aristotle, a thing (τὸ ὄν) = something that "is" or "has being,"[5] something that is "real." But, of course, this prompts the question of what "real" means—which is the core question of all metaphysics: "What constitutes the

1. GA 45: 29.28–29 = 29.18–19: "Philosophie [ist] das Wissen vom Wesen der Dinge." This focus on the "essence" or being [*Sein*] of things is what distinguishes philosophy from the sciences: "[D]as Seiende kann untersucht werden, ohne ausdrücklich nach dem Sein zu fragen," GA 22: 8.11–12 = 6.20–21.

2. *Metaphysics* VI 1, 1026a30 and XI, 4, 1061b19: φιλοσοφία πρώτη. Also *On the Motion of Animals* 6, 700b9.

3. Respectively, Thomas Prufer, "A Protreptic," 2; and GA 19: 212.2–3 = 146.32: "das Ganze hinsichtlich seiner Ursprünge."

4. *Metaphysics* VI 1, 1003a22–23: ἐπιστῆμαι ἐν μέρει λεγόμεναι.

5. GA 22: 7.14–15 = 5.36: "Es [das Seiende] ist, es *hat Sein*." Heidegger's emphasis.

realness of the real?" To articulate this "realness of the real," Heidegger (like most all other philosophers) employs the two most formally indicative words in the lexicon, in his case, "*das Sein*" for "realness" and "*das Seiende*" for "the real." As formally indicative, all such words (and their equivalents in any other language) are only placeholders, stand-in terms, for whatever Aristotle or Heidegger or any other philosopher *thinks* the realness of the real consists in. For Plato the realness of a thing consisted in its "ideal intelligible appearance" (εἶδος). Aristotle thought the realness of a thing consisted in its possession of or its functioning unto perfection (ἐντελέχεια, ἐνέργεια), whereas Aquinas thought it lay in the thing's participation, via creation, in the very life of God. In other words, the terms "realness" or *Sein* or *esse* or "being" are only formal indications of what philosophers will argue is the *content* or meaning of the "realness" of things. For Heidegger, as we shall see, *das Sein* is only a formal indication of what *he* will argue is the content of that term—namely, the meaningful presence of something in and for human intelligence. Therefore, in what follows I will use the words *Sein*, *Seiendheit*, and "realness" as *ex aequo* formal indications of the specific, not-yet-determined content that Plato, Aristotle, Aquinas, Heidegger—and we ourselves—have yet to argue for.[6]

The circularity here is obvious. To ask for the realness of whatever-is-real promotes that question to the level of a second one: What is meant by—what constitutes—the "realness" that things are said to "have" to the degree that they are "real"? Two questions converge here: What is *a thing* insofar as it is real? What is the *very realness* that such a thing is said to have? These two questions comprise the work of traditional *ontology*. Asking and answering a third question—"What is the highest instance of the real-in-its-realness?"—is the work of "natural" (i.e., philosophical) *theology*. Insofar as metaphysics traditionally comprises both ontology (general metaphysics) and natural theology (special metaphysics), Heidegger refers to it as "onto-theology."

Aristotle opens up the ontological moment of metaphysics when he declares that "there is a certain science that investigates things insofar as they are real at all."[7] But he also hints (and only that) at the second and more important question at the beginning of Book VI of the *Metaphysics*, when he says in effect that we will not find an adequate answer to the first question, focused on real *things*, until we first answer the second question: What do we mean by "realness as such"?[8]

---

6. "Realness": an entity's existence in what one takes to be "the nature of things"; see GA 84, 1: 396.9–10 and Suarez, *Disputationes metaphysicae*, XXXI, section I, 2: "esse aliquid in rerum natura" and "aliquid reale."

7. *Metaphysics* IV 1, 1003a21: a science of τὸ ὂν ᾗ ὄν. Also ibid., VI 1, 1026a31–32.

8. See SZ 11.18–19 = 31.25–26: Answering the second question would explain the a priori conditions not only of the ontic sciences but of ontology as such.

> The question that was raised of old and is raised now and will always be raised, the question that is always a puzzle—"What is a real thing?" [τί τὸ ὄν;]—comes down to the question "What is realness itself?" [τίς ἡ οὐσία;].[9]

If the second question, about realness as such, *were* systematically asked, one possible solution would be to trace all instances of realness back to the entity that is the most real of all, God as *das Seiendste*.[10] However, to anchor realness in some thing or person, even theologically in the highest divine thing or person, is to leave unresolved the question of what constitutes the realness of *that* thing as well as the nature of realness *at all.*

But what do we mean by translating Aristotle's word οὐσία as "realness"? Figuring out what that key philosophical term means—both in Aristotle (οὐσία) and in Heidegger (*Seiendheit*)—requires a brief review of the Greek words that underlie it.

❖ ❖ ❖

The Greek verb "to be" (εἶναι) declines the nominative of its present participle as:

MASCULINE	FEMININE	NEUTER
ὤν	οὖσα	ὄν
he, *being* [e.g., tall],	she, *being* [tall],	it, *being* [tall]

To form the word "a thing," Greek takes the neuter present participle ὄν, combines it with the definite article, and thereby turns it into the noun τὸ ὄν, parallel to the German neologism *das Seiende*, the Italian *l'ente*, and the article-less Latin *ens*. Τὸ ὄν can express either a *single* thing that is real or *all* things that are real. We may translate τὸ ὄν into English as "a thing," or "things" or "the real," when it refers in general to whatever "has realness." "Things-that-are-real" is sometimes expressed by the plural, τὰ ὄντα.

On the other hand, to express the *realness* that these things "have," Greek takes the feminine present participle οὖσα and turns it into a noun: οὐσία, which means "realness" (that which makes the real *be* real) or, inelegantly, "being-ness" (*Seiend-heit*), analogous to the way one might say that "treeness" makes a tree be a tree and not a loaf of bread. In the citation above (*Metaphysics* VI 1, 1028b2–4), Aristotle said that the answer to the question "What

9. *Metaphysics* VI 1, 1028b2–4.

10. GA 73, 2: 991.13: "Das Seiendste des Seienden ist der Gott."

is a real thing?" comes down to what one means by realness, or, in Greek, what one means by οὐσία, the very "is-ness" of "what-is," or the "being" of "what-has-being." Heidegger rejects the usual translation of οὐσία as "substance," from the Latin *substantia* (even though he might have appreciated its etymology: the rare verb *substo*, the basis of *substantia*, has the sense of "to be present"). Medieval translations of οὐσία as *essentia* (the "*esse*-ness" of what-has-*esse*) tend to understand that Latin term as "essence" in contradistinction to "existence," whereas in Aristotle οὐσία covers both essence *and* existence. Therefore, to express the οὐσία of τὸ ὄν (the realness of the real) while avoiding those translation traps, Heidegger translates οὐσία as the "beingness of things" ("*die Seiendheit des Seienden*," which is exactly the same as *das Sein des Seienden* in its traditional sense).[11] But again, this usage still leaves open the question of what Heidegger thinks *Sein*/*Seiendheit*/realness cashes out as in Aristotle *and* in his own work.

Οὐσία was a common Greek term before Plato and Aristotle brought it into the province of philosophy. In its primary sense it refers to a *thing* or *things*. But the philosophers used it to refer also to the *realness* of a thing; and one has to be clear on which of the two usages is operative in a given case—that is, whether in a text from Plato or Aristotle οὐσία means a particular thing or the very realness of that thing. When Heidegger refers to οὐσία, he means it predominantly in the second sense: as the *Sein* or realness of a thing.

In classical Greek, regardless of whether οὐσία is used *non*-philosophically to refer to the real, or philosophically to refer to the realness of the real, the notion of "real" has two connotations: a thing's *presence* and its *stability*: being as the stable presence of something. Here "presence" means *availability*, with overtones of what *belongs* to a person. In its pre-philosophical sense, οὐσία meant what is one's own: property in the form of goods or wealth, livestock, land, or even a worker's tools. Οὐσία refers to one's stable possessions or holdings, something that one *has a stake in*, as with John Locke's "to have a property in something."[12] Heidegger's argument is worth citing at length.

> In Greek οὐσία means things—not just any things but things that in a certain way are *exemplary in their realness*, namely the things that *belong* to you, your goods and possessions, house and home (what you own, your wealth), what

11. See GA 15: 344.13–15 = 46.35–36: "Frage nach dem Sein des Seienden, mit anderen Worten: Frage nach der Seiendheit des Seienden." GA 66: 200.32 = 176.35: "die Seiendheit als das Sein." GA 74: 6.3: "Seiendheit ist das Sein." GA 66: 316.25–27 = 281.31–33: "Unverborgenheit des Seienden und Offenbarkeit des Seienden besagt griechisch: Anwesung und d.h. Sein und d.h. Seiendheit und d.h. Seiendes als solches." Aquinas calls this Seiendheit "entitas" in his commentary on Aristotle's *Metaphysics*, Book VII, lectio 2, no. 35 (1304).

12. John Locke, *Two Treatises*, chapter V § 25, 111.

> is at your disposal. These things—goods and possessions—are able to stand at your disposal because they are *fixed, steadfastly within your reach*, at hand, present in your immediate environment. . . .
>
> What makes them exemplary? Our goods and possessions are invariantly within our reach. Ever at our disposal, they are what lies close to us, they are right here, presented on a platter; they are *steadfastly presented to us.* They are the closest to us, and as steadfastly closest, they are in a special sense *at-hand*, present before us, *present to* us. Because they are exemplarily here, and because they are present to us, we call our goods, possessions, and wealth our *estate*—this is what the Greeks meant by οὐσία: our *present holdings*.[13] In fact with οὐσία the Greeks meant nothing but *steadfast presence*, and this is what we understand by realness. This steadfast presence or present steadfastness is what we mean by the *realness* [of something]. Whatever measures up to this notion of realness as steadfast presence, whatever is *always at hand*, is what the Greeks called a thing in the proper sense.[14]

Clearly this "presence" (the presence *of* the thing, or equally, the thing *as* present) indicates not merely the fact that something is just "objectively out there" (*vorhanden*) in front of us. More significantly it indicates that something is "proper" to us, our property, something we are involved with, indeed something we own. Such a thing is not just present "alongside us" in physical space (*neben uns*) but also *to* us (*bei uns*): we are *interested in* and *involved with* it.[15] Such presence entails an interested "dative," an involved "recipient" of that presence. In this Greek meaning of οὐσία as παρουσία (παρά + οὐσία: "presence *unto*") Heidegger espies an implicit phenomenological correlation in Greek philosophy and especially in Aristotle: to ask *what* something is, is to ask how someone is involved with it, interested in it—that is, how that thing is significant and meaningful to that person. Thus, the question "What makes up the οὐσία or realness of a chair?" comes down to how *we understand* the chair in its (usually tacit) relation to us.[16] Heidegger understands οὐσία as the relatedness of something *to* someone *within* the world of one's interests and concerns. Thus he will interpret Aristotle's use of οὐσία as

13. See Plato, *Theaetetus*, 144c7: Theaetetus' father, Euphronius, left behind "an exceedingly large fortune" (οὐσίαν μάλα πολλήν). Also *Republic* VIII, 551b2–3: No one shall hold office whose property or possessions (οὐσία) do not reach the required amount. (Heidegger comments on this last text at GA 34: 326.1–4 = 231.6–7.) Heidegger translates οὐσία at *Phaedrus* 240a2 as "das vorhandene Verfügbare": GA 83: 118.8. See "zur Verfügung anwesend" at GA 33: 179.25–26 = 154.6.

14. GA 31: 51.11–15 and 51.31–34 = 36.8–11 and .21–25, my translation. See also GA 9, 260.7–18 = 199.20–29 and GA 40: 65.17–24 = 66.17–25.

15. The translations of "Sein bei" in *Being and Time* as "being alongside" (Macquarrie-Robinson) and "being together with" (Stambaugh) entirely miss this point.

16. GA 31: 56.13–16 = 39.23–25.

proto-phenomenological. In this view the ontological status of things is not "objective" in the sense of being indifferent to human beings. Rather, it is the phenomenological presence (the personally experienced relatedness and significance) of something to and for a person, in correlation with the interests that person has in the thing.

The remainder of this chapter spells out the specifics of Heidegger's reading of Aristotle as a proto-phenomenologist. We do so by studying Heidegger's re-interpretations of key terms in the Aristotelian lexicon: φύσις, ἀλήθεια, πέρας, ἀεί, εἶδος, ἐνέργεια, and ἐντελέχεια, along with Aristotle's interpretation of being as disclosedness, as he worked that out in *Metaphysics* IX 10.

❖ ❖ ❖

Before going into further detail about the relatively late (fourth century BCE) Platonic-Aristotelian term οὐσία, we will first investigate what Heidegger claims are among the oldest philosophical terms in the Greek lexicon: φύσις and ἀλήθεια.[17] Heidegger speaks of "the unique essential relation between φύσις and ἀλήθεια,"[18] and he argues that the two terms go together: "Φύσις points to ἀλήθεια itself."[19] Taken as a unity, φύσις/ἀλήθεια or emergence-as-disclosedness bespeaks the emergence *of some thing* (not of φύσις or ἀλήθεια in and for itself) from a state of concealment-from-us into one of dis-closedness to us—that is, manifestation and availability.[20] Thus in the following text Heidegger is referring to *things* emerging into availability *thanks to* φύσις/ἀλήθεια.

> In the age of the first and definitive unfolding of Western philosophy among the Greeks, when questioning about the real as such and as a whole received its true inception, things were called φύσις. [. . .] But what does the word φύσις mean? It indicates something that emerges from itself (e.g., the emergence, the blossoming, of a rose), the unfolding that opens itself up, something's

17. GA 4: 56.15–16 = 79.1–2, re φύσις: "Dieses Wort ist das Grundwort der Denker im Anfang des abendlänidschen Denkens."

18. GA 40: 109.26–27 = 121.12–14. See GA 66: 111.18–19 = 93.6–7: "im ersten Anfang verborgen φύσις und ἀλήθεια dasselbe und einzige 'sind.'"

19. GA 15: 344.5 = 46.30. See GA 45: 68.7 = 61.25–26: "beständiger sich auftuender und sich zeigender Anwesenheit"; ibid., 68.23–24 = 62.5–6: aufgehendes sich zeigendes Anwesen (italicized in the original).

20. GA 15: 331.5–7 = 38.16–18: "Hervorkommen-[des-Seienden]-aus-der-Verborgenheit (im Sinn der φύσις)" and "Aufgehen-[des-Seienden]-in-die-ἀλήθεια." For an entity's "aus der Verborgenheit heraustreten" see GA 40: 109.16 = 112.3–4; ibid., 122.4 = 126.8–9. Re "to us": GA 38: 80.17–18 = 69.1–3: "Der Zusatz 'wahr für uns' hat aber gar keinen Sinn, da ja der Bezug auf uns zur Wahrheit gehört."

> coming-into-appearance in such unfolding, and holding itself and persisting in appearance.[21]

We note two distinct meanings of φύσις here, one referring to things, the other referring to the being of those things. In the beginning of Greek philosophy, Heidegger says, φύσις in one sense was a name for things, indeed *all* things, whether they are natural things or artifacts; and in a second sense, φύσις is not a thing but is that which *allows* all those things to emerge as what and how they are. Heidegger also points out the etymological connection between the Greek φυ- and φα-, which are the respective roots of φύειν and φαίνεσθαι ("to grow" and "to show"), which in turn are the etymons of φύσις (the unfolding-emergence of a thing into visibility and availability) and φαινόμενον (that which *has* unfolded and emerged and so is visible and available). Note that the following two texts are referring to the self-showing (or intrinsic availability) of things, but not of φύσις in its second sense, as the being of things.

> Recently, the radical φυ- has been connected with φα-, φαίνεσθαι. Φύσις would then be something that emerges into the light; φύειν: to light up, to shine forth, and therefore to appear.[22]

> The roots φυ- and φα- name the same thing. Φύειν—the emerging [of a thing], an emerging that reposes in itself—is φαίνεσθαι, being lit up, showing up, appearing.[23]

In other words, φύσις does what ἀλήθεια does:

> it makes something manifest. This already implies that the being [of something], i.e., its appearing, is letting-that-thing-step-forth from hiddenness. Insofar as a thing as such *is*, it is placed into and stands in *disclosedness,* ἀλήθεια.[24]

It is important to be clear on this point: Such unfolding, emerging, and appearing is *that of a thing* and not of φύσις itself. In the origins of Western

21. GA 40: 15.25–28 and 16.23–26 = 15.1–4 and 15.28–32; see ibid., 134.5–6 = 138.14–15: "das aufgehende Walten." GA 66: 87.2–3 = 72.28–29: "Im ersten Anfang: *der Aufgang* (φύσις), die sich entfaltende (öffnende) Anwesung."

22. GA 40: 76.13–16 = 78.19–22: "das ins Licht Aufgehende"; leuchten, scheinen, erscheinen. See Friedrich Specht, "Beiträge zur griechischen Grammatik," 61.35–62.4. "Such an active φαύειν [= φάειν, to shine] would have to coincide in meaning with φύειν and thus be a kind of causative verb to φύεσθαι [i.e., to *make* something come forth]." Fried and Polt provide a helpful reference to this article at p. 78, note 14, of their translation of GA 40.

23. GA 40: 108.9–11 = 110.20–22: "das in sich ruhende Aufgehen."

24. GA 40: 109.15–18 = 112.3–5; see 147.21–22 = 154.17–18: "Sein besagt: im Licht stehen, erscheinen in die Unverborgenheit treten." All of these verbs name what an *entity* does thanks to its being-*qua*-φύσις.

philosophy, Heidegger says, "we see that φύσις is the self-unfolding emergence [of a thing] wherein and whereby a thing first is what it is."[25] He is speaking here of the early Greek vision where all things are viewed under the rubric of their emergence from some form of hiddenness. Later, however, Aristotle will limit such intrinsic emergence (φύσις) to only "natural" things (φύσει ὄν) rather than all things including artifacts (τέχνη ὄν). Moreover, within the realm of "nature" Aristotle distinguishes between φύσει ὄν (natural *things*) and their φύσις itself as their emergence-into-appearance, just as, in the realm of the artifactual, he distinguishes between τέχνη ὄν, on the one hand, and τέχνη as their being, on the other.

Thus the two meanings that Heidegger draws out from φύσις and intensifies by the connection with ἀλήθεια are the *emergence* and the *appearance* of a thing, indeed the thing's emergence *as* "self"-showing.[26] (The *faux* reflexive "*self*-showing" means the *intrinsic* showing-up of a thing, of and by itself.) In this Greek view, things, when wrested from non-accessibility into accessibility, are open and available to us. What makes a thing be real is that thing's very openness to human concerns, its availability to human knowing and acting.[27]

❖ ❖ ❖

Along with emergence and appearing, another significant ontological characteristic of things is their *Ständigkeit*, their steadfastness. "Φύσις is the emerging power [of a thing], its standing-there-in-itself: steadfastness."[28] The German noun *Ständigkeit* is usually translated as "permanence," but Heidegger

25. GA 73, 1: 85.18–20: "zeigt sich: φύσις—das *Sichentfaltende* [sic] *Aufgehen*, worin und wodurch erst das Seiende ist, was es ist." I have omitted the italics in this translation.

26. All of the following texts refer to the "activities" (of emerging, appearing, coming-to-presence) that a *thing* does, thanks to its being-*qua*-φύσις: GA 40: 16.22–24 = 15.31–32: "das sich eroffnende Entfalten, das in solcher Entfaltung in die Erscheinung-Tretten"; ibid., 65.34–35 = 67.5–6: "das aufgehende Sichaufrichten, das in sich verweilende Sichentfalten"; ibid., 76.12–13 = 78.18–19: "aufgehen, das wiederum vom Anwesen und Erscheinen her bestimmt bleibt"; ibid., 117.8–9 = 120.15–16: das aufgehende Sichzeigen; ibid. 122.4 = 126.8–9: "aufgehendes Erscheinen, aus der Verborgenheit heraustreten"; ibid., 122.31–123.1 = 127.7–8: "aufgehend-erscheinendes Anwesen, Nichtsein als Abwesen"; ibid., 191.8 = 203.2: aufgehendes Scheinen (italicized in the original). GA 45: 68.23–24 = 62.5–6: "aufgehendes sich zeigendes Anwesen" (italicized in the original).

27. When Heidegger speaks of being (*Sein*/*Seiendheit*) as the manifestness of a thing, we must remember that he means this *phenomenologically*. Such manifestation happens only in correlation with human beings understood as "having λόγος." See GA 5: 74.3–4 = 55.26: "Sein aber ist Zuspruch an den Menschen und nicht ohne diesen." SZ 152.11–12 = 193.31–32: Heidegger's inquiry "fragt nach ihm selbst [= das Sein selbst], sofern es in die Verständlichkeit des Daseins hereinsteht."

28. GA 40: 191.21–22 = 203.14–15: "Φύσις ist das aufgehende Walten, das In-sich-dastehen, ist Ständigkeit." Also ibid., 189.32–33 = 201.10–11.

deflects that meaning by emphasizing the rootedness of the word in the verb *stehen*, to stand. When a thing emerges into the state of disclosedness, it *takes a stand*, with the double meaning of "standing there" and "staying there." The being of such a thing is both its *stability* and its *staying power*.

> For the Greeks, "being" bespeaks steadfastness in the double sense of:
>
> 1. the standing-in-itself as the arising-and-standing-forth [of a thing] (φύσις),
> 2. yet doing so "con-stantly," that is, enduringly, as a staying-there-awhile (οὐσία).[29]

To take stability first: Being is a thing's intrinsic power (*das Walten*), which enables that thing to "stand on its own," to take "an upright stand"[30] and, in appearing, to show up *as* steadily present. For the Greeks such steadfastness entails that a thing has "run up against the necessity of its limit, its πέρας"[31] in the sense of "being placed into its form" (μορφή).[32] This means "self"-limitation: a thing's "holding itself together" in such a way that it can stand of and by itself and so be real.

> This πέρας [the so-called "limit" of a thing] is not something that first comes to a thing from outside. Much less is it some deficiency, in the sense of a detrimental restriction. Instead, the self-restraining "hold" that comes from a limit, the having-of-itself in which the steadfast thing holds itself, is the being of that thing. It is what first makes a thing *be* a thing as opposed to not-a-thing. Therefore, for something to take such a stand means for it to attain its limit, to de-limit itself.[33]
>
> Πέρας in Greek philosophy is not "limit" in the sense of the outer boundary, the point where something ends. The limit is always that which limits, defines, gives footing and stability, that by which and in which something begins and is.[34]

---

29. GA 40: 68.7–10 = 70.1–4. Here Heidegger is using Ent-stehendes in the double sense of the "arising" and the "coming-forth" of a φύσει ὄν.

30. GA 40: 68.24 = 70.17: ein aufrechtes Stand. Ibid., 116.11 = 119.13–14: "Being" in the sense of "[das] Gerade-in-sich-aufrecht-dastehen [des Seienden]."

31. GA 40: 64.18–20 = 65.15–17: "Was dergestalt zum Stand kommt, in sich *ständig* wird, schlägt sich dabei von sich her frei in die Notwendigkeit seiner Grenze, πέρας."

32. Cf. GA 40: 67.7–8 = 68.18–19: "das in Grenzen Geschlagen [d.h. in seine Gestalt Gestellte]."

33. GA 40: 64.20–27 = 65.17–24. *See Zollikoner Seminare* 40.1–4 = 32.19–22; GA 7: 156.22–24 = 154.18–20; GA 36/37: 93.28–30 = 75.4–6.

34. GA 9, 269.21–24 = 206.9–12. See Plotinus *Enneads* V 1: 7.25–26: steadfastness (στάσις) is equated with limitation (ὁρισμός) and form (μορφή), and these are related to ex-sistence (ὑπόστασις). (All references to the *Enneads* are to the standard *Plotini opera*, ed. Henry and Schwyzer.) For the relation of limit and limitation to human ex-sistence: GA 15: 359.34–35 = 56.25–26: "Aber die wesentliche Beschränkung, die Endlichkeit, ist vielleicht Bedingung der echten Existenz."

The stability of an emergent-appearing thing is thus its "con-stancy," its ingatheredness (*con-*) into a stand (Late Latin *stare*), into its "form"—that is, its intelligible appearance. Here "constancy" is to be understood primarily as *steadfastness-in-appearance* rather than as permanent presence. Heidegger puts *Ständigkeit* and ἀλήθεια together: "The standing [of a thing] is the constancy of [the thing's] shining."[35]

> This self-unfolding emergence is the standing-in-φύσις of the thing that is present within [that dynamism]—it is the occurrence of the presence [of the thing]: its coming to presence. But that entails two things. The intrinsic unfolding from out of itself—whatever is stable-in-itself—has absolutely no need of anything else [in order to come to a stand as itself]. But at the same time the emergence thanks to which everything has its permanence and enduring, is what is constant in itself.[36]

After the first meaning of a thing's "taking a stand" the second meaning that Heidegger retrieves from *Ständigkeit* as steadfastness is *staying power*. Having taken a stand within its limits and in its form, a thing "stays around" for a while. In itself steadfastness does not necessarily entail that the thing is *permanently* present (although it can gain that sense: see below). Rather, steadfastness, as an entity's being, refers to the staying power whereby a thing holds itself in appearance and "stays there for a while."[37]

In this regard Heidegger offers an illuminating interpretation of the Greek adverb ἀεί, which is usually translated as "forever" or "eternally."[38] At *Physics* 193a21–28 Aristotle starkly contrasts two Greek terms: ἀΐδιον (usually "eternal," from ἀεί) versus ἀπειράκις ("without limit": compare ἀ + πέρας, and the Latin translation *in-finities*). Heidegger argues that in the context of *Physics* II 1, ἀΐδιον is *not* to be understood as "persisting, continuing" (*das Fortwähren*)[39] or even "everlasting" in the sense of limitless duration or sempiternity. That would be the meaning of ἀπειράκις (ongoing without limit), which is the very opposite of ἀεί. Rather, ἀΐδιον refers to a thing's *current* (*jeweilig*) presence within its πέρας, but a "presence that *is in itself.*"[40] A thing that is ἀΐδιον is not

---

35. GA 5: 71.2–3 = 53.12–13: "'Stehen' ist (vgl. S. 21) die Ständigkeit des Scheinens." Ibid., 21.30–31 = 16.15–16: "Das Sein des Seienden kommt in das Ständige seines Scheinens."

36. GA 73, 1: 85.20–22: "Das Sichentfaltende [*sic*] Aufgehen aber ist das Hereinstehen von darin Anwesendem—Geschehnis der Anwesenheit—Anwesung."

37. Verweilen is usually (but a bit too preciously) translated as "to tarry" or "to while."

38. GA 9: 268.18–270.13 = 205.17–206.32.

39. GA 73, 1: 86.10.

40. GA 73, 1: 86.10. "das *In-sich-wesende* Anwesen." Heidegger continues: "die Ewigkeit—das ἐξαίφνης (Dialog Parmenides)," ibid., 86.10–11. He is referring to his interpretation of "eternity" (see immediately below) and to Plato's *Parmenides* 156d3, "the instant" or "the

one that is forever ongoing but rather one that, as self-contained, is authentically present *for the time being*. When Aeschylus' Prometheus refers to Zeus as ὁ ἀεί κρατῶν[41] ("the one who is ruling ἀεί"), he means the deity "who is *currently* in power." Prometheus could not be calling Zeus the "eternal ruler" after having just predicted that Zeus would soon be cast off his throne.[42] The same holds for when Herodotus speaks of ὁ ἀεί βασιλεύων Αἰγύπτου: he does not mean some "eternal" Egyptian Pharaoh but rather "the one who reigns in Egypt *at the time*."[43] Insofar as ἀεί and ἀίδιον can refer to the being of things, these terms do not primarily designate chronological permanence—"there for all time"—but rather an entity's *current stability* within its πέρας. And that is the reason why, in other contexts and in the right circumstances, ἀΐδιος can take on the meaning "everlasting."[44]

In short, Heidegger is arguing that φύσις and ἀλήθεια, taken together, bespeak (1) an entity's emergence from "un-disclosedness," whatever that will turn out to mean, and (2) its steadfast, delimited appearance as present and disclosed—or to put it phenomenologically, as accessible to us as meaningful.

> This says that whatever shows itself in the power [of its being] stands in [the sphere of] the disclosed. The disclosed entity as such comes to a stand in showing itself. . . . Dis-closedness is not an addendum to being.[45]

❖ ❖ ❖

With Plato (and later, but in a different valence, with Aristotle) the emergent, disclosed, steadfast, delimited appearance of something comes to be read as εἶδος and ἰδέα, the "intelligible appearance" of something (εἶδος from ἰδεῖν: to see; cf. εἰδέναι: "having seen, to know").[46] With that, says Heidegger, φύσις

---

moment," using the nominalized adverb derived from ἄφνω, "suddenly, unawares, in the moment."

41. Aeschylus, *Prometheus Bound*, line 937: τὸν κρατοῦντ᾽ ἀεί.

42. Cast off his throne: ibid., lines 907–10.

43. Herodotus, *Histories*, II, 98, 345: τοῦ αἰεὶ βασιλεύοντος Αἰγύπτου (http://www.sacred-texts.com/cla/hh/hh2090.htm). In context: The city of Anthylla in lower Egypt was especially assigned "to the wife of whoever happens to be ruling Egypt at the time."

44. GA 9: 269.13–16 = 206.3–5.

45. GA 40: 109.31–32 = 112.17–18: "Die Wahrheit ist als Un-verborgenheit nicht eine Zugabe zum Sein."

46. *Metaphysics* I 1, 980a1. Augustine at Cassiciacum continued the tradition of the εἴδη as intelligible appearances by speaking of them as "quae intelligibiliter lucent"—that is, the eternal meanings [of things] that appear ("shine") only to the intellect: *Soliloquies* I, 3, *Patrologia Latina* 32, 870.17–18. See GA 19: 70.1–5 = 48.17–20. Heidegger first encountered the etymology of εἶδος in Braig, *Die Grundzüge der Philosophie*, 20.1–10.

in its unity with ἀλήθεια began to get covered over.[47] Plato understood being as εἶδος, the intelligible appearance or knowability of something, such that the thing can be "seen" in the whatness in which and as which it comes to stand steadfastly in presence. "In the intelligible appearance [εἶδος], the thing is present and stands there in its whatness and howness."[48] But with the introduction of Platonic εἶδος a subtle shift takes place with portentous consequences. Ἰδέα and εἶδος become characteristics of whatever stands there only insofar as they stand in relation to a human seeing. "The Greek word ἰδέα [means] what is seen *in the act of seeing*, the intelligible appearance, the thing's appearance as placed there in a placing-before-one."[49] As Heidegger reads him, Plato understands the individual thing as offering this intelligible appearance as a kind of "foreground" of itself, a "surface" that tells the person looking at it how and as what the thing is to be intellectually apprehended.[50] Correlatively, and in keeping with the fifth-century BCE "turn to the human,"[51] this Platonic whatness becomes the "possession" of an intellectual apprehension. "It is the *what-is-held* in [an act of] taking-in, it is the *available* presence of what is present: οὐσία."[52] The result of this Platonic over-valorization of essence is that the individual concrete *thing* gets demoted to second rank, overshadowed, as it were, by its εἶδος, which, as "the being-est element of the thing," is then taken to be alone the "really real" (ὄντως ὄν).[53] This Platonic shift regarding the being of things is where Heidegger locates the origin of the later distinction between *existentia* and *essentia*.

> If we understand the ἰδέα, the intelligible appearance, as [the thing's] presence, then presence shows itself as [a thing's] steadfastness in a double sense. On the one hand, the intelligible appearance entails the standing-forth-from-concealment, the simple ἔστιν ["it is"]. On the other hand, what shows itself in the intelligible appearance is that which looks a certain way, i.e., *what* stands

47. GA 65: 222.12–14 = 174.4–6: "φύσις . . . verdeckt in eins mit ἀλήθεια durch die ἰδέα."

48. GA 40: 190.2–3 = 201.14–16. Note the conjunction (and functional equivalence) of ἀλήθεια, πέρας/μορφή, and εἶδος /ἰδέα as terms for being/*Seiendheit*: "etwas erscheinen, in seinem Umriß [= πέρας/ μορφή], in seinem 'Aussehen' (εἶδος, ἰδέα) sich zeigen und so je als Dieses und Jenes anwesend sein kann": GA 4: 56.28–30 = 79.13–14.

49. GA 42: 158.15–17 = 91.37–39, my emphasis.

50. On "foreground" and "surface" (das Vordergründige, Vorderfläche, Oberfläche), see GA 40: 191.1 = 201.13 and 191.29 = 203.22.

51. See Jaeger, *Paideia,* I, 237ff. and vol. II passim; also his *Humanism and Theology*, 42ff.

52. GA 40: 190.4–5 = 201.16–19, my emphasis.

53. GA 40: 193.1–7 = 205.4–11. Also GA 45: 85.24–25 = 76.28. For ὄντως ὄν, see, for example, *Timaeus* 28a3–4, *Phaedrus* 249c4, *Philebus* 59d4, *Republic* 490b5, etc. For τὸ παντελῶς ὄν, see *Republic* V, 477a3.

> here, the τί ἔστιν [what-it-is]. Thus the ἰδέα [the whatness or essence of a thing] constitutes the being of the thing.[54]

The Greeks, as we have intimated, experienced things fundamentally as appearances (φαινόμενα), as emerging from out of themselves so as to "show up" as they are in their δόξα, their effulgence. Professor John H. Finley's classic *Four States of Greek Thought* expresses this view when he describes the archaic Greek world of Homer as a "brilliant world" characterized by "the show and impression of things" in their "bright particularity."[55] Plato's εἶδος is certainly an echo of this. "In fact, it cannot be denied that the interpretation of being as ἰδέα results from the fundamental experience of being as φύσις."[56]

> The reason why the Greeks understand essence as *whatness* is that they generally understand the being of things (οὐσία) as what is *con-stant* and, in its con-stancy, is *steadfastly present*, and as present shows itself, and as self-showing offers its intelligible appearance—in short, as the intelligible appearance of something, as ἰδέα. Only on the basis of this understanding of being as the con-stant self-opening and self-showing presence [of a thing] is the interpretation of the being of things (and thus the interpretation of οὐσία) as ἰδέα possible and necessary.[57]

Although this Platonic shift to reading φύσις as εἶδος is authentically Greek, the consequences of this transformation, as Heidegger sees it, are momentous and not entirely happy. "What [now] remains decisive is not the fact in itself that φύσις was characterized as ἰδέα, but that the ἰδέα comes forth as the sole and definitive interpretation of being."[58] Plato's shift to being as the intelligible look of something entails a correlative intellectual looking at the ἰδέα. Parmenides had prepared for this vision when he articulated the correlation between the seen and the seeing as τὸ αὐτό (the togetherness) of τὸ εἶναι (being) and τὸ νοεῖν (perception, widely construed).[59] In Heidegger's interpretation, whereas the Greeks previously understood φύσις as the emergent and steadfast appearance of a thing, Plato now understands the intelligible ἰδέα—the whatness as seen—as "a determination of the steadfast thing insofar as, and only

54. GA 40: 190.14–20 = 202.1–8, my translation.

55. *Four Stages*, respectively 5.7; 31.29; 29.5–6. See ibid., 29.3–4: "the brilliant world that draws to brilliant action."

56. GA 40: 191.5–7 = 202.28–29.

57. GA 45: 68.1–9 = 61.21–28.

58. GA 40: 191.14–17 = 203.8–10.

59. Parmenides, fragment 3: τὸ γὰρ αὐτὸ νοεῖν ἐστίν τε καὶ εἶναι. Plotinus reformulates this at *Enneads* V 1: 4.30–32: ἅμα ἐκεῖνα καὶ συνυπάρχει . . . νοῦς καὶ ὄν: "These are simultaneous and exist together . . . mind and being." However, Heidegger interprets this as "Seyn und Lichtung ist dasselbe" at GA 66: 313. 23 = 279.9.

insofar as, it stands over against an [intellectual] seeing."[60] "If the whatness is characterized as something seen, then it is determined only with regard to the way we encounter it and grasp it—with regard to the way it stands over against us, and not as it is in itself."[61]

In Plato, therefore, the factors of emergence and current appearance recede into the background, while οὐσία, now understood as the *whatness* of a thing, comes to refer to the ever-present and in fact *eternal* εἶδος that endures immutable throughout change. To the degree that a thing lacks such presence, it is relatively unreal (μὴ ὄν). It is an εἴδωλον, a mere "image" of true reality as seen, for example, in a mirror or a dream.[62] The philosophical connotations of the "really real" now become *identity*, *unchangeability*, and *permanent presence*, as we can see from the question that Plato attributes to Socrates, with the expectation of an affirmative answer:

> That very οὐσία, of whose being (τὸ εἶναι) we are giving an account by question and answer—is it always in the same way and in the same state?[63]

For Plato, to the degree that a thing has permanent, unchangeable, self-identical, and intelligible presence, it has οὐσία. Thus the οὐσία or being of things can indeed be called the realness of those things, so long as one remembers that, in the Parmenidean framework that Plato appropriated, reality means permanence in self-identity.[64] Thus, "From a rigorous Platonic way of thinking, the essence of a thing is *impaired* by its entanglement with an [individual] actuality, it loses its purity and so in a certain sense its universality."[65] For Plato, of course, the realm of οὐσία was the world of ideal forms (εἶδη) as the really

60. GA 40: 191.23–24 = 203.15–17. At ibid., 191.31–192.8 = 203.23–204.2. Heidegger spells out the difference between the concepts of space in a pre-Platonic and in a Platonic view. In the first, the appearing thing "creates space for itself," whereas in the second, it merely emerges from "an already prepared space" and is viewed within "the already fixed dimensions of this space."

61. GA 45: 68.18–22 = 62.1–4. But Heidegger stresses that "the perceiving of beings as such is an ἰδεῖν only because a thing as such is self-showing: ἰδέα": ibid., 68.25–27 = 62.7–9.

62. *Sophist*, 240a7–8 and 266b6–8. An εἴδωλον for Plato is a "knock-off" of an εἶδος, which is what something really is: GA 34: 68.25–28 = 50.36–51.3.

63. *Phaedo* 78d1–3.

64. Parmenides, 8, 4: ἀτρεμές (motionless) and ἀτέλεστον (without end); 8, 3: ἀγένητον (not coming-to-be) and ἀνώλεθρον (without destruction); 8, 5–6: οὐδέ ποτ' ἦν οὐδ' ἔσται, ἐπεὶ νῦν ἔστιν ὁμοῦ πᾶν, / ἕν, συνεχές ("It neither has been nor will be, because it is now, entirely whole, / one, continuous"). Heidegger translates συνεχές as "holding itself together in itself" at GA 40: 145.8–9 = 151.16–17: "das sich in sich zusammenhaltende." Parmenides' view is repeated by Plotinus, who describes the νοῦς as ἔστι μόνον, καὶ τὸ "ἔστιν" ἀεί: "it only is, and its 'is' is eternal": *Enneads* V 1: 4.22.

65. GA 45: 69.14–17 = 62.27–29.

real, in contrast to the concrete things of this constantly changing world. As Heidegger puts it:

> Overwhelmed, as it were by the essence, Plato understood εἶδος [the intelligible appearance of the whatness of a thing] as something independently present and therefore as something common (κοινόν) to the individual "things" that "stand in such an appearance." In this way individuals, as subordinate to the ἰδέα taken as what properly is, were displaced into the role of non-things.[66]

❖ ❖ ❖

Aristotle likewise carries over into his own philosophy the connotation of οὐσία as steadfast stability and staying power, but he radically changes the paradigm within which he uses οὐσία. He, too, investigates the stable reality of things: for example, he speaks of things as συνιστάμενα and συνεστῶτα, that which has taken a stand.[67] Contrary to Plato, however, Aristotle's vision of the world valorizes motion and change as ἐνέργεια τίς[68]—as real in their own way. "Real" admits of degrees.[69] Aristotle recognizes the reality of the as-yet-incomplete, and he affirms what is incomplete *as* real to the degree that it appears (cf. εἶδος) and makes sense to us (cf. τὸ ὂν λεγόμενον). He valorizes the radiance and effulgence (δόξα: the shining appearance) of something *even* when it is still in the process of striving for the full perfection of its essence. Aristotle understands movement as always for the sake of a goal; whatever is in movement strives for full appearance and stable constancy.[70] His genius was to see the "not-yet" dimension of something in motion as "im-perfect" (*ad perfectionem*) in the sense of being *on the way to* perfection or fulfillment.[71]

> This expression ["imperfection"] is not purely and simply negative but is negative in a particular way. That which we designate as imperfect does not have nothing at all to do with perfection. On the contrary, it is precisely oriented

---

66. GA 9: 275.19–25 = 210.27–31.

67. *Physics* II 1, 192b13 and 193a36.

68. *Physics* III 2, 201b31.

69. GA 34: 33.16–18 = 26.5: "Das Seiende hat ebenfalls *Grade*! Seiend und seiend ist nicht ohne weiteres dasselbe."

70. What Aristotle says about the nutritive faculty applies to all movement. *De anima* III 9, 432b15–16: ἀεί τε γὰρ ἕνεκά του ἡ κίνησις αὕτη: This movement [of nutrition] is always for the sake of something [viz., its τέλος]. See *On the Parts of Animals* I 1, 640a18: ἡ γὰρ γένεσις ἕνεκα τῆς οὐσίας ἐστίν: Coming-to-be is for the sake of actually being. *Topics* VI 2, 139b20: ἡ γένεσις ἀναγωγὴ εἰς οὐσίαν: Becoming is the bringing of something into being.

71. See Thomas Aquinas, *Scriptum super sententiis* IV, distinctio 47, quaestio 2, articulus 2, quaestiuncula 1, corpus: "motus, qui est via ad perfectionem." http://www.corpusthomisticum.org/snp4047.html.

> toward perfection: in relation to perfection it is not all that it could be. . . . Hence the imperfect is that whose being entails a definite orientation towards perfection. "Imperfect" means that the thing of which it is predicated does not have the perfection it could have, should have, and is desired to have.[72]

Movement is ἐνέργεια ἀτελής, the *incomplete* completion of something, or better, its *im*-perfection as a functioning-*unto*-perfection. As moving or being moved, a thing already possesses *to a degree* the full appearance disclosedness that it is striving for. In a way that is (only) analogous to Nietzsche, Aristotle stamped becoming with the characteristics of being.[73] Aristotle is the philosopher of the "on-the-way" (*Unterwegs*) and of the "re-lative" in the sense of "what is borne unto" (πρός τι) perfection. Like Heraclitus he valorized ἀγχιβασίη (frag. 122), "approximation"—a thing's "towardness" or anticipation of its fullness—as itself real in its own way.[74] He saw a thing's functioning-unto-perfection as already suffused, to a degree, with the blessings of perfection.

At issue in Aristotle's world are not disembodied ideal forms but the concrete and particular, the τόδε τι, "this thing here." Such things are in movement in one way or another, and Heidegger insists that Aristotle was the first Greek philosopher to conceptualize movement as real being. Unlike Plato he refused to relegate moving things to the status of less-than-real (μὴ ὄν) in contrast to the forms as the really real (ὄντως ὄν). Unlike the Eleatic Sophist Antiphon (fl. 410 BCE), Aristotle saw that being-in-movement (e.g., a tree that is growing) or being changed (e.g., a table under construction) does not exclude a thing from the realm of the real but rather belongs to the very being of the thing.[75] Thus Aristotle asks what it is *about* these changing or changeable things that makes them participate to some degree in self-identical presence or reality.

It would be simplistic and misleading to interpret Aristotle as somehow bringing the Platonic forms "down to earth" and "infusing" them into things as "energies" or "powers."[76] Surely Aristotle first had to have understood

---

72. GA 19: 15.18–23 and .28–31 = 10.30–34 and 11.1–4. Cf. Aquinas, *Summa theologica* I, 5, 1, c.: "est autem perfectum unumquodque, inquantum est actu."

73. Compare "Dem Werden den Charakter des Seins *aufzuprägen*," Nietzsche, *Sämliche Werke* VIII, 1, 320.15 = *The Will to Power* no. 617, 330.88.

74. Re ἀγχιβασίη: Bekker, *Suidae Lexicon*, 20a, s.v. ἀγχιβατεῖν; also Diels-Kranz, *Die Fragmente der Vorsokratiker*, I, 178.6–7, no. 122. Further: Dreyfus and Wrathal, *A Companion to Heidegger*, 213 n. 71. GA 77: 152.18ff. = 99.37ff.: "Herangehen": to approach; GA 15: 215.25–26 = 133.9–10, Fink: "In die Nähe kommen."

75. *Physics* II 1, 193a9–28.

76. GA 6, 2: 372.12–15 = 9.10–14.

concrete things as real before he could supposedly "bring down" Plato's forms to earth and "embed" them in those concrete things. Moreover, to think of individual things as real, he first had to have a different notion of realness from Plato's, one that included movement and change *within* self-identity. Instead of reducing Aristotle's philosophical contribution to a simple inversion of Plato, let us see how he revolutionized metaphysics by conceiving the individual as the primary bearer of reality. We take up, first, Aristotle's location of primary reality in concrete things and then his valorization of movement as real.

❖ ❖ ❖

Aristotle says that "being real" (ὄν) has many meanings and is neither an equivocal nor a univocal term, but an analogical one. That is, it is not a homonym, where the same word has different meanings (the bark of a dog, the bark of a tree), nor a synonym, where a generic term applies to all its species (both the ox and the human being are "animals," one rational and the other not).[77] Rather, the word ὄν has a variety of meanings that all refer to some one thing, in what was later called an analogy of attribution.[78] "Having-being [i.e., having-reality]" he writes, "is meant in more than one way, but [all the meanings point] toward one thing or nature" (πρὸς ἕν καὶ μίαν τινὰ φύσιν), that is, "towards one principle" (πρὸς μίαν ἀρχήν) which serves as the common referent that applies to the others in different ways.[79] In comparison with Parmenides, for whom all reality was one (ἕν) without differentiation, and with Plato, for whom being was a genus common to many (γένος, τὸ κοινόν), Aristotle's analogical approach to having-reality marks "a *transformation* of the entire question."[80] But how does Aristotle arrive—if he ever does—at that single meaning of "realness" that explains all the others?[81]

77. *Topics* VI 6, 144a6–b11. At *Metaphysics* II, 3 Aristotle argues that although "being" and "oneness" are the two characteristics most predicated of all things (998b20–21; see X 2, 1053b20–21), neither one of them can be a genus of entities, because whatever might serve to differentiate each species within that genus (each "specific difference") would, of course, itself also have the characteristics of being and oneness (998b23–24), which would be illogical.

78. At *Metaphysics* IX 1, 1045b27 the verb referring to such "attribution" is ἀναφέρω, to carry (refer) up and/or back. At XI 3, 1061a11 the noun is ἀναγωγή, a leading up and/or back.

79. *Metaphysics* IV 2, 1003a33–34. Re one principle: ibid., 1003b6; see IX 1, 1046a9: πρὸς τὸ αὐτὸ εἶδος.

80. GA 33: 27.24–25 = 22.14–15. See SZ 3.23–24 = 22.26: "eine grundsätzliche neue Basis."

81. GA 11: 145.28–146.10 = x.7–20.

In *Metaphysics* Aristotle offers at least four different lists of the multiple ways "real" (ὄν) is said and meant.[82] For present purposes, however, we may refer to his text at *Metaphysics* VI 2, where he provides two distinct lists, one of them embedded inside the other. The first list is a broad fourfold set of meanings; the second (number 3 below) is made up of the ten categories. The bracketed numbers are my own.

> The unqualified term ὄν ["real"] has several meanings, one of which we have seen to be [1] the accidental. Another is [2] the true (with the false as not-real). Beyond these two there are [3] the modes of predication (for example, the "what," quality, quantity, place, time, and any similar meanings that "real" may have). Again, besides those there is [4] being-in-δύναμις and being-in-ἐνέργεια.[83]

This unsorted array (even when adjusted by dropping "real *qua* accidental" and "real as true and false in the judgment")[84] is never systematized by Aristotle; nor, it would seem, does he ever answer the question about the single meaning to which these four refer.[85] However, the traditional medieval commentaries on the analogy of "real," as well as nineteenth-century interpretations of that same topic, did that job for him. Whether properly or not, they worked out the common referent of "real" within the third meaning above, the "modes of predication," by which Aristotle is referring to the ten categories. (He provides a complete list at *Categories* 4, 1b25–2a4.) Within the ten, there is a further division into two: (1) the concrete *something* that is what it is (οὐσία) and (2) the other nine categories as modifications of that οὐσία.[86] It is οὐσία that serves as the prime analogue to which the other nine refer—because one can speak of being-this-way-or-that only in relation to a concrete something that can bear those properties.[87] Thus:

---

82. The lists are as follows: *Two*fold (IX 1, 1045b28–34): the categories, along with potency and actuality. *Three*fold (IX 10, 1051a34–1051b1): the categories, along with potency and actuality, and the true or false. *Four*fold (VI 2, 1026a34–1026b2): the accidental, the true, the categories, and potency and actuality. (This same fourfold list appears, in a different order, at V 7, 1017a7ff.)

83. *Metaphysics* VI 2, 1026a34–1026b2. See GA 84, 1: 474.2–4: potentia-actus, Eignung-Verwendung/Verwirklichung. On potential as Eignung: GA 83: 12.15–22.

84. See *Metaphysics* XI 8, 1065a21–26.

85. SZ 3.24–25 = 22.26–27: "Gelichtet hat das Dunkel dieser kategorialen Zusammenhang freilich auch er nicht." But see below in this chapter re ἀλήθεια in *Metaphysics* IX 10.

86. The ten categories are οὐσία, quantity, quality, relation, place, time, position, state or condition, action, and being-affected.

87. See GA 33: 42–48 = 34–39, where Heidegger argues that the analogy of being-real is questionable with regard to both lists of its multiple meanings. Those issues are not our immediate concern here.

> Οὐσία, in the predominant and primary and most definite way in which we mean the term is that which neither is predicated of some present thing [i.e., of a ὑποκείμενον] nor inheres in some present thing [as a property], but rather is this individual person, this individual horse.[88]

What-is-real is first and foremost the concrete thing itself, the τόδε τι, of which we may then predicate incidental and supervenient ways of reality such as quantity, quality, and so forth. For Aristotle the particular thing, and not the ideal forms in the purely intelligible world, is primary reality. But having established the τόδε τι as the primary bearer of reality, he has to account for the apparent tension—if not disjunct—between the changeableness of concrete things and the steadfastness that is a hallmark of the Greek sense of the real. His genius consisted in the insight that constituted "a *revolution* in understanding the sense of being up until then" and that found expression in the question: "How does the realness of what is *not fully* real become present and evident?"[89]

❖ ❖ ❖

Heidegger sees Aristotle's philosophical works as a late reflection of the pre-Socratic world of emergence and luminous appearance—along with the element of stability and presence as the defining characteristic of the real. But Aristotle's sense of stability stands over against Plato's view of eternal fixity: Aristotle's includes change as well. His world is certainly one of movement, but of movement that reaches towards stable perfection. In a classic formulation: movement is incomplete reality; reality is completed movement.[90] And "incomplete reality," when it is in the movement of becoming, "is, on the one hand, no longer nothing, but, on the other hand, it is not yet what it is destined to be."[91] Aristotle's thought managed to hold together both incompletion and completion under the aegis of οὐσία, while reserving absolute stability and permanence—in fact, absolute self-presence—to the self-coincident Unmoved Mover. In Aristotle, Heidegger says, "All determinations of things can be led back, if necessary, to an everlasting entity and are intelligible on that basis."[92]

---

88. *Categories* 5, 2a11–14.

89. GA 19: 192.22–23 = 133.18–19: "eine *Revolution.*" Ibid., 193.15–17 = 133.42–134.1 (here paraphrased): "Auf welchem Weg wird das Sein des Nicht-Seienden präsent und evident?"

90. Ross, *Aristotle*, 82.

91. GA 40: 122.18–20 = 126.23–24: "Was sich im Werden aufhält, ist einerseits nicht mehr das Nichts, es ist aber auch noch nicht das, was zu sein es bestimmt ist."

92. GA 19: 34.4–6 = 23.40–42.

The deity, as the ideal of unchanging reality, moves everything else in the world via "final causality"—that is, by being desired by all nature (κινεῖ ὡς ἐρώμενον),[93] just as the desired object (ὀρεκτόν) initiates and moves the desire for it (ὄρεξις).[94] The two notions of movement and stability come together in Aristotle's understanding of a natural thing as *gathering* itself into a relatively stable appearance (εἶδος).

To see how movement in Aristotle comes into its own as a kind of realness, we take a step back into some implicit presuppositions of his metaphysical view. This requires that we adjust our sights from a "bottom-up" vision of the real to one that proceeds "top-down." Aristotle shares the classical Greek conviction of the normativeness of the perfect and the whole over the imperfect and the partial, of the state of repose over a still-incomplete movement unto repose, and of the one over the many.[95] It is clear, Aristotle says, that whatever has achieved its fulfillment has ontological priority over what is still on-the-way to fulfilment.[96] He reads reality "backwards," as it were: he discovers *what* a thing is and *where* it is on the scale of perfection by measuring it against its τέλος, working from the *de jure* perfect back to the *de facto* imperfect, from the prior to the posterior.[97] He begins by implicitly "projecting" the fulfilled or "per-fect" form of something (how else would he know a particular thing as im-perfect?) and then, in order to understand that particular thing, tacitly moves from the ideal to the actual, from the fully achieved to what is still on-the-way, from the whole to what merely participates in it. In *Being and Time* Heidegger will argue that this is analogous to what any τεκνίτης—any person who produces something—does. He or she first projects the what-is-to-be-achieved and then looks around for whatever is suitable to achieve it. Another famous Aristotelian would agree:

> A spider conducts operations that resemble those of the weaver, and a bee would put many a human architect to shame by the construction of its honeycomb cells. But what distinguishes the worst architect from the best of bees is that the architect has first built his structure in his head before building it in

---

93. *Metaphysics* XII 7, 1072b3.

94. See *De anima* III 10, 433b10–11: κινοῦν τὸ ὀρεκτόν.

95. Whole prior to part: *Politics* I 1, 1253a20: τὸ γὰρ ὅλον πρότερον ἀναγκαῖον εἶναι τοῦ μέρους. Fulfillment (repose) over movement: *On the Parts of Animals* I 1, 640a18: ἡ γὰρ γένεσις ἕνεκα τῆς οὐσίας ἐστίν. One over many: *De anima*, II 1, 412b8–9, where τὸ ἕν, τὸ εἶναι, and ἐντελέχεια are equated.

96. *Metaphysics* IX 8, 1049b5: φανερὸν ὅτι πρότερον ἐνέργεια δυνάμεώς ἐστιν.

97. This is the case even when an investigation goes from what is better known to us to what is better known in itself: *Physics* I 1, 184a16–18.

> reality. At the end of every labor-process we get a result that already existed as an ideal in the imagination of the laborer at the very beginning.[98]

In *Being and Time* Heidegger will argue that this movement of aheadness-in-the-"ideal" and return-to-the-actual is operative also in apophantic statements: the pre-understanding of a thing's possible whatness and howness precedes adjudging the thing to be this or that. And finally he even will take this movement to be the very structure of human ex-sistence. (See chapter 5.)

To return to Aristotle: The presupposition of Aristotle's implicit movement from ideal to actual is his "teleological" view that holds that everything strives for its τέλος, its own perfection, and above all for its *appearance* as perfect. Heidegger says:

> A basic characteristic of a thing is its τέλος, which does not mean goal or purpose but end. Here "end" does not have any negative sense, as if "end" meant that something can go no further, that it breaks down and gives out. Instead "end" means completion in the sense of coming to fulfillment. Limit and end [πέρας and τέλος] are that whereby things first begin to *be*.[99]

It was Aristotle's achievement to have understood the positive relation between τὸ ἀ-τελές and τὸ τέλειον, between that which is not yet in its τέλος and that which is. The τέλος is the state of something that is fully "worked up into its perfection" (*per* + *factum*) and thus is fully present-in-reality as what and how it is. The ἀ-τελές, on the other hand, is something claimed and appropriated by the τέλος and therefore in movement towards it (*in* + *perfectum*: the imperfect as *functioning unto* perfection). By "perfection" Aristotle means *self-possession in what and how something is by its essence*. Thus a thing is perfect and complete when "it possesses its τέλος"—that is, "when not the least part of the thing can be found outside of it."[100] Such perfect self-possession is also called "wholeness" (τὸ ὅλον) in the sense of "ownness." A thing is whole and its own, Aristotle says, when "it lacks no part of what is said to belong to it by its nature."[101]

98. Karl Marx, *Das Kapital* MEGA II 5, 129.31–36 = *Capital* I, 178.6–13 (tr. Moore and Aveling) and 284.1–8 (tr. Fowkes): "die Zelle in seinem Kopf gebaut hat, bevor er sie in Wachs baut"—literally, "has built the honeycomb cell in his head before he builds it in wax."

99. GA 40: 64.27–32 = 65.24–30.

100. Respectively, *Metaphysics* V 16, 1021b24–25: κατὰ τὸ ἔχειν τὸ τέλος τέλεια. ("Things are complete in virtue of having attained their fulfillment"); and ibid., b12–13: Τέλειον λέγεται ἓν μὲν οὗ μὴ ἔστιν ἔξω τι λαβεῖν ἓν μόριον (When there is not even one part of a thing to be found outside of it, that thing is called "fulfilled."): see also ibid., b31–32.

101. *Metaphysics* V 26, 1023b26–27: μηθὲν ἄπεστι μέρος ἐξ ὧν λέγεται ὅλον φύσει.

These ideas converge in Aristotle's key terms, ἐντελέχεια, "being wholly fulfilled" and ἐνέργεια, "being finished and operative." Heidegger goes back behind the medieval translation of these terms (the Latin *actus* and *actualitas*) and gets to the Greek etymons underlying them. Here again we see the priority of the perfect over the imperfect. For Aristotle, to be perfect means to have arrived at and to possess one's τέλος. It is to have come into one's own and to stand there in fulfillment: ἐν τελει ἔχειν: ἐντελέχεια: "proper being in the sense of self-holding in con-stant presence."[102] Likewise with the word ἔργον, which underlies ἐνέργεια.[103] While ἔργον has many meanings, including "work" in the sense of labor, Heidegger takes it as referring to the desired and perhaps actualized *outcome* of production—not unlike the way we speak of a "work of art."

> What is produced, what is intended for production, is the ἔργον. This does not result arbitrarily and by chance from any work or activity whatsoever; for ἔργον is always that which is intended to stand there and be available.[104]

An ἔργον is what has either "placed itself" (natural things) or been placed by someone else (artifacts) into the manifestation of its own εἶδος, its "self-showing" that announces how and as what it exists. The ἔργον is what is finished, complete: τὸ γὰρ ἔργον τέλος.[105] It is what is currently *im Werk*—completely or incompletely "operative": ἐν τῷ ἔργῷ, ἐν-έργ-εια: ἐνέργεια. To the degree that something is currently operative, it shows up in its present appearance. Thus Aristotle equates ἐν τῷ ἔργῳ with ἐν τῷ εἴδει (1050a16).

> Ἐνεργείᾳ, ἐντελεχείᾳ ὄν [a thing that is in ἐνέργεια or in ἐντελέχεια] means the same as ἐν τῷ εἴδει εἶναι [to be in an intelligible appearance as what-it-is]. Whatever is present by virtue of "being-operative-as-such" has its presence in and through its intelligible appearance. Ἐνέργεια is the οὐσία (the presence) of the τόδε, i.e., of this or that thing that is *currently here*.[106]

But again: What about the im-perfect, that which has not yet arrived at, but is in movement towards, its perfection? For Aristotle, "perfection," "wholeness," and "ownness" are not univocal but analogous terms. Therefore, we must say that every entity is fulfilled *to the degree* that it has come into its own. Thus on the one hand God is perfectly perfect insofar as it is a thinking that thinks

102. GA 31: 93.15–17 = 66.5–6.

103. *Metaphysics* IX 8, 1050a22–23: τοὔνομα ἐνέργεια λέγεται κατὰ τὸ ἔργον. The name ἐνέργεια is formulated and meant in accordance with ἔργον.

104. GA 33: 137.31–138.2 = 117.23–26.

105. *Metaphysics* IX 8, 1050a21.

106. GA 6:2: 369.5–9 = 6.9–13. I use "being-operative-as-such" to translate "im-Werk-als-Werk."

of nothing except the highest and best object of thought—namely, itself: God as the thinking that thinks itself as thinking itself: νόησις νοήσεως νόησις.[107] There is no becoming in God because God has no unrealized potential (μὴ ὕλην ἔχει).[108] God has always-already come into its own and therefore is supremely at rest in its self-coincidence. But on the other hand, the cosmos as a whole is populated by things that are only partially fulfilled and yet still show up as things of such and such an intelligible appearance (ἐν τῷ ἔργῳ / ἐν τῷ εἴδει εἶναι)—that is, as things that have *imperfect* presence and are in movement to full presence—whether they are in a state of as-good-as-it-gets (the fixed stars, moving in perfect circularity) or as ever striving for perfection (in the sub-lunar realm). The latter have their being as ἐνέργεια ἀτελής (they are actual and operative, but not fully). Such things are real *to the degree* that they possess ἐνέργεια. The imperfect as the *approximation* (ἀγχιβασίη) of the perfect is, to that extent, real. "It seems that movement is a kind of ἐνέργεια, but one that has not yet fully reached its τέλος."[109] Two kinetic tropes recur in Western philosophy and art from Parmenides (fragment 1.29: ἀλήθεια εὔκυκλος)[110] down to Nietzsche: the emergence of things into light from out of darkness, and the yearning of movement for repose. This vision (broadly Greek, and even Dantesque) is what T. S. Eliot captures in the first of his *Four Quartets* when he speaks of

daylight
Investing form with lucid stillness
Turning shadow into transient beauty
With slow rotation suggesting permanence.[111]

In summary: For Aristotle, even things in movement participate in the real. To the degree that a thing stands there (συνεστῶτον, συνιστάμενον) or lies there (ὑποκείμενον), and is held in presence (οὐσία) in its self-limitation (πέρας) and shows itself as what it is (εἶδος) in at least implicit conjunction with λόγος (cf. τὸ ὂν λεγόμενον)—to that degree such a thing has gathered itself up and "has itself" (ἔχειν) in its relatively stable fulfillment (ἐντελέχεια) and thus is real. And because all of these meanings can also be expressed by the Greek ἔργον, the word ἐνέργεια bespeaks the same emergence and in-gathering into stable appearance in λόγος and thus the same degree of realness as does ἐντελέχεια.[112]

107. *Metaphysics* XII 9, 1074b34–35.

108. *Metaphysics* XII 9, 1075a4.

109. *Physics* III 1, 201b31–32: ἥ τε κίνησις ἐνέργεια μέν τις εἶναι δοκεῖ, ἀτελὴς δέ. Heidegger treats Aristotelian κίνησις at GA 83: 5–20, passim.

110. Diels-Kranz, I, 230.11.

111. "Burnt Norton" (III), *The Complete Poems and Plays,* 173.

112. See *Physics* III 1, 201a10–11, where ἐντελέχεια is the equivalent of ἐνέργεια.

❖ ❖ ❖

We are still faced with the question "What is the *unity* of the various ways in which something can have being—that is, be real?" It seems (we have said) that Aristotle provides no clue for answering this question. Or does he? It appears that Heidegger *did* find the fundamental meaning of having-being in *Metaphysics* IX 10 (Θ 10), where Aristotle argues that τὸ ὄν ὡς ἀληθές—the real *insofar as it is disclosed*—is the most authoritative and proper instance of the real (τὸ κυριώτατα ὄν: 1051b1).[113] Thus what constitutes the realness of the real (the οὐσία of τὸ ὄν) is a thing's openness to human intellect (the ἀλήθεια of τὸ ὄν). Whereas some scholars have disputed the authenticity and/or the location of this treatise,[114] Heidegger argues in favor of both:

> In Θ 10 there is concentrated the most radical conception of the basic problem of Θ. In a word: Θ 10 is not a foreign appendix, but rather the *keystone of Book Θ,* which itself is the center of the entire *Metaphysics*.[115]

As previously mentioned, I translate *Wahrheit*, *Entborgenheit*, and *Unverborgenheit*, along with their cognates, by variations on the word "disclosedness" (sometimes hyphenated as dis-closedness in order to show its relation to ἀ-λήθεια) as well as by "accessibility," "availability," and "openness." All of these terms refer strictly to *intelligible* disclosedness, availability, and so on, and not disclosedness to the senses alone. I interpret *Unwahrheit*, *Verborgenheit*, and cognate terms by "closedness" or "inaccessibility."

Earlier in the *Metaphysics* Aristotle had already declared that each thing "has as much intelligibility [ἀλήθεια] about it as it has being [εἶναι]."[116] There, as well as in *Metaphysics* IX 10, Aristotle is speaking of the disclosedness of things *not* in the way it occurs in the judging and asserting intellect (ἐν διανοίᾳ),[117] where it would be a matter of logic, epistemology, and correctness (*adaequatio intellec-*

113. Ross's Greek edition of the *Metaphysics* places κυριώτατα ὄν in brackets with the note "seclusi: an post μὲν (a34) transpondenda?"—that is, "to be cut out, or [perhaps] transposed and placed after μὲν at 1051a34?"

114. Heidegger's argument with Albert Schwegler and Werner Jaeger is spelled out at GA 31: 81–84 = 57–60.

115. GA 31: 107.29–34 = 75.29–32.

116. *Metaphysics* II 1, 993b30–31: ὥσθ' ἕκαστον ὡς ἔχει τοῦ εἶναι, οὕτω καὶ τῆς ἀληθείας. See Thomas Aquinas, *Summa theologiae* I–II, 3, 7 c: "Eadem est dispositio rerum in esse sicut in veritate." Also *Summa contra gentes*, I, 71, 16: "quantum habet de esse, tantum habet de cognoscibilitate." See GA 45: 122.3–5 = 106.26–28: "Oft steht auch ἀλήθεια einfach anstelle von ὄν. Die Wahrheit und das Seiende in seiner Seiendheit sind dasselbe."

117. On ὄν ὡς ἀληθές ἐν διανοίᾳ see *Metaphysics* VI 3, 1027b27 and IX 8, 1065a21–22: τὸ δ' ὡς ἀληθὲς ὄν . . . ἐν συμπλοκῇ διανοίας.

tus et rei). Rather, this text deals with disclosedness as an intrinsic ontological characteristic of things themselves (ἐπὶ τῶν πραγμάτων).[118] Heidegger maintains that in *Metaphysics* IX 10 Aristotle reaffirms the implicit Greek tradition of ἀλήθεια as the *availability of things to the intellect*. In this text Aristotle gives that tradition "its first and radical expression" insofar as "the chapter is concerned to unfold the proof of the thesis that *Wahrsein* [a thing's being open to, available to, intellect] *constitutes the most proper being of proper beings*."[119] Heidegger summarizes the argument of the chapter in Joycean catechetical form:[120]

> *Question*: When can a thing be properly disclosed as such? . . .
> *Answer*: When every possibility of concealment is excluded in every respect from the thing.
>
> *Question*: When is that? . . .
> *Answer*: When disclosedness belongs essentially to the thing's being.
>
> *Question*: How is that possible?
> *Answer*: When being-disclosed [*Wahrsein*] constitutes what is most proper to the very being of the thing.
>
> *Question*: But what is a thing's being?
> *Answer*: Its steadfast presence.
>
> *Question*: What is the most proper disclosedness that absolutely excludes the possibility of misrepresentation? When is that the case?[121]
> *Answer*: See *Metaphysics* Θ 10.

He concludes by stating the goal of Aristotle's argument in this chapter:

> Thus, when disclosedness is nothing but the highest possible and most proper presence, then there [really] is disclosedness. This is a metaphysical question—indeed, of the purest kind—and has nothing to do with so-called epistemology.[122]

Aristotle's treatment of ἀλήθεια in *Metaphysics* IX 10 progresses through three scenarios in which the adjective ἀληθές ("dis-closed"—open qua intelligible) is attributed more and more purely to three distinct kinds of things:

---

118. *Metaphysics* IX 10, 1051b2.

119. Respectively, GA 31: 82.33 = 58.32 and 87.21–23 = 62.2–4.

120. GA 31: 92.6–18 = 65.8–13, paraphrased. Joyce's catechesis: *Ulysses* episode 16 (Ithaca), 666–738.

121. GA 31: 101.2–4 = 71.6–7.

122. GA 31: 92.18–22 = 65.13–16. The disclosedness under discussion here is, of course, that *of an entity*.

***composites*: σύνθετα**
1. with accidental predicates: συμβεβηκά
2. with essential predicates: ἀεὶ συγκείμενα

***non-composites*: ἀσύνθετα**
3. essences, being (ἁπλῆ οὐσία: εἶδη, ὄν)

Heidegger's argument is thick and complex, and we can best convey it by staying close to his own (and Aristotle's) exposition.[123]

1. *Regarding composites* (σύνθετα) *with non-essential properties* (συμβεβηκά: "accidental" elements, those that merely happen to "go together with" something else: σύν + βαίνω)—for example, John as pale (1051b6–9). In a case like this, if we synthesize S and P into the affirmative statement "John is pale," our speech discloses John as he is if and only if John is in fact pale. Our speech likewise discloses him as he is if we correctly assert in the negative that "John is not blushing" when in fact he is not blushing. On the other hand, if we say that he is blushing when he is pale or that he is pale when he is blushing, we do not disclose (ἀληθεύειν) but rather misrepresent him (ψεύδεσθαι). The important principle underlying these simple cases is that the *primary basis* for either disclosing or misrepresenting John lies not in our speech about him but *in his condition itself.* "[John] is pale not because we correctly take him to be such; rather, we correctly take him to be pale because he is in fact pale" (1051b4–7). In other words, the actual state of affairs (John's paleness) is what makes our statements about him be true or false. John's condition *makes* the truth whereas our proposition *bears* the truth.[124]

In such cases, the properties in question are not essential to the subject, and therefore could change. At any given time John's visage could be pale or blushing or just normal. Our statement that John is pale could be correct in the morning (i.e., disclose him as he is when he wakes up), and the same unchanged statement could be incorrect and misrepresent how John is in the evening after he has had a few drinks. "The same statement can disclose him at one moment and misrepresent him at another" (1051b14–15).

The upshot: In statements that (affirmatively or negatively) link subjects with changeable, non-essential properties, the purest and plenary use of the adjective ἀληθές is not operative. A statement with a merely contingent predicate does not necessarily preclude the misrepresenting of the subject. Because it

123. Heidegger's major treatments of *Metaphysics* X 10 are in GA 21: 170–182 = 143–154 and GA 31: 87–109 = 61–76.

124. Mark Textor, "States of Affairs."

involves the constant possibility of misrepresentation (non-disclosedness), this kind of ἀλήθεια is not itself the proper form of disclosedness.[125]

2. *Regarding composites with essential properties* (ἀεὶ συγκείμενα: elements that "always lie together")—for example, chalk and materiality or the diagonal of the square as incommensurate with the side of the square (1051b15–17; 20–21; 33–35). This takes a step beyond the non-essential ("accidental") properties of a thing. "Chalk" and "whiteness" are not necessarily conjoined any more than John and the conditions of blushing or going pale are. (There is such a thing as orange chalk.)

> By contrast, the very materiality [*Stofflichkeit*] of an existing piece of chalk does not just occur now and again, συμ-βεβηκός, but is a συγκείμενον—it goes together with the chalk—συν-κείμενον [lying together] with the ὑποκείμενον [the underlying thing]. In this case chalk and materiality are ἀδύνατα διαιρεθῆναι [1051b9–10], impossible to separate.[126]

Chalk and its essential property "materiality" are not merely given together; they are in fact inseparable in their being.

> The verb συγκείσθαι does not mean merely "to lie together" in the sense of just happening to be given together [like John and paleness]; rather, it refers to constant togetherness—an a priori remaining together—i.e., constant co-presence of one with the other.[127]

To that degree:

> Seen from the side of things as unveiled in their whatness, things and the properties that are essential to them [ἀεὶ συγκείμενα] are not sometimes uncovered and sometimes covered over. Thus they are not exposed to the possibility of concealment.[128]

Thus, with essential properties we have taken a step closer to the pure disclosedness of a thing. However—and this is the important caveat—insofar as the piece of chalk has its essence as chalk-ness, it excludes *other* essences—wood-ness, for example. However, it still is a composite entity (put together: σύν-θετον) insofar as the particular thing is not the same as and perfectly interchangeable with its essence, but rather "has" its essence—that is, it is there *together with* its essence. Therefore, someone could attribute the *wrong*

125. GA 31: 98.21–23 = 69.18–20: die ständige Möglichkeit der Unwahrheit; nicht eigentliche Wahrheit.

126. GA 31: 95.8–14 = 67.13–17.

127. GA 31: 96.6–10 = 67.34–68.2.

128. GA 31: 98.26–29 = 69.23–25.

essence to the chalk and thus misrepresent it, for example by synthesizing this white thing over there with "wood-ness" and thus seeing it not as chalk but as a piece of wood. In the real world, on the other hand, the property of "materiality" is *essential* to ("always lies together" with) a piece of chalk. Therefore, in this or any other case, a thing's essence, its essential whatness, is *inherently* disclosive of the thing. (And, as a result, to see an essence for what it is, is to have the thing as *unerringly disclosed* as what it is.) Thus the whatness of a thing would seem to qualify as the highest form of disclosedness/ἀλήθεια. As Aristotle puts it (1051b15–17), mentally conjoining (for example) chalk and its essential property of materiality does not sometimes disclose the thing as it is and sometimes misrepresent it. Rather, the two elements that are synthesized in these examples always belong together in reality and cannot be otherwise.

But there is a catch. The piece of chalk and materiality do indeed always go together (ἀεὶ συγκείμενα) in what we will call the world of "objective reality." However, this piece of chalk and its essence are not one and the same (just as in the statement "Socrates is an Athenian" Socrates himself does not exhaust the class of "Athenians"); and therefore this-piece-of-chalk-and-its-materiality is a composite phenomenon (σύνθετον), as was John-as-pale. Therefore, when we want to know what this white thing is, we must *synthesize* "this thing here" and "chalk-ness"—but with the possibility that we just might get it wrong and take this four-inch white cylinder as a plastic tube instead of as a piece of chalk. For Aristotle such a *possibility* of incorrect disclosure in thought and speech *disqualifies* the essence or whatness of a thing from being the absolute and unmistakable instance of disclosedness. As long as the thing does not perfectly and exhaustively coincide with its being, such a synthetic phenomenon harbors within itself the possibility of misrepresentation.

> Anything [e.g., a piece of chalk] that has the way-of-being of the [ἀεὶ] συγκείμενον also has an essential [even if only possible] relation to what *cannot* belong to it. The possibility thus arises of attributing to it something that does *not* belong to it—that is to say, the possibility of misrepresentation. . . . Thus with respect to that with which it [always] belongs together, the thing is constantly disclosed; but the thing is constantly [able to be] distorted [by synthesizing it with an essence] that does not belong with it.[129]

From both of the foregoing cases, John and the piece of chalk, Heidegger derives the principle that

> the more the being of a thing is proper to that thing, the purer and more constant is the thing's presence, i.e., the more disclosedness belongs to the thing as such

129. GA 31: 99.4–16 = 69.32–70.3.

> and the more misrepresentation is ruled out. Yet as long as the disclosedness [of something] remains bound up with the possibility of non-disclosedness, that [kind of] disclosedness is not the proper and highest [kind of] disclosedness.[130]

Thus if the essence of a thing coincided with the thing, that thing would not be a composite and therefore would be completely disclosed to an intellect that was adequate to that essence (the way Aristotle's God, as knowing, completely knows itself as knowing).[131]

The question now becomes: "What is the most proper disclosedness that absolutely excludes the possibility of misrepresentation? When is that the case?"[132]

3. ***Regarding non-composites*** (ἀσύνθετα: "what is *not* put together," 1051b17ff.). We leave composite entities behind now and turn to what excludes all synthesis—namely, the very being or intelligible presence of things seen in and by itself.[133]

> The being of a thing does not just sometimes belong to a thing and sometimes not, but belongs to the thing constantly and before everything else. Being as such, simplicity, unity—these cannot be analyzed further back. Being is the simple itself, and as such it is the primary and ultimate ground of the possibility of every actual and conceivable thing. That which is most simple is also that which is most proper to things.[134]

> The disclosedness of something simple can never be distorted by something else that does not belong to that simple something. This disclosedness cannot change over into distortion—not because what belongs together with it is constantly revealed but precisely because the simple does not admit of any togetherness [= compositeness] at all. The disclosedness of the simple completely excludes the possibility of non-disclosedness.[135]

Moreover, insofar as being/presence is not composed, it cannot be revealed by way of a declarative statement, a λόγος ἀποφαντικός, which, whether correctly or not, necessarily synthesizes a subject and one of its alleged properties, while at the same time keeping the subject and the properties distinct.

130. GA 31: 99.29–100.4 = 70.13–17.

131. *Metaphysics* XII 9, 1074b34–35: νόησις νοήσεως νόησις. The same holds analogously for Aquinas' God: "Deus se per seipsum intelligit" (*Summa theologiae* I, 14, 2, corpus) insofar as "Deus est suum esse": ibid., I, 45, 5, ad 1 and I, 61, 1, corpus.

132. GA 31: 101.2–4 = 71.6–7.

133. *Metaphysics* IX 10, 1051b26–27: περὶ τὸ τί ἐστιν and περὶ τὰς μὴ συνθετὰς οὐσίας. GA 21: 179.33 = 152.11: εἴδη.

134. GA 31: 103.13–20 = 72.27–32, slightly paraphrased.

135. GA 31: 101.30–102.3 = 71.26–31.

("Socrates is an Athenian" = composition/σύνθεσις; but Socrates as not exhausting the class of Athenians = distinction/διαίρεσις.) But in the case of the being of things, when it is taken by itself, there is nothing to synthesize and nothing to keep apart (1051b18–20). The being or intelligible presence of a thing is ἁπλοῦν, simple, with no compositeness about it at all. Nothing else accompanies being that might function as a property of being and thus serve as a predicate within declarative sentences. The being of something can be known only by an unmediated intuition that directly addresses and grasps it. Aristotle speaks of this intuition as simply "touching" (θιγεῖν) and "addressing oneself to" (φάναι) the being of a thing. Heidegger paraphrases Aristotle (1051b23–31; 30–32):

> In the case of non-synthetics, disclosedness entails just touching and addressing oneself to the disclosed. Affirmation [κατάφασις] is not the same as purely and simply addressing oneself to it [φάσις]. In the case of non-synthetics, not-apprehending is the same as not-touching [τὸ δ' ἀγνοεῖν μὴ θιγγάνειν] . . . .
>
> Regarding whatever is present in and of itself [ὅσα δή ἐστιν ὅπερ εἶναί τι καὶ ἐνεργείᾳ]—of such things there is no deception but only apprehension or non-apprehension.[136]

Or as Heidegger puts it:

> The disclosedness of the simple can never be distorted by something not belonging to the simple.[137]

> Primary and proper disclosedness is the very manifestness of something that can present itself as itself. The disclosedness of something simple like the being of a thing is the presence of that simple being [*Sein*] in and of itself. This presence is absolutely unmediated, i.e., nothing can intervene between the seer and the seen. Further, this unmediated presence of being [*Sein*] is prior to all other presence—for example, the presence of *things*,. It is the highest and most original kind of presence. Above all, however, this completely unmediated constant presence of being, of itself and for itself, *this most constant and purest presence, is nothing else but reality in its highest and most proper sense.*[138]

---

136. See GA 21: 176.14–19, .24–26 = 148.14–15, .17–22, and .26–27. In this paraphrase I follow Bekker rather than Ross at 1051b31 (ἐνεργείᾳ rather than ἐνέργειαι). Re θιγεῖν: compare Plotinus' use of that word at *Enneads* VI 9: 7.4, and of ἐπαφή ("touching") at VI 7: 36.3–4. Augustine concurs with Aristotle on "no deception": "At vero in illis intellectualibis visis [anima] non fallitur: aut enim intelligit, et verum est; aut si verum non est, non intelligit," the latter being "errare quia non videt": the soul does not err in those intellectual intuitions or sightings; it either intuits [its object], and the thing is disclosed; or the soul does not intuit [it] if it is not disclosed. It is one thing to err when one sees something, quite another to err by not seeing it: *De genesi ad litteram* XII, 25, 52, *Patrologia Latina* 34, 476.7–9 and .10–11; also op. cit., XII, 14, 29, 465.25–26.

137. GA 31: 101.30–31 = 71.26–27.

138. GA 31: 102.11–21 = 72.1–8, slightly paraphrased.

Being, when viewed in and for itself, is *the* most disclosed: “if things are to be discoverable and determinable at all, their being must be constantly disclosed.”[139] On this reading, the nature of disclosedness in its most proper sense is nothing but the constantly available intelligible presence of the thing, *whereby* the thing is seen as this or that. To the degree that something is intelligibly present, to that degree it is disclosed; and to the degree that something is disclosed, it is intelligibly present. *Metaphysics* IX 10 has thus spelled out and demonstrated Aristotle’s earlier thesis: The being (εἶναι) of a thing and the intelligible disclosedness (ἀλήθεια) of that thing are one and the same.[140] Thus, within the limits of metaphysics Aristotle has shown that disclosedness—the intelligibility and availability of things (implicitly: to human beings)—is the very highest form of reality and thus the analogical unity of all modes of the being of things.[141]

It is crucial to point out here that *for Heidegger* the sub-text of *Metaphysics* IX 10 is not only Aristotle’s proto-phenomenological vision, which is implicit and yet discernible, but also a very important distinction between “levels” of ἀλήθεια. We take this up in the next chapter but may allude to it here. We saw that *Metaphysics* IX 10 is *not* about “truth in the intellect” (ἐν διανοίᾳ) but rather the disclosedness of things (ἐπὶ τῶν πραγμάτων).[142] The “truth in the intellect” that Aristotle excludes is the truth of correspondence between mental propositions (or their expression in declarative sentences) and states of affairs, the storied *adaequatio intellectus et rei*. But the disclosedness of things is *not at all* the truth of correspondence—that is, a matter of “getting it right” in the sense of seeing these things correctly as what they “really are.” We should reserve the word “truth” (*Wahrheit*) for such *adaequatio* or correctness and refuse to follow Heidegger in his misleading use of that word for the disclosedness of things (and, even worse, for the openedness of ex-sistence). The kind of disclosedness that Heidegger retrieves from *Metaphysics* IX 10 is not “truth” but *meaningfulness*. Aristotle did not thematize this point, but Heidegger does.

When a thing is “disclosed” pre-theoretically, that is, prior to becoming the subject matter of a declarative statement, it does indeed present itself *as* this or that. However, such a presentation can be incorrect from the standpoint of truth as correspondence. Heidegger gives the example of someone walking through the forest at dusk and mistaking a bush for a deer. The bush was indeed

139. GA 31: 103.29–30 = 73.4–5: “muß das Sein überhaupt im vorhinein und ständig schlechthin entborgen sein,” italicized in the original.

140. *Metaphysics* II 1, 993b30–31.

141. GA 65: 93.3–4 = 74.1–2: “Diese Wahrheit des Seyns ist gar nichts vom Seyn Verschiedenes, sondern sein eigenstes Wesen.” GA 83: 21.6–7: “Weil ‘Sein an sich’ durch *Wahrheit* bestimmt ist.”

142. For ἐν διανοίᾳ: *Metaphysics* V 4, 1027b27; ἐπὶ τῶν πραγμάτων: ibid., IX 10, 1051b2.

"disclosed-as-something" to me when it appeared as a deer, but on investigation I see I got it wrong the first time. Now it is disclosed as a bush. But wait: What if, as I get closer, it turns out to be not a bush at all but a large boulder? In all three instances—as deer, as bush, as boulder—the thing is disclosed (i.e., is *meaningful*), even if I happened to get the meaning wrong in two out of the three instances. The point: When something "has ἀλήθεια" or "is ἀληθές," that means (in terms of Heidegger's reading of *Metaphysics* IX 10) that the thing is *meaningful* in one way or another. When I construct propositions about the disclosed/meaningful thing, I may get the meaning wrong, or I may get it right, in which case my proposition is either false or true. But *in order to* be false or true with regard to the subject matter, that subject matter must first be disclosed meaningfully—*as* something that I can understand. For a human being everything is meaningful, either actually so or potentially. Even when I don't understand something but merely ask "What *is* a gluon?" I have already situated "gluon" in the realm of the intelligible. Everything is meaningful, but not everything is true.

Heidegger's re-reading of *Metaphysics* IX 10 was only a stepping stone to what he took to be the truly primary sense of ἀλήθεια—let us call it provisionally "ἀλήθεια-prime." It, too, has to do with meaningfulness: it is the *reason why* there is meaning at all—and yet it itself is not understandable. But that is a matter for later chapters.

❖ ❖ ❖

As he pointed out in private seminars dating to 1973, Heidegger's path to these insights was paved not only by Aristotle but also by Husserl's *Logical Investigations* VI, chapter 6, "Sensuous and Categorial Intuition." By distinguishing two kinds of intuition, sensuous and categorial, and the objects given to them, Husserl had opened the possibility of a *phenomenological* approach to the *ontological* question of the being of things as their availability-to-man that Aristotle had taken up in *Metaphysics* IX 10.[143] Take, for example, an inkwell. The object of a sensuous intuition of it is what Husserl called the *hyle* (cf. Aristotle's ὕλη)—in Heidegger's words, "the sense data (blue, black, spatial extension, etc.). What is perceived sensibly? The sense data themselves."[144] But your dog Fido perceives as much. We, however, also see, in addition to the sense data and founded upon them, the phenomenon of the "presence-as-meaningful" of the data, something that Fido presumably cannot do. This fact—that

143. GA 15: 373–78 = 65–67. See the masterful treatment of these matters in Daniel Dahlstrom, *Heidegger's Concept of Truth*, 74–97.

144. GA 15: 374.24–27 = 65.29–31.

the sense data are *present-as-meaningful* (whatever meaning may be ascribed to them)—does not arise from a sensuous intuition, and yet it is immediately intuited.[145] In opposition to Kant's restriction of intuition to merely sense intuition (since, given his position on the *Ding an sich*, the intellectual intuition of essences is impossible), Husserl, by way of an analogy with sensuous intuition, argues for a *categorial* intuition, to which is given the sheer fact of "present-as-meaningful" (regarding whatever appears in sense intuition). The protocol of Heidegger's 1973 seminar reports (here paraphrased):

> We encounter here the Husserlian idea of "surplus" [*Überschuss*].[146] Heidegger explains: In a sentence like "The inkwell is black," the "is," through which I observe the presence of the inkwell *as* object or substance, is a "surplus" in comparison to the sensuous affections. But in a certain respect the "is" [i.e., the "it-is-meaningful"] is given *in the same* [if analogous] *manner* as the sensuous affections. But the "is"—i.e., the sheer fact of meaningfulness—is not *added* to the sense data; rather, it is "seen" [i.e., intuited]—even if it is seen *intellectually* and thus differently from what is sensibly visible. In order to be "seen" in this way, "being"—the sheer fact of the thing's meaningfulness—*must* be *given.*[147]

Husserl's doctrine of the categorial intuition of the presence-as-meaningful of a thing helped Heidegger discover a phenomenological clue for understanding the classical Greek understanding of being as the steadfast intelligible presence of a thing. "The Greeks are those people who lived immediately in the openness of phenomena"[148] (i.e., of things understood as "τὰ ἀληθέα, that which is revealed as disclosed and available"[149]). "In their essence the Greeks belong to ἀλήθεια, in which things unveil themselves in their phenomenality."[150] What, then, does ἀλήθεια name, and what is it that the Greek wonder at (θαυμάζειν)?[151] "It is the *overabundance*, the *excess* beyond whatever is present"[152]—namely, meaningful presence *as such.* It was this "excess" that Husserl rediscovered in the "surplus" that the categorial intuition presents, the surplus of a thing's meaningful presence, given prior to and beyond the mere

145. GA 15: 374.32–33 = 65.33–34.

146. *Logische Untersuchungen, Husserliana* XIX/2, 660.7–9 = II, 775.26: "es bleibt ein Überschuß in der Bedeutung, eine Form, die in der Erscheinung selbst nicht findet, sich darin zu bestätigen."

147. GA 15: 375.28–376.4 = 66.13–19. My translation.

148. GA 15: 330.7–9 = 37.31–33.

149. GA 15: 327.23 = 36.4–5. As disclosed and available: "das Offenbare in der Unverborgenheit."

150. GA 15: 330.23–25 = 38.1–2.

151. Plato, *Theaetetus* 155d3; Aristotle, *Metaphysics* I 2, 983a13.

152. GA 15: 331.9 = 38.19: Überfulle, Übermaß; see ibid., 330.23 = 38.1: Übermaß.

assertoric "is" of the copula with the sense of just "exists." In the following text Heidegger signals the threshold of his own insight into "the thing itself." It was not "being" in any form, but rather that which allows for ("gives") being as meaningful presence.

> With his analyses of the categorial intuition, Husserl freed being from its attachment to judgment. With that, the entire field of investigation gets re-oriented. When I pose my own question about *how* being is intuitable, I must already be beyond being when it is understood as the being *of things*. More precisely still: in the question of the intuitable intelligibility of being, the subject of the inquiry—*das Befragte*—is being, i.e., the being of things. But the desired outcome of the question—*das Erfragte*—concerns *what allows for* the *intuitability* of being (which I will later call the immediate dis-closedness of being). In order to unfold the question about the intuitability of being and to inquire about its intelligibility, being must be *given* to us immediately and non-discursively.[153]

Like the Greeks before him, Heidegger could now "intuit" the givenness of meaningful-presence-as-such. But unlike the Greeks, he chose to question *behind* this meaningful presence so as to discover why it is necessary and how it is possible. Neither the Greeks nor Husserl had taken such a step. The Greeks, on the one hand, were so fascinated and absorbed by the bright phenomenality of things that they did not ask what brings about this effulgence. Husserl, in turn, "having reached, as it were, being as *given*, does not inquire any further into it . . . since for him it goes without saying that 'being' means being-an-object [of consciousness]."[154] We can now see, therefore, how Heidegger could write in 1963:

> What occurs for [Husserl's] phenomenology of the acts of consciousness as the self-manifestation of phenomena is thought more originally by Aristotle and in all Greek thinking and ex-sistence as ἀλήθεια, the disclosedness of present things, their being revealed, their showing themselves. What [Husserl's] phenomenological investigations rediscovered as the supporting attitude of thought proves to be the fundamental characteristic of Greek thinking, and indeed of philosophy as such.
>
> The more decisively this insight became clear to me, the more pressing became the question: How and on what grounds are we to determine that which, according to the principle of phenomenology, is to be experienced as "the thing itself"? Is it consciousness and its objectivity? Or is it the being of things in its disclosedness and hiddenness?[155]

153. GA 15: 377.24–378.5 = 67.18–28, strongly paraphrased. "Intuitable intelligibility" and "intuitability": Sinn.

154. GA 15: 378.11–16 = 67.33–37.

155. GA 14: 99.1–15 = 79.18–31. How it is disclosed and closed off: "in seiner Unverborgenheit und Verbergung."

❖ ❖ ❖

Let us summarize some key points of this chapter. Heidegger's re-reading of Aristotle begins with the phenomenological insight that the realness of things implies their openness and availability and, with that, their relatedness to man (cf. οὐσία as "stable *possessions*"). Probing behind οὐσία Heidegger finds a kinetic dimension to this availability, the emergence (φύσις) of a thing from out of hiddenness and unavailability into stable (ἀεί) presence (εἶδος) in an implicit conjunction with human intelligence (cf. τὸ ὂν λεγόμενον). By such emergence-into-presence Heidegger clearly is not referring to the pre-human natural emergence of things in the spatio-temporal universe during, say, the Jurassic Period, some 200 to 150 million years ago: the blooming of conifers, the birth of reptiles, or the physical presence of things on the supercontinent Pangaea. He means, rather, the emergence of things into meaningful availability to human beings in what he will call *der Welteingang des Seienden*, "the entry of things into world," where "world" means the world of meaning.[156] Such emergence into meaningful availability entails two things: that the thing (1) has "taken a stand" within its defining limits (πέρας) as what and how it is, and that, as such, (2) it can "show up" in an "intelligible appearance" (εἶδος: what the thing "looks like" to the mind). Even from this much it is clear that Heidegger reads Aristotle as a proto-phenomenologist rather than as a naïve realist who considers things merely as "objects" out there in the world.

Plato's thematization of εἶδος as the knowable whatness of a thing runs a double risk: that of banishing emergence in favor of a notion of realness as the stable identity, unchangeability, and permanent presence—the essence—of a thing; and that of reducing the particular thing to a state of relative unreality (μὴ ὄν, εἴδωλον). Aristotle, on the other hand, valorizes incomplete ("kinetic") realness as a thing's progress towards and participation in fulfillment. Movement is the incomplete completion of something. In Aristotle's theory of analogy, to-be-real admits of degrees. He offers four lists of what "real" means, and he settles on the concrete and kinetic particular—this-thing-here (τόδε τι)—as the primary bearer of realness. A particular thing's functioning-unto-completeness (its ἐνέργεια ἀτελής) is its *degree* of realness, its measure of having come into its own.

The genius of Aristotle lies in his implicit thematization of "being-real," on an analogical scale, as the availability of something to human intelligence (i.e., to νοῦς *qua* λόγος) in a broad sense that encompasses both practical and theoretical activities. With this doctrine of the givenness *of things*, Heidegger

156. GA 14: 87.1 = 70.10–11: "Es gibt sie [= Anwesenheit] nur, wenn Lichtung waltet." Welteingang: GA 26: 250.32 = 194.27; and Wahrheit: GA 83: 21.8–11. World as meaningfulness: SZ 87.17–18 = 120.23; 334.33–34 = 384.1.

was able to raise the question of how the givenness (being) of things is itself given. With that he found the subject matter of a question that would take him, first, back to the pre-Socratic insight into the *open realm* that makes possible such givenness (Parmenides' "untrembling heart of well-rounded ἀλήθεια," fragment 1.29)[157] and into the *intrinsic hiddenness* of that realm (Heraclitus' φύσις, which remains ever concealed). This step back into the pre-Socratics then allowed him to ask for the whence and why of that intrinsically hiddenness of what makes possible ("gives") all configurations of meaningfulness. He found the "answer" in the a priori thrown-openness of human being (*Geworfenheit*), the fact that ex-sistence has always already been brought into its proper state of openedness (ex-sistence's ap-*propri*-atedness: *Ereignetsein*) as the space of intelligibility. Aristotle had taken Heidegger to the threshold of a question that neither Aristotle nor Parmenides nor Husserl—in fact, the whole of metaphysics—had ever raised.

157. Diels-Kranz, I, 230.11.

3

Heidegger beyond Aristotle

Heidegger frequently said that his own philosophical endeavors were rooted in Aristotle's metaphysics and yet went significantly beyond that to a question Western philosophy had never raised.

> My own philosophical evolution began already in high school as a preoccupation with Aristotle, which I took up again later. On that basis the question τί τὸ ὄν; [What is a thing?] has always remained for me the guiding question of philosophy.
>
> As my engagement with ancient philosophy as a whole become ever more clear, one day I realized in that connection that at the beginning of Western philosophy, as well as in all philosophy since then, the guiding question was, "What is a thing as such?" [τί τὸ ὂν ᾗ ὄν;]. However, it was never asked, "What is being itself? [τίς ἡ οὐσία;] What does the openness of being and its relation to man consist of, and what is it grounded in?"[1]

In 1937, on the tenth anniversary of the publication of *Being and Time*, Heidegger took stock of how he had arrived at his own question about the "whence" of being and how far he had gotten over the last ten years. In an important text titled "The Question about Being" he states:

> Right off, "the question of being" has two meanings. It can refer to the question about the being of things—what a thing as such is. . . . Asked in this way it is *the* question with which Western philosophy originates and by which it is guided progressively to its end. It is the guiding question with which Western philosophy began and through which its progress and goal were guided. [. . .]
>
> But the question of being can also refer to the *essence* of being itself—what *being* (not this or that thing) is. This is *the* question that, over against the guiding question, must be posed first and made to be experienced in its necessity. It seeks the essence of being itself: that whence and through which [*von woher und wodurch*] being as such occurs. This question is the *basic* question, to which the heretofore guiding question must be brought back.

1. GA 16: 423.3–15 = 4.3–14.

> It is the *authentic* question. From out of it the rightness, nature, and urgency of the guiding question are determined.[2]

This "basic question" goes back to the very foundation that makes metaphysics possible. It "seeks not the being of things but rather being itself in *its* essence"[3]—that is, it seeks the whence and why of meaningful presence at all.

> All "ontology." which ostensibly deals with being itself, completely fails to ask about being itself. For its part, what this ontology does deliver counts merely as *metaphysica generalis*—as a *forecourt* and as a formal framework.[4]

But as we have seen, Aristotle was aware of being (οὐσία), and his guiding question about things in their being (the real as regards its realness) did in fact convey Heidegger to the threshold of the basic question. Granted, Aristotle's metaphysics looks to the being of things only insofar as it sheds light on those things and lets them be understood at all. Nonetheless, metaphysics does in fact step across the threshold and

> avails itself of a region into which it moves being, and from out of which it places being in the open and thereby into openness. But it does all of this without really knowing about that [region] or needing to know it.[5]

In raising the question "Whence being?" Heidegger distinguishes two levels of human "transcendence." On the one hand, Aristotle's ontology transcends the real in the direction of its realness and as such is meta-physical: μετὰ τὰ φυσικά εἰς τὴν φύσιν.[6] Heidegger's question, on the other hand, is *meta*-meta-physical: it takes a further step, beyond realness/ουσία itself: μετὰ τὴν φύσιν εἰς τὸ "X." Metaphysics asks, "How come beings?" whereas Heidegger asks, "How come being—that is, meaningful presence—at all?" In that regard Heidegger's question, analogous to Plato's, goes ἐπέκεινα τῆς οὐσίας (beyond being) to the "X" that *enables* being.[7] The preliminary answer to Heidegger's question is

---

2. GA 73, 1: 82.3–6 and .11–17. My emphasis. See GA 74: 7.3–5: "die Unterscheidung der Frage nach dem Sein des Seienden (nach der Seiendheit) von der Frage nach der Wahrheit des Seins."

3. GA 40: 183.21–22 = 194.22–23: "das Sein selbst in *dessen* Wesen."

4. GA 73, 1: 87.4–7: "fragt gar nicht nach dem Sein selbst." At SZ 11.21 = 31.28 Heidegger calls such ontology "blind." GA 73, 2: 1064.28: "Keine Ontologie denkt das Sein selber."

5. GA 73, 1: 84.32–35: "beansprucht sie einen Bereich, in den hinaus sie das Sein rückt, aus dem her sie das Sein ins Offene und damit in die Wahrheit stellt."

6. Heidegger, "Zum 'Brief' über den 'Humanismus,'" 15.6. Cf. μετὰ τὰ ὄντα, ibid., 15.5.

7. *Republic* VI 509b9. Heidegger calls the power that enables εἶδος "das Ermöglichen und Tauglichmachen": GA 9: 228.8–9 = 175.6.

this: What accounts for being at all is the appropriated clearing (*das Offene, die Lichtung*). But Parmenides had already discovered that openness with his insight into "well-rounded ἀλήθεια" (fragment 1.29). So Heidegger's question turns out to be

1. not "Whence beings?"—the answer to that is: being;
2. nor even "Whence being at all?"—the answer to that is: the open clearing;
3. but rather "Whence and how is there 'the open'?"[8] or equally "Whence and how is there the clearing?"[9]

And the answer to that question will be *Er-eignis*: the ap-*propri*-ation of ex-sistence to its *proper* state of thrown-openness.[10]

> The *basic question* about the essence of being itself (not merely about things) now places being itself in question and from the very start moves being back into a region that is yet to be determined [= "X"], whence being receives the *openness* of its own essence: its disclosedness.[11]

> When the being-question is understood and posed in this way, one must have already gone beyond being itself. Being *and another* now come into language. This "other" must then be that wherein being has its emergence and its openness (clearing—disclosing)—in fact, wherein openness itself has its own emergence.[12]

We note here again the two elements of Heidegger's own question: (1) the move "beyond being" to its "whence"—namely, the clearing; and (2) the move "beyond the clearing" to *its* "whence"—namely, *Ereignis* as the appropriation of ex-sistence.

As Heidegger put it in his 1930 "Preface" to the Japanese translation of "What Is Metaphysics?":

---

8. GA 14: 46.4–5 = 37.14–15: "von woher und wie es 'das Offene' gibt." Also GA 77: 112.20–21 = 73.1: "Was ist diese Offene selbst?"

9. GA 14: 90.3–4 = 73.3: "Woher aber und wie gibt es die Lichtung?" Also GA 66: 422.5–6 = 373.6–7: "wie west die Wahrheit des Seyns."

10. GA 71: 211.9: "Das Da bedeutet das ereignete Offene—die ereignete Lichtung," which ex-sistence itself, as thrown open, is.

11. GA 73, 1: 82.20–24: "rückt es also im voraus noch in einen, noch zu bestimmenden Bereich, aus dem es die *Offenbarkeit* seines eigenen Wesens empfängt—seine *Wahrheit*."

12. GA 73, 1: 83.1–5: "Das Andere muß dann jenes sein, worin das Sein die Wesung und die Wahrheit (Lichtung—Verbergung) hat—ja jenes, worin die Wahrheit selbst—ihre Wesung hat." Heidegger continues (ibid., 83.5–6): "(more in detail –; clarification of the *meaning-question* [*Sinn-frage*])." This parenthetical material may be a *pro memoria* to Heidegger himself to work out the question of the *essence* of being more in detail as the question of the *intelligibility of being*.

> The author believes he has recognized that the *more original elaboration* of the traditional question guiding Western metaphysics—"What is a thing?"—depends on the basic question that supports and leads that traditional question, namely "What is being?" But that latter question likewise entails asking: What is the ground of the inner possibility and necessity of the openness of being?[13]

This "ground" is what Heidegger heuristically refers to the *Urphänomen* or *Ur-sache*.[14] This "primal phenomenon" turns out to be the "open space" that allows us to take things *as* this-or-that and thus to understand their "being"—that is, how and as what they are currently meaningful.

How did Heidegger arrive at the "X" that makes being possible and necessary? Not surprisingly the answer is: by way of a turn to history and specifically to Greek philosophy. Again, in his 1937, tenth-anniversary text, he asks:

> *But that [dimension] wherein being itself has its emergence-into-presence—how are we supposed to know it?* If we are not to find it arbitrarily, then we must search. And if the searching is not to disperse itself aimlessly, it requires a direction. But this direction can come only from what supports and guides us historically—from the manner in which the openness of being prevails throughout Western history.[15]

That last sentence hints at what Heidegger will call (not unambiguously) the "history of being," a topic that will occupy us in chapter 9. In the remainder of this present chapter our goal is more modest. Insofar as classical metaphysics at least *names* being—for example, as the ἀλήθεια, εἶδος, and οὐσία of things—we will sketch out how Heidegger retrieved from each of those terms some major elements of his own meta-metaphysical question. As Heidegger put it, within those names "a hint lies concealed for us, whose directive power must be forced into the light."[16]

> What clue does the beginning and history of the guiding question of Western thinking offer for questioning the openness of *being itself*? The guiding question [of metaphysics] seeks the being of *things*. And in so doing, it does bring

---

13. GA 16: 66.11–16 (emphasis added). That is, what brings about the immediate (if hidden) presence of meaningfulness as such?

14. GA14: 81.13–14 = 65.30–32.

15. GA 73, 1: 83.9–15: "Worin aber das Sein selbst die Wesung hat—wie sollen wir das wissen?" All italicized in the original.

16. GA 73, 1: 85.8–10.

> being to speech—but [only] with a view to *things*, for the sake of comprehending *them* as such. Nonetheless, even in [merely] naming being, [metaphysics' guiding] question is already giving an interpretation of being—right there, in the essential word with which it names being.[17]

To see how Heidegger sorted out the meta-metaphysical thrown-open clearing that makes the very being of things possible, we investigate three crucial terms that guided his retrieval: (1) ἀλήθεια, (2) ἰδέα/εἶδος, and (3) οὐσία.[18]

1. ἀλήθεια

How should we translate the Greek noun ἀλήθεια and the adjective ἀληθής? Throughout much of his career Heidegger unfortunately rendered ἀλήθεια by the German word *Wahrheit*—that is, "truth"—and he did so despite his own warnings in *Being and Time* and elsewhere that to do so was to distort what ἀλήθεια originally meant.

> To translate this word as "truth" . . . is to cover up the meaning of what, for the Greeks, constituted the "self-evident" pre-philosophical basis for understanding the use of the term ἀλήθεια.[19]
>
> Neither the Latin word *veritas* nor our German word *Wahrheit* contain the least echo of what the Greeks saw in advance and experienced when they spoke about . . . ἀλήθεια.[20]

It was only at the end of his career that Heidegger acknowledged his mistake.

> Ἀλήθεια thought as ἀλήθεια has nothing to do with "truth"; rather, it means disclosedness. What I said back in *Being and Time* about ἀλήθεια already goes in this direction. Ἀλήθεια as disclosedness had already occupied me, but in the meantime the word "truth" slipped in between.[21]
>
> In any case one thing becomes clear: To raise the question of ἀλήθεια, of disclosedness as such, is not the same as raising the question of truth. For this reason, it was inadequate and consequently misleading to call ἀλήθεια, in the sense of the clearing, by the word "truth."[22]

---

17. GA 73, 1: 84. 24–31.

18. Heidegger names these terms at GA 73, 1: 85.13–14 and spells them out through ibid., 87.7. I supplement his treatment with other texts of his.

19. SZ 219.33–37 = 262.26–29: verdecken den Sinn; vor-philosophisches Verständnis; selbst-verständlich.

20. GA 45: 98.8–12 = 87.20–24: "Weder . . . veritas noch. . . . Wahrheit."

21. GA 15: 262.5–10 = 161.31–34: "nichts zu tun" and "schob sich dazwischen."

22. GA 14: 86.16–20 = 70.2–5: "nicht sachgemäß und demzufolge irreführend."

But what is the "self-evident pre-philosophical basis" for understanding what ἀλήθεια means? Heidegger finds within the root of the word ἀλήθεια an implicit negative sense (-λήθ-) that is related to the verbs λήθω/λήθομαι and λανθάνω, "to escape notice, to remain hidden."[23] When that negative element is canceled out by the addition of an alpha-privative (ἀ-), the word ἀ-λήθ-εια conveys to Heidegger a *double* negative sense: a thing's condition of "no longer going unnoticed"—or to state it positively: a thing's having become noticed. For Heidegger, the verb ἀληθεύειν means "*to bring something to light*, to bring into our vision something that heretofore was not seen at all."[24] In short, for the Greeks ἀλήθεια was the condition of a *thing* insofar as it is now present-and-visible, and not just spatio-temporally present to one's eyes but *meaningfully* present to one's mind.

We can confirm this reading indirectly in the texts of Aristotle when he speaks of friendship in *Nicomachean Ethics*. One can feel goodwill (εὔνοια) for another person, he says, but that does not constitute friendship unless and until the goodwill is reciprocated, and not only reciprocated but also mutually *recognized*. The Greek verb Aristotle uses here for "to recognize" is μὴ λανθάνω ("not" + "to be hidden, unnoticed"), hence, to be not-hidden—or, in a word: noticed or known.[25] The same Greek usage continues some seven centuries later in Plotinus.[26] He defines sensation (τὸ αἰσθάνεσθαι) as "being aware of what affects you." But the Greek expression for such awareness is τὸ τὸ πάθος μὴ λανθάνειν—"to have what affects you not be hidden from you" (again, a double negative). Moreover, later in that text Plotinus places μὴ λανθάνειν, "to not be hidden." in apposition to the (late Greek) verb γινώσκω, "to know." Given such examples, the "'self-evident' pre-philosophical basis" of the ancient Greek understanding of ἀλήθεια is a thing's condition of being open and available for knowledge, whether theoretical or practical.

---

23. GA 54: 61.30–31 = 42.7–8: λανθάνει: "unbemerkt." See Wilhelm Luther, *"Wahrheit" und "Lüge" im ältesten Griechentum*, 11–13: unbemerkt; hence verborgen, verdeckt, verhüllt; Unverborgenheit. Also Robert Beekes, with Lucien van Beek, *Etymological Dictionary of Greek*, I, 65f., s.v. ἀληθής.

24. GA 45: 94.9–10 = 83.38–39: "Hervor-bringen heißt hier *Ans-Licht-bringen*, etwas bisher überhaupt noch nicht Gesichtetes zu Gesicht bringen."

25. *Nicomachean Ethics* VIII 2, 1155b34: μὴ λανθάνουσαν: when the goodwill is "not hidden" (in Bekker's Latin, "non occultam neque incognitam." III: 574a11) and 1156a4: μὴ λανθάνοντας: the mutual goodwill and benevolence must "not be hidden"—that is, must be recognized ("cognitum," Bekker, III: 574a19). See also *Physics* III 1, 200b13–14: If we are to understand φύσις, the meaning of κίνησις must "not be hidden." μὴ λανθάνειν (Bekker: "non lateat nos." III: 110b29), which Aristotle couples with ἀγνοεῖσθαι, "to not know, to be ignorant of." Cf. Aquinas: *Commentaria in octo libros Physicorum*, liber III, lectio 1, no. 279: "ignorato motu, ignoratur natura."

26. Plotinus, *Enneads* I 4: 2.3–6.

In his better moments Heidegger translates ἀλήθεια not by *Wahrheit* ("truth") but by neologisms like *Erschlossenheit* and *Unverborgenheit*. The first is usually brought into English as "disclosedness," which in fact parallels the structure of the alpha-privative: ἀ-λήθεια, dis-closedness. *Unverborgenheit* is usually rendered as "unhiddenness" or "unconcealedness." which likewise parallels ἀ-λήθεια. However, the double negative in those terms fails to capture the *positive* and more vivid image of the English word "openness." As Heidegger puts it (misusing the word *Wahrheit* to translate ἀλήθεια), "By the term *Wahrheit* we understand the openness/manifestness of things."[27] It is important to remember two things: (1) In Plato and Aristotle ἀλήθεια is the openness or intelligibility of *things*, and (2) such ἀ-λήθεια/dis-closedness is phenomenological—that is, it occurs *only* when there is a correlative human act of ἀ-ληθεύειν (the dis-closing of something). When Heidegger speaks of the "dis-closedness of an entity" he is saying that the entity is opened up as meaningful only in and for a human act of apprehension (*Vernehmen*). Heidegger always preserves the phenomenological correlation between whatever is open/intelligible and the apprehending of what is open/intelligible. So, on the one hand, the kind of disclosedness of *things* is their meaningful (not just their sensible) disclosedness, and this occurs not off by itself in some pre- or extra-human scenario but only in and with the human apprehension of those things.[28] On the other hand, when Heidegger speaks of the disclosedness of *the clearing*, he means the hidden presence of the openness that lets things be intelligible ("have being").[29] Heidegger simply wants to know why and how that is the case.

Heidegger interprets ἀλήθεια philosophically as an analogical term with three distinct and in fact layered meanings, which we may designate as ἀλήθεια-1, ἀλήθεια-2, and ἀλήθεια-3. Taking these three in the reverse order:

ἀλήθεια-3 refers to the correctness of a statement, the de facto agreement of a proposition with the state of affairs to which it refers—what has traditionally been called the correspondence of intellect and thing (*adaequatio intellectus*

27. GA 38: 79.21–22 = 68.12–13: "Unter Wahrheit verstehen wir die Offenbarkeit von Seiendem."

28. GA 9: 442.30–31 = 334.28–29: "[Wir] müssen daran erinnern, daß die ἀλήθεια, griechisch gedacht, allerdings für den Menschen waltet." GA 87: 103.2: "Das Sichzeigen [ist] schon bezogen auf ein Vernehmen."

29. This intelligibility is not yet the truth of correspondence. Things show up as *meaning something or other*, whether that meaning is correct or not.

et rei).[30] This kind of truth can occur only when we make a claim about a state of affairs in a declarative sentence. I might claim (rightly or wrongly) that I am presenting something in speech just the way it appears "in reality," just as it shows up in and of itself (i.e., "from" itself: ἀπο-φαίνεσθαι, *de-clarare*), rather than expressing my feelings, intentions, and wishes about the thing (in the subjective or optative moods, expressing my *attitude* toward what I'm saying). The Greek name for a declarative sentence—one that makes such a claim—is λόγος ἀποφαντικός or simply ἀπόφανσις. If our claim conforms to the state of affairs, it is possessed of apophantic truth (correctness). If our claim does not hold up, we're stuck with apophantic falsehood (incorrectness). I *maintained* that the spatula was in the drawer, and sure enough it was. I *declared* that it was a deer I saw in the forest at twilight, but on closer observation it turned out to be a bush.[31] In other words, the fact that a sentence is apophantic (= is in the declarative mode) does not guarantee that it is true, only that it *could be* true—or false.

However, the state of affairs against which an apophantic claim is measured must itself be already disclosed to us in one way or another if our statement about it is to be either correct or incorrect. This means that apophantic truth or falsehood necessarily presumes a prior disclosedness *qua* intelligible availability of the subject matter of the statement. Therefore the possibility of correspondence truth depends on:

ἀλήθεια-2, which is the prior, pre-propositional (pre-apophantic) intelligibility of a thing or a state of affairs. This prior intelligibility, which is always already operative in our everyday world, is what Heidegger initially called "ontic truth."[32] However, that phrase can be misleading insofar as "ontic *truth*" might seem to imply that our pre-propositional awareness of things always discloses those things as what they "really" and "correctly" are. But that would be ἀλήθεια-3. Yes, things are always disclosed meaningfully *as something*, even if the "something" turns out to be wrong (e.g., we see the bush as a deer). The ἀλήθεια-2 of a thing is its unavoidable *meaningfulness* rather than its disclosedness as it "truly" and "correctly" is. And finally, at the root of ἀλήθεια-3 and -2, and making both of them possible, there is:

ἀλήθεια-1 (or ἀλήθεια-prime), the thrown-open/dis-closed "space" that ex-sistence itself is and that makes possible both the intelligibility of things

30. Aquinas, *Quaestiones disputatae de veritate*, quaestio 1, articulum 1, corpus. See SZ 214.26–36 = 257.24–35.

31. GA 21: 187.17–20 = 158.14–17.

32. GA 3: 13.15–16 = 8.40: "Offenbarkeit des Seienden (ontische Wahrheit)." GA 5: 37.17–18 = 28.10–11: "᾿Αλήθεια[-2] heißt die Unverborgenheit des Seienden." Re ἀληθής as the "disclosedness" (not the "truth") of something, see above, chapter 2, note 136, on Augustine's use of verum in *De Genesi ad litteram*.

(ἀλήθεια-2) and the correctness of propositions (ἀλήθεια-3). This is what Heidegger initially called "ontological truth,"[33] a phrase that can be just as misleading as "ontic truth" and for the same reason. Ἀλήθεια-1 is what makes possible both ontic disclosedness and apophantic truth, without being either one. This most basic level of ἀλήθεια is what Heidegger means by "the clearing" in both his earlier and later work.[34]

In short, the common denominator of all three levels of ἀλήθεια is not "truth" but *openness* with regard to *meaning*. Ἀλήθεια-1 is the "open space" in which we can take things *as* . . . and thereby disclose their meaningful presence. Ἀλήθεια-2 is the pre-propositional meaningful presence of a thing. Ἀλήθεια-3 is the propositionally correct meaning of something—at least correct for now, until a more correct meaning comes along. A few more remarks, therefore, on these three levels of openness as regards meaningfulness, but now in the proper order.

First, ἀλήθεια-1: This names the very structure of ex-sistence insofar as it is "world-open,"[35] "*openness* as such (ex-sistence),"[36] and "openness in itself, as originally occurring: ex-sistence."[37] "Only with the *openedness* of ex-sistence do we reach the *most original* phenomenon of the alethic."[38] Without this ever-operative openedness of ex-sistence it would be impossible to relate something to something else (a tool to a task, or a subject to a predicate) and thus to understand the thing's current being. However, precisely as *thrown*-open, ex-sistence *qua* ἀλήθεια-1 remains a mystery, *das Geheimnis des Da-seins*—in fact, the "forgotten" mystery, *das vergessene Geheimnis des Daseins.*[39] This mystery is not praeter-human, but simply is the fact that how and why there is openedness at all is unknowable. The mystery that Heidegger is referring to is the unique presence-*by-absence* of the thrown-open clearing. As Heidegger puts it, the clearing, as ἀλήθεια-1, is opened up to

33. GA 3: 13.16–17 = 8.40–9.1: "die Enthülltheit der Seinsverfassung des Seienden (ontologische Wahrheit)." On ἀλήθεια-1 and -2: GA 9: 134.1–2 = 105.22–23: "liegt in der Unverborgenheit vom Seiendem je schon eine solche seines Seins."

34. SZ 133.5 = 171.22. GA 14: 85.32–33 = 69.21–22: "Die Ἀλήθεια, die Unverborgenheit im Sinne der Lichtung." Ibid., 82.9 = 66.26: "die Lichtung des Seins."

35. GA 21: 164.12–3 = 137.28–29: "die Weltoffenheit des Daseins."

36. GA 45:154.27–28 = 134.19: "die *Offenheit* als solcher (Da-sein)." See GA 65: 13.10–11 = 13.7–8: "die Gründung des Wesens der Wahrheit als Dasein" and GA 45: 193.25–27 = 167.20–22: "in ihm [Da-sein] *als* dem vom Seyn Ereigneten der Grund der Wahrheit sich gründet."

37. GA 45: 223.11–12 = 187.9–10: "die Offenheit in sich: ursprünglich wesend: das *Da-sein.*"

38. SZ 220.38–221.1 = 263.26–27: "wird erst mit der *Erschlossenheit* des Daseins das *ursprünglichste* Phänomen der Wahrheit erreicht."

39. Respectively GA 9: 197.26 = 151.9 and 195.23 = 149.28.

us as "an *abyss*"[40] or as a χώρα.[41] That is, the clearing (1) is always already present-and-operative wherever ex-sistence ex-sists, but (2) metaphorically speaking, it is "hidden" (or "absent") insofar as the reason *why* it occurs is unknowable. The mystery of the clearing-*qua*-abyss is what Heidegger calls "facticity" in the proper sense of the term: the fact that we cannot question back behind this thrown-openness (which is ourselves) to find its "cause," without presupposing this very thrown-openness as what first makes such questioning possible. This primal, always operative openedness is usually overlooked precisely because, as the ultimate presupposition of everything human, it is necessarily unknowable ("hidden," "absent") in its why and wherefore. And yet it is "more real and more efficacious than all historical events and facts," because it is their ground.[42] Only within this openedness can there be "understanding, that is, the projecting [of something *as* something], bringing it into the open"[43]—the understanding of the thing's current being *qua* meaningful presence.

Next, ἀλήθεια-2: This meaningful openness *of things* in our pre-propositional involvement with them

> signifies the un-coveredness [*Entdecktheit*] of some thing, and all such un-coveredness is grounded ontologically in the primordial case of the alethic, the openedness [*Erschlossenheit*] of ex-sistence.[44]

Here Heidegger makes a terminological distinction—which he soon stopped observing—between

1. *Erschlossenheit* (dis-closedness): the primal openedness of ex-sistence itself [= ἀλήθεια-1]; and, founded on that:
2. *Entdecktheit* (un-coveredness/dis-coveredness): the resultant intelligible availability of things [= ἀλήθεια-2].

Insofar as ex-sistence, as dis-closed, makes possible and is in correlation with the un-coveredness of things, Heidegger calls the being of ex-sistence *Entdeckendsein*, "the uncovering of things," usually translated awkwardly as ex-sistence's "being-uncovering" (Macquarrie-Robinson) or "being-revealing" (Stambaugh). What Heidegger means is simply that ontologically (*-sein*)

40. GA 45: 193.27 = 167.22. See GA 9: 174.13 = 134.17: "der *Ab-grund* des Daseins." See GA 26: 234.5–9 = 182.11–15 on ex-sistence's transcendence as opening up the abyss.

41. GA 83: 157.5 and .12 on χώρα as "Von wo her etwas [i.e., a thing in its being] anwest" (italicized in the original).

42. GA 45: 44.22–24 = 41.31–33: "ein *Geschehen*, das wirklicher und wirksamer ist als alle historischen Begebenheiten und Tatsachen."

43. GA 16: 424.21–22 = 5.15–16: "Verstehen, d.h. Entwerfen (ins Offene bringen)."

44. SZ 256.7–9 = 300.8–10.

ex-sistence is always un-covering (*entdeckend*) things by taking them as meaning something or other. Eventually, however, Heidegger discarded this distinction between "disclosed" (ex-sistence) and "un-covered/ dis-covered" (entities) and spoke instead of ex-sistence as *erschließend erschlossenes*, "disclosed [in itself] and disclosive [of entities]."[45] As a priori opened up, ex-sistence in turn opens up (renders meaningful) everything it meets, including itself *qua* existentiel. We cannot encounter anything, not even ourselves, except under the rubric of meaningfulness. Even if we merely puzzle over what an unknown something might be ("What is a meson after all?"), we have already brought the thing into the realm of the knowable ("Let X stand for whatever a meson is"). If it were not already disclosed as at least a *knowable something*, we could not search for, much less find out what it is (if it is at all), and we certainly could not make correct or incorrect propositional statements about it.[46]

Finally, ἀλήθεια-3: This third level of ἀλήθεια refers to that particular state of disclosedness that consists in the agreement of a proposition with the already (priorly and perhaps only preliminarily) disclosed state of affairs that it refers to.

> In order to be what it is (namely, an assimilation to the object), truth as correctness-in-representing-things [= ἀλήθεια-3] presupposes the openedness/availability of things [= ἀλήθεια-2] by which they become capable of being ob-jects in the first place. . . . Consequently this openedness [= ἀλήθεια-2] shows itself to be the [proximate but not ultimate] ground of the possibility of correctness [i.e., of ἀλήθεια-3].[47]

The translation of ἀλήθεια as "truth" should be strictly and exclusively confined to this third level: apophantic correctness. This is the locus of the traditional (Aristotelian, Thomistic, Kantian) doctrine of truth as the conformity of the judgment and the judged, the agreement of mental or verbal propositions and worldly states of affairs.[48] This is what Aristotle called the ὁμοίωσις

45. GA 27: 135.13. (Already at SZ 207.12–13 = 251.3–4 and 365.21 = 416.32 Heidegger used "erschlossen" of innerworldly entities.) See GA 45: 227.10–13 = 188.35–38: "Man is both 'der *Wächter der Offenheit des Seyns selbst*' and 'der Bewahrer der Unverborgenheit des Seienden.'"

46. See Plato, *Meno*, 80d5–8 (Meno's paradox) and 86b6–c2 (Socrates' tentative response).

47. GA 45: 92.3–9 = 82.8–14. See GA 27: 78.5–6": "[Das Seiende] ist an ihm selbst unverborgen [= ἀλήθεια-2]. Weil es das ist, können wir Aussagen darüber machen." Re "proximate but not ultimate": The ultimate ground of ἀλήθεια-3 is ἀλήθεια-1, the openedness of ex-sistence.

48. *Metaphysics* IV 7, 1011b26–28; Aquinas, *De veritate* I, 1, respondeo ("Prima"): "et in hoc formaliter ratio veri perficitur": the nature or structure of truth has its formal perfection in such correspondence; Kant, *Critique of Pure Reason*, A 58 = B 82. For a list of terms for "correspondence": GA 45: 16.16–27 = 16.4–14.

or "assimilation" of τὰ παθήματα τῆς ψυχῆς (the so-called "impressions" the soul has of things) to τὰ πράγματα (the things themselves).[49] The word "truth" (*Wahrheit*) properly pertains *only* to such correct apophantic-declarative claims, and we should never follow Heidegger's mistaken employment of that term for the other two meanings of ἀλήθεια—that is, for what he wrongly called the pre-propositional "truth" of entities and, worse yet, the "truth" of being itself.

Heidegger argued that Aristotle was oblivious of ἀλήθεια-1 and knew only ἀλήθεια-2 and -3: the intelligibility of things and the correctness of statements. Heidegger would reserve to himself the discovery—or at least the re-thematization—of the hidden but ever-operative ἀλήθεια-1. Parmenides did indeed have a sense of ἀλήθεια-1 as the aboriginal all-enabling openness ("well-rounded ἀλήθεια": fragment 1.29), but he failed to inquire into what accounts for that openness: the thrown-openness or appropriation of ex-sistence. Likewise Heraclitus: The farthest he got was the *intrinsic hiddenness* of that φύσις/ἀλήθεια-1. He declared, "φύσις prefers to remain hidden" (fragment 123). Heidegger renders that phrase as follows: "Intrinsic concealment is the innermost essence of the movement of appearing,"[50] where "the movement of appearing" refers to the emergence of being, understood as the φαίνεσθαι of things. Heraclitus knew that the dimension that accounts for all forms of *Sein* (whatever that dimension might be) was intrinsically hidden, but he failed to understand *why*. It remained for Heidegger to see that *Ereignis*, the thrown-openness of ex-sistence, can never come into the open (a fact that Heidegger called *Ent-eignis*) precisely because it is the necessarily presupposed reason why there is an open at all.[51] Thus Heidegger can claim, with regard to both the pre-Socratics and the classical fourth-century philosophers, "With appropriation one is no longer thinking with the Greeks at all."[52] Therefore, it is important to note the crucial difference Heidegger sees between ἀλήθεια-1 in the pre-Socratics and ἀλήθεια-2 in Aristotle.

49. Aristotle, *De interpretatione* 1, 16a6–8.

50. GA 15: 343.24–25 = 46.18–19: "das Sichverbergen ist das innerste Wesen der Bewegung des Erscheinens [eines Seienden]." See his various paraphrases of this at GA 15: 343.23–31 = 46.17–24. Heidegger expresses the *intrinsicness* of the unknowability of the clearing with the statement (which is potentially misleading because of the faux reflexive) "diese Verborgenheit *sich in sich selbst* verbirgt": GA 6:2: 319.1–2 = 214.8, my emphasis.

51. As that which accounts for everything human, Ereignis (the appropriation of ex-sistence to its thrown-openness) is, in itself, "Enteignis," which is Heidegger's way of saying that appropriation is intrinsically hidden ("withdrawn") and does not appear at all: GA 14: 27.35–28.5 = 22.31–23.3. Translating "Enteignis" as "expropriation" says nothing at all.

52. GA 15: 366.31–32 = 61.4.

Parmenides and Heraclitus understood ἀλήθεια/φύσις (they are the same) as the hidden source of the being of things, whereas Aristotle first separates ἀλήθεια and φύσις and then takes each of them down a notch or two.

1. In Parmenides ἀλήθεια is always ἀλήθεια-1, and it refers to the *clearing* wherein and whereby all forms of the being of things become manifest. In Aristotle, on the other hand, ἀλήθεια-1 is lost, and ἀλήθεια-2 names only the *being* of things.
2. In Heraclitus φύσις names the *intrinsically hidden source* of all forms of the being of things. In Aristotle, however, φύσις names only the *being* of things (not their hidden source) and in fact the being of only a *particular realm* of things, those we call "natural" entities as contrasted with artifacts.

Aristotle's φύσις is thus only a faint echo of Heraclitus'. It still bespeaks "emergence" (*Aufgang*), but now it is no longer the emergence of *being* but only of *things*, and specifically of those things (the things of nature) that "do" their own emergence without extrinsic help: "the *self-unfolding emergence*, in and through which alone the thing is what it is."[53]

Another important note: When speaking of the Greeks in general, Heidegger does say that "φαίνεσθαι means: to be brought into appearance and to appear therein."[54] However, the "that" which "is brought into appearance" is the appearing *thing*, τὸ φαινόμενον in its φαίνεσθαι; and the φαίνεσθαι (or being) of the thing is that by which the thing appears. If, like Heidegger, one were to go "behind" such things-in-their-appearance and ask what brings the very *being* or φαίνεσθαι (of the thing) into appearance, one would have to go beyond Aristotle to the pre-Socratics, and ultimately to Heidegger. This point is of capital importance. The φύσις and ἀλήθεια that Aristotle (not the pre-Socratics) knew of was only that of *things*: ἀλήθεια-2; and the movement of becoming-disclosed that he articulated with those two Greek words was always *a thing's* emergence, unfolding, and appearance as what and how it is. Heidegger articulates this exclusively *ontic* nature of ἀλήθεια-2 as follows:

> We translate ἀλήθεια[-2] as the disclosedness of things, and in so doing we already indicate that disclosedness—i.e., "truth" as the Greeks understood it—is a determination of things themselves. . . . The disclosedness of things and the being of things are the same.[55]

53. GA 73, 1: 85.19–20: "das *Sichentfaltende* [*sic*] *Aufgehen*, worin und wodurch erst das Seiende ist, was es ist."

54. GA 12: 125.10–11 = 38.4–5.

55. GA 45: 121.27–30 and 122.4–5 = 106.16–19 and .27–28. The last sentence is a slight paraphrase to maintain rhetorical balance. In a strictly literal reading: "Disclosedness and things in their being are the same."

Heidegger the phenomenologist insists that a thing's emergence into meaningful appearance cannot happen apart from human beings. The ἀλήθεια-2 of things, their appearance as knowable and usable, occurs only in an actual encounter with a human being.[56] In fact, the disclosedness of a thing does not belong to the *thing* but to *ex-sistence*.[57] As Heidegger puts it, "Disclosedness is a determination of things—insofar as they are *encountered*."[58]

> Something can be settled about things with reference to their being, only *insofar as things are present*, that is, as we say, [note the definition of "being present"] insofar as things can be *encountered* at all.[59]

The encounter mentioned here is an encounter with human beings as intelligent and not merely as sentient. For Aristotle there *is* a sentient disclosedness of things, and Heidegger notes that in *Being and Time*: " Ἀἴσθησις, the straightforward sense-apprehension of something . . . is alethic."[60] However, human beings live in the ἀλήθεια of <u>λόγος</u>: "[For human beings] ἀληθεύειν shows up first of all in λέγειν."[61] Hence "presence as encounterability" is a thing's intelligible, meaningful presence insofar as we take the thing (correctly or incorrectly) *as* something or other. Like Aristotle before him, Heidegger investigates being

> insofar as the encountered things (= "the world" in naïve ontology) are met and are present to everyday ex-sistence insofar as it speaks about the world in such a way that discoursing and addressing become at the same time a further guideline orienting the question of being.[62]

---

56. GA 83: 22.1–4: "Nur sofern es Welt gibt, d.h. sofern Dasein existiert, kann das Seiende . . . sich *als Seiendes* in seinem Sein bekunden!"

57. GA 27: 133.25–26: "Die Unverborgenheit des Vorhandenen gehört nicht zum Vorhandenen, sondern zum Dasein."

58. GA 19: 17.1–2 = 11.35–36: "Die Unverborgenheit ist eine Bestimmung des Seienden, sofern es begegnet" (my emphasis); ibid., 23.6–7 = 16.21. See SZ 28.36–37 = 51.15–17: "nach der Zugangsart zu ihm." GA 83: 21.3–23 discusses disclosedness *qua* Bekundlichkeit (manifestness) as a thing's Welteingänglichkeit (its condition of having entered the world of meaningfulness).

59. GA 19: 205.7–10 = 141.27–30, where the ET omits Heidegger's two italicizations within the German text.

60. SZ 33.30–32 = 57.11–12: "'Wahr' ist . . . die αἴσθησις, das schlichte, sinnliche Vernehmen von etwas."

61. GA 19: 17.26 = 12.12: "Das ἀληθεύειν zeigt sich also zunächst im λέγειν."

62. GA 19: 205.16–20 = 142.2–5. In the margin of his text Heidegger annotates the phrase "speaking about the world" with "the 'is' in simple saying and asserting."

Thus as regards ἀλήθεια-2 in Aristotle:

> Ἀληθές means literally "uncovered." It is primarily things, the πράγματα, that are uncovered: τὸ πρᾶγμα ἀληθές. This uncoveredness does not apply to things insofar as they just *are* ["in the universe"] but insofar as they are *encountered*, insofar as they are objects of our dealings.[63]
>
> Where and how is this disclosedness [= ἀλήθεια-2]? We see it as an *occurrence*—an occurrence that happens "with *man*."[64]
>
> At the origin of the disclosedness of things, [that is] at the point where being "lets things come through [to us]," our perceiving is just as much involved as is the thing that is perceived in our perceiving. . . . *Together* they constitute disclosedness.[65]

There are two significant issues related to this position, one regarding λόγος, and the other regarding the extra-mental existence of things. In the first case: As Heidegger reads Aristotle, λόγος as discursive apprehension plays an essential role in the appearance of the being of things. Aristotle asks, "How do things look insofar are they are addressed and spoken of, insofar as they are λεγόμενα?"[66] This sentence is referring to a thing insofar as it is *taken-as*-something in discursive apprehension. When that occurs, the thing is present to us in terms of its current whatness and howness, its being *qua* meaningful presence.

> Philosophy aims at things insofar as they are and *only* insofar as they are. But this means philosophy is not concerned with what we call the ontic, with things themselves in such a way that philosophy would become utterly engrossed in them. Instead, philosophy is concerned with things in a way that addresses the ὄν as ὄν—the ὂν λεγόμενον ᾗ ὄν [the thing as discursively addressed with regard to the fact that it *is*].[67]

---

63. GA 19: 24.29–33 = 17.25–33: "begegnet . . . Gegenstand eines Umgangs." My emphasis.

64. GA 34: 73.32–33 = 54.30–31: "ein Geschehnis, das 'mit dem *Menschen*' geschieht."

65. GA 34: 71.17–21 = 52.36–38: "Sie [das Er-blicken und das Erblickte] machen Unverborgenheit *mit* aus." The phrase "lets things come through [to us]" is my paraphrastic interpretation of Heidegger's shorthand "Durchlaß desselben [= des Seienden]."

66. GA 19: 205.21–22 = 142.5–7: "Angesprochenes . . . λεγόμενον."

67. GA 19: 207.19–23 = 143.18–24, emphasis added. Heidegger continues at .25–28 (all italicized): "This idea of 'onto-logy,' of λέγειν, of the addressing of things with regard to their being, was exposed for the first time with complete acumen by Aristotle." See ibid., 224.5–10 = 154.36–155.2: "Here we arrive at a concluding characteristic of the fundamental science of the Greeks, πρώτη φιλοσοφία—this science is ultimately oriented toward λόγος, precisely because its theme is things insofar as they are ὂν λεγόμενον, hence things as addressed [discursively], things insofar as they are themes for λόγος."

> Hence, λόγος, discourse about the world and things, plays the role of the guiding thread insofar as things are present in the λεγόμενον [i.e., in what is said and thus revealed about them]. Even (as is the case with Aristotle) when research into being goes beyond dialectic, that is, beyond confinement to things as addressed, toward a pure grasping of the ἀρχαί, toward θεωρεῖν—even there it can be shown that λόγος is still fundamental for the final conception of being. Even Aristotle, although he overcomes dialectic, still remains oriented toward λόγος in his entire question of being.[68]

So close are ὄν and human λόγος in this proto-phenomenological ontology that Aristotle can say that it is the human being who performs the act of bringing the encountering thing into its state of uncoveredness. Heidegger comments on Aristotle, "Uncoveredness [the *Unverdecktsein* of things] is a specific accomplishment of ex-sistence, an accomplishment that has its being in the soul: ἀληθεύει ἡ ψυχή."[69] That is, human beings disclose things in their being, and this disclosing (*Erschließen* as ἀληθεύειν) is "a *determination of the being of human ex-sistence itself*."[70] Thus, when it comes to discovering the being of things, "λόγος is and remains the guiding thread."[71]

Along with the crucial role of λόγος, the second significant issue regarding ἀλήθεια is Heidegger's insistence that things do in fact "exist out there" on their own apart from their knownness or knowability by human beings. Heidegger cuts the Gordian knot: "Questions like 'Does the world exist independent of my thinking?' are meaningless."[72] It is true that "things are uncovered [i.e., "have being" in Heidegger's sense of the word] only *when* ex-sistence *is*; and they are disclosed only *as long as* ex-sistence *is*."[73] Nonetheless, that does not mean that a thing "can only be what it is in itself when and as long as ex-sistence ex-sists,"[74] because "things *are* quite independent of the expe-

---

68. GA 19: 206.8–16 = 142.22–29; see ibid., 224.14–225.5 = 155.6–23. Heidegger's mention of the "pure grasping of the ἀρχαί" refers to the θιγεῖν or θιγγάνειν, the "touching" of *Metaphysics* IX 10, 1051b24–25. See chapter 2, note 136.

69. "The soul discloses [things]": GA 19: 24.33–25.1 = 17.28–30. The reference is to *Nicomachean Ethics* VI 3, 1139b15.

70. GA 19: 23.6–8 = 16.21–23: "eine *Seinsbestimming des menschlichen Daseins selbst*" with ibid., 17.11–14 = 12.1–3: "Das Erschließen . . . ist . . . eine Seinsweies des Seienden, das wir als menschliches Dasein bezeichnen."

71. GA 19: 206.20 = 142.31–32: "der λόγος Leitfaden ist und bleibt."

72. GA 58: 105.15–16 = 84.5–6: "sinnlos." See GA 26: 194.30–31 = 153.28–29; 216.28–30 = 169.12–14. *Zollikon Seminare* 222.1–5 = 176.24–27.

73. SZ 226.28 = 269.21–22. See ibid., 57.34–37 = 84.19–20: An entity "can 'meet up with' ex-sistence only insofar as [the entity] can, of its own accord, show up within a *world*."

74. SZ 212.1–3 = 255.8–9: "nicht . . . wenn und solange Dasein existiert."

rience, knowledge, and grasping by which they are disclosed, uncovered, and determined."[75] Thus:

> The uncoveredness or disclosedness [i.e., the ἀλήθεια-2 of a thing] reveals the thing precisely as it already was beforehand, regardless of its being uncovered or not uncovered. As uncovered, the thing becomes intelligible as what it is *just as* it is-and-will-be regardless of every possible uncoveredness of itself. Nature does not need disclosedness, revealedness [= ἀλήθεια-2], to be as it is.[76]

Further in that vein, when Heidegger discusses the relation between the human senses and their objects (αἴσθησις and its αἰσθητόν), he notes that "the actual existence [*Wirklichkeit*] of the perceptible as such does not depend on the performance of an act of perception."[77]

Nonetheless we can see the complexity of the matter. Heidegger remarks on "the wonder" that, although the act of perception is related to something that stands there independently in and for itself, the fact that the thing is related to perception "does not deprive the entity of its independence but precisely enables the entity to secure its independence in being disclosed."[78]

> The independence of things from us human beings is not altered by the fact that this very independence as such is possible only if human beings ex-sist.[79] Without the ex-sistence [*Existenz*] of human beings, the being-in-themselves of things becomes not only unexplainable but also utterly unintelligible. Nonetheless, this does not mean that the things themselves are dependent upon human beings.[80]

> Physical nature can occur as innerworldly [i.e., as meaningful] only when world, i.e., ex-sistence, ex-sists. However, nature can certainly "be" in its own way without occurring as innerworldly, i.e., it can "be" without human ex-sistence—and thus a world—ex-sisting. In fact only because nature is objectively present *of and by itself* can it also encounter ex-sistence within a world.[81]

---

75. SZ 183.28–29 = 228.10–12: "unabhängig von Erfahrung."

76. GA 24: 314.31–315.3 = 220.40–221.2. My emphasis. See also SZ 227.6–8 = 269.36–38: "das vordem schon war."

77. GA 33: 201.11–13 = 172.27–28. All italicized in the original.

78. GA 33: 202.13–16 = 173.25–27. See GA 34: 70.22–25 = 52.14–16.

79. This writer's note: See SZ 212.5–7 = 255.11–12: "When human being does not exist, there 'is' neither 'independence' nor the 'in itself.'"

80. GA 33: 202.23–29 = 173.34–174.3: "diese Unabhängigkeit . . . nur möglich . . . wenn der Mensch existiert"; "völlig sinnlos ohne die Existenz des Menschen."

81. GA 25: 19.26–32 = 14.20–24. At SZ 14.23–24 = 34.39–40 Heidegger insists that tying ἀλήθεια-2 to a human act of ἀληθεύειν "has nothing in common with a vicious subjectivizing of the totality of beings."

That is, the being/meaningfulness of things—not their mere existence-out-there-in-the-universe—occurs always and only in correlation with human λόγος. In Heidegger's phenomenological sense of the term, *Sein* is given only in human understanding.[82] In fact, being is *dependent* on man's understanding of being.[83]

> Ἀλήθεια[-2] is a peculiar ontological characteristic of things insofar as things stand in relation to a "looking" that is aimed at them, to a disclosing that notices them, to a knowing. On the other hand, the ἀληθές [the disclosed thing] is certainly also in ὄν [in being] and [to that extent] is a characteristic of being itself, specifically insofar as being = the presence [of a thing] and this presence is taken up in λόγος and "is" in it.[84]

Or again, with regard to "being" in Plato, Heidegger says:

> An ἰδέα is what-is-sighted. What-is-sighted *is* sighted only in and *for an act of seeing*. An "unsighted sighted" is like a round square or a piece of iron made out of wood. We finally have to get serious about the fact that Plato gave the name "ideas" to being [*das Sein*]. "Being sighted" is not an add-on to the ideas, a predicate subsequently connected to them, or something that occasionally happens to them. Instead it is what characterizes them first of all and as such. They are called "ideas" precisely and primarily because they are understood to be that: to be what-is-sighted. Strictly speaking, the "sighted" *is* only where there is a seeing and a looking.[85]

In other words, the only *Sein* to which we have access is the intelligibility of things, their ἀλήθεια-2 or disclosedness to us. While this does not deny that things "exist out there," that is not what is at stake in Heidegger's phenomenology, particularly after one has performed a phenomenological reduction, as Heidegger always does (see chapter 4). For Heidegger the phenomenologist, things are indeed "manifest in themselves." but not the way they are in naïve realism or in Husserl's transcendental idealism.

---

82. SZ 183.29–31 = 228.12–14: "Sein . . . nur im Verstehen des Seienden." Ibid., 212.4–5 = 255.10–11: "Allerdings nur solange Dasein *ist*, das heißt die ontische Möglichkeit von Seinsverständnis, 'gibt es' Sein." GA 26: 194.32–33 = 153.30: "Sein gibt es nur, sofern Dasein existiert."

83. SZ 212.13–14 = 255.19–20: "Abhängigkeit des Seins . . . von Seinsverständnis." GA 66: 138. 32 = 118.24: "Das Seyn nur vom Da-sein." Ibid., 139.18 = 119.6: "Das Seyn is vom Menschen abhängig." See GA 26: 186.22–23 = 147.35–36: "[Sein:] was nie fremd, sondern immer bekannt, 'unser' ist."

84. GA 19: 17.4–11 = 11.33–42; also GA 24: 240.17–31 = 169.2–18, where Heidegger denominates beings *outside* the world as vorhanden. Also *Zollikoner Seminare* 350.27 = 281.16: "Weltlosigkeit bloß vorhandener Dinge."

85. GA 34: 70.22–32 = 52.14–22.

> What occurs in [Husserl's] phenomenology of the acts of consciousness as the self-showing of phenomena was thought more originally by Aristotle and in all Greek thinking and ex-sisting as Ἀλήθεια[-2], the dis-closedness of what-is-present, a thing's having been brought out of hiddenness, its being made manifest. What phenomenological research rediscovered as the basic stance of thinking turns out to be the fundamental characteristic of Greek thinking, if not indeed of philosophy as such.[86]

For Heidegger, *Sein*—the ἀλήθεια-2 of entities—shows up always and only in and to a correlative human act of disclosing (ἀληθεύειν).[87]

This brief look at the three different levels of ἀλήθεια has turned up important clues that Heidegger found in the Greeks for his own question about the possibility and necessity of *Sein* as the meaningful presence of things to man. However, to achieve a satisfactory answer to that question Heidegger would have to do at least four things:

1. explain the intrinsic hiddenness (the presence-as-absence) of ἀλήθεια-1;
2. show how such hiddenness makes possible ἀλήθεια-2, the intelligible presence of things;
3. show that this ἀλήθεια-2 is not an ontic "given" but must be actively "brought forth" by human ex-sistence; and thus
4. explain what the so-called "wresting from hiddenness" (represented by the hyphen between the ἀ- and the -λήθ of ἀ-λήθεια-2) is all about.

In Heidegger's telling, these four issues were not thematically addressed by Greek philosophy and in fact could be raised only by going beyond metaphysical thinking—or, as he put it, "stepping back" from metaphysics into a region that is prior to and the basis for it.

2. ἰδέα/εἶδος

We continue to follow Heidegger's effort to retrieve from the ancient names for "being" some clues for his own basic question about the "whence" of being. When he considers ἰδέα/εἶδος as another name for οὐσία, he picks up the third and fourth issues mentioned above—namely, the wresting of a thing from hiddenness and the bringing of it forth into disclosedness. (Note: Properly speaking, we do not wrest the *disclosedness* of the thing from un-disclosedness. We wrest the *thing* into disclosedness.)

86. GA 14: 99.1–9 = 79.18–25: "dis-closedness" = Unverborgenheit; "having been brought out of hiddenness" = Entbergung [because things do not "come out of hiddenness" on their own]; "being made manifest" = sich-Zeigen.

87. See the correlation of "Anwesenheit und Gegenwärtigung" at GA 14: 87.21–22 = 71.1. Also GA 21: 414.26–28 = 342.39–41.

Heidegger is emphatic that the meaningful presence of things—their knowability, usability, enjoyability—is not gleaned from the *de facto* empirical presence of things themselves. Yes, in Aristotle the knowability of a thing as what and how it is, *is* the thing's ἰδέα/εἶδος. However, this intelligibility is not somehow ontically embedded *in* the thing, such that an epistemological X-ray vision could read off the thing's essence. As Heidegger puts it, "The ideas are not present-but-somehow-hidden objects that we could lure out through a kind of hocus-pocus."[88] Of course, the appearance of a thing that Heidegger is talking about is not the physical presence of that thing with all its sensible features but the thing's intelligible appearance, which only the intellect (practical or theoretical) can discern. And insofar as "being is not a thing, nor any existing ingredient of things,"[89] we will never discover a thing's whatness and howness by staring at the thing, no matter how intently or how intelligently. Rather, if one holds to the Greek position that the essence must be pre-understood if we are to understand any of its instances, then "what else can this mean except that in some way the essence is brought before us and we bring ourselves before the essence?"[90] In fact, Heidegger argues that we play a very active role in bringing about the meaningful appearance—the being—of the thing. "The grasping of the essence." Heidegger says, "is a kind of bringing-forth of the essence."[91] What kind of bringing-forth or pro-duction is this unique ποίησις?

The Greeks understood the whatness of a thing as its "form" or intelligible structure. Plato, of course, would deny that ἰδέα/εἶδος—eternal and unchanging as it is—could ever be brought forth by human doing. Aristotle, however, holds that in addition to being the intelligible-ontological structure of things, essences are indeed brought forth into actual knownness by man. What Aristotle has in mind by this pro-duction (ποίησις: leading something forth) is not a "making" in the sense of bringing something into existence for the first time. Rather, it is a matter of taking a thing that is already there and wresting it out of obscurity and into the light, in this case, into the light of intelligibility. "To bring forth means to bring out into the light, to bring into view something which, up to then, was not seen at all."[92] The undisclosedness from which something is wrested, Heidegger says, can be threefold:

88. GA 34: 71.24–26 = 53.4–5: "keine vohandenen, irgendwo versteckten Objekte . . . Hokuspokus."

89. GA 40: 93.31–32 = 96.8–9: "nicht Seiendes . . . kein seiendes Bestandstück des Seienden."

90. GA 45: 83.16–17 = 74.28–30: "vor uns gebracht."

91. GA 45: 83.18–19 = 74.31–32: "Her-vor-bringen"; also ibid., 83.32–84.1 = 75.8–9.

92. GA 45: 94.9–10 = 83.38–39: "*Ans-Licht-bringen.*"

1. the unknownness of the real meaning of something, due to common opinions;
2. a thing's not-being-known at all;
3. a thing's *no longer* being known, due to our having forgotten something we once knew.[93]

The kind of existentiel-personal ποίησις whereby we lead the whatness or being of the encountering thing into the light is made possible by our existential-structural "irruption" into the midst of otherwise undisclosed things

> in such a way that, in and through this in-break, things break open and show what and how they are. The in-break that breaks things open, in its way helps things to themselves.[94]

This "breaking open" of things refers to their appearance as intelligible. As a phenomenon—and that always means: in correlation with an enactment of human λόγος—the thing always appears (correctly or incorrectly) *as* something meaningful: for Homer perhaps as the shield that the warrior can use, as the god he can reverence or challenge, as the home to which he returns. The "as" of "something-*as*" is what human λόγος brings to the phenomenon in order to let it "become" what it is. This contribution of the as-structure—which is what Heidegger means by "world"[95]—marks the arrival of meaning in the universe of entities, and the "*that*-as-which" a thing shows up (the shield, the god, the home) embodies the meaning of the thing in question.[96]

In one of the most discussed passages in his works, Aristotle speaks of ὁ [νοῦς] τῷ πάντα ποιεῖν,[97] "the mind that makes all things"—to which we must add the important word νοητά: "the mind that makes all things *intelligible*" (i.e., knowable and useable). Aristotle's Greek phrase refers to the νοῦς ποιητικός,

93. Heidegger, "Dasein und Wahrsein nach Aristoteles," 9.3–18 = 225.9–25. See the corresponding forms of disclosedness in the ET: 237.20–35.

94. GA 9: 105.8–11 = 83.32–35: Einbruch, aufbricht. (See below, this chapter, note 170.) To use a later word from a different context, this in-breaking ποίησις is very much a μεταποίησις in the sense of changing something into a better state. See Procopius of Gaza, *Commentarii in Deuteronomium* [32:6], *Patrologia Graeca* 87 (Pars Prima), 956.52–54: in Migne's Latin: "non solum rei primitivam essentiam dare, verum in meliorem conditionem commutare."

95. Thus he can speak of ex-sistence as "in das 'als' geworfen": GA 73, 1: 233.23.

96. SZ 151.25–26 = 193.1–2: "Sinn ist das, worin sich Verständlichkeit von etwas halt." Perhaps: Intelligibility in the broad sense of meaningfulness-at-all (i.e., "the world" in Heidegger's sense) is where the *particular* knowability or meaning (here Verständlichkeit = Bedeutung) of something is found.

97. *De anima* III 5, 430a15. See appendix 2.

or "activating intellect"[98]—that is, the mind—insofar as it allows what is only potentially intelligible to become actually intelligible, analogous to the way the invisible diaphanous, when illuminated, makes colors that lie in the dark (and hence are only potentially visible) become actually visible.[99] Heidegger's retrieval of Aristotle's activating intellect consists of reinterpreting the νοῦς ποιητικός in terms of the clearing, thanks to which we can existentielly take a thing as this or that and thus bring it from unknownness into knownness. Heidegger speaks of such an existentiel act as a "productive seeing" (*Er-sehen*) of the essence of the thing, an active intellectual seeing that is a *Herausstellen* (ποίησις as pro-duction: bringing forth) of the thing's εἶδος or meaning. Here Heidegger is referring to the act of taking something *as or in terms of* one of its possible uses or meanings, what Heidegger calls *etwas entwerfen auf*. . . . Unfortunately, both Macquarrie-Robinson and Stambaugh translate this by the unintelligible phrase "projecting something *upon*," as if one were throwing a book on a table or pitching a horseshoe. The underlying Aristotelian term is τὶ κατὰ τινὸς λέγειν: showing something (correctly or incorrectly) *as* this-or-that.[100] Such an existentiel act of "pro-jecting something *as*" (taking it in terms of this or that meaning) is possible only because ex-sistence itself is already structurally pro-jected, thrown ahead as possibility into possibilities. Thrown-open and thereby clearing the space for taking-as, ex-sistence is the reason why we can actively "bring forth" the current being (*Was-sein*, *Wie-sein*) of something. Heidegger's interpretation of the νοῦς ποιητικός or activating intellect is worth citing at length.

> The essence of something is not at all to be discovered simply like a fact; on the contrary, it must be *brought forth*, since it is not directly present in the sphere of immediate [i.e., sensible] representing and intending. To bring forth is a kind of making [ποίησις; hence νοῦς ποιητικός], and so there is something creative residing in all grasping and positing of the essence. The creative always appears to be violent and arbitrary . . . [because] it is bound to a higher lawfulness that must be protected against the intrusion of common opinion . . . which abhors the exception.[101]

98. The phrase νοῦς ποιητικός (Latin: intellectus agens) is one that Aristotle in fact never used, although it is correctly modeled after the ποιητικόν at *De anima* III 5, 430a12.

99. Responsible for: τὸ αἴτιον, *De anima* III 5, 430a12; light: τὸ φῶς, 430a15, 16; potential, actual: δυνάμει, ἐνεργείᾳ: 430a16–18. On the diaphanous (τὸ διαφανές) see *De anima* II 7, 418b7—not to mention Stephen Dedalus' gloss of it as the "ineluctable modality of the visible": Joyce, *Ulysses*, Episode 3 (Proteus), 43.21. Also GA 4: 56.34 = 79.18: "Durchsichtigkeit der Helle" and Appendix 2.

100. See *De interpretatione* 5, 17a21 and 10, 19b5; *Metaphysics* VIII 3, 1043b30–31.

101. GA 45: 93.28–94.4 = 83.25–34.

> This bringing-into-view is a peculiar kind of seeing. It does not see by merely staring at what is objectively present or otherwise already accessible. Instead, this seeing first brings before itself that which is to be seen. It is a seeing that *draws something forth*, not a mere looking at what is standing about waiting for people to come across it as they go on their way. It is not a mere noticing of something previously unheeded though otherwise observable without further ado. The seeing of the intelligible appearance that is called the "idea" is a seeing that draws it forth, a seeing that, in the very act of seeing, compels what-is-to-be-seen to stand before the seeing. Therefore we call this seeing, which first brings forth into visibility that which is to be seen, and pro-duces it before itself, "productive seeing" [*Er-sehen*: ποιητικῶς νοεῖν].[102]

Here we have a further clue to the question of the essence or "whence" of being. The existentiel act of wresting something from obscurity into intelligibility is neither a supra-human divine activity as it is in Avicenna, Averroes, and Maimonides, nor an event that happens in some fantasized realm of "Being Itself." Rather, it requires an existentiel act of "productive seeing" made possible by the existential clearing. Without ex-sistence, the being or meaningfulness of things simply does not appear.

A further word on ἰδέα/εἶδος, specifically on its structural correlation with human being. Heidegger lays out some of the particulars of Aristotle's proto-phenomenology in his 1940 seminar on the meaning of φύσις in *Physics* B 1. At first blush it might seem that Heidegger is simply spelling out what Aristotle meant by φύσις as the being of "natural" things. However, what is actually going on in Heidegger's text is a subtle re-description of naturalistic φύσις precisely in phenomenological terms. It soon becomes clear that Heidegger's reading of Aristotle (1) goes beyond φύσις as the being of natural things and reinterprets it as the being of *all* things, and (2) retrieves from Aristotle's φύσις Heidegger's own notion of the *phenomenological* emergence of things into intelligibility and not their objective-natural emergence within the universe.

In the *Physics* Aristotle investigates the particular kind of οὐσία that befits natural things (τὸ φύσει ὄν), entities that have the source of their movement within themselves, as contrasted with artifacts (τὸ τέχνῃ ὄν) that have the source of their movement in something external—namely, the artisan's skill/τέχνη. Natural things have their reality as an intrinsic emergence (*Aufgang*) into their appearances as phenomena. But what kind of appearance? And how does that appearance come about?

102. GA 45: 85.9–20 = 76.11–23; ibid., 169.22 = 146.27. On Heidegger's violence (Gewalt) in interpreting Kant in GA 3: GA 65: 253.10–14 = 199.20–24.

At *Physics* B 1, 193a28–31, Aristotle introduces into his discussion of φύσις the elements of ὕλη and μορφή, which are usually translated as "matter" and "form." A phenomenon is by definition an appearance-to-man—that is, it has an εἶδος, an intelligibility that can be "sighted" by the mind, whether theoretical or practical. To leave ὕλη aside for now, Heidegger understands μορφή as saying the "same" as εἶδος, but with the kinetic nuance of a natural thing's "*self*-placement into appearance" (*die Gestellung in das Aussehen*).[103] This movement into appearance and knowability marks the difference between Aristotelian and Platonic εἶδος. Plato understands the ideal form of a thing as standing off on its own as the "really real," in comparison with which individual things are subordinated to the role of the relatively not-real. Aristotle, however, grasps the individual this-thing-here, the τόδε τι, as something that is real of and by itself insofar as it "places itself" (μορφή), as intelligible, into its own εἶδος. But how does this placement come about?

It is crucial that we understand how Heidegger reads Aristotle's primary definition of φύσις as ἡ μορφὴ καὶ τὸ εἶδος <u>τὸ κατὰ τὸν λόγον</u> (193a 30–31). The key issue here is the meaning of the underlined Greek words. Some translations of this key phrase into English are:

- "the shape or form that is specified <u>in the definition of the thing</u>" (Hardie and Gaye).
- "the form [of the thing], that is to say, the 'kind' of thing it is <u>by definition</u>" (Wicksteed and Cornford).
- "'shape' or 'form' as expressed <u>in a definition</u>" (Hope).
- "the shape or form <u>according to formula</u>" (Apostle).[104]
- "the form, or the look <u>that is disclosed in speech</u>" (Sachs).[105]

Translations into Latin include:

- "forma, <u>secundum quam sumitur</u> ratio definitiva rei (<u>per quam scimus</u> quid est)" (Aquinas).[106]

---

103. GA 9: 281.14–15 and .28–29 = 214.38–39 and 215.10. Compare Gestellung as a soldier's "reporting for duty" upon being "called up" for military service.

104. Respectively (see bibliography): Hardie and Gaye, 269.19–21; Wicksteed and Cornford, 113.23–24; Hope, 25.9–10; Apostle, 26.35. The line numbers here refer not to the Bekker lines but to the lines on the English page.

105. Sachs, *Aristotle's Physics*, 50.33–34.

106. Aquinas, *Commentaria in octo libros Physicorum,* liber II, lectio 2 [re *Physics* II 1 193a9–b21], no. 151, found at http://www.dhspriory.org/thomas/Physics2.htm. I have adapted this definition from Aquinas' sentence: "id quod est potentia caro et os, non habet naturam carnis et ossis antequam accipiat formam, secundum quam sumitur ratio definitiva rei (per quam scilicet scimus quid est caro vel os)." Roughly, "What is flesh and bone in potency does not have the nature of flesh and bone before it receives the form in keeping with which the thing's definitive nature is grasped (through which we of course know what

Roughly: the thing's intelligible form, in keeping with which the thing's definitive structure [or nature: *ratio*] can be grasped (through which we know what the thing is).

- "ipsa forma et species, quae rationi accommodatur" (Bekker).[107] Roughly: the thing's intelligible structure-and-appearance, which is available to reason [= λόγος].[108]

From Heidegger's perspective, Sachs' English and Bekker's Latin translations would be the most faithful to the Greek, with Aquinas a close runner-up. Unlike the other four English renderings, these three preserve the implicit phenomenological correlation between a thing's being (its μορφὴ/εἶδος) on the one hand, and the human act of bringing that being to light (λόγος/λέγειν) on the other. Heidegger himself interprets the passage as follows: φύσις is "μορφή, and this means the εἶδος that is in accordance with the λόγος."[109] There are three points to note here.

First of all, Heidegger argues that μορφή and εἶδος stand in apposition to one another. Therefore, like Wicksteed and Cornford above, he correctly renders the Greek word καί (usually "and") as "*das will sagen*": "μορφή, and, *that is to say*, the εἶδος." The μορφή-moment of the thing's emergence and the εἶδος-moment of the thing's appearance go together as one—emergence-into-appearance—just as do φύσις-and-ἀλήθεια or φύειν-and-φαίνεσθαι.[110]

Secondly, Heidegger follows both the specific Aristotelian view that natural things are always κινούμενα (in movement *as moved*) and the general Greek view that things appear by being gathered into luminous stability and intelligibility. Therefore, Heidegger reads μορφή dynamically as a thing's emergence-into-meaningful-presence (*Anwesung*).

> By translating μορφή as a thing's "self"-placement into the appearance, we mean to express initially two things that are of equal importance to the meaning of the Greek term but that are completely lacking in our word "form." To begin with, placement into the appearance is a mode of the presence [of a thing]: οὐσία. Μορφή is not an *ontic* property present in matter, but a kind of *being*. Moreover, "self"-placement-into-the-appearance is a matter of being-moved, κίνησις, which "moment" is radically lacking in the concept of form.[111]

---

flesh and bone is)." The "quam" of "per quam" can refer to either forma or ratio, both which finally come down to the same thing.

107. Bekker, *Aristotelis opera*, III, 106b, just south of line 30.

108. The "rationi accommodatur" could also be translated as "adapted/suitable to reason."

109. GA 9: 275.4–5 = 210.14–15.

110. See chapter 2, notes 18, 20, and 22.

111. GA 9: 276.14–21 = 211.14–20, my emphasis.

Third, and of greatest importance for his interpretation of Aristotle, Heidegger insists on the *phenomenological correlation* between εἶδος and λόγος. What and how something is (its being) shows up only in and to the human intellect, which is ineluctably discursive—λόγον ἔχον and μετὰ λογοῦ, respectively, "having λόγος" and "according to λόγος."[112] *We* are the sole site of intelligibility: "the locus of intelligible appearances" (τόπος εἰδῶν), the place where "intelligible appearances show up" (εἶδος εἰδῶν).[113] Whatever emerges, emerges into a knowable appearance (ἐις τὸ εἶδος),[114] one that shows up only in acts of taking-as. And when man's discursive powers are operative (ἐνεργείᾳ, "in act"), the potentially intelligible phenomenon becomes actually known. In short, the rule is:

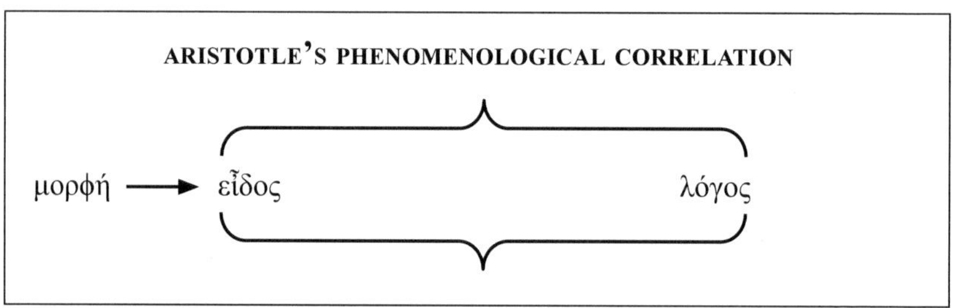

> Μορφή must be understood from εἶδος, and εἶδος must be understood in relation to λόγος.[115]
>
> The clue by which we can understand εἶδος—and so also μορφή—is λόγος.[116]

But what, then, is λόγος? Heidegger cuts through the term's usual meanings—"word" and "language" or, in mathematics, "relation, proportion, analogy, correspondence"[117]—and goes to its etymological roots in λέγειν: to gather, join together, and bring to light. For Heidegger, λέγειν, "to collect," means the same as ἀληθεύειν: to bring into intelligible presence.[118]

112. *Nicomachean Ethics,* respectively VI 1, 1139a4 and VI 4, 1149a7.

113. *De anima*, respectively, III 4, 429a27–28 and III 8, 432a2. GA 51: 91.28–29 = 77.9–10: "Der Mensch ist das wesende Tier (– animal rationale–)," where "das wesende Tier" means "the animal that renders [things] present."

114. *Metaphysics* IX 8, 1050a15.

115. GA 9: 275.5–6 = 210.15–16.

116. GA 9: 275.35–276.1 = 210.40–211.1.

117. SZ 32.12–14 = 55.30–31.

118. See SZ 33.16–18 = 56.37–39.

> "To collect," to gather, means: to bring various things together into a unity, and at the same time to bring this unity *forth* and hand it *over* (παρά). Into what? Into the undisclosed dimension of presence. . . . Λέγειν means to bring together into a unity and to bring forth this unity as gathered, i.e., above all as present; thus it means the same as to open up what was formerly closed off, to let it be manifest in its presence.[119]

Here the language of ἀληθεύειν—to open something up (*offenbar machen*), to let it be manifest in its presence (*in seiner Anwesung sich zeigen lassen*)—bespeaks knowability, which in turn invokes the human questioning and interpreting (the λέγειν) that issues in what something currently means and thus *is* for us. And this occurs across the spectrum of human activities, from the heights of a faith-inspired declaration that "God exists!" to the quite ordinary and barely articulated insight that this tool will do the job.

As earlier with ἀλήθεια *qua* φύσις, so too now with εἶδος and λόγος, Heidegger's investigation of the Greek terms for "being" has offered him directives about how to broach his own question about the possibility and its necessity of "being" within the human world. His re-reading of Aristotle on εἶδος and λόγος confirmed what he had learned from Husserl's early phenomenology: that the uniqueness of human being among other entities is that with us there arrives intelligibility. Indeed, we have access to things only in terms of their meanings—first of all, owing to the existent*ial* λόγος that is our very structure; and then consequently in existent*iel* acts of λέγειν whereby we (correctly or incorrectly) take something *as being* this or that. In turn, Heidegger's analysis of νοῦς ποιητικός in Aristotle's *De anima* showed him that what his earlier study of Thomism had called "the abstraction of intelligible species"[120] was actually a matter of existentielly *wresting* something from unintelligibility into intelligibility in an act of pro-jective understanding (or "taking-as") that is made possible by the existential clearing. Thus Heidegger retrieved the notion of ex-sistence as itself the clearing within which and whereby things can become intelligible—that is, can "have being" in Heidegger's sense of the term.

> The ontic image of the *lumen naturale* in man refers to nothing else but the existential-ontological structure of this entity, the fact that it *is* in such a way

119. GA 9: 279.1–7 = 213.10–15. See GA 33: 5.8–21 = 2.33–3.14.

120. Cf. Aquinas, *Summa theologiae* I, 12, 13, corpus, on the activating intellect as a "lumen naturale intelligibile, cuius virtute intelligibiles conceptiones ab eis [= phantasmatis] abstrahimus." Roughly: the natural light of the intellect whereby we abstract intelligible concepts from the sensible phantasms. See ἀφαίρεσις: Aristotle, *Metaphysics* XI 3, 1061a29.

> as to be its openness . . . the fact that it itself *is* the clearing. Only for such an entity—one that is existentially cleared in this way—do things that are objectively present become [existentielly] *accessible* in the light [of intelligibility] or hidden in the darkness [of unintelligibility].[121]

Things do not carry around signs stamped with their proper essence that we merely need to read off in order to understand them. Nor are the true meanings of things hidden inside them, waiting to be pulled out by the magic of epistemological abs-traction. Rather, as λόγον ἔχοντες[122] we have not only the ability but also the obligation to decide for ourselves what the current significance of things—their current being—is for us and others[123] and to do so without appealing to a divinely bestowed "ontological truth" or a Platonic ἀνάμνησις or an Augustinian *illuminatio* that would show us what things "really are." To have things meaningfully present requires a "productive seeing"—or better, a productive *doing*, a finite and fallible "taking-as" on the part of ex-sistence. This entails the ever-present possibility of taking something incorrectly, as well as the need to always *re*-take things over and over again as new evidence and new hermeneutical possibilities emerge. And with that goes the ineluctable fact that we will never, ever, get the "being" of something as the unchanging truth of that thing, much less ever see the "truth" of "being itself."

With regard to these "epistemological" matters, as well as in the decisions of everyday life, personal freedom in Heidegger is every bit as radical as freedom in Sartre, and every bit as groundless and absurd. Sartre and Heidegger both agree that we are condemned to be radically and groundlessly free precisely because our "essence," which is our ex-sistence, is to be thrown ahead *as* possibility *into* possibilities, mortally, finitely, and without hope of rescue from this fate. Heidegger was a bad reader of Sartre when he claimed in 1946 that the difference between them was that Sartre had declared, "We are precisely in a situation where there are only human beings," whereas for Heidegger, "We are precisely in a situation where principally there is Being."[124] The alleged difference collapses once one realizes that the *es* in *es gibt Sein* or the *il* in *il y a l'Être* (i.e., that which makes possible or "gives" the clearing) is the appropriation of ex-sistence to its proper situation as the groundless clearing. The givenness of the clearing in no way changes the fact that our "situation"

121. SZ 133.1–7 = 171.17–24, my emphasis; also ibid., 170.24–25 = 214.25–26. Cf. Heidegger's retractatio at GA 14: 82.7–12 = 66.25–29. Re φῶς: *De anima* III, 5, 430a15, 16. Aquinas on intellectus agens: *Summa theologiae* I, 79, 4. On all this, see appendix 2.

122. *Nicomachean Ethics* VI 1, 1139a4.

123. A fact that terrifies members of the Swooning *Seinlassen* School.

124. GA 9: 334.12–16 = 254.29–34. I follow Heidegger's hyperbolic capitalization of "l'Être" in this text and at GA 9: 334.18 = 254.36: "il y a l'Être."

(Sartre: *plan*) is entirely and exclusively human. "Being" is not some "higher dimension" added on to and surpassing ex-sistence. It is simply what we do, finitely and mortally, in our groundless freedom.

3. οὐσία/παρουσία

We continue to sort out the "whence" of being as Heidegger retrieved clues about that from the early Greek names for "being." What about Plato's and Aristotle's most general name for being: οὐσία as stable presence? Heidegger espies in that term a hint of what he will eventually call by the (potentially misleading) term "time."

> And finally the basic term οὐσία (which is decisive for the future terms "substance" and *essentia*) harbors within itself the relation to "time": it has the character of presence in itself (more pointedly: οὐσία—παρουσία as "one's holdings," something at one's disposal, one's possessions, something stable in itself and constant).[125]

> "Presence" for the Greeks is παρουσία [παρά, "unto" + οὐσία], shortened to οὐσία; and "presence" for the Greeks means being. To say that something *is* means that it is present, or better, that it is (as we must say in German) present-to [*west an*] in the present moment [*Gegenwart*].[126]

And in speaking of being as a thing's stability he says:

> The stable constancy [of a thing] is [its] pure presence—*being-present in the full sense*. . . . This entails a gesture toward the present [*Gegenwart*] and thus toward "time."[127]

Heidegger argues that the so-called "temporal" character of οὐσία can be gathered from Plato's designation of the "really real" (ὄντως ὄν) as ἀεὶ ὄν and ἀΐδος οὐσία (usually "eternal being"),[128] although Heidegger argues that "the more sharply οὐσία is grasped and associated with the [Aristotelian] 'categories,' the more the relation to time gets shrouded."[129] In fact, Heidegger's own

125. GA 73, 1: 86.12–16: "birgt . . . ουσία . . . den Zeitbezug."

126. GA 34: 51.20–24 = 38.29–32. <u>An</u>wesen translates the Latin <u>prae</u>sentia.

127. GA 73, 1: 85.25–27 and .30: "In-sich-ständige Beständigkeit ist reine Anwesenheit—*Anwesung im vollen Sinne*. . . . Hierin liegt der Wink auf Gegenwart und damit auf die Zeit."

128. Respectively, *Symposium* 211a1, *Timaeus* 27d6–a1 and 37e5. See chapter 2, note 41.

129. GA 73, 1: 86.16–18: "Aber je schärfer . . . um so mehr verhüllt sich der Zeitbezug."

notion of "time" differs radically from what he found in the Greeks. The classical philosophy of time (χρόνος) worked out in Aristotle's *Physics*, for example, was of no use to Heidegger in his search for the source of being, because Book IV of that treatise focuses on time as a continuous series of "nows" and considers time as a *thing* that *is*. Thus the *Physics* is caught up in the classical question about the being of *things* rather than about being taken for itself.[130]

> The customary ideas of time—as well as those that work out time as "experienced" time—will not get to what is being sought after in the [basic] question, since each of these ideas apprehends time as an entity and as something that is in a state of becoming.[131]
>
> [I]t became clear that the traditional concept of time was in no way adequate even for correctly *posing* the question concerning the time-character of presence, to say nothing of *answering* it. Time became questionable in the same way as being did.[132]

Greek notions of time were utterly inadequate—if, that is, one relied only on fourth-century philosophy. But there was also fifth-century tragic poetry, and Heidegger saw in Sophocles' *Ajax* (646–647) something close to the radical notion that he was searching for: "time" as that which lets what was heretofore hidden (ἄδηλα) emerge (φύειν as ἀληθεύειν).[133]

> ἅπανθ᾽ ὁ μακρὸς κἀναρίθμητος χρόνος
> φύει τ᾽ ἄδηλα καὶ φανέντα κρύπτεται
>
> Great and measureless time
> discloses all that is hidden and hides all that is disclosed.[134]

---

130. See GA 24: 327–361 = 231–256.

131. GA 73, 1: 90.10–13. "Experienced" time: literally, the time of "experience," "die Zeit des 'Erlebens.'"

132. GA 11: 147.16–20 = xii.23–27, my emphasis. Time-character: "Zeitcharacter."

133. In this regard, see Bernini's unfinished group "La Verità svelata dal Tempo" ("Truth unveiled by Time"), Galleria Borghese, Rome, http://www.galleriaborghese.it/borghese/it/verita.htm. (While "truth" is certainly unveiled in Bernini's sculpture, the planned companion statue of "time" was never begun.)

134. GA 73, 1: 134.8. In 1946 Heidegger cited this text in a letter to Prof. Eduard Baumgarten in an effort to apologize (?) for a secret, blackballing letter that Heidegger had written in 1933, accusing Baumgarten of "associating with the Jew Frankel," not being a National Socialist, and so on (see GA 16: 774–775 and 417–418). In his 1946 letter to Baumgarten Heidegger suggested letting bygones be bygones, and he translated line 647 as follows (my English rendering of his German): "[Time] leaves tasks unopenable [! ἄδηλα] and takes appearances back into itself." See Sheehan, "Heidegger and the Nazis," note 14.

Such a non-"temporal" meaning of "time" in Heidegger's work is the chief reason why his early use of "temporal" language can easily mislead the reader. I am referring to such words as:

Zeit: the "time" of the title *Sein und Zeit*;
Temporalität: the "time-character" of the clearing. (It is equivalent to *Zeit* in the title *Sein und Zeit*.)
Zeitlichkeit: the so-called "temporality" of ex-sistence.

In Heidegger's texts these three terms have nothing specifically or directly to do with time in our usual sense of the word or with what Aristotle called χρόνος.[135] Rather, Heidegger used those terms as only provisional names either for (1) ἀλήθεια-1 as the clearing (= *Zeit* and *Temporalität*) or for (2) the opening-up or holding-open of the clearing (= *Zeitlichkeit*). In other words, these so-called "temporal" terms actually refer to the *openness* that makes intelligibility possible. For that reason I will always put "time," "temporality," and "temporal" within scare quotes.

In that same vein, the terms *Zeitigung* and *Sich-zeitigung* should never be translated by such barbaric neologisms as "temporalization" (Macquarrie-Robinson) or "temporalizing" (Stambaugh) but rather always in terms of "opening-up." If one were to follow the usual way of translating Heidegger, the phrase "*Zeitigung als Sich-zeitigen*" would come out as "temporalization as self-temporalizing," which says absolutely nothing, not even in Heideggerspeak. According to Heidegger's own gloss on this phrase, it means "unfolding, going forth, appearing,"[136] and thus it might be interpreted (without the faux reflexive of "*self*-unfolding") as "an opening-up as an intrinsic unfolding." In any case, in his later writings Heidegger was finally clear: these so-called "time" words were only preliminary attempts to name the thrown-open or dis-closed clearing, ἀλήθεια-1.

"Time" is a preliminary name for the openness of the clearing.[137]

---

135. See *Schellings Abhandlung*, 228.28–229.6 = 188.24–40 for notions of time that Heidegger excludes (numbers 1–3), and for the one he accepts (number 4).

136. *Zollikoner Seminare,* 203.7–8 = 158.10–11: "Zeitigung als Sich-zeitigen ist Sich-entfalten, aufgehen und so erscheinen."

137. GA 9: 376.11 = 285.26–27: "die 'Zeit' als der Vorname für die Wahrheit des Seins." GA 49: 57.2–3: "Der Name 'Zeit' is hier der *Vorname* für die Wahrheit des Seins." GA 65: 331.23–24 = 263.1–3: "ἀλήθεια—Offenheit und Lichtung des Sichverbergenden . . . verschiedene Namen für dasselbe." GA 14: 36.11–12 = 28.20–21. GA 65: 74.10–11 = 59.20–23: "'Zeit' ist . . . Wahrheit der Wesung des Seins." GA 66: 145.25 = 124.6: "Lichtung (Zeit)." GA 73, 1: 758.2: "'Zeit' hier als Zeit-Raum im Sinne der Gegend."

> "Time" as a preliminary name for the thrown-open domain.[138]
>
> The unfolding of *Temporalität* is a preliminary name for the openness of the clearing.[139]
>
> "Time" is . . . the clearing of being itself.[140]
>
> "Temporality" [*Zeitlichkeit*] and its [correlative, the] *time-character* [of the clearing,] as a way of announcing the open-ness of the open.[141]
>
> "Temporality" constitutes the clearedness of the open [the *Da*] in an thrown-open, horizon-forming way.[142]

We note two things: (1) *Zeitlichkeit*—"temporality" as ex-sistence's ("ex-static") maintaining of the openness of the open—is always in correlation with *Zeit* and *Temporalität* (see chapter 7). And (2) these latter two terms—"time" and the "time-character of the clearing"—are co-equal names for what *Being and Time* called the "horizon" for all forms of the being of things, and what the later Heidegger re-articulated as the clearing.[143] Thus in Heidegger's early work "time" refers to the "horizonal" space within which being as the meaningful presence of things occurs,[144] and "temporality" refers to ex-sistence's thrown-openness as sustaining that open space.[145]

---

138. Heidegger, *Schellings Abhandlung*, 229.4 = 188.38.

139. GA 9: 159 note a = 123 note a: "Zeitigung der Temporalität als Vorname der Wahrheit des Seyns." Also: GA 69: 95.3–5: "Zeitlichkeit zeitigt den Lichtungsbereich für das Sein (die dort [in *Sein und Zeit*] sogennante 'Temporalität'). Zeitlichkeit ist der Vorname für die Wahrheit des Seyns." GA 68: 36.11–12: "Das Offene des Da (Da-heit)."

140. Heidegger, *Schellings Abhandlung*, 229.4 and .6 = 188.38–40. Here Heidegger himself puts "Zeit" in scare quotes.

141. GA 88: 46.7–8: "(Zeitlichkeit und ihre *Temporalität* als Anzeige der Da-heit des Da.)"

142. SZ 408.7–8 = 460.20–21: "Weil die Zeitlichkeit die Gelichtetheit des Da ekstatisch-horizontal konstituiert . . ." italicized in the original; ibid., 411.25–26 = 464.20–21: "als ekstatisch-zeitliches je schon erschlossen"; ibid., 410.34–35 = 463.29–30: "Zeitlichkeit . . . Erschlossenheit des Da" (italicized).

143. After 1931 the term "Temporalität" no longer appears in Heidegger's lecture courses.

144. GA 14: 40.10–11 = 32.8–9: "jenes Eigene der 'Zeit' . . . von woher sich 'Sein' als Anwesen er-gibt." GA 65: 451.4–5 = 355.15–16: "'Sein und Zeit' ist aber doch darauf angelegt, die 'Zeit' als den Entwurfsbereich für das Seyn zu erweisen." See the equation of "Zeit" and "Lichtung" in the chiasmic phrase at GA 14: 90.1–2 = 73.1–2.

145. Re "sustains": *Zollikoner Seminare*, 273.31–274.1 = 218.14–15: "'existieren' mit 'aus-stehen eines Offenheitsbereiches' zu übersetzen." Also GA 65: 352.28–29 = 278.37–38: "Ausstehen der Lichtung"; and GA 66: 217.9–10 = 191.10: Ausstehen der Lichtung. In another formulation: GA 66: 308.13 = 274.21 (et passim in GA 65): "[die] Gründung der Lichtung im Da-sein." "Ausstehen" should never be translated as "to withstand" as at GA 9: 374.7 = 284.4, but always as "to sustain."

> In *Being and Time* I have attempted to develop a new concept of "time" and "temporality" in the sense of thrown-openness.[146]

> Meaningful presence (being) belongs in the intrinsically concealed clearing. The intrinsically concealed clearing ("time") brings forth meaningful presence (being).[147]

Thus Heidegger's phenomenological interpretation of "time" as the ever-hidden openedness-for-the-sake-of-intelligibility explains an otherwise enigmatic text from 1964. In a lecture he presented in France, titled "The End of Philosophy and the Task of Thinking," Heidegger suggested that a more accurate title for the whole of his major work (and not just of SZ I.3) should be not *Sein und Zeit* but rather *Zeit und Sein*, "'time' and being." But he then paraphrased *Zeit und Sein* as "*Lichtung und Anwesenheit*"—that is, "clearing and meaningful presence."[148]

Moreover, the question of "time" as the thrown-open-but-hidden clearing plays a fundamental role in what Heidegger called his "history of being." He unfortunately misspoke when he taxed Western metaphysics with *Seinsvergessenheit*—"the forgottenness of being"—when in fact metaphysics from Plato to Nietzsche spoke of virtually nothing else *but* "being." Indeed, absent a familiarity with being, no one could be human. ("Being is the atmosphere we breathe, without which we would descend to [the level of] the mere beast.")[149] What Heidegger meant to say, rather, was that metaphysics overlooks or forgets the so-called "temporality-and-time" correlation—that is, the clearing sustained by appropriated ex-sistence. It was in terms of this overlooking and forgetting that Heidegger charted the devolution of Western culture that begins with Parmenides' "original and in fact necessary failure to experience 'time' as the openedness of the clearing" and eventually became "necessarily and unconsciously a suppression of this region and of every impetus to question in this direction."[150] This oblivion and suppression becomes thicker, Heidegger claims, with the "in-break of Christianity into Western thinking" with its notion of God as "eternal truth."[151] And further along in the history of philosophy:

146. GA 16: 708.10–11 = 85.39–44: "[Ich habe] in 'Sein und Zeit' einen neuen Begriff der Zeit und Zeitlichkeit im Sinne der ekstatischen Offenheit zu entwickeln versucht." GA 49: 54.28–29: die ekstatische Offenheit der "Zeit."

147. GA 11: 151.26–28 = xx.31–33: Heidegger's 1962 letter to William J. Richardson.

148. GA 14: 90.1–2 = 73.1–2: "statt 'Sein und Zeit' Lichtung und Anwesenheit."

149. GA 42: 169.22–25 = 98.13–14. "Being" here translates Seyn.

150. GA 73, 1: 86.26–29.

151. GA 73, 1: 86.30–32.

> The merely ostensible de-Christianizing of this relation in modern times—when the ground of being is taken as reason, consciousness, absolute spirit, life, and will to power—only further *intensifies* the suppression. . . . Thus finally the forgottenness of [the clearing for] being grows, the most obvious sign of which is the belief that "being" is the most general, most empty, and most self-explanatory "concept."[152]

At the end of this centuries-long devolution Heidegger found his work cut out for him: to articulate for the first time in Western philosophy the ever-operative yet hidden clearing as the reason why there is any meaning at all.

This is as far as Heidegger goes with οὐσία and the question of "time" in his 1937 text "The Question about Being." But we have to ask: Why did Heidegger settle on "time" at all?—even when it is properly understood as the throw-openness of the clearing?

For Heidegger the human need to understand things discursively—that is, as mediated to us *qua* meaningful—is an epistemological deficiency and a sign of ontological imperfection, at least by comparison with the highest model of perfection, the self-coincident and thus self-intuiting God of *Metaphysics* XII 7–9.[153] God cannot do ontology. Here the word "ontology" does not refer to the science that considers things insofar as they are real ("have being"). Rather, it refers to the necessity of raising questions and answering them—that is, knowing things not directly through an intellectual intuition but mediately, through their meanings. Insofar as we are thoroughly determined by (and in fact are) λόγος, we know something only by synthesizing it with one or more of its possible meanings, while at the same time keeping those meanings distinct from the thing in question. For example, "Aristotle is a philosopher": here we have a σύν-θεσις or putting-together of the man Aristotle and the predicate "philosopher." However, as good as he was (and for Aquinas he was even *the* philosopher), Aristotle does not exhaust the class of "all philosophers." Here we have διαίρεσις or dis-tinction (διά + αἵρεσις), a keeping-separate of Aristotle and the class of "all philosophers," and by this act of synthesizing-and-distinguishing we come to know Aristotle *as* a philosopher—that is, as *one* of the class "philosophers." God does not do such synthesizing and distinguishing,

152. GA 73, 1: 86.32–87.4.

153. Re highest model: GA 3: 21.27 = 15.22: "Erkennen ist primär Anschauung." The principle applies beyond Kant. See SZ 33.35–38 = 57.20–22 and GA 83: 80.8; also Aquinas, *Scriptum super sententiis* I, distinction 3, quaestio 4, articulum 5, corpus: "Intelligere . . . dicit nihil aliud quam simplicem intuitum intellectus in id quod est praesens intelligibile."

because God cannot. As perfectly self-coincident, with no unrealized potential (μὴ ὕλην ἔχει),[154] Aristotle's God is the apex of immediacy, perfectly closed in upon itself in a divine narcissism of pure self-presence.

This reference to a theological limit-situation helps clarify why "time"—thrown-openness—is associated with the understanding of being. In order to know anything at all we must synthesize and distinguish the thing and its possible meanings; and in order to do that, we must (metaphorically speaking) "traverse an open space" (*eine offene Weite zu durchgehen*) within which the synthesizing-and-distinguishing can take place.[155] This "open space" is what Heidegger calls the clearing that lets us relate things and meanings.[156] As thrown-open, human beings are a priori thrown into the labor of mediation, condemned to (or better, liberated for) making sense of things both practically and theoretically. This fatedness to mediation is emblematic of finitude, proof positive that we are not completely self-present and thus are bereft of a godlike intuition of the "unchanging reality" of things. Meaningful presence is never pure presence and actuality, but always open-ended, suffused with further possibilities. Our knowing is not perfect light but chiaroscuro, not the divine's eternal rest but an ever ongoing movement of disclosure coupled with an inevitable failure-to-disclose.

At the very beginning of his 1915 inaugural habilitation lecture, "The Concept of Time in the Science of History." Heidegger placed an epigram taken from Meister Eckhart that defines time in terms of possibility: "Time is what *changes* and becomes *multiple*. Eternity remains simple."[157] Before Eckhart, St. Augustine had likewise drawn a contrast between the concentrated unity of the eternal God and the dispersion and distraction of human beings (*inter te unum et nos multos in multis per multa*),[158] which is further evidenced in the simplicity of eternity versus the distention of time: "Nothing passes away in eternity; all is present. Time, on the other hand, is never completely present, but the past is always driven on by the future."[159] Over against God's ever-actualized self-coincidence there is the dispersion and stretching out of the human spirit, the *distentio animi*, a

154. *Metaphysics* XII 9, 1075a4.

155. GA 15: 380.6 = 68.43. See GA 14: 81.35 and 84.3–4 = 66.19 and 68.9; and GA 7: 19.12 – 18.32.

156. Also "world." Cf. "Die Lichtung des Seins, und nur sie, ist Welt": GA 9: 326.15–16 = 248.37–38. GA 38: 168.13–14 = 140.7–8: "Das Sein im Ganzen . . . ist die *Welt*." GA 79: 51.34–52.1 = 49.18: "Die Welt ist . . . das Sein selber."

157. GA 1: 415.1–3 = 61.2–4. Heidegger's italics.

158. Augustine, *Confessiones* XI 29, 39, *Patrologia Latina*, 32, 825.8–9.

159. *Confessiones* XI 11, 13, *Patrologia Latina*, 32, 814.48–51: "non autem praeterire quidquam in aeterno, sed totum esse praesens; nullum vero tempus totum esse praesens; et videat [quisquis] omne praeteritum propelli ex futuro."

phrase that Augustine borrowed from Plotinus' διάστασις ζωῆς, the "spreading out of life."[160] This is a perspective that Heidegger took over in *Being and Time* under the rubric of "*die 'zeitliche' Erstreckung des Daseins*." the so-called "temporal" stretch of ex-sistence.[161] For Heidegger, this "stretchedness" was not a matter of multiple now-moments strung out in a line (hence his scare quotes around the word "*zeitliche*"), but rather a two-pulse movement of

1. living "ahead" as possibility among possibilities and
2. "returning" from that aheadness to synthesize one of those possibilities with whatever one encounters in the present.

The aheadness-moment (*sich schon vorweg-sein*) "carries us away and gives us distance [διάστασις, *distentio*]"[162]—it opens up the clearing. Thus, in keeping with Augustine, Heidegger defines "time" as "the fact that I am dis-closed."[163] But along with this "distance," human being also "returns to" (i.e., remains with) itself and the things it encounters as it renders them meaningfully present in terms of one or another possibility (*Sein bei* as *Gegenwärtigung*). Our structural κίνησις—a combination of absence and presence, of living ahead and returning—is what allows us to make sense of ourselves and of whatever we meet. That is, the interpretive "as" functions existenti*elly* in human thought and practice only because it functions existenti*ally* as the very structure of human ex-sistence. Here Heidegger's argument reflects the medieval Scholastic axiom *operari sequitur esse*: activities are consonant with and derive from natures; or in the reverse: natures determine activities.[164] In the present case,

160. Respectively: *Confessiones* XI 26, 33, *Patrologia Latina*, 32, 822.47–49: "mihi visum est, nihil esse aliud tempus quam distentionem: sed cuius rei, nescio; et mirum, si non ipsius animi"; and *Enneads* III 7: 11.42. "The spreading out of life" is A. H. Armstrong's translation in his Plotinus, *Enneads*, III, p. 341.11–12. Heidegger translates distentio as "Ausgestrecktheit" at GA 83: 69.2.

161. SZ 371.32 = 423.15. GA 26: 173.34 = 138.17: "Dasein als Erstreckung." See GA 66: 315.18 = 280.31: "er-streckt und aus-streckt." Heidegger first encountered the alleged etymology of Zeit in terms of "[ich] strecke mich" in Braig, *Die Grundzüge der Philosophie*, 88.32. Braig claims Zeit is traceable to τανύω, to stretch (see *Iliad*, XVII, 393: τάνυται, [a hide] is stretched). However, "Zeit" is more likely related to the Indo-European root dā-, "divide, division," and the Greek δαίω, to divide.

162. GA 26: 285.18–19 = 221.17–18: uns entrückt und die Ferne gibt; Wesen der Ferne. SZ 192.4 = 236.19: Sich-vorweg-sein."

163. "The fact that I am dis-closed": "das 'Offenbarmachen' *meiner selbst*": GA 83: 72.9–10. See SZ 147.2–3 = 187.13–14: "[die] Gelichtetheit, als welche wir die Erschlossenheit des Da charakterisierten."

164. For example, Thomas Aquinas, *Summa theologiae*, I, 75, 3, corpus, ad finem: "similiter unumquodque habet esse et operationem." Or, to reverse the direction, "qualis modus essendi talis modus operandi": a thing's way of being determines its way of acting. See GA 4: 65.26–28 = 87.27–29: "Jegliches . . . je nur das leistet, was es ist."

our being stretched between the actual thing and its possible meanings *follows from* our kinetic bivalence, the fact that we have our actuality as our stretched-ahead-ness as possibility.

But how exactly do we sustain the openedness of the clearing that we ourselves are? The movedness of human life is analogous to the bivalent movedness of any living thing: a matter of being relatively self-absent—stretched beyond itself (*Weg-von-sich*)—while remaining relatively self-present (*bei-sich-selbst einbehalten*).[165] In the case of man, Heidegger calls this movedness a *fortnehmende Zukehr*, a being carried away into possibilities (*fortnehmende*) that is always "returning to" itself (*Zukehr*), in the sense of always remaining with itself.[166]

> This being-ahead-of-oneself as a returning [*Sich-vorweg-sein als Zurückkommen*] is, if I may put it this way, a peculiar kind of movement that ex-sistence *qua* "temporal" constantly makes.[167]

Being carried away into possibility and returning to oneself as actuality opens the discursive space that Heidegger calls the world, the clearing, or the open. "To ex-sist." Heidegger says, "might be more adequately translated as 'sustaining a realm of openness.'"[168] Within that existential space we carry out our existentiel mediations. The "re-turn" or turning back to our here-and-now selves from out of the possibility that we are is also a "re-turn" to the things we currently encounter as we render them meaningfully present in terms of this or that specific possibility. This dynamic structure of ahead-and-return is what Heidegger is getting at with his notion of "temporality" as thrown-openness. We are an ec-centric self, an incompletely self-present aheadness-in-possibility that "returns" to make sense of ourselves and of things.

In 1930 Heidegger interpreted that structural movement of thrown-ahead-and-returning in terms of existential thrown-openness ("thrown projectedness": *geworfener Entwurf*) that makes possible the existentiel synthesizing of things with possible meanings. First, the existential structure:

---

165. GA 29/30: respectively 343.4 = 235.24–25 and 342.19 = 235.9. See chapter 5.

166. GA 29/30: 527.35 = 363.15–16. See Thomas Aquinas, *Summa theologiae* I, 14, 2 ad 1: "Redire ad essentiam suam nihil aliud est quam rem subsistere in se ipsum." Aquinas here draws on Proclus, *The Elements of Theology*, proposition 82 (p. 76.29–30): Πᾶν τὸ ἑαυτοῦ γνωστικὸν πρὸς ἑαυτὸ παντῃ ἐπιστρεπτικόν ἐστιν. "All that is capable of self-knowledge is capable of completely returning to itself."

167. GA 21: 147.23–26 = 124.19–20. I here correct my earlier reading (ibid.) of "Zeit" in place of "Dasein."

168. *Zollikoner Seminare*, 274.1 = 218.15: "aus-stehen eines Offenheitsbereich." See the translators' note on the English page. GA 45: 169.24 = 146.28. GA 49: 41.25–28: "Ent-wurf besagt: "Er-öffnung und Offenhalten des Offenen, Lichten der Lichtung, in der das, was wir Sein (nicht das Seiende) nennen und somit unter diesem Namen auch kennen, eben als *Sein offenkundig* ist."

> [Existent*ial*] projection is a simple, unified "occurrence" that can be formally characterized as σύνθεσις and διαίρεσις, both at the same time. Projection is διαίρεσις—i.e., as "taking away," it takes us away as projection. In a certain sense it stretches us apart from ourselves, endows us with a stretching [*Erstreckung*]. It takes us away into the possible, not so as to lose ourselves there but rather so as to let the possible, *as the rendering-possible of the actual*, speak back precisely upon ourselves as projection, as binding—uniting and binding: σύνθεσις.[169]

From this existent*ial* structure there follow existent*iel* acts of making sense of things, whether by way of the apophantic "as" of declarative sentences or the hermeneutical "as" of practical activity. Our ever-operative existential identity as stretched-ahead (being present to ourselves *as* living ahead in possibilities) is what makes possible the discursive "as" whereby we understand what and how things currently are. Thus the thrown-openness that is our very being

> is also that "occurrence" in which the thing we problematize as the as-structure has its origin. The "as" is the expression for what breaks open in the in-break [of us among things]. . . . Only because we have broken into the dimension of this distinction between the actual and the possible—between things and being in the broadest sense—do we have the possibility of grasping and understanding something as something.[170]

Ex-sistence as appropriated to sustaining the clearing is the basic occurrence of openedness: *das Grundgeschehnis der Wahrheit.*[171] We are structurally dis-closed (*erschlossen*) and thus sustain the space within which the "as" can function and the discursive understanding of things can take place.[172] As such, we are pan-hermeneutical. Our lived environment is not just a natural encircling ring of instinctual drives that befits an animal, but an open-ended as-structured world of possible meanings that we can talk about, argue over, and vote on. Whatever we meet, we meet under the rubric of "is manifest

---

169. The emphasis in the ET is my own. I cite Heidegger's words spoken in the classroom (Thursday, 27 February 1930) from the typescript of the Simon Moser Nachschrift, p. 703.12–13, corresponding roughly to the much abbreviated passage at GA 29/30: 530.23–28 = 365.14–19. The Nachschrift is available at the Simon Silverman Phenomenology Center (see bibliography).

170. This text is from the Nachschrift (see previous note), 703.28–704.6, corresponding roughly to GA 29/30: 530.30–531.7 = 365.21–30. See above, this chapter, note 94.

171. GA 36/37: 178.3–5 = 138.38–40: "Grundakt . . . Grundgeschehnis der Wahrheit"; ibid., 178.20–22 = 138.9–10: "Grundgeschehen im Wesen des Menschen."

172. At GA 9: 377.22 = 286.29 and 377.28–378.1 = 287.2 "geworfene Entwurf" is defined as "entwerfende Offenhalten der Wahrheit des Seins."

as"—that is, "is accessible as" and therefore "is meaningful as." Our existential thrown-openness entails that we can and must make sense of whatever we meet. We *are* ur-ἑρμηνεία.[173]

Heidegger's 1937 review of his path of thinking shows how he probed various Greek terms for "being" with an eye to retrieving from them the core issue that Greek philosophy had left unthematized. His interpretations of Aristotle deliver a consistently insightful, abundantly rich, and highly plausible reading of at least some of his corpus. And dominating that retrieval was Heidegger's *phenomenological* approach.[174] If one grants that Aristotle's proto-phenomenology already had an inkling of "the openedness of being and its relation to man," Heidegger wanted to find out "wherein that is grounded."[175] In his effort to retrieve the "unsaid" from Greek philosophy, one element constantly came to the fore: "The basic question of being and 'time' forces us into the question about human being."[176] Or, again, "The basic words νοῦς, λόγος, ἰδέα, ἰδεῖν [to which we could add: φύσις, ἀλήθεια, and οὐσία] show that the essence of man is the decisive place for determining the essence of being in general."[177] Thus Heidegger begins his own work by turning to the human being as the one entity that understands being—that can engage with the meaning of things. "With us—i.e., with human beings—being comes into play." Indeed, we stand "in the play of being," even if "we do not know who we ourselves are."[178] "Being itself has an exceptional relation to humans," he continues, "and consequently we must try to understand human being, originally and in advance, out of its relation to being and out of the essence [i.e., the whence] of being itself."[179] In short, the general take-away from his reading of Aristotle is this: "If correctly

173. GA 21: 150.26–27 = 126.31–33: "das Verstehen, das dabei verstanden werden muß als eine Grundart des Seins unseres Daseins." Ibid., 146.29–31 = 123.32–33: "ich bin—qua Dasein . . . verstehender Umgang."

174. At GA 19: 62.23–25 = 43.37–40 Heidegger defended himself against the charge of reading contemporary phenomenological insights back into antiquity.

175. GA 16: 423.14–15 = 4.12–4: "die Offenbarkeit des Seins and seines Verhältnisses zum Menschen" and "worin [sie] gründet und besteht." See ibid., 704.1–5 = 82.30–33.

176. GA 31: 121.8–9 = 84.22–23.

177. Heidegger, *Schellings Abhandlung* 116.11–14 = 96.26–28. The first seven words of the phrase above are omitted at GA 42: 166. 26–27.

178. GA 73,1: 90.28, .31 and 91.2.

179. GA 73,1: 91.13–16. See GA 16: 423.14–15: Heidegger's central topic is the appropriated clearing "worin gründet und besteht die Offenbarkeit des Seins und seines Verhältnisses zum Menschen."

posed, the question about being as such presses, by its very content, into the question about man."[180]

From the very early 1920s, when Husserl "put phenomenological eyes in my head,"[181] Heidegger saw in Greek thought the correlation of man and the intelligible presence of things. This presented him with two tasks. The first one, which he executed brilliantly in his early lecture courses, was to retrieve and spell out Aristotle's proto-phenomenology with an emphasis on the correlation of λόγος with οὐσία as φύσις, ἀλήθεια, μορφή, εἶδος, ἐνέργεια, ἐχτελέχεια, πέρας, and so on. The second task, which took up the rest of his career and was his greatest contribution, was to raise and answer what he called the fundamental question (*die Grundfrage*): Why οὐσία *at all*? What accounts for it, and why is it necessary in human experience? If, within a phenomenological perspective, "being" is the *significance* of things for us, then why do we need significance at all?

Heidegger did all of his work on the question of being *as phenomenology*. This is a fundamental, show-stopping fact that naïve realist interpretations of his philosophy entirely miss. He argued that this phenomenological approach, far from being a *res nova* in the history of ontology, in fact ran through all of Western philosophy, from the pre-Socratics down to Nietzsche—even though it was only implicit and therefore, in Heidegger's view, was just begging to be thematized. In his 1927 contribution to Husserl's *Encyclopedia Britannica* article on phenomenology Heidegger wrote:

> Something striking comes to light even in the very first steps of the science of the being of things. Philosophy seeks to clarify being by way of a reflection on one's *thinking* about things (Parmenides). Plato's disclosedness of the ideas takes its bearings from the *soul's soliloquy* (λόγος) with itself.[182] The Aristotelian categories originate with regard to *reason's* assertoric knowledge. Descartes explicitly founds First Philosophy on the *res cogitans*. Kant's transcendental problematic operates in the field of *consciousness*.[183]

180. GA 31: 123.11–12 = (omitted at 85.36): "Die recht gefragte Seinsfrage als solche drängt ihrem Fragegehalt nach in die Frage nach dem Menschen." See ibid., 121.8–9 = 84.22–25.

181. GA 63: 5.22–23 = 4.19–20: "die Augen hat mir *Husserl* eingesetzt." Also GA 14: 147.31–32 = 201.14–15: "mit dem inzwischen [in the 1920s] eingeübten phänomenologischen Blick."

182. The reference is to *Sophist* 263e3–4, where Plato defines διάνοια (thought) as ὁ μὲν ἐντὸς ψυχῆς πρὸς αὑτὴν διάλογος ἄνευ φωνῆς γιγνόμενος—that is, "the interior dialogue of the soul with itself, which happens without sound." Heidegger comments on this passage at GA 19: 607.32–608.3 = 420.31–34.

183. Heidegger in *Husserliana* IX, 256.13–22 = 108.5–11.

Heidegger puts a question to this implicit "turn to the subject" in Western thought. He asks: Is this turning around (cf. περιαγωγή)[184] of the philosophical gaze—from things as objectively-present-out-there to things in relation to the human intellect—merely an accident within the history of Western philosophy? Or does this implicit λόγος-οὐσία correlation show that

> in the final analysis such a turn is *demanded* by the very thing that has constantly been sought for as the problematic of philosophy, under the specific name of "being"?[185]

In other words, from now on must philosophy, and in particular ontology, be done strictly and exclusively as phenomenology?

---

184. See Plato, *Republic* VII 515c7: περιάγειν τὸν αὐχένα, "to turn one's head [literally: one's neck] around."

185. *Husserliana* IX, 256.24–25 = 108.13–15 (my emphasis), echoing *Metaphysics* VII 1, 1028b2–4, a text that Heidegger cites at GA 3, 246.28–29 = 173.7–8. See chapter 2, note 9.

PART TWO

The Early Heidegger

4

Phenomenology and the Formulation of the Question

The most astonishing thing about everyday life is not that things exist out there in the world, standing over against us as independent objects, but that they impinge on us, touch us, intrude on our lives, concern us, in short, are *significant* to us.[1] In the normal course of our daily lives, things are not indifferently "out there in the universe," located within some neutral coordinates of space and time. Rather, they are *meaningfully present* to us. They do not just exist; they make sense, and the sense they make is their "being."

Things are present and available.[2] I take note of them, name them, admire them, perhaps possess them. I may also fear and flee them, but even so, I am still involved with them. They still have a place within the world of meaning in which I live. As far as I can see or think or do, whatever I meet (or could meet) is understandable to one degree or another, whether it is currently so, or once was, or will be when I figure it out.

Meaningfulness is the mostly unnoticed dimension through which alone I can encounter whatever shows up. Thus everything I meet is in a sense "mine." It is familiar to me, part of my "family," a participant in the meaningful narrative that is my life.

Or if they are not immediately familiar—if the only sense I can make of them is that I do not immediately understand them—I can still make *interrogative* sense of them by dealing with them as potentially intelligible phenomena whose specific meaning I do not yet grasp: "How many members comprise the lepton family?" "Is this an opisthokont?" In both cases I have already introduced "the lepton family" and "opisthokonts," however tentatively, into my world of meaning

At least since Homo sapiens came on the scene some 200,000 years ago, "to be" has meant "to be meaningful." Meaningfulness is inevitable for us. I

1. "Obtrude": see Aufdringlichsten, GA 45: 2.9 = 4.5, and das Überdrängende und Vordrängende, ibid., 130.21–22 = 113.25–26.

2. GA 33: 179.25–26 = 154.6: zur Verfügung anwesend.

have contact with things only through this mediating medium, and without it I would not be human. This is the "wonder of all wonders"[3]—not that things merely exist in space and time but that *they make sense to us.*

> Being itself is understood in a definite way, and as something so understood, it is open to us.[4]

> Whatever we understand, and in whatever way it is *opened up* to us in understanding, we say that it has intelligibility.[5]

For Heidegger, "being" refers not to the mere physical presence of a thing to the sense organs. Rather, it refers to the meaningful presence of things, which is given only with human beings. "Being comes into play with us, with humankind."[6] There is no way I can get around meaningfulness or outside of it—I cannot step out of my pan-hermeneutical skin. Nor should I want to, because for humans, "outside" of meaningfulness there is only death. I am ineluctably thrown into meaningfulness simply by being human, and I am human only to the degree that I am immersed in meaning. I a priori "exceed" things insofar as I am always already "beyond them," related to their significance. The different and constantly changing worlds I live in—as student, worker, parent—are saturated with meaning, as is everything that shows up within those meaning-giving worlds. Everything I attend to—everything I can "mind"—turns out to make sense, whether actually or potentially.

Vague and indeterminate though it may be, this acquaintance with meaningfulness is what guides us in everything we do. We do not first of all understand things "empirically"—that is, by merely bumping up against them with our senses—but the other way around: only because we are a priori engaged with their possible significance can we relate to things at all. Meaning is closer to us than are the things we deal with. It is not only "more real" than they are, but in fact constitutes their realness-at-all for us. And yet, we constantly ignore or remain unaware of such meaningfulness in and for itself. It seems to be a necessary element of our makeup that we look *through* meaning without noticing it, whilst focusing instead on (meaningful) *things.* The transparent medium of meaningfulness is so much in evidence that I rarely attend to it, any more than I normally focus on the air I breathe. I overlook the meaningfulness of things as I go about dealing with (meaningful) *things* in the usual way. I

3. GA 9: 307.23–24 = 234.17–18, where "*ist*" means "anwest." See Husserl, *Ideen*, III 75.23 = 64.31. GA 4: 52.34 = 75.26: "das Einfache des Wunderbaren."

4. GA 40: 125.11–12 = 129.17–19.

5. GA 40: 89.20–24 = 91.24–26.

6. GA 73, 1: 90.28: "Bei uns—den Menschen—kommt das Sein ins Spiel."

overlook the cardinal fact that every time I say "is" I mean "is meaningful as" or "makes sense as."

Meaning is the barely heard white noise enveloping everything I meet, and the unnoticed gleam that lets everything shimmer with reality. I have—indeed, am—a familiarity with meaning, even though I need not explicitly say to myself that something "is meaningful as" this or that. Yet I do operate with such an implicit understanding in my silent comportment towards everything, whether in theoretical reflection on things or in the practical use of them. Meaningfulness is already self-evident to me prior to all thematic understanding and speech. And this pertains not only to things in my external environment but also to myself. Without this pre-conceptual familiarity with meaning, I could not understand myself, much less anything else. Without it I could not say "I," "you," or "it."

(Of course, I could become a philosopher and doubt that anything in the world has meaning. But then, in spite of myself, I would be making sense of the world and, as Leopold Bloom said, I would meet myself coming around again: "So it returns. Think you're escaping and run into yourself."[7])

Intelligibility is the name of the world I inhabit as I live into and out of an array of possibilities that I am thematically aware of or not, that I welcome or am indifferent to, that excite or bore me, possibilities that in a sense I myself *am* in the inevitable process of always having to become myself (cf. *Zu-sein*).[8] But if meaning is to occur, my ex-sistence as the clearing is required. On the one hand, the clearing determines the concrete, existentiel me: it is the reason why I exist at all.[9] But, on the other hand, without my ex-sistence there is no clearing: I am its *sine qua non*. That bondedness, wherein the "two" are one, is the very heart of what we mean by "human."[10] It is the ineluctable if hidden fact that determines my life and that I can never get back behind. That my ontological fate is to *be* the clearing is evidenced time and again as I talk with others, manage the things of my life, imagine the future, or remember the past: I cannot *not* make sense of everything I meet because I cannot *not* be a priori opened up. By our very nature we are both the demand for and the reason for intelligibility, for a meaningfulness that determines us and yet has no reality apart from us. And there is no way out but death. In fact, the whole process of making sense is mortal.

7. Joyce, *Ulysses*, Episode 13 (Nausicaa), 377.20–21.

8. SZ 42.4 = 67.9.

9. GA 88: 26.9–11: "das Wesen des Menschen aus der Wesung des *Seins als solches*." GA 15: 280.4 = 6.36: "Alles Denken ist 'umwillen des Seins.'"

10. On the clearing as das Brauchende (and nötigend), and on man as der Gebrauchte, see GA 6, 2: 354.14–17ff. = 244.30–32ff. Also GA 7: 33.10–1 = 32.5–6.

Why "mortal"? To answer that we step back once again into Heidegger's philosophical narrative about the original, non-subjective Greek sense of meaningful presence, an experience available to us as well. We find the things of the world already opened up, accessible, and meaningful before we ourselves have any chance to make it so. The wondrous fact is that things *already* make sense and that "something" (although the Greeks knew not what) has antecedently opened the world for human use and enjoyment, knowledge and exploitation, creativity and appreciation. Plato and Aristotle were quite aware of the wonder of meaningful presence (τὸ ὄν ὡς ἀληθές = ἀλήθεια-2), but what they did not know is how and why that is the case. They missed the fact that it is our own nature—the very way we are: thrown-open/appropriated—that has "preceded" us and, as ἀλήθεια-1, has always already opened up the world of ἀλήθεια-2. But the poets and tragedians of ancient Greece were attuned to this basic human fact to the degree that they understood our desperate need to hold things together against the onslaught of chaos, to gather them into a coherent whole within which we strive to fulfill our needs and desires. Sustaining and living in such a world is our response to the fact that all around us things are changing, going their own way, unfolding in multiple directions, and at the same time falling apart. Everything is in a state of flux, everything is becoming. And becoming not only generates novelty but also leads things to their demise.

On the one hand, in the return of things and seasons, in the world's "slow rotation suggesting permanence,"[11] the Greeks saw some hope of constancy and eternity—what Heidegger calls "stable presence." But on the other hand, their tragedians had a strong sense of the struggle to the death, the πόλεμος, that underlies such ultimately transient stability. We are enveloped both by riotous becoming and by death-dealing entropy, and nowhere is this more evident than in our own lives, which ever shoulder up against mortality: *nascendo et moriendo.*[12] Our urge to survive resists death and the chaos of things going their own way apart from us—and yet our mortality is our very bondedness to the chaos that will finally swallow us. We struggle for a secure space where we can, at least for a while, hold things together. We are born as λόγος, the need and ability to gather disparate things into a tentative unity of sense and thereby secure a shared human world (perhaps overseen and guaranteed by the gods) that we can inhabit for these few years. Our inescapable need of meaning is both the passing remedy for and the surest sign of our mortality. We cannot have one without the other. Ours is a fight to the death *against* death in the

11. T. S. Eliot, *Four Quartets*, "Burnt Norton," III. See chapter 2, note 111.

12. A favorite phrase of Augustine's: *De vera religione* liber unus, XLVI, 88: *Patrologia Latina*, 34, 161.35 (repeated, *Retractationes,* liber primus, XIII, 8: ibid., 32, 605.18). Also: *De natura boni contra manicheos*, liber unus, VIII: ibid., 42, 554.39; *De sermone domini in monte*, liber primus, XV, 40 and 41: ibid., 34, 1249.57–58; etc.

name of a fragile and ultimately futile stability. And out of this struggle come the glory of creativity and the grandeur of accomplishment, the openness of things in all their bright innocence and dark terror, as well as the tragedy of ultimate defeat. Meaning staves off chaos for a brief stretch of time in the losing battle of life.

Realizing all this is crucial for understanding the phenomenological turn that underlies Heidegger's work, and thus the central role played by first-person experience. To continue in that vein:

I begin to see that I "mind" whatever I meet, whether in the sense of caring about something for my own sake ("Yes, I mind if you smoke") or minding people for their own sake ("I'll mind the baby while you're out"). I also "mind" the things in my immediate world of purposeful activity in the sense that I understand and am involved with what they can do and what they are for. I am structurally a matter of minding (*Besorgen, Fürsorge*), of being concerned about whoever and whatever comes into my ken.[13] In my everyday ex-sistence I do not perceive things as objects standing over against me. Rather, I am involved and concerned with them. In fact, structurally I *am* such concern (*Sorge*), and this structure cuts across the disastrous mind-body split (νόησις/αἴσθησις). I am a bodily minding, which is the same as a minding body. I mind people and things *as meaningful* in different ways. The "object" of minding is the meant. And the meant is always meaningful.

Just as I usually do not thematize the meanings of the things I mind, so too I usually overlook *myself* as both a priori immersed in meaning and necessary for there to be meaning at all.[14] Occasionally I may thematically recognize that I am interpreting this literary text or that historical event—that is, actively figuring out how they fit within certain coordinates of significance. But it would be quite a different occasion, and no doubt rare, for me to ask why it is that on this side of death I cannot *not* make sense of things. I virtually never ask why there must be meaning at all. Yes, perhaps I do during a second-order "philosophical reflection," when I ask why there are things at all rather than nothing. Or perhaps in rare, shocking moments when meaning seems to drain out of everything, such that my very ex-sistence is threatened, and I anxiously wonder "what it's all about." But ask as I might, the question will always remain aporetic: everything is intelligible except why there is intelligibility at all.

13. On "Selbstsorge" as a tautology: SZ 193.8–11 = 237.26–28. Richardson argues, quite correctly in my opinion, for translating "Sorge" as "concern" rather than "care": *Heidegger*, 40, note 35.

14. On ex-sistence as nearest to yet farthest from itself: SZ 15.25–27 = 36.19–22.

And above all, the more I focus on the meaningful, the more I forget that I am the thrown-open clearing that makes meaning possible and necessary. This is what *Being and Time* means by "fallenness" (*das Verfallen*), which is the quite ordinary fact of overlooking the clearing despite the fact that "what is closest [= the clearing] is the farthest, and what is farthest [= meaningful things] is closest."[15] The clearing is "the innermost fire of human ex-sistence,"[16] just as meaning is the invisible air I breathe, absent which I would be dead. And yet, although I am a priori defined by—and indeed am—the clearing, I cannot grasp and conceptualize it, much less say why it is necessary for being human. In that sense the clearing is intrinsically "hidden": always present-and-operative but unknowable in its why and wherefore.

Heidegger argues that the ancient Greeks lived in a similar situation. They also lived within the world of meaning, but rarely thematized that fact. However, the thinkers among them were struck by the astonishing fact that everything in the world is powerfully present (*anwesend*, παρόν)—not just existing in space and time, indifferent to the people who live with those things, but always present to them (although not like objects to Kantian subjects).[17] Their philosophers called this presence "being" (τὸ εἶναι, οὐσία). However, in re-reading the Greeks Heidegger puts a twist on the word and finally dismisses it. "I no longer like to use the word '*Sein*'," he said,[18] and in fact William J. Richardson noted of the later Heidegger that the word *Sein* "has almost completely disappeared from his vocabulary."[19]

> "*Sein*" remains only the provisional term. Consider that "*Sein*" [= οὐσία] was originally called "presence" in the sense of a thing's staying-here-before-us-in-disclosedness.[20]

---

15. GA 45: 82.22–23 = 74.2–3; see ibid., 82.6–7 = 73.26–28: "closer than so-called 'reality' [i.e., 'real things'] is the essence of things, *which we know and yet do not know*." See also GA 9: 331.12–14 = 252.20–21.

16. GA 33: 20.5 = 16.5–6.

17. GA 8: 241.14–17 = 237.21–26: "Das παρά im εἶναι . . . meint die Nähe [etc.]."

18. GA 15: 20.8–9 = 8.34.

19. Richardson, *Heidegger*, 633.16–17; also 633 note 30: "Even in SZ, presumably, Heidegger sensed the inadequacy of the term but could find no other way to designate the process under discussion."

20. GA 7: 234.13–17 = 78.21–24; cf. GA 83: 213.24–25: "*Her-an-während, her* in die Unverborgenheit." Re "before us": ibid., 214.8: "Unverborgenheit wo, wie? D.h. wofür an? Für den Menschen."

"Staying-here-before-us-in-disclosedness" (*her-vor-währen in die Unverborgenheit*) is Heidegger's term of art for "phenomenality"—that is, for the meaningful presence of something to someone. The phrase expresses three things: (1) the relative *stability and constancy* of the meaningful thing (*währen*); (2) the *locus* of its meaningful appearance—namely, the world of human concerns (*-vor-*); and (3) a certain *movement into appearance*, from an undisclosed, merely potential intelligibility into an actually operative one (*in die Unverborgenheit*). He emphasizes the elements of light and brightness that characterize the Greek vision, an element (as we noted earlier) that classics scholar John Finley noted with regard to Homer's epic poems:

> [E]verything that he describes keeps a flashing concreteness and beautiful knowability.[21]
>
> Each [thing] . . . keeps its inherent nature, and a chief marvel of the poems might be said to be the ineffable act of concentration whereby men and women, great people, small people, towns, fields, animals, seas, rivers, earth, sky, and the lucent gods themselves, remain each distinct while jointly comprising the brilliant world.[22]

Finley speaks of Homer's universe as "the brilliant world that draws to brilliant action," attuned by "an outgazing bent of mind that sees things exactly, each for itself, and seems innocent of the idea that thought discerps and colors reality."[23] In Heidegger's view the brilliant "presence" of things (*Anwesen*, παρουσία) bespeaks the Greeks' proto-phenomenological view of the world.

One of Heidegger's first tasks in reading the Greeks was to re-enact the phenomenological attitude at work in Greek philosophy and culture and thereby thematize the rich but implicit sense of meaningful presence within which the Greeks lived their lives. To that task, beginning with his early Freiburg courses, he brought to bear on Greek thought, and particularly on Aristotle, the phenomenological way of seeing that he was then learning from Husserl. The keystone of that phenomenological vision was the inevitable fact of meaning in human comportment—this as over against a supposed dumb encounter with isolated sense data that are only subsequently gathered into a unified sense. Human beings always encounter things within an intelligible ensemble

21. Finley, *Four States of Greek Thought*, 54.1–2.

22. Finley, *Four States of Greek Thought*, 5.1–7.

23. Finley, *Four States of Greek Thought*, respectively 29.3–4 and 3.22–24.

of other meaningful things. Significance accrues to the things of this ensemble due to their orientation to the human concerns and interests that define that intelligible whole. Heidegger designates such a context by the technical term "world"—a specific context of significance, such as the world of the business woman or the world of the cleaning staff.

> [T]o live means to care. What we care for and about, what caring adheres to, is equivalent to what is meaningful. *Meaningfulness* is a categorial determination of the world; the objects of a world—"worldly" or "world-some" objects—are lived inasmuch as they embody the character of meaningfulness.[24]

In his first course after the Great War Heidegger used the example of the lectern from which he was speaking in the classroom. He took the occasion to make one of the earliest presentations of what he would later articulate as the contextualizing world of meaningfulness (*Welt als Bedeutsamkeit*), which occurs a priori in and with human being.

> In the experience of seeing the lectern something is given *to me* from out of the first-hand world around me [*Umwelt*]. This lived world (teacher's lectern, book, blackboard, notebook, fountain pen, beadle, student, fraternity, streetcar, automobile, and so on) does not consist of mere things, objects, which are then conceived of as meaning this or that.
>
> Rather, what is primary and what is immediately given to me without some mental detour through a conceptual grasp of the thing is *something meaningful* [*das Bedeutsame*]. When we live in the first-hand world around us, everything comes at us loaded with meaning, all over the place and all the time. Everything is within the world of meaning: *the world of meaning holds forth* [*es weltet*].[25]

Which means: If things are the meaningful (*das Bedeutsame*), their being is their meaningfulness (*Bedeutsamkeit*).[26] Heidegger equates "the question of the meaningfulness of things" with "the question of the being [of things]."[27] Whether in Heidegger's reading of the Greeks or in his own philosophy, his implicit phenomenological reduction of things to their meaningful presence recasts their being as their significance to human beings.

---

24. GA 61: 90.7–12 = 68.6–10.

25. GA 56/57: 72.31–73.5 = 61.19–28. My emphasis.

26. Heidegger defines "world" as "meaningfulness" (Bedeutsamkeit). See William J. Richardson, *Heidegger*, 167, n.15: "World is equivalent to Being"; "the term 'Being' replaces the term 'World.'"

27. GA 19: 205.13–14 = 141.33–34: "die Frage nach dem Sinn des Seienden, nach dem Sein."

The lectern, of course, appears in a meaning-giving context: the classroom, where the students and the professor already know their way around and are familiar with what fits and doesn't fit.

> Coming into the lecture-room, I see the lectern. . . . What do "I" see? Brown surfaces, at right angles to one another? No, I see something else. Is it a largish box with another smaller one set on top of it? Not at all. I see the *lectern at which I am to speak*. You see the lectern from which you are to be addressed and from which I have previously spoken to you.[28]

It is a bad reading of the situation, Heidegger insists, to pretend to see de-contextualized "things" that subsequently get meanings slapped on them,

> as if I first of all would see intersecting brown surfaces that then reveal themselves to me as a box, then as a desk, then as an academic lecturing desk, a lectern, so that I attach lectern-hood to the box like a label.[29]

> It is not the case that objects are at first present as bare realities, as objects in some sort of natural state, and that they then in the course of our experience receive the garb of a value-character, so that they do not have to run around naked.[30]

In other words, there is a priori operative a context of lived experience that already "places" things in relation to my needs and interests.

> I see the lectern in one fell swoop, so to speak, and not in isolation, but as adjusted a bit too high for me. I see—and immediately so—a book lying upon it as annoying to me (a *book*, not a collection of layered pages with black marks strewn across them), I see the lectern in a certain orientation, within a certain light, against a background.[31]

Even if someone from an entirely different lived context—"a farmer from deep in the Black Forest"—enters the room, he does not see, in Heidegger's words, "a box, an arrangement of boards." Instead, "He sees 'the place for the teacher,' he sees the object as *fraught with a meaning*."[32] Suppose, likewise, that someone from a tribe remote from Western civilization enters the classroom and notices the lectern. It is possible that he would not immediately understand what it is.

---

28. GA 56/57: 71.2–9 = 59.34–60.6. My emphasis.
29. GA 56/57: 71.10–14 = 60.7–10.
30. GA 61: 91.22–25 = 69.6–9.
31. GA 56/57: 71.16–22 = 60.11–16.
32. GA 56/57: 71.29–31 = 60.23–24, "mit einer Bedeutung behaftet." My emphasis.

> It is difficult to say precisely what he would see: perhaps something to do with magic, or something behind which one could find good protection against arrows and flying stones. . . . Even if he saw the lectern as a bare something that is just there [*bloßes Etwas, das da ist*], it would have a meaning for him, a moment of signification. [Even if the tribesman is entirely perplexed by the lectern,] he will see the lectern much more as something "that he does not know what to make of." The meaningful character of "instrumental strangeness" [for the tribesman] and the meaningful character of "lectern" [for the professor and students] are in their essence absolutely identical.[33]

Heidegger's early lectures are replete with his insistence that every encounter with a thing is an encounter with something meaningful. For example, in his lecture course of 1921–1922 on "Phenomenological Interpretations of Aristotle":

> The category of meaningfulness indicates how objects are in life according to the basic sense of their content and how and as what they hold themselves and comport themselves in a world.[34]

We do not meet things by taking on board dumb sense data; rather, we always encounter things *as* something or other, even if (as in the example above) it is as something we cannot figure out.

> The as-what and the how of the encounter may be designated as *meaningfulness*. This itself is to be interpreted as a category of being.[35]

Heidegger continued with this theme in his 1919–1920 course "Basic Problems of Phenomenology." He advises his students:

> You should put aside all theorizing and reject what epistemologists say about the matter. Instead, see the sense in which factical experience ever and anew has what it experiences in the character of meaningfulness. Even the most trivial thing is meaningful (even though it remains trivial nonetheless). Even what is most lacking in value is meaningful.[36]

There is nowhere else for a human being to live except in meaning.

> I live factically always as a *prisoner of meaningfulness*. And every instance of meaningfulness has its arena of new instances of meaningfulness. . . . I live in

33. GA 56/57: 71.35–72.3; 72.19–21 and .26–30 = 60.27–30; 61.8–10 and .14–18.
34. GA 61: 92.31–34 = 70.1–4.
35. GA 63: 93.7–9 = 71.10–12.
36. GA 58: 104.19–24 = 83.19–23.

> the factical as in an entirely particular *matrix* of meaningfulnesses. . . . In this unobtrusive character of meaningfulness stands whatever is factically experienced in factical life-contexts.[37]

Meaningfulness is a thing's relatedness-to-oneself (*Mich-Bezogenheit*),[38] and the phenomenologist studies this relatedness of the subject matter and the person involved with it. Phenomenology, as Husserl said, is "correlation research," and for Heidegger "the philosophizing individual belongs together with the matters being treated."[39] In the everyday, meaningfulness mostly remains implicit and unnoticed and need not be thematically known or expressed. In one's daily life "[m]eaningfulness as such is not explicitly experienced, even though it can be experienced."[40] In fact, "The phenomenon of meaningfulness is not what we originally see."[41] But that in no way speaks against the reality that "factical life lives in factical relations of meaningfulness."[42] Indeed, "In factical life the meaning of 'ex-sistence' lies in forms of meaningfulness, whether actually experienced, or remembered, or awaited."[43]

> Even "just anything" that I experience . . . as indefinite and without determination, *I nonetheless experience in the indeterminacy of a determined context of meaningfulness*—as a noise in the room "which I can't understand" ("Something's not right," "it's something eerie").[44]

This meaningfulness functions at every moment and in every comportment. Taking "world" not as a technical term (as in *Being and Time*) but as referring to "whatever's out there," Heidegger says, "I experience the world by living in contexts of meaningfulness. The world announces itself as actual and real in those contexts."[45] Indeed, "the 'objective' comes forth in the meaning-context of one's factical life-situation."[46] In fact, I do not live *in* a given meaningful context; rather, I *live it*.[47]

37. GA 58: 104.32–105.1–9 = 83.30–38: Heidegger's emphases.

38. GA 58: 105.12–13 = 84.3.

39. GA 9: 42.25–27 = 36.35–36.

40. GA 61: 93.8–9 = 70.11–12: "Nicht ist Bedeutsamkeit als solche erfahren, ausdrücklich; sie kann aber erfahren werden."

41. GA 58: 108.18–19 = 86.10–11.

42. GA 58: 105.22 = 84.10.

43. GA 58: 106.12–14 = 84.31–32.

44. GA 58: 106.27–31 = 85.2–6.

45. GA 58:107.12–13 = 85.18–19.

46. GA 58: 113.6–8 = 89.8–9.

47. GA 58: 117.20–21 = 92.12–13.

This position is again enunciated in Heidegger's lectures and writings of 1924—for example, in his course "Basic Concepts of Aristotelian Philosophy":

> For a long time now, I have been designating the ontological character of human ex-sistence as *meaningfulness*. This ontological character is the primary one in which we encounter the world.[48]

Or in reading through his essay "The Concept of Time" (1924; the essay meant for publication, not the Marburg address), one can hardly take a step without stumbling over the word *Bedeutsamkeit*.

> The lived world is present not as a thing or object, but as meaningfulness.[49]

> We have now identified the basic character of encountering the world: meaningfulness.[50]

> We identify meaningfulness as the world's primary ontological characteristic.[51]

> . . . the primary character of encountering the world—meaningfulness.[52]

That same year Heidegger explicitly identifies being and meaningfulness in his course on Plato's "Sophist," when he speaks of metaphysics as

> the inquiry into the *intelligibility* of things, that is, the inquiry into *being*.[53]

And the following year, on the verge of writing *Being and Time*, he again signals the centrality of meaningfulness in his course on logic and truth:

> The very being of ex-sistence is to make sense of things, and therefore ex-sistence lives in meanings and can express itself in and as meanings.[54]

Thus, for Heidegger, whether in his own phenomenology or when reading the Greeks, his first move is to focus on meaning. But the question then becomes: What kind of meaning? In his earliest course after World War I, Heidegger's main attack was on the primacy that Husserl attributed to theory over lived experience and to the pure transcendental ego over what Heidegger at

48. GA 18: 300.15–17 = 203.27–29.

49. GA 64: 65.18–19 = 55.15–16.

50. GA 64: 23.32–33 = 17.25–26.

51. GA 64: 24.2–3 = 17.30–31.

52. GA 64: 25.13–14 = 19.1–2.

53. GA 19: 205.13–14 = 141.33–34: "die Frage nach dem Sinn des Seienden, nach dem Sein." My emphasis.

54. GA 21: 151.4–5 = 127.30–32.

this point was calling the "historical ego" and the "ego of the situation."[55] "We find ourselves at a methodological crossroads," he remarked, "where it will be decided whether philosophy shall live or die."[56] And survival depends on first getting clear about what philosophy's true issue is. "What is distorting the real problematic is not just naturalism as some people think," he said with obvious reference to Husserl, "but the overall dominance of the *theoretical*."[57]

To keep the focus on our lived world as where we primarily experience meaningfulness, Heidegger radically recasts the "principles" that Husserl had laid down for phenomenology in Section 24 of his *Ideas for a Pure Phenomenology and a Phenomenological Philosophy* (1913).[58] If, according to Husserl, firsthand intuition is the starting point of phenomenology, such intuition—"even though Husserl does not say this in so many words"—is not some theoretical comportment towards objects but an "understanding intuition, a *hermeneutic intuition*," from which theory is but a precipitate.[59] This hermeneutic intuition, which already understands the world as meaningful in a lived way prior to any theorizing, and which is the basis of all the rigor that phenomenology claims for itself, is

> the primordial intention of genuine life, the primordial bearing of lived experience and of life as such, the absolute *sympathy with life* that is identical with lived experience. Prior to anything else—that is, if we take this path away from theory and more and more free ourselves from it—we *see* this basic comportment all the time, we have an orientation *to* it. This basic comportment is absolute, but only if we live in it directly. And no conceptual system, no matter how elaborately constructed, can reach it. Only phenomenological living, as it gets continually more intense, can get to it.[60]

Heidegger carries into his *magnum opus* the conviction that phenomenology is strictly about meaning. In *Being and Time* he designates the very structure of world (*Welt*) as meaningfulness (*Bedeutsamkeit*),[61] and he referred implicitly to

55. See the letter of Gerda Walther to Alexander Pfänder, June 20, 1919: Husserl Archives, R III Walther 20.VI.19.

56. GA 56/57: 63.16–18 = 53.14–16.

57. GA 56/57: 87.25 = 73.33–34.

58. Husserl, *Ideen I*, Husserliana III, 1, 52.6–14 = 44.19–23.

59. GA 56/57: 109.30–110.1 = 92: 27–28: "wenn auch Husserl darüber sich nicht ausspricht"; ibid., 117.13 = 99.10.1: "die verstehende, die *hermeneutische Intuition*."

60. GA 56/57: 110.2–11 = 92.29–93.6.

61. SZ 87.17–18 = 120.13; 334.33–34 = 384.1.

SZ I.1 as his "doctrine of meaning" (*Bedeutungslehre*).[62] He explicitly equates being and intelligibility when he says that ontology, which deals with the *being* of things, is in fact "the explicit theoretical inquiry into the *intelligibility* of things."[63] And he calls the (usually unnoticed) being of things their "intelligibility" (*Sinn*).[64] With such formulations, Heidegger was announcing his phenomenological re-interpretation of the central topic of "first philosophy" as not the being (*existentia* and *essentia*) of things but their meaningfulness.

At the core of that doctrine is the phenomenology of ex-sistence as "being-in-the-world." But since the essence of world is meaningfulness, we should interpret *In-der-Welt-sein* more precisely as *In-der-<u>Bedeutsamkeit</u>-sein*: the very structure of ex-sistence is its a priori *engagement with meaning and its source*, expressed as "ex-sistence . . . in its familiarity with meaningfulness."[65] Absent that engagement, we cease to exist. When we can no longer relate to meaning, we are dead. This a priori engagement with intelligibility—as our only way to be—entails that we are ineluctably hermeneutical. We necessarily make some sense of everything we meet, and if we cannot make any sense at all of something, not even interrogative sense, we simply cannot meet it. We can have no encounter with things that lie outside our hermeneutical horizon of meaningful *Anwesen*.

As we saw, Heidegger insists that meaning—which is always discursive—is confined to the realm of the human. But then how exactly do things become meaningful to us? In *Being and Time* Heidegger writes:

> Intelligibility is a structural characteristic of ex-sistence, not a property attaching to things. . . . Only ex-sistence "has" intelligibility.[66]

And at the same time:

> When things within the world are discovered with the being of ex-sistence—that is, when they come to be understood—we say they *make sense*.[67]

---

62. SZ 166.9–10 = 209.26–27; see GA 64: 24.4–7 = 17.34–35.

63. SZ 12.14–15 = 32.23–24 (my emphasis in the English): "[Ontologie als] das explizite Fragen nach dem Sinn des Seienden." This text stood from 1927 until 1977—through some seventeen editions of SZ. But then, without notification or explanation, GA 2 (which at v.1 and 579.12 claims to be the "unveränderter Text") changed it to "nach dem Sein des Seienden" (16.23 = Stambaugh 11.15). This is nothing short of a travesty of editing.

64. SZ 35.25 = 59.31.

65. See SZ 87.19–20 = 120.25: "Dasein . . . in seiner Vertrautheit mit der Bedeutsamkeit."

66. SZ 151.34–36 = 193.11–13: Structural characteristic: "ein Existential." On worldhood as an existential: ibid., 64.19–20 = 92.34–36:

67. SZ 151.22–24 = 192.35–37. "Make sense": "hat Sinn." The text continues at 151.24–25 = "But strictly speaking what is understood is not the meaningfulness but the thing, or

That is, we alone have the ability to make sense of things, and we do so by connecting a possibility of ourselves (a need, interest, or purpose) with a possibility of something we encounter. We take whatever we meet as related to our everyday concerns and goals. When things are discovered in such a relation with human beings within a given context or world, they make sense. And world is what brings that about.[68]

THE WORLD AS A REALM OF MEANINGFULNESS

possibilities of things ↘

→ **HUMAN CONCERNS AND POSSIBILITIES** → **MEANINGFULNESS**

↗ **possibilities of things**

Heidegger says, "As existing, the human being *is* its world."[69] That is, the world is ourselves writ large as a matrix of intelligibility. It is our thrown-openness structured as a set of meaning-giving relations. The world consists of lines of referral to our concerns and possibilities (represented by the arrows above) that in turn establish the meaningfulness of things. We are a hermeneutical field of force, like a magnet that draws things together into unities of sense insofar as these things are connected with a possibility of ourselves as the final point of reference.[70] Anything outside the scope of our embodied hermeneutical ken does not make sense.

"The world," as Heidegger understands the term, is the prior "open space" or "clearing" that we need in order to understand X *as* Y or use something *in*

---

alternatively the being [of the thing]." That last phrase refers to when being rather than things is the Befragte of the question, as in Heidegger's Grundfrage.

68. See Heidegger's summary of his world-analysis: SZ 297.15–26 = 343.32–344.9.

69. SZ 364.34–35 = 416.8: "Dieses [= das Dasein] *ist* existierend seine Welt." GA 9: 154.18–19 = 120.24–25: "Welt ist in all dem die Bezeichnung für das menschliche Dasein im Kern seines Wesens." Also SZ 64.9–20 = 92.32; 365.38 = 417.11; 380.28–30 = 432.17–18. GA 24: 237.8–10 = 166.33–35.

70. GA 9: 279.1–4 = 213.10–12: "zusammenbringen auf Eines . . . Wohin? In das Unverborgene der Anwesung."

terms of one of its possibilities. In doing so we make sense of the thing—or, in traditional language, we "understand its being." But why do we need such a prior openness in order to make sense of something? Making sense of something is a matter of synthesizing it with a possible meaning: "Socrates is a Theban"—no, wait: *that* possible meaning is wrong. So we might try another possible meaning: "Socrates is an Athenian." The need to synthesize a thing with a possible (correct or incorrect) meaning is an index of our finitude. The highest form of knowing, says Heidegger, is not a matter of synthesis (which entails the possibility of getting things wrong) but direct and unerring intuition of what a thing actually is. But traditionally it is God, not man, who has such an intellectual intuition. God does not *make sense of* things but simply *makes* them. Heidegger describes Kant's position:

> [W]hat remains closed off to us are the things themselves insofar as they are thought as objects [i.e., noumena] of an absolute knowledge, i.e., as objects of an intuition that does not first need an interaction with the things and does not first let them be encountered, but rather lets them first of all *become* what they are through this intuition.[71]

In our case, things do not show up directly as what and how they are, the way they might to a divine intellectual intuition. Rather, they appear only to a mediating and dis-cursive intellect, one that must "run," so to speak, from subject to predicate, or from tool to task, and back again (*dis-currere*: to run to and fro) in order to synthesize two things that lie apart one from the other: subject and predicate or tool and task.[72] According to the classical tradition, a perfect intellectual intuition requires a fully actualized and self-present subject, whether that be the self-coincident act-of-thinking-about-itself-as-thinking, the νόησις νοήσεως, of Aristotle's *Metaphysics*, or the perfect *reditio completa in seipsum* (the perfect return to itself) of Aquinas' God.[73] But for Heidegger, discursivity, unlike the "closure upon itself" of Aristotle's self-thinking God, requires *openness*. Human reason must traverse an open "space" (constituted by ex-sistence

71. GA 25: 98.22–27 = 68.5–9.

72. SZ 34:1–4 = 57.25–28: "rekurriert." Here Heidegger is following the tradition: see Aquinas, *Summa contra gentes*, I, 57, 27: "Ratiocinatio autem est quidam motus intellectus transeuntis ab uno in aliud." Discursive thinking as a kind of movement of the intellect, going from one thing [the subject] to another [the possible predicate]. Also *Summa theologiae* I, 58, 3, ad 1. Thus GA 29/30: 447.6–7 = 308. 39–40: "Es gibt Sprache nur bei einem Seienden, das seinem Wesen nach *transzendiert*"—that is, with the entity that is thrown ahead and returns discursively to things. Also GA 84, 1: 50.1–6: beziehendes Unterscheiden.

73. Respectively, Aristotle, *Metaphysics* XII 9, 1074b34–35 and Aquinas, *Summa theologiae* I, 14, 2, obj. 1 and ad 1. Aquinas applies such self-presence *analogously* to God, angels, and man.

as thrown-open) within which alone reason can synthesize disparate things. This prior openness is "the realm a person traverses every time he or she, as a subject, relates to an object."[74]

> Apprehension and presence—in order for both to be possible and at the same time to be for one another—require a free space and an open domain, within which they pertain to one another.[75]

But we *are able* to do such "traversing of an open space" in existentiel knowledge and action only because we *already are* such an open space in our existential essence (a priori and structurally, of course, and not of our own volition). Our essence is to be the existential wiggle-room required for existentiel acts of taking-as.

> We [erroneously] think that a thing becomes accessible when an "I" as subject represents an object. But in fact prior to that, there must be already operative an open region within whose openedness something can become accessible *as* an object *for* a subject and in which the accessibility itself can be traversed and experienced.[76]

Over the course of Heidegger's career this open domain would ride under various titles: the clearing, ἀλήθεια-1, the thrown-open realm (*Entwurfbereich*) for being, and so on. This open region—along with *the opening of it* by our being thrown-open or "brought into our own" (ap-*propri*-ated)—is the core fact, *die Sache selbst*, of all Heidegger's philosophizing.

To return to the question of the being of things: As we have seen, Heidegger never understood it as the raw existence of things out there in space and time. That was what he called *existentia*, the ontological "substance" of things when they are considered apart from human involvement with them, which is to say, before the enactment of a phenomenological reduction. It is wrong to think that Heidegger refused the phenomenological reduction and instead conducted his early investigations of the everyday world within the natural attitude. Husserl, however, thought that was the case, and he always accused

74. GA 7: 19: 11–13 = 18.31–33. See GA 15: 380.5–7 = 68.42–44: "die für das Menschenwesen grundlegende Möglichkeit, eine offene Weite zu durchgehen, um bis zu den Dingen zu gelangen."

75. GA 15: 401.24–27 = 93:23–25: "Beide . . . bedürfen . . . eines Freien und Offenen." See GA 34: 59.22 = 44.20: "Durchgang."

76. GA 48: 177.21–28 (also at GA 6, 2: 121.12–19) = 93.17–23.

Heidegger of not understanding the reduction. Heidegger himself gave Husserl reason enough to doubt his protégé when in October of 1927 Heidegger drafted significant sections for Husserl's eventual *Encyclopedia Britannica* article, specifically on the idea of phenomenology and the method of pure psychology, including the phenomenological reduction.[77] In that draft Heidegger argued that the proper topic of phenomenology is being (*das Sein*), but always in correlation with some form of human being[78] (hence as *Anwesen*). When that correlation is made explicit by way of a phenomenological reduction, the things out there in the universe come to be seen as meaningfully present phenomena: the perceived of a perception, the loved of an act of love, the judged of an act of judgment—that is, always in correlation with a human concern or practice. In his early work, of course, Heidegger focused the reduction on practical action, and there the phenomena are the things with which we engage (τὰ πράγματα) in our practical dealings (πρᾶξις, *Umgang*).

A few months before composing that draft for Husserl, Heidegger had clarified the phenomenological reduction in his course "Basic Problems of Phenomenology," where he contrasted (4 May 1927) his own understanding of the reduction with that of Husserl. For Husserl, he said, it means leading things back to "the transcendental life of consciousness and its noetic-noematic experiences, in which objects are constituted as correlates of consciousness." On the other hand:

> For *us* phenomenological reduction means leading the phenomenological vision back *from* the apprehension of a thing, whatever may be the character of that apprehension, *to* the understanding of the being of the thing (i.e., understanding the thing in terms of the way it is disclosed).[79]

We see here that "being" in Heidegger's sense does not stand on its own with no relation to ex-sistence. Even prior to the reduction the being (= meaning) of the things is already operative in our everyday understanding. The phenomenological reduction merely draws the reflective philosopher *explicitly* into the already-operative correlation between the φαινόμενον on the one hand and the λόγος that lets it be seen on the other: the reduction thematizes for the phenomenologist the meaningful disclosedness of the thing. In other words, leading one's philosophical vision away from a thing and onto its "being" means seeing the thing in terms of its current form of meaningful presence.

77. Husserl, *Phänomenologische Psychologie, Husserliana* IX, 256–263 = 107–116.

78. See also "Der Weg," 15.19–20: "die Erfassung des Seins als solchen (d.h. der Bezug des Menschen zum Sein, nicht nur zum Seienden)."

79. GA 24: 29.15–19 = 21.26–30. GA 19: 8.25–26 = 6.8–10: "Phänomen bezeichnet das Seiende, so wie es sich zeigt, in den verschiedenen Möglichkeiten seines Erschlossenwerdens."

The reduction "puts the breaks on" (see epoché) our natural tendency to overlook meaningfulness as we look through it to the entity—even though meaning is the most ob-vious (etymologically, "in-the-way") element of the process.[80] The reduction takes us back reflectively and thematically to where we always already stand in our everyday lives: in relation to the thing *as meaning* this or that. Therefore, as long as we take the word λόγος in the broad sense in which Heidegger meant it—as encompassing every kind of intelligent activity ("minding"), whether practical, theoretical, or whatever—we may say that the thing's presence, which the phenomenologist focuses on in and through the reduction, is the thing's current meaningfulness and never its mere "out-thereness" apart from human engagement.

Of course, neither Husserl nor Heidegger doubt that things remain "out there" after the reduction. Husserl explicitly said that

> we must not overlook the *most essential thing of all*, namely that even after the purifying epoché, perception still remains perception of this house, indeed, of this house with the accepted status of "actually existing."[81]

We have seen that for Heidegger "Questions like 'Does the world exist independent of my thinking?' are meaningless."[82] He added that the thing in nature

> shows up in the reducing gaze that focuses on the act of perceiving, because this perceiving is essentially a perceiving *of* the thing. The thing *belongs* to the perceiving *as its perceived.*[83]

For Heidegger as well as for Husserl, a thing is still out-there (*vorhanden*) after the reduction; it's just that, as such, it is not the focus of their philosophy. The subject matter of a phenomenological inquiry is things only insofar as we are in some way meaningfully engaged with them. After the phenomenological reduction, the only philosophical problems one may properly pursue are those of sense and meaning–that is, hermeneutical questions.

In its most basic form, the phenomenological reduction is a matter of learning to stand thematically where we always already stand in lived experience. The upshot of Heidegger's phenomenological reduction is that we engage with

80. GA 8: 113.8–10 = 110.11–13: "Das Sein des Seienden ist das Scheinendste; und doch sehen wir es gewöhnlich überhaupt nicht." Heidegger references Aristotle, *Metaphysics* II 1, 993b9–11: we are as blind as a bat to that which is, by nature, most evident of all: τὰ τῇ φύσει φανερώτατα πάντων.

81. Husserl, *Phänomenologische Psychologie*, *Husserliana* IX, 243.30–34 = 91.12–14.

82. GA 58: 105.15–16 = 84.5–6. GA 26: 194.30–31 = 153.28–29: "Seiendes ist an ihm selbst das Seiende, was es ist und wie es ist, auch wenn z.B. Dasein nicht existiert."

83. Husserl, *Phänomenologische Psychologie*, *Husserliana* IX, 261.6–9 = 113.13–15.

things from a contextualized, first-person, embodied-experiential involvement with things, which inevitably makes sense of them. Even if I get information about a thing from someone else, it is still *I* who get that information in the first person. (This is the unavoidable truth of Descartes' *ego cogito*.) And no matter where I get that information from, I cannot *not* make sense of it. (In other words, human being is pan-hermeneutical.)[84] No matter how much we forget about meaningfulness and get absorbed in things, we always remain, by our very structure, phenomenological. This first-person experiential sense-making is where I already stand prior to any subsequent move into the theoretical or the practical.

In *Being and Time* Heidegger refocuses and crowns his earlier investigations into meaningfulness by grounding it in human being. "The doctrine of meaning is rooted in the ontology of ex-sistence."[85] He sees human being as *possibility* (i.e., as ex-sistence: "being made to stand out and beyond") while at the same time, as always related to itself (mineness).[86] Ex-sistence is a form of movement of the self in which possibility always outrides actuality.[87] Man is a unique kind of κίνησις that, of and as itself, is related to itself: a self-related relation (i.e., its self-understanding is part and parcel of what man is) that *is* itself in its incompleteness (it will never fulfill all its possibilities). For Heidegger that movement is grounded in the most basic fact of human being, its a priori understanding of meaningfulness.[88] If we cannot encounter anything except by *understanding* it, then our facticity—the necessity that determines the structure of our being—is our bondedness to the world of meaning and, a fortiori, to what makes that world possible.[89]

Heidegger begins his analysis of the world of meaning with where we live our ordinary lives, the "everyday," as he calls it, where we deal with things by

84. GA 66: 325.30–32 = 289.18–19: "ist 'Dasein' von Anfang an 'hermeneutisch', d.h. als Entworfenes eines *ausgezeichneten* Entwurfs."

85. SZ 166.9–10 = 209.26–27.

86. GA 49: 21.5–6, referencing Kierkegaard: As "subjects" we are related "bewußt zu den Dingen und selbstbewßt zu uns selbst." Mutatis mutandis, Heidegger could accept this in his own work as a "psychological" adaptation of the reditio completa in seipsum mentioned earlier.

87. SZ 38.29–30 = 63.2.

88. For Heidegger man's κίνησις is a "being-moved" or "mov*ed*ness" (Bewegtheit) insofar as man is *thrown* open. See SZ 375.2–3 = 427.10: "Bewegtheit des *erstreckten Sicherstreckens*," Heidegger's emphasis.

89. GA 36/37: 100.20–21 = 80.8–9: "*Dieses Gebundenheit in die Übermacht des Seins* ist uns das *tiefst Wesen des Menschen*."

handling them, using them, and managing them as extensions of ourselves, rather than merely observing them as objects of theory or speculation. Whether we attend to this fact or not, all such things are significant to us, meaningful in a practical way. We use them instrumentally to achieve a purpose: cooking dinner, painting the garage, researching an event. They are not merely "available" for mental observation but are functionally accessible and usable. Hence we call these things "the useful" (Heidegger's *das Zuhandene*). They fulfill a need, achieve a purpose, help us to reach a desideratum. Before functioning as mere observers of our world, we work in it to satisfy our needs. We are lacking, and we seek satisfaction; we are concerned and seek to work things out. We want to change some things, accomplish others, and do away with yet others.

Another characteristic of human being is that we usually see things not as scattered and unrelated but rather within wholes or sets, as somehow unified and interacting with each other—perhaps because we are de facto the perspectival center that defines our encompassing horizon, perhaps because we see our own selves as a whole, an open-ended narrative unity that gathers things into significance for ourselves and manifests them in such a way that we can relate to them. We live in meaningful contexts, worlds of meaning shaped by our interests and concerns, which confer meaning on the things that inhabit those contexts. We live in *many* such contexts at the same time. In the evening, for example, a woman returns business calls from home while sipping a Scotch and rocking her child to sleep. In a matter of seconds she might reach for a notepad to jot down a number, hold up her glass to ask for a refill, and put her finger to her mouth to signal for silence, since the child has just dozed off. Each of those three worlds of meaning is organized around a purpose traceable to that woman, to her complex life and needs as lawyer, wife, and mother; and each specific purpose organizes various things into distinct ensembles of significance. What she is intent upon has evoked the possibilities of the things around her—the cradle and baby blanket; the glass and ice cubes; the phone and notepad.

But the point is that she is *de facto* engaged with many different worlds of meaning only because *de jure*—that is, as a human being—she is a priori and inescapably the very clearing that makes all of this possible. She is "in-the-world," in fact, "in" (i.e., familiar with) many worlds of meaning at once. In the phrase "being-in-the-world," the "world" refers to an ensemble of suitabilities: this pad as suitable for recording a phone number, this gesture as suitable to signal for silence, this upraised glass as suitable to signal for a refill. Those worlds of purposefulness are fraught with meaning, and yet are mostly tacit—familiar but implicit—until perhaps something goes wrong: the cell phone battery dies, the pen won't write, there's no more Scotch, or the baby suddenly wakes up with a blasting wail. Then those heretofore tacit worlds "light up," as

Heidegger puts it. They become explicit, along with the various purposes that gathered together the things within them. A disappointed purpose reveals what we have been about without attending to it: setting an appointment, getting the child asleep, hoping for a refill.

That conjunction of the possibilities of things satisfying the possibilities of ourselves is what allows us to use things straightaway and, on reflection, to explicitly see them as meaningful. That conjunction, the common structure of any world of meaning, is what Heidegger calls the "worldhood" (or better, the essential structure) of a world; and he designates such "worldhood" as meaning-giving. In turn, the fact that we ourselves sustain such contexts he calls "being-*in*" a world—that is, being inescapably familiar with it and its source. Lest "being-in-the-world" sound like the banal fact of just being extant within certain spatio-temporal coordinates of the universe and in mute contact with certain objects—the way a stone is "in the world"—we have designated that existential structure by the phenomenologically more adequate term "engagement with meaning." This is the core of all of Heidegger's work. Over the half-century following the publication of *Being and Time*, Heidegger will stretch and compress and christen this phenomenon with a plethora of variously nuanced titles—from *Lichtung* to *Ereignis* to *die Wesung der Wahrheit des Seins*—but he will never get beyond ex-sistence as being-in-the-world, nor did he need to, nor could he if he had wanted to.

5

Ex-sistence as Openness

Heidegger's basic question about the source of intelligibility was very much a post-Nietzschean inquiry. In an age when there is no Ground of Being under our feet and no Divine Ideas above our heads, how does meaning come about at all? Without invoking a divine standard of truth, or the myths of Platonic ideas or extractable essences, Heidegger's question about *Sein*, aka *Anwesen*, becomes "the question of how meaningful presence as such can be given."[1]

We have seen that the metaphysical tradition's οὐσία or *esse* or *Sein* is always the being *of things*—"Being never occurs without things"[2]—and further that, within Heidegger's phenomenology, the word "being" no longer refers to *existentia* and *essentia* as the guiding concern of traditional metaphysics but rather means the intelligibility of things in correlation with human intelligence. But Heidegger's own question went a step further than that to what he called the basic question: Granted that being is the meaningful presence of things to man, how does such meaningful presence come about at all? What makes it both possible and necessary in human experience? And given the necessary correlation of being and man, the question of the "whence" of being is inseparable from the question of what makes possible man's understanding of being at all.

Thus Heidegger's basic question is actually about what makes intelligibility possible. But since intelligibility occurs only with human beings, the question about what makes it possible turns the tables and begins by putting questions to the human being who asks such questions: Why are we condemned to making sense of things? Why are we structurally required to mediate between things and their meaning? Can meaningfulness collapse, and what happens if it does? By understanding being as the meaningfulness of things

1. GA 14: 86.24–87.1 = 70.9–10: "[Die Grundfrage] nach dem Sein als Sein, d.h. die Frage, inwiefern es Anwesenheit als solche geben kann."

2. GA 9: 306.17–19 = 233.28: "Das Sein nie west ohne das Seiende." SZ 37.12 = 61.26–27: "Sein aber je Sein von Seiendem ist." GA 73, 2: 970.3: "Sein und Seiendes sind unzertrennlich." Also SZ 9.7 = 29.13 and GA 73, 2: 975.24.

and as correlative to human being, *Being and Time* stands in the centuries-long tradition of the transcendental turn to the subject (*die Wende zum Subjekt*), which reaches back at least as far as Descartes and, for Heidegger, arguably as far back as Parmenides.[3] In that transcendental tradition, the way to solve a philosophical problem is to turn the inquiring subject into the subject of the inquiry.[4] Heidegger's place within that tradition is defined from the outset by the debate he initiated over what is meant by the "subject" (which he interprets as the "e-ject": thrown-open ex-sistence). As located formally within the transcendental tradition, *Being and Time,* Part I, had three distinct tasks, each task corresponding to one of the Part I's three divisions:

- first (SZ I.1): to establish what the existential e-ject is and how it makes sense of things, and to ground such sense-making capabilities in man's radical thrown-openness as ἀλήθεια-1.
- second (SZ I.2): to show that thrown-openness is mortal, to argue that it can be "taken over" in an act of resolve, and to interpret it in terms of "temporality," which is the basis for human historicity.[5]
- third (SZ I.3): to show how "temporality" generates the "temporal" horizon for all forms of being—this under the rubric of "clearing and meaningful presence" (*Lichtung und Anwesenheit*) or "time and being."[6]

In short, "fundamental ontology" (SZ I *in toto*) was to show that and how meaningful presence—"being in general"—is made possible by and occurs only within human openedness as the clearing.[7] The early Heidegger articulated this thrown-open clearing as the hermeneutical "horizon" sustained by ex-sistence as "transcendence."[8] Later and more adequately he spelled it out as

3. See chapter 3, note 183, and GA 26: 179.20–21 = 143.24–5: "insofern bei Parmenides zum erstenmal zur Sprache kommt, daß Sein subjektsbezogen ist."

4. SZ 7.24–27 = 27.7–9. Plotinus thematizes the "transcendental turn" at *Enneads* V 1: 1.31–32: τί ὂν ζητεῖ γνωστέον αὐτῇ, ἵνα αὐτὴν πρότερον μάθῃ, εἰ δύναμιν ἔχει τοῦ τὰ τοιαῦτα ζητεῖν: "It [the soul] should know what it is as an investigating soul, so that it may learn first about itself, whether it has the power to investigate things of this kind" (Armstrong). More literally: "It is necessary for the soul to know what kind of being is doing the searching . . . (etc.)."

5. See chapter 3, notes 137–42.

6. "Clearing and meaningful presence": GA 14: 90.2 = 73.2 and GA 11: 151.21–28 = xx.25–33. Heidegger summarized other topics to be covered in SZ I.3 at GA 24: §6 (on 4 May 1927). See chapter 7.

7. GA 7: 186.31–32 = 185.25–26: Being arrives "in den geöffneten Bereich des Menschenwesens." On fundamental ontology, see chapter 7, below. On ex-sistence's openness as "existential spatiality" see SZ 132.32–33 = 171.8 and §§ 22–24.

8. Heidegger understands "transcendence" (= ex-sistence qua being ahead and beyond—that is, open) as "das Offenhalten des Horizontes, in dem das Sein des Seienden vorgängig erblickbar wird": GA 3: 123.28–30 = 87.24–25. See GA 9: 172.18–19 = 132.35–36: "in der

"the realm of dis-closedness, the clearing (that is, the realm of intelligibility)"[9] opened up by man's ap-propri-ation.

In turn, *Being and Time*, Part II, was to carry out a phenomenological "dismantling" of the history of ontology, running in reverse chronological order from Kant (SZ II.1) through Descartes (SZ II.2) to Aristotle (SZ II.3). The following diagram outlines the plan of the book, with the shaded areas indicating the divisions that were actually published.

SZ I.1	**SZ I.2**	**SZ I.3**
What ex-sistence is (ch. 1–2) How it makes sense of things (ch. 3) How it is the clearing (ch. 5–6)	Mortality (ch. 1) Resolve and authenticity (ch. 2–3) Temporality and historicity (ch. 3 and 5)	How time (i.e., the temporal "horizon") determines all formations and regions of being as the meaningful presence of things.

SZ II.1	**SZ II.2**	**SZ II.3**
Kant (= GA 3)	Descartes	Aristotle

Let us review some earlier remarks about terminology. Heidegger's term for any concrete, personal instance of hermeneutical openedness is *Dasein,* whereas his precise word for the "essence" or ontological structure of any concrete, personal ex-sistence is *Existenz* or *Da-sein* (usually hyphenated, but Heidegger is not always consistent). I translate both terms equally as ex-sistence (the context tells whether *Dasein* or *Da-sein*/*Existenz* is meant), intentionally misspelled and hyphenated so as to call attention to the etymology of the word: *ex* + *sistere*: "to be made to stand ahead [of oneself] and beyond [whatever one encounters]"—that is, to stand "open."[10] What one is ahead and beyond *into* is meaningfulness as such and, as the basis for that, the clearing. We note that the verb *sistere* does not mean "to stand" (by one's own power, as it were) but "to be *made* to stand," which in the present case draws attention to the

ontologischen Wahrheit, d.h. aber in der Transzendenz selbst." GA 27: 207.13–14: "gründet die ontologische Wahrheit in der Transzendenz."

9. GA 16: 424.20–21 = 5.14–15: "der Bereich der Unverborgenheit oder Lichtung (Verstehbarkeit)." See GA 9: 199.21 = 152.24: "[das] Offene des Begreifens."

10. See Heidegger's own intentional misspelling at GA 83: 69.4 and 73.5.

inexorable *thrown*-openedness of both ex-sistence as one's ontological structure and ex-sistence as one's own personal life.[11]

The distinction between ex-sistence as personal and ex-sistence as structural is supremely important. The first refers to any one of us as living ahead in a range of concrete possibilities, whereas the second refers to our very essence as possibility. To be a *Dasein* means that, as possibility, one has always already (i.e., structurally, by one's very essence) exceeded oneself-as-actuality. Human being is structurally ἐπέκεινα, an *excessus.* "Higher than actuality is possibility," Heidegger wrote, not just as a jab at Husserl[12] but more importantly as an inversion of the classical metaphysical tradition (Aristotle, Augustine, Aquinas) according to which human beings are in movement toward full actualization (whether or not they ever reach that goal) in imitation of God as pure act.[13] Such movement is the dynamism of filling out the limits/πέρας of one's essence; and in that project, actuality (to *actually* be) stands higher than possibility (the *ability* to be), just as a hundred real thalers make one richer than a hundred possible thalers.[14] But Heidegger reverses that. Now the maxim that governs human being is no longer μηδὲν ἄγαν ("Nothing in excess") but rather πὰν ἄγαν: human being is *fundamentally* a matter of excess.[15] With that, we reach the end of the worldview that stretches from Platonic ἔρως and Aristotle's κινεῖ ὡς ἐρώμενον, through Gregory of Nyssa's ἐπέκτασις and Augustine's *donec requiescat in te*, all the way down to Hegel's "development and realization of Spirit."[16]

The *Da* of *Da-sein* should never be translated as "here" or "there," as is customary in the current scholarship (for example: being there, being here, being

11. "Inexorable": that which you cannot beg your way out of: in + ex + orare. Beginning with SZ I.1, chapter 5, he often uses the hyphenated "Da-sein" (with the sense of "structurally being the openedness") as another way of saying "Existenz." Unfortunately, Heidegger frequently uses "Dasein" when he means "Existenz."

12. SZ 38.29–30 = 63.2: "Höher als die Wirklichkeit steht die *Möglichkeit.*" Heidegger's emphasis. He was not so subtly hinting that phenomenology as "actualized" by Husserl still had further and very different possibilities—namely, Heidegger's own work.

13. See, for example, Aquinas: "Intantum est autem perfectum unumquodque, inquantum est actu": Everything is perfect insofar as it is actual. (*Summa theologiae*, I, q. 5, a. 1, c.) Moreover, man's perfection lies in the vision of the divine essence: ibid., I/II q. 3, a. 8, c.: "ultima et perfecta beatitudo non potest esse nisi in visione divinae essentiae." In fact, the perfection of *all* things consists in their being like God: "ultimus rerum finis sit Deo assimilari," *Summa contra gentiles*, III, 19, 1.

14. Kant, *Critique of Pure Reason*, B 627.

15. Nothing in excess: Plato, *Protagoras* 343b3.

16. Aristotle, *Metaphysics* XII 7, 1072b3: God moves [the world] by being desired. Gregory: *De vita Moysis* in *Patrologia Graeca* 44, 401A.9–11: [ἡ ψυχὴ] συνεπεκτεινομένη: the soul striving for perfection (see Philippians 3:13). Augustine, *Confessiones* I. 1. 1, *Patrologia Latina* 32, 661.4–6: the unquiet heart seeks rest in God. Hegel, *Philosophie der Weltgeschichte*, 938: "dieser Entwicklungsgang und das wirkliche Werden des Geistes."

t/here). Heidegger insists that "*Da ≠ ibi und ubi*"[17] (the *Da* of *Da-sein* is not a locative adverb at all: "here" or "there"). Rather, the *Da* should always be interpreted as "openedness" or "the open" in the sense of man's being *thrown*-open, "[being] brought into one's openedness but *not* of one's own accord."[18] "The *Da* means appropriated openness—the appropriated clearing of [i.e., for] being."[19]

> "*Da-sein*" is a key word of my thinking and thus the occasion for major misunderstandings. For me, "*Da-sein*" does not mean the same as "Here I am!" but rather—if I might express it in a perhaps impossible French—*être le-là*. And the *le-là* is precisely 'Αλήθεια: disclosedness—openness.[20]

Heidegger speaks of "our question about *openness* as such (*Da-sein*),"[21] and he writes that the *Da* of *Dasein*

> should designate the openedness where things can be present for human beings, and human beings for themselves.[22]
>
> . . . being human, as such, is distinguished by the fact that to be, in its own unique way, is to be this openedness.[23]
>
> The human being occurs in such a way that he or she is the "*Da*," that is, the clearing of being.[24]

17. GA 71: 211.5: "Da does not mean 'there' or 'where.'" "Die 'Seinsfrage' in *Sein und Zeit*," *Heidegger Studies* 27, 2011, 9.27–30: "'Da' nicht demonstrative (wie 'dort) ontisch, / sondern: ekstatisch—dimensioniert / die Lichtung des Anwesens für jegliches Hier und Jetzt und dergleichen."

18. SZ 284.11–12 = 329.35–36: "Seiend ist das Dasein geworfenes, *nicht* von ihm selbst in sein Da gebracht."

19. GA 71: 211.8–9 = 180.1–2: "Das Da bedeutet das ereignete Offene—die ereignete Lichtung des Seins."

20. Heidegger, "Lettre à Monsieur Beaufret, (23 novembre 1945)," 182.27–184.3: "'Dasein' bedeutet für mich nicht so sehr 'me voilà!' sondern, wenn ich es in einem vielleicht unmöglichen Französisch sagen darf: être-le-là. Und le-là ist gleich 'Αλήθεια: Unverborgenheit—Offenheit."

21. GA 45: 154.27–28 = 134.18–19.

22. *Zollikoner Seminare*, 156.35–157.3 = 118.22–24: "[Das Da des Daseins] soll die Offenheit nennen, in der für den Menschen Seiendes anwesend sein kann, auch er selbst für sich selbst." GA 27: 136.13–15: "Das Dasein is dasjenige Seiende, das so etwas wie ein 'Da' ist. Das 'Da': ein Umkreis von Offenbarkeit." Ibid., 137.7–8: "eine Sphäre von Offenbarkeit."

23. *Zollikoner Seminare*, 157.31–32 = 121.14–15: "das Menschheit [ist] als solches ausgezeichnet, auf seine Weise diese Offenheit selbst zu sein." GA 2: 216, note a = 157 note: Draußensein: "das Da; Ausgesetztheit als offene Stelle."

24. GA 9: 325.20–21 = 248.11–12: "Der Mensch west so, daß er das 'Da,' das heißt die Lichtung des Seins, ist." *Zollikoner Seminare* 351.14–17 = 281.31–282.1: "Die Offenständigkeit des Da-seins 'ist' das Ausstehen [= sustaining] der Lichtung. Lichtung und

> The *Da* refers to that clearing in which things stand as a whole, in such a way that, in this *Da*, the being of open things shows itself and at the same time withdraws. To *be* this *Da* is a determination of man.[25]

> [Ex-sistence] *is* itself the clearing.[26]

> The clearing: the *Da*—*is* itself *ex-sistence.*[27]

> The point is to experience *Da-sein* in the sense that human being itself *is* the *Da*, that is, the openedness of being, in that a person undertakes to preserve it, and in preserving it, to unfold it (See *Sein und Zeit*, p. 132f. [= 170f.]).[28]

> Ex-sistence must be understood as being-the-clearing. *Da* is specifically the word for the open expanse.[29]

> Ex-sistence [*das Da-sein*] is the way in which the open, the clearing, occurs, within which being as cleared is opened up to human understanding.[30]

> *To be—the clearing*—to be cast into the clearing as the open = to-be-the-*Da.*[31]

The distinction between ex-sistence as personal/existentiel and ex-sistence as structural/existent*ial* (which, unfortunately, Heidegger tends to blur) comes into its own in Heidegger's discussion of "decision" or "resolve" (*Entschluss*) in *Being and Time* § 62. My ex-sistence is always mine alone, and this fact

---

Da-sein gehören im vorhinein zusammen und die bestimmende Einheit des Zusammen ist das Ereignis." GA 14: 35.23 = 27.33: "[die] Lichtung des Da-seins."

25. GA 45: 213.1–4 = 180.6–9. GA 66: 321.12 = 285.28: "Das Da lichtet sich im Da-*sein.*"

26. SZ 133.5 = 171.22: "daß es [= Dasein] selbst die Lichtung ist." GA 66: 328.1–2 = 291.13–14: "Das Da-sein ist der aus dem Er-eignis ereignete geschichtliche Grund der Lichtung des Seyns." Italicized in the original. GA 69: 101.12–13: "*Die Lichtung—sein*—in sie als Offenes sich loswerfen = das *Da*-sein." GA 66: 129.5 = 109.7–8: "das 'Da', die Lichtung." Heidegger will go so far as to say that the Da "gehört zum Sein selbst, '*ist*' Sein selbst und heißt darum das Da-sein": GA 6:2: 323.14–15 = 218.4–5.

27. "Die 'Seinsfrage' in *Sein und Zeit*," 9.23: "die Lichtung: das Da—*ist* selbst *das Dasein.*" See GA 14: 35.23–24 = 27.31–33. GA 3: 229.10–11 = 160.32–33: "ist der Mensch das Da, mit dessen Sein der eröffnende Einbruch in das Seiende geschieht." GA 70: 125.12: "[die] Lichtung des Da-, die als Da-sein west."

28. GA 15: 415.10–13 = 88.18–21: "Es gilt, das Da-sein in dem Sinne zu erfahren, daß der Mensch das 'Da', d.h. die Offenheit des Seins für ihn, selbst *ist*, indem er es übernimmt, sie zu bewahren und bewahrend zu entfalten." (Vgl. "Sein und Zeit," S. 132f.)

29. GA 15: 380.11–12 = 69.4–5: "Dasein muß als die-Lichtung-sein verstanden werden. Das Da is nämlich das Wort für die offene Weite." At SZ 147.2–3 = 187.13–14 Heidegger speaks of "[die] Gelichtetheit, als welche wir die Erschlossenheit des Da charakterisierten." GA 66: 100.30 = 84.11: "Das Offene der Lichtung."

30. GA 49: 60.25–27: "Das Da-sein ist vielmehr die Weise, wie das Offene, die Lichtung west, in der 'das Sein' als gelichtetes dem menschlichen Verstehen sich öffnet."

31. GA 69: 101.12: "*Die Lichtung—sein*—in sie als Offenes sich loswerfen = das *Da*-sein."

entails that the responsibility for choosing how I am to live rests exclusively with me and with no one else. I have a choice: I can either embrace my dynamic and mortal structure as ex-sistence, along with all that it entails, or I can flee it. When (personal) ex-sistence embraces its (structural) ex-sistence, Heidegger says, one is "authentic," the self-responsible author of his or her own finite life. When ex-sistence flees its ex-sistence, it is "inauthentic," insofar as it refuses to fully understand and embrace itself and "become what it already is."[32] (See the following chapter.)

Heidegger did not pull out of thin air his notion of ex-sistence as possibility: ahead and open. Rather, some of that can be glimpsed *in ovo* by comparing what he had to say about life in general, and animal life in particular, with what he holds regarding ex-sistence. As we broach the centrality of human openedness with regard to intelligibility as such, we begin with a discussion of four aspects of life as Heidegger presents them in his 1929–1930 course, "Basic Problems of Metaphysics."

1. *Life as possibility and self-disclosure.*

For Heidegger as for Aristotle, life, whether it be the ζωή of plants and animals or the βίος of human beings, is necessarily bound up with possibilities of itself. Life in general is an *Entheben in das Mögliche*: a being lifted up and away into the possible. Life's actuality is to be caught up in possibility.[33]

> In the last analysis, potentiality and possibility belong precisely to the essence of the [living thing] in its actuality, in a quite specific sense.[34]

In its most basic form, life is a natural drive to be underway to more of itself, an ongoing unfolding of itself (*Sich-zeitigung*) so as to appear in a new εἶδος, which in turn generates ever more possibilities, including its ever-present possibility of death.[35] Insofar as life consists in constantly bringing forth

32. SZ 145.40–41 = 186.4–5, implicitly referring to γένοι' οἷος ἐσσί μαθών: Pindar, *Pythian Odes* II, 72 (also GA 40: 108.26–28 = 111.12–14). For Heidegger, "inauthenticity" is a matter of being alienated from one's essence: SZ 281.20–21 = 326.30: "das 'Wesen' nicht trifft."

33. GA 29/30: 528.4 = 363.19: Entheben; 321.26–30 = 220.3–6: Möglichkeit-Haben . . . nicht anderes ist als dieses; 343.22–24 = 235.42: Fähigkeit gehört zum Wirklichsein.

34. GA 29/30: 343.18–20 = 235.38–40.

35. GA 29/30: 331.1 = 226.31: Drängen zu; 334.1–3 = 228.33–35: treibt sich; Vorgetriebensein; 335.25–26 = 230.5–6: Hineintreiben zu. (As noted in chapter 3, *Zeitigung* or *Sich-zeitigung* should never be translated as "temporalization" but always in terms of unfolding and opening up.)

something new of itself, it is a natural process of disclosure.[36] The reason? Life is a kind of φύσις (*Sich-zeitigung*: self-unfolding), and φύσις is a kind of κίνησις (a being-moved), and κίνησις is a kind of μεταβολή (change whereby something hidden comes to light), and μεταβολή is a kind of ἀλήθεια.[37] Φύσις/κίνησις = μεταβολή/ἀλήθεια, the single process of a natural thing's bringing-forth from itself what was heretofore hidden.

But the living thing is not thrown or appropriated into just any possibilities. Most basically it is a *Selbst-ermöglichung*, an enabling of *itself*, in the sense that it is the very possibility of becoming its own future-possible self. A living thing naturally sets forth its own what-for (*Wozu*) and sets itself forth into it, while always remaining with itself as the source of this drive.[38] Unlike a tool, which gets its capacity to serve a purpose from its maker, living things pro-duce their own ability to achieve their what-for. They are self-enabling acts of becoming.[39]

2. *Life as having to be.*

Every living thing—and not just a human being—is stamped with the essential characteristic of *Zu-sein*, which means both having to be as possibility and having to become itself as possibility in order to stay alive. A living thing has its τέλος as self-preservation (*Selbst-erhaltung*).[40] It is driven to sur-vive, to keep on keeping on, until its ability to supply its own self-sustaining self-empowerment runs out naturally or is cut off. This also entails that whatever is alive is able to die at any moment. Here we are not referring to the obvious fact that the living thing, whether plant, animal or human being, moves diachronically in the direction of its future demise. Rather, the living thing is *always at-the-point-of-death: zum Ende, zum Tode.*[41] For any living thing, to live is to live mortally, that is (consciously or not), ever shouldering up against its own ultimate possibility, which is to have no more possibilities and so to be dead.[42]

---

36. GA 45: 94.9–10 = 83.38–39: "Hervor-bringen heißt Ans-licht-bringen." This is said properly of human being but *mutatis mutandis* applies to all life.

37. GA 9: 249.19–29 = 191.6–17.

38. GA 29/30: 339.17–18 = 232.33–35: Sich-*vor*-in das eigene Wozu; 339.35 = 233.6: Sich-in-sich-selbst-Vorlegen. GA 9: 258.16–17 = 198.6: in seine ἀρχή zurückstellen.

39. GA 29/30: 325.11 and .16–7 = 222.27–28, 32: seine eigene Bewegtheit leitet, einleitet und umleitet; wiederherstellt und erneuert; Selbstherstellung, Selbstleitung, Selbsterneuerung.

40. GA 29/30: 339.23 = 232.38, and 377.22 = 259.34.

41. Being-at-the-point-of-death: SZ 329.37–38 = 378.20–21: "Es [Dasein] hat nicht ein Ende, an dem es nur aufhört, sondern *existiert endlich*."

42. GA 29/30: 343.24–26 = 236.1–3: "Nur was fähig ist und noch fähig ist, lebt; was nicht mehr fähig ist . . . das lebt nicht mehr." See GA 27: 331.33–332.2–3: "[Dasein] existiert ständig entlang diesem Rande des Nicht." This is said properly of human being but analogously fits plant and animal life.

All of this is structural and essential to life—it is of a priori necessity. When we speak of the living thing as "thrown" or "appropriated" into possibility, both of those terms indicate a living thing's "facticity": that which it cannot not be. (The term "facticity," like "being at the point of death," applies properly only to human beings, but analogically to all life. The analogy here is one of proper proportionality rather than of πρὸς ἕν attribution.) Life entails always being more than it is *de facto* but never more than it is *faktisch*, never more than the self-possibilizing that it is "obliged" to be.[43]

3. *Life as a bivalent movement.*

Another aspect of the structure of life is the *bivalence* of its movement. Living is not only an instinctual movement that is stretched out into possibility (*Hin zu, Weg-von-sich*).[44] It also *remains one with itself*: "an exiting from itself in the essence of its being, yet without abandoning itself."[45] Life is a constant presence to itself, a "retaining itself within itself."[46] A living thing, Heidegger says,

> does not lose itself in the sense that an instinctual impulse to something would leave itself behind. Rather it retains itself precisely in such a drive and remains "its self," as we might say, in this drive and driving.[47]

On the one hand, life is bound to its future, to a further becoming beyond what its previous becoming has already achieved. On the other hand, it constantly remains with the source of such movement, a source that in fact it itself is. This is what Heidegger calls a living thing's "self-like character" or "ownness" throughout change.[48] To take the plant as an example: Out of its roots and stem emerge the leaves, then the bud, which opens up as the flower, which in turn gives way to the fruit. The plant actualizes new possibilities for itself while still remaining the same plant, rooted in its ἀρχή, the source of its own growth.[49] Its *Weg-von-sich* or being-ahead-of-itself is always a *return to itself* in the sense of remaining *bei sich*: with itself. It is ever ahead-as-returning.

---

43. See SZ 145.32–36 = 185.22–27.

44. GA 29/30: 343.2–3 = 235.24–25.

45. GA 29/30: 531.15–16 = 365.36–37: "ein Heraustreten aus sich selbst ist, ohne sich doch zu verlassen." This is said properly of human being but applies analogously to animal life.

46. GA 29/30: 342.19 = 235.9: bei sich selbst einzubehalten.

47. GA 29/30: 340.29–32 = 233.32–234.2.

48. GA 29/30: 339.34 = 233.5: Selbstcharakter; 342.16 = 235.7: Eigen-tumlichkeit: ownness (McNeill: "proper peculiarity"); 347.25–26 = 238.40: Bei-sich-sein.

49. GA 9: 293.9–11 = 224.5–7: φύσις as "ein In-sich-*zurück*-Gehen, zu *sich*, das ein Aufgehen bleibt."

4. *Life as openness.*

When it comes to animals, the a priori stretch into possibility wherein the animal retains its ownness has a certain (delimited) character of openness about it. As an instinctual drive to more of itself, animal life has

> the character of a traversing, of a dimension in the formal sense. . . . Dimension is not yet understood in a spatial sense here, although the dimensional character of drive is . . . presumably the condition of the possibility of the animal's being able to traverse a spatial domain in a quite determinate manner.[50]
>
> We must say that the animal is related to . . . and that its captivation and behavior display an *openness* for.[51]

This "dimension" names the animal's limited openness that "clears the way" for sense perception. In their very different ways of being ψυχή, both animals and humans are open and intentional in the quite broad sense of (1) going beyond any supposedly monadic self-enclosure and (2) being disclosive of what is other than themselves.[52] For Heidegger, the nature of ψυχή—that is, of life—is *entbergen*, dis-closing something heretofore hidden.[53] To live is to be beyond any supposed encapsulation. It is to be open to and disclosive both of itself and of something other, which in the animal's case is the sensible object (αἰσθητόν) of the corresponding sense-faculty (αἴσθησις).[54]

In contrast to human ex-sistence, Heidegger speaks of the animal *qua* sentient as *captivated* by what it is open to. The sense organs "have no choice," as it were, about their corresponding objects. The eye sees light, no matter what. The alternative to seeing light is not to see at all. We noted that animals as sentient are, in a limited way, open, and to that degree "alethic," disclosive of their corresponding objects.[55] Or to reverse the trajectory, the senses are *opened up by* their respective objects in a process that Heidegger calls *Enthemmung* ("dis-inhibiting"). However, the animal's sense-openness is restricted to taking merely what the sensible appearances offer and dealing with it only within the

50. GA 29/30: 334.9–15 = 229.1–8.

51. GA 29/30: 361.31–33 = 248.31–32; see 377.5–6 = 259.22: immer im Offensein zu dem, wofür es offen ist.

52. Regarding animal "intentionality": GA 29/30: 350.3–5 = 240.22–24: eine Bewegung nach; ein Greifen nach; Das Sehen ist das Sehen des *Gesichteten*, das Hören ist das Hören des *Gehörten*.

53. *Zollikoner Seminare*, 47.16–21 = 37.25–31. For human beings as disclosive, *Nicomachean Ethics* VI 2, 1139b12: Of both parts of the "rational soul" (τὸ λόγον ἔχον, 1102a28), ἀλήθεια τὸ ἔργον.

54. SZ 33.30–35 = 57.11–17; 147.8–9 = 187.19–20.

55. SZ 33.30–32 = 57.11–13: "die αἴσθησις, das schlichte, sinnliche Vernehmen von etwas."

limitations of instinct. The animal "behaves" (*benehmen*) rather than properly "relating itself to" (*sich verhalten zu*) in the way a human being does. "Instinctual activity is not a recognitive self-directing toward objectively present things, but a *behaving*."[56]

> We can see more and more clearly in particular respects the essential contrast between the animal's being open and the *world-openness* of man. Man's being open is a being held toward . . . whereas the animal's being open is a matter of being-taken-by . . . and thereby a being absorbed in its encircling ring.[57]

This confinement to behavior is what Heidegger means by "captivation" (*Benommenheit*). He also calls it "putting aside" (*Beiseitigung*)—that is, the animal does not recognize those appearances *as* what and how they are but rather "leaves those meanings aside." The objects *as such* remain withdrawn from animal perception, unable to be apprehended as something intelligible. In that sense, "the animal is separated from man by an abyss."[58]

In summary: Anything, including human being, that has life (1) has its actuality as possibility and self-disclosure (*Sich-ermöglichung*, ἀλήθεια); (2) has to be and become the possibility it is (*Zu-sein*); (3) is a bivalent movement of aheadness while remaining with itself (*Weg von sich, bei sich*); and (4) is to some degree open (*offen*) and thus disclosive. We may now examine how these elements, which pertain to life in general, get transformed as we cross the abyss and encounter human ex-sistence.

Much of what Heidegger has to say about ex-sistence derives from Aristotle's notion of movement (κίνησις), a thing's intrinsic suitability for and anticipation of a state of affairs which it has not completely realized or at which it has not yet fully arrived. (The "anticipation" can be either the thing's own intending of that state of affairs, as with living things, or its being *intended for* it—for example, by a craftsman.) Heidegger indirectly expresses the centrality of movement by placing possibility higher than actuality.[59] In the case of human being, the "actuality" of ex-sistence consists entirely in living *as* possibility (as existential) *into* possibilities (as existentiel). Our actuality resides in our

56. GA 29/30: 353.32–34 = 243.10–11.

57. GA 29/30: 498.3–7 = 343.12–15.

58. GA 29/30: 384.3–4 = 264.10. This, of course, has to be read and corrected in the light of contemporary studies of animal intelligence.

59. See above, this chapter, note 12.

being structurally *pulled open*, drawn out ahead of ourselves.[60] The "itself" that we are ahead of is the common-sense self—what I shall call the "crowd-self" (*das Man*, usually translated as the "they-self").[61] Rather than accepting *that* as our true way of being, Heidegger insists that our actuality is our structural capacity to be and to do (*Seinkönnen*), including our capacity to die. The question of authentic selfhood has to do with how we relate to that ultimate possibility.

The possibility which we structurally are is also a strict necessity. It is not a power that we occasionally exercise, but rather is what we have to be (*Zu-sein*), what we cannot *not* be.

> Ex-sistent human being does not encounter itself as something just out there in the world. . . . As thrown it has been thrown *into ex-sistence*. It ex-sists as an entity that has to be as it is and as it can be.[62]

The "essence" of a human being (insofar as we can speak of an essence here at all) consists in its *having to be constitutionally ahead of itself*, as possibility, amidst possibilities.[63] Such essential stretched-out-ness is what Heidegger calls "thrownness." And since being thrown ahead = being pulled *open*, the stretch into possibilities is thrown-*open*-ness. But with us, being thrown-open always entails living into meaning-giving possibilities. Ex-sistence thus unfolds as—is thrown open as—the open region of possible meaningfulness.

In its most basic sense, openedness as the possibility of intelligibility remains the one and only *factum*, τὸ πράγμα αὐτό, of all Heidegger's work.[64] He also called this the question of the dis-closedness (ἀλήθεια-1) of the clearing.

> The question about the "intelligibility of being," i.e., about the thrown-open realm, the openness wherein being-at-all (not just things) is first disclosed to an understanding—*that* is the question about the "disclosedness of being."[65]

If the thrown-open clearing is the core of Heidegger's thought, we may expect to find it at the heart of *Being and Time*. In that work Heidegger treats such hermeneutical openedness first in terms of its structure and implications (SZ I.1)

60. On "pulled" or "drawn out" see GA 8: 11.6–10 = 9.13–17. Here "open" is a metaphor that, along with "non-closure," indicates "the still-possible" in contrast to "closure" in the sense of actuality without further possibility.

61. SZ 193.25–26 = 238.2–4: "das Selbst im Sinne des Man-selbst."

62. SZ 276.13–18 = 321.8–12: "Seiendes, das, wie es ist und sein kann, zu sein hat."

63. SZ 42.4–6 = 67.10–12, and GA 2: 56, notes c and d = 41, notes ‡ and §.

64. GA 49: 56.20: "die Offenheit, die Lichtung."

65. GA 49: 56.31–34: "Die Frage nach dem 'Sinn von Sein', d.h. nach dem Entwurfsbereich, dem Offenen, darin einem Verstehen 'Sein' überhaupt (nicht erst ein Seiendes) sich enthüllt, ist die Frage nach der 'Wahrheit des Seins,'" my emphasis. See GA 9: 201.30–33 = 154.12–15 and 377.22–26 = 286.30–33 for other formulations of this position. GA 66: 84.13–14 = 70.17: "Diese Lichtung ist die *Wahrheit* des Seyns, welches Seyn selbst die Wahrheit *ist*."

and then in terms of how human beings can embrace it and become authentically "temporal" and "historical" (SZ I.2). The unpublished SZ I.3 was to show that, once we personally take over our existential openedness, it functions as the hermeneutical horizon for a transformed and transforming understanding of how meaningful presence is possible at all.[66]

Heidegger describes the openness of ex-sistence as a bivalence that may be illustrated by the diagram below. The larger arc, which moves from left to right, describes ex-sistence as stretched out beyond the actuality of the common-sense self and thrown ahead as possibility. (Heidegger calls this aheadness an ἐπόρεξις, a "being stretched towards").[67] This arc also describes the area of "the open"—that is, the "*Da*" of *Dasein* or the "ex-" of ex-sistence. The smaller arc, which moves from right to left, indicates what Heidegger calls the *Zurückkommen*, the "return" of ex-sistence to itself, which in fact is ex-sistence's *always remaining* with itself *in* its stretched-forwardness. We noted this above as a structural aheadness-*as*-return (*Sich-vorweg-sein als Zurückkommen*).[68] That is, it is not a matter of one moment (return) occurring after the other moment (aheadness), "chronologically," as it were. Rather, the diagram presents what Heidegger described as the always-already-operative structure that constitutes human being. It illustrates the existential structure of ex-sistence as the basis for existentiel acts of making sense of things.

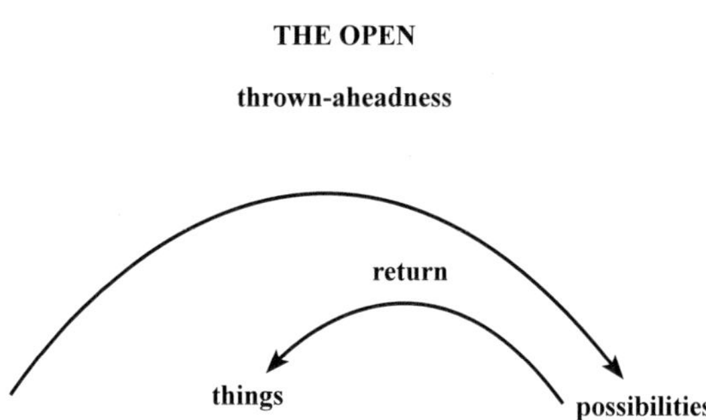

66. Re transformed and transforming, see GA 14: 69.3–4 = 61.3–4: The answer to Heidegger's basic question "müßte. . . in einer Verwandlung des Denkens bestehen, nicht in einer Aussage über einen Sachverhalt." See GA 45: 214.18 = 181.7–8: "eine *Verwandlung des Menschseins* selbst." Also GA 29/30: 423.2–4 = 292.6–7. But this is rare: GA 26: 253.10–11 = 196.14–15; GA 27: 336.4–6; and GA 69: 56.9–10: selten. This is Plato's περιάγειν, *Republic* VII, 515c7.

67. GA 26: 181.8 = 143.31—that is, ἐπί + ὄρεξις. (To my knowledge, the term does not appear in Greek literature or philosophy.) It is important to remember, however, that this is the *structure* of ex-sistence (it is existential), not a human act (existentiel). GA 36/37: 177.19 = 137.19: "herausgetreten sein in die Auseinandersetzung des Seins."

68. GA 21: 147.24–26 = 124.19–20.

This a priori openedness is the same as our ineluctable engagement with meaningfulness and with the clearing that makes such meaningfulness possible—what is usually called "being-in-the-world" (*In-der-Welt-sein*). But we saw earlier that when properly interpreted, this phrase comes out as *In-der-Bedeutsamkeit-sein* in the sense of our structural familiarity with the world of meaningfulness. Being-in-the-world-of-meaningfulness is what makes possible the existentiel-personal aheadness-and-return of our everyday activities. In practical matters, for example, we understand this-thing-here in terms of the purpose we have already projected, and we do so within a world of meaningfulness that shapes our understanding of things. Thus,

> in taking hold of a tool, we return to the tool and understand it in terms of the work-world that has always already been opened up.[69]

And in general:

> Factical ex-sistence, understanding itself and its world ec-statically in the unity of this openedness, comes back *from* those horizons *to* the things encountered within them. Coming back to these things understandingly is the existential meaning of letting things be encountered by making them [meaningfully] present.[70]

We have already seen that intelligibility is not a property that attaches to things but an essential characteristic (an "existential") of ex-sistence alone. This entails that things attain to their meaningfulness only when they are discovered *with* human ex-sistence—that is, when they come to be understood.[71] We can be involved with things only because we are first engaged with meaningfulness as such. In other words, the togetherness of the current (*jeweilig*) possibilities of things with the current possibilities of our ex-sistence is what gives those things the meanings they have. Put schematically: In the practical realm, our needs serve as final purposes (= 1). They are the basis of the task we need to perform (= 2) and thus are the final reason why things get the meanings they have (= 3).[72]

69. SZ 352.35–36 = 404.2–3: "kommt aus der je schon erschlossenen Werkwelt im Zugriff auf ein Zeug zurück."

70. SZ 366.14–19 = 417.30–34, my emphasis. See ibid., 107.39–108.2 = 142.26–28; 296.21–22 = 344.4–6; 353.27–29 = 404.34–36; 359.41–360.2 = 411.15–17. Also GA 77: 111.26–27 = 72.21–22: Transcendence: "das sich auf die Gegenstände und auf das Vorstellen der Gegenstände zurückbezieht." GA 21: 192.27–28 = 162.19–20: "Dieses Gegenwärtigen, *in dem ich ständig lebe*."

71. SZ 151.22–24 = 192.35–37.

72. SZ 297.15–26 = 344.1–9. In the theoretical realm, subjects (analogous to no. 3) get their meanings from possible predicates (analogous to no. 2), which in turn get their meaning from the world of possibilities that we are familiar with (no. 3). In that case, one takes

HOW MEANING IS ASSIGNED

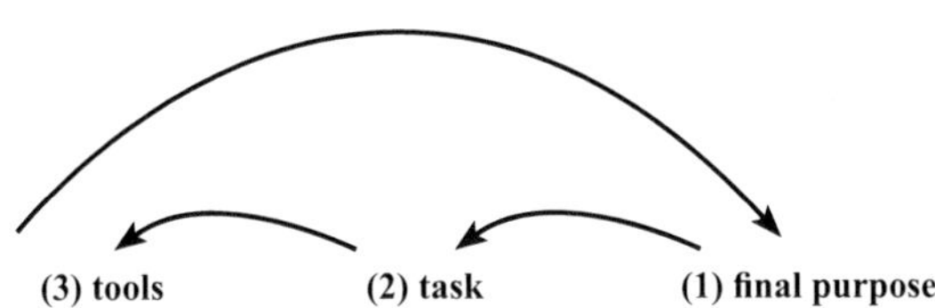

In our practical experience, things come in ensembles, and what holds things together in such wholes is their suitability for (*Bewandtnis*) and referral to (*Verweisung*) some ultimate purpose (*Worumwillen*) of ours. Heidegger famously describes a concatenation of such referrals in the practical order: hammers are referred to nails, which are referred to fastening boards together, which is referred to making a *house*. The house is the task-to-be-done (the ἔργον), from which the hammer, nails, and boards derive their meanings. But that task (no. 2 in the above diagram) in turn derives *its* meaning from some need of ours, drawn from among our possibilities—for example, the need for shelter. That need serves as the final purpose (the τέλος: no. 1 in the diagram) whence both tools and task get their meaning in this (broadly speaking) "teleological" theory of meaning.

To summarize: Early on, Heidegger conceived of ex-sistence as intrinsically meta-physical (μετὰ τὰ φυσικά).[73] That is, we are intentional in the full sense of having both sensuous and categorical intuitions; and therefore we do not just bump up against things but in fact have always already transcended them by (1) understanding their possible meanings and in terms of that (2) returning to those things in order to render them present in terms of those meanings. Say I'm camping and need to pound in tent pegs to set up some shelter against the coming rain. I live "ahead" in the need of shelter—and then, coming "back" from that need, I look around for my mallet . . . and realize I have forgotten it. So, instead, I "come back" from my purpose ("gotta hammer in those tent pegs") to that stone over there, which I can use for that purpose and which I therefore "make meaningfully present" as an ersatz mallet. "Com-

something *as* something (the subject *in terms of* a predicate) rather than as *for* a practical task.

73. GA 9: 118.27, 30–32 and 121.34–35–122.1–3 = 93.32, 34–36 and 96.7–10; GA 7: 111.11–16 = 420.10–14.

ing back to things with understanding means . . . letting ourselves encounter them by rendering them meaningfully present."[74] This example illustrates the "meta-physics" that we structurally are in the practical order (analogous to what Kant called "natural metaphysics").[75]

Soon enough, however, it became clear to Heidegger that, more fundamentally, ex-sistence is *meta*-metaphysical. That is, we transcend things *not only* in the sense of already understanding their possible meanings and then returning to the things to give them meaning, but also and above all by being already "beyond" things-*and*-their-meanings and in touch with what makes the meaningfulness of things possible at all. We are not just fully intentional—present to both things *and* their meanings. More basically, we "transcend" things-and-their-meanings *to*—that is to say, we in fact *are*—the thrown-open clearing that makes possible our "natural metaphysical" relation to things-in-their-meanings.[76] Ex-sistence is not only "transcendental" but also "trans-transcendental" or "transcendental to the second power."[77]

No matter how much our engagement with intelligibility may be parsed out into its component moments, it is a strict and original unity that cannot be resolved into anything more primal.[78] If we were to ask what we might be *prior* to our engagement with meaning, such an inquiry would entail that we *already have enacted* an engagement with meaning by simply asking the question, and hence would be moving in a vicious circle. Our very ex-sistence is such an engagement, and absent that, we would not be human, much less able to ask any questions at all. However, without breaking up its unified structure, engagement with the world of intelligibility can be analyzed into its three constitutive moments:

1. the world of meaningfulness: SZ I.1 chapter 3;
2. the self that is engaged with the world of meaningfulness: SZ I.1 chapter 4; and
3. the very *engagement with* the world of meaningfulness: SZ I.1 chapter 5.

74. SZ 366.17–19 = 417.33–34: "Das verstehende Zurückkommen auf . . . ist der existenziale Sinn des gegenwärtigenden Begegnenlassens von Seiendem."

75. *Critique of Pure Reason*, B 21.

76. On "thrown-open clearing," see GA 65: 448.24–25 = 353.27: "die Geworfenheit einer zum Stand gekommenen Lichtung." GA 5: 59.22 = 44.28–29: "die in der Geworfenheit ankommende Offenheit."

77. See *potenziert*: chapter 7, note 118.

78. SZ 53.12 = 78.22: "ein *einheitliches* Phänomen."

We now analyze the third moment above, that of *engagement with* the world of meaningfulness, which Heidegger calls "*In-sein*" in the sense of "being familiar with." In so doing, we are spelling out the structure of *the way ex-sistence holds the clearing open*. Ex-sistence sustains the openedness of the clearing via its bivalent structure of already-aheadness and return. The matter may seem complex but finally is easy to grasp.

THE BIVALENT STRUCTURE OF EX-SISTENCE
AS
SUSTAINING THE CLEARING

1. already ahead	
a. ahead *as* possibility	(*sich vorweg*)
b. already engaged with the world of meaningfulness	(*schon in*)
2. returning to render things meaningfully present	(*Sein bei*)

1. *Already-aheadness*: Ex-sistence is always ahead as possibility among possibilities and thus is already in touch with a range of needs and purposes. In turn, those needs and purposes are meaning-giving insofar as they are the possible meanings of whatever things might satisfy those needs and fulfill those purposes. Heidegger designates this single moment of (a) being ahead as possibility and (b) being already engaged with the world of meaning by the phrase (a) *Sich-vorweg-sein . . . im . . .* (b) *schon-sein-in*.[79] Insofar as we are possibility, we are "away" (*vorweg*) from ourselves-as-actual by being already thrown into (*schon-sein-in*) the realm of possible needs, purposes, and meanings.[80] Being ahead as possibility and being already engaged with meaning are two sides of the same coin: already-ahead-ness.
2. *Return*: In the second moment of its bivalence, ex-sistence is a return from the possible to the actual in order understand (render meaningfully present) the things we meet, and to do so *in terms of* one or another of those possibilities. Heidegger calls this second moment *Sein bei* as

79. SZ 192.11 = 237.11.

80. The aheadness emphasizes our ex-sistentiality, our living *as* possibility. The alreadiness emphasizes facticity: our unfathomable thrownness into a range of meaning-giving possibilities.

Gegenwärtigen. Unfortunately, Macquarrie and Robinson translate *Sein bei* as "being alongside" things, and Stambaugh renders it as "being together with" things. Neither of those phrases captures Heidegger's sense of *rendering things meaningfully present*, which is how we shall interpret the phrase.

Aheadness-and-return, the two unified moments of ex-sistence's engagement with the world of intelligibility, come down to one thing only: λόγος as the structural possibility of making sense of things and of ourselves. Heidegger translates λόγος by the German term *Rede*; but here *Rede* does not mean "speech, talk, discourse" in the sense of a string of sounds endowed with meaning: φωνὴ σημαντική, *vox significativa.*[81] Nor does it mean "language" as a rule-governed system of communication. *Rede*/λόγος refers, rather, to the dis-cursive structure of ex-sistence itself—that is, to the twofold movement whereby we transcend things and then return to render them meaningfully present by taking them in terms of one or another possibility.[82] In fact, in SZ § 67 Heidegger equates *Rede*/λόγος with ex-sistence itself when he places discursivity and ex-sistence in apposition to each other:

> [*die*] *Zeitlichkeit der Rede, das heißt des Daseins überhaupt.*
>
> the thrown-openness of λόγος, that is, of ex-sistence in general.[83]

Heidegger understands λόγος in terms of the verb λέγειν: to collect, synthesize, unite. Ex-sistence as λόγος/*Rede* is first of all the holding together of one's own existential structure as both possibility (thrown-aheadness) and actuality (return). In turn, λόγος/*Rede* as the existent*ial* structure of ex-sistence makes possible the existent*iel* act of holding together (synthesizing) a thing with its meaning. In ontological language this is the act of understanding something in terms of its being.

---

81. Respectively, *De Interpretatione* 4, 16b26, and Thomas Aquinas, *Expositio libri Peryermeneias*, Proemium 3, citing Boethius, *Patrologia Latina*, 64: 301.33 ("De nomine"). See GA 9: 74.24–25 = 59.14–15: "eine Abfolge akustisch objektivierbarer Töne, die mit einer Bedeutung behaftet sind." Also GA 19: 18.33–35 = 13.4–5: "Das Sprechen is also φωνή, ein Verlautbaren, das in sich eine ἑρμηνεία hat, das über die Welt etwas sagt, welches Gesagte verstanden werden kann."

82. Here λόγος is understood not "als der *Aussage*" but rather "als *Grundwesen des Menschen*": GA 83: 168.18–19.

83. SZ 349.32 = 401.2–3: "Aus der Zeitlichkeit der Rede, das heißt des Daseins überhaubt."

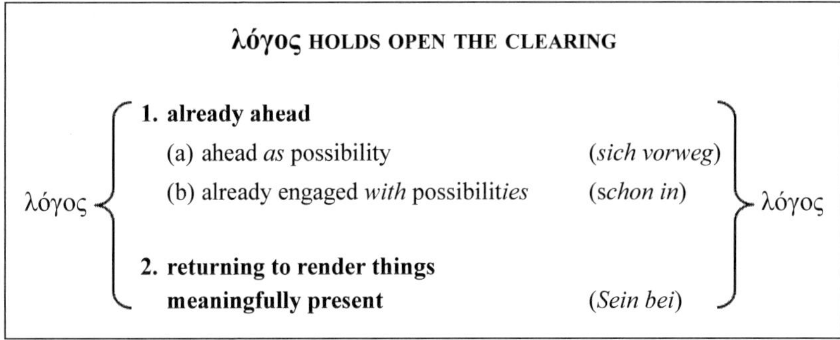

However, despite what we have argued above, the received tradition of Heidegger scholarship holds that ex-sistence does not have a *bivalent* structure of aheadness-and-return but rather a *trivalent* structure comprised of the moments of *Verstehen*, *Befindlichkeit*, and *Rede*, usually translated as understanding, attunement (or disposition, or state-of-mind), and discourse. Apparently that tradition first surfaced in Alphonse de Waehlens' *La Philosophie de Martin Heidegger* in 1942, a work that strongly influenced a generation of Louvainians in the 1950s and 1960s. However, the doctrine first came to North America via another channel, Werner Brock's "An Account of *Being and Time*," in Martin Heidegger, *Existence and Being* (1949). By 1961 it had settled in with Thomas Langan's *The Meaning of Heidegger*, and by 1963 it was confirmed by William Richardson's *Heidegger: Through Phenomenology to Thought* and by Otto Pöggeler's *Der Denkweg Martin Heideggers*. Schematically, the received tradition holds to the following threefold structure of ex-sistence:

THE DE WAEHLENS TRADITION

(1) already ahead as possibility *Verstehen*	(*sich vorweg*)
(2) already engaged with the world *Befindlichkeit*	(*schon in*)
(3) discourse / λόγος *Rede*	(*Sein bei*)

In the scholarship today this received tradition remains, with a few notable exceptions, the settled doctrine about the constitutive moments of ex-sistence as engagement with the world of meaning. However, the de Waehlens tradition is wrong on six important points.

In the first place, the received threefold structure of *Verstehen*, *Befindlichkeit*, and *Rede* is at odds with the full text of *Being and Time*.

a. It is one thing to say that these three phenomena are equiprimordial, as Heidegger does,[84] but quite another to say that they are three *ex aequo* "components" of openness, as Heidegger does not.
b. It is one thing to say that *Verstehen* and *Befindlichkeit* are defined and determined by λόγος, as Heidegger does,[85] quite another to say that, alongside those two, *Rede* is the third structural component of the *Da*, as Heidegger does not. (This is a complicated but finally resolvable matter: see appendix 1.)

Second, the received doctrine turns *totum* into *pars:* it takes *Rede*/λόγος, which is the whole of ex-sistence, and reduces it to merely one component of that whole. But engagement with the world of intelligibility is not merely one element of human being. It constitutes our complete raison d'être, outside of which there is nothing human.

Third, the received doctrine, by wrongly reducing λόγος to one moment within a supposedly triadic structure of human openness, suppresses the true second moment of that whole—namely, *das Sein bei*, our meaningful involvement with things, which always risks absorption in them.

Fourth, and as a corollary, the received doctrine misses the fact that in the final analysis there are not three constitutive moments of the thrown-open clearing (*Verstehen*, *Befindlichkeit*, and *Rede*), but only two, insofar as *Verstehen* and *Befindlichkeit* (like *Entwurf* and *Geworfenheit*), taken *together*, constitute the first moment: thrown-aheadness. (*Verstehen* and *Befindlichkeit* are only two sub-moments—two aspects—of the first moment of the engagement with intelligibility.) Thus, when it comes to ex-sistence's openedness, (1) being-already-ahead (*Sich-vorweg-im-schon-sein-in*) is one moment, and (2) returning to render things meaningfully present (*Gegenwärtigung* as *Sein bei*) is the other. In Heidegger's understanding, there are only *two* basic moments of ex-sistence, not three.

Fifth, even the correct *two* moments of ex-sistence finally reduce to *one* simple structure of "being-in-the-world": λόγος as man's engagement with meaningfulness as such.

Sixth, given this tripartite confusion in the structure of ex-sistence as being-in, the structure of care (*Sorge*) and "temporality" (*Zeitlichkeit*) will likewise be skewed. As is obvious from even a superficial look at SZ § 68

84. SZ 161.5–6 = 203.34: "Die Rede is mit Befindlichkeit und Verstehen existenzial gleichursprünglich," italicized in the original.

85. SZ 133.26–27 = 172.4–5: "Befindlichkeit und Verstehen sind gleichursprünglich bestimmt durch die *Rede*."

("The 'temporality' of openedness in general"), *Rede* will not fit the supposed threefold structure of either care or "temporality." *Rede* does not correspond to *Sein bei* as *Gegenwärtigen*. Rather, dis-closedness/ἀλήθεια-1 as a whole is constituted by *Verstehen, Befindlichkeit*, and *Sein bei*, and "*Rede* does not unfold and emerge primarily in *any specific* ec-stasis"[86] but rather is the *whole* of the clearing.

Heidegger's vision of the bivalent structure of ex-sistence is the backbone of *Being and Time* and arguably continues into his later view of the two moments of appropriation—namely, *Brauch* and *Zugehörigkeit*. (See chapter 9.) The bivalent structure of ex-sistence rewrites Aristotle's notion of κίνησις (for Heidegger, possibility stands higher than actuality) and underwrites Heidegger's *Bedeutungslehre* based on ex-sistence as the a priori engagement with meaning-at-all. It shows the sameness of (1) the unfolding of thrown-openness (*die Zeitigung der Zeitlichkeit*) and (2) the possibility of the meaningful presence of whatever we meet. It allows, in turn, for "authentic temporality" as our personal entry into what Heidegger calls the "situation."[87] Once the erroneous trivalent view of care and temporality is overcome, the structural parallels of care, temporality, and authenticity—and their unity—finally become clear.

Heidegger's philosophy (as one might hope all philosophy would be) was not just about knowing something, getting the answer to a question, no matter how profound that question might be. In the spirit of what we might call Greek "existential wisdom," his philosophy was also, and in fact above all, an exhortation to self-transformation. We turn now to that issue.

86. SZ 349.5–8 = 400.16–19, my emphasis. I translate "zeitigt sich" with the hendyadis "unfold and emerge."

87. SZ 326.17–18 = 374.7–8: "Zukünftig auf sich zurückkommend, bringt sich die Entschlossenheit gegenwärtig in die Situation." See the following chapter.

6

Becoming Our Openness

The lifelong task that Heidegger set himself can be divided into two moments: analytic and protreptic. The analytic moment was intended to unfold in two steps. Heidegger proposed (1) to disclose the *source* of meaningfulness at all (= SZ I.1–3); and then (2) to confirm and broaden that analysis by showing that whereas the thrown-open clearing had been glimpsed by the pre-Socratics, it went unquestioned by them as regards its source and thereafter had increasingly eluded metaphysics from its inception in Plato to its culmination in our day (= SZ II, plus the "history of being" in his later thought). The second, or protreptic, moment of Heidegger's task was to show how one could, and should, personally embrace one's finite and mortal thrown-openness, with transformative consequences in one's life. Although this transformation is somewhat muted in Heidegger's later writings, it remained the ultimate goal of his philosophical project, the reason why he taught and wrote at all.

On his first day of teaching after World War I he urged upon his students the words of the German preacher Angelus Silesius (1624–1677): *Mensch, werde wesentlich!* "Become what you essentially are!" (which he coupled with Jesus' challenge, "Accept it if you can!").[1] Eight years later, in *Being and Time* he echoed the same exhortation, this time in the words of Pindar: *Werde, was du bist!* "Become what you already are!"[2] And yet again, in mid-career (1937–1938) he told his students:

> Over and over we must insist: In the question of "truth" as posed here, what is at stake is not only an alteration in the traditional conception of "truth" nor a complement of its current representation. Rather, what is at stake is a transformation in man's way of being.[3]

1. GA 56/57: 5.34–35 = 5.14–15: literally, "Become essential." Matthew 19:12: ὁ δυνάμενος χωρεῖν χωρείτω (in the singular).

2. SZ 145.41 = 186.4, echoing Pindar's γένοι' οἷος ἐσσί μαθών, in *The Works of Pindar*, III 56.

3. GA 45: 214.15–18 = 181.5–8. See also GA 70: 93.22–24: "die Wandlung des Menschenwesens aus dem Bezug zum Sein durch dieses and für dieses in den Bezug zu ihm." GA 66: 144.18–19 = 123.7–8: "in einer Verwandlung des Menschen aus der Entscheidung zum *Seyn*." GA 65: 439.27–28 = 347.2–3: "in einer Wesensverwandlung des

Heidegger understands the first or "analytic" moment of his project, which comprises virtually the entirety of his corpus, as only a preparation for (*Vorbereitung*) and an exhortation to one's own personal, existentiel act of "becoming what one already is" by embracing and living out of one's appropriation—what he called the "entry into *Ereignis*."[4]

> Therefore, let us say cautiously that thinking [i.e., the analytic moment] begins to prepare the conditions for such an entry. In other words . . . this thinking above all prepares man for the possibility of corresponding to such an entry.[5]

As regards the analytic moment taken for itself *alone*—if for example, one were to master all the texts of the *Gesamtausgabe*, write brilliant books about them, but not hear the protreptic or take the transformative plunge—Heidegger would seem to agree with the poet:

> The meaning doesn't matter
> If it's only idle chatter
> Of a transcendental kind.[6]

The first division of *Being and Time* and significant chapters of the second division are devoted to spelling out the structure of ex-sistence—namely, thrown ahead as possibility into possibilities, right up to the ever-present possibility of the end of all possibilities. As thrown-open, we are always face-to-face with our ultimate possibility, death; and in experiencing that, we are able to know and accept ourselves as radically mortal: Plotinus' θνητάτονον.[7] We may gloss Heidegger's protreptic to become what we already are—to personally embrace and become our essence—with Augustine's *vivere moriendo*, "to live mortally," whatever that might happen to mean in each individual's life.[8]

---

bisherigen Menschen." GA 66: 239.1–2 = 211.25: "[die] Versetzung des Menschen in das Da-sein." Also GA 69: 99.24–28. The steps of this transformation are outlined at GA 66: 237.3–10 = 210.3–8.

4. GA 14: 51.33–34 = 42.30–31: "[die] Einkehr in das Ereignis"; see ibid., 50.23 = 41.24 and GA 15: 390.12 = 75.6.

5. GA 15: 390.18–22 = 75.10–13, with ibid. 390.8–9 = 75.3: "bei ihm einzutreten, in ihn einzukehren."

6. W. S. Gilbert, Bunthorne's song "Am I Alone?" from *Patience*, Act I: Bradley, *The Annotated Gilbert and Sullivan*, II, 149.

7. *Enneads* V 1: 1.21. For Heidegger human beings alone can experience death as death: GA 12: 203.18–19 = 107.32–33.

8. Vivere moriendo, "to live as dying": *Epistula XCV*, no. 2, *Patrologia Latina*, 33: 352.38. What Heidegger calls "anticipation of death" (Vorlaufen in den Tod: SZ 305.32 = 353.25–26) was expressed by Augustine, although with a different valence: "Mortem invocat; id est,

In this chapter we sketch out the elements that constitute the act of resolve—appropriating one's *whole* self ("whole" because it includes one's mortality)—and the grounding of that in thrown-openedness, the existential structure that Heidegger provisionally called "temporality."

The early Heidegger carried out this program by asking: What happens when meaning fails? As the form of life that is defined by λόγος, we are made for meaning, but we are also able to experience its collapse. That can occur on various levels. There is the failure of practical-ontic meaning when, for example, a chosen tool no longer fits its appointed task because the tool either breaks down or is found unsuitable (too light, too heavy). There is also the failure of logical and epistemological meaning when, for instance, a declarative sentence, which purports to show something apophantically (i.e., as it is in itself), proves not to do so: the pen is not in the drawer, as I had claimed it was. More globally, a specific paradigm of meaning can fail to adequately explain and predict its range of phenomena, not just provisionally but definitively: medieval cosmology gives way to modern views. Finally—but *really* finally—there is the moment when one's life, suffused as it is with meaning, fails to go on. I die, and with me disappears my relation to meaning at all.

But short of death I can experience another, crucial failure of meaning, one that issues in what Heidegger calls "dread" (*Angst*). Here a complete collapse of meaning in the very midst of my life lets me see the absurdity, the utter groundlessness, of my engagement with meaning.[9] (I use the word "absurdity" in a Heideggerian-phenomenological sense based on the word's Latin etymology, *surdus*: that which is "deaf " to any efforts to make sense of it.) In that moment I come face-to-face, however briefly, with the fact that I am ever at the edge of death (*Sein zum Tode*) and not just "towards" it as an inevitable but still future event. "Death is a way of being, that you take over as soon as you exist. 'As soon as you are born, you are old enough to die.'"[10] In this condition, says Heidegger, one may sense an invitation or summons ("the call of conscience") to understand and accept the groundlessness of oneself and thus to assume authorship of one's own life. To take that decision is to "double" one's ex-sistence: already structurally thrown open (*erschlossen*), I take it over and become *resolutely* thrown-open (*entschlossen*). How does that happen and what does it entail?

---

sic vivit ut mortem ad se vocet." "He invokes death, i.e., lives in such a way as to call death to himself." *Enarratio in Psalmum XLI*, no. 13 [re verse 8], Augustine, ibid., 36: 473.35–36.

9. At GA 66: 229.11–12 = 203.13–14 Heidegger says that dread as Ent-setzten (horror) "die Abgründigkeit des Seyns um ihn [Dasein] wirft." On the Lichtung as Abgrund, ibid., 87.8 = 72.33. On Seyn as Abgrund, ibid., 312.23–24 = 278.13–14. GA 88: 35.16–17: "Warum Ab-grund? Weil Da-sein Endlichkeit!"

10. SZ 245.25–27 = 289.35–36.

We are indeed made for meaning, but that very fact is glaring proof of our finitude. By our very nature we are onto-logists, caught on the hyphen between the ὄν and the λόγος—between what we encounter and its possible meanings—and condemned to mediate between the two. As we mentioned in chapter 3, the God of traditional theology is not an onto-logist, because God does not mediate.[11] In fact, God does not do meaning at all. "Ontology is an index of finitude. God does not have it. . . . Only a finite being requires ontology."[12] Here "ontology" refers to *metaphysica naturalis*,[13] our need and ability to discursively interpret things (τὰ ὄντα λέγειν) in terms of their possible whatness and howness, something that God does not have to (and arguably cannot) do. Ontology in this broad sense is the purview only of the human subject as λόγον ἔχων, as endowed with the need and the ability to bind together things and their possible meanings.

Heidegger pierces through human discursivity to the underlying finitude that makes it possible. He was after the source of intelligibility, but unlike traditional metaphysics he sought a non-theistic, non-subjective, non-substantive source, the correlative of which was not an ontological subject, either divine or human, but a phenomenologically experienced "e-ject," a self-concerned thrown-openness. Heidegger placed in question the "subject" that is correlative to meaning, first by strongly thematizing the ineluctable finitude of all the meaning that this subject can know. In Heidegger's telling, the correlativity of man and being has long been known to philosophy. However, the open space (*Lichtung*) which makes such correlation possible, as well as the opening up (*Lichten*) of that space—or better, its ever-openedness (thrown-openness)—has long been overlooked by metaphysics because of the intrinsic hiddenness of that openness. Heidegger's goal was to find and announce (*kundgeben*, κηρύσσειν) the ever-opened yet hidden clearing that makes possible the correlation of minding and the meant. The path to that goal led through the fundamental finitude of ex-sistence, and his early name for that finitude was thrownness (*Geworfenheit*).

11. See Aquinas, *Scriptum super sententiis* I, distinctio 25, quaestio 1, articulum 1, ad 4: "rationale est differentia animalis, et Deo non convenit nec angelis." Roughly: The term "rational" has to do with a difference between species of animals [i.e., it differentiates man as the *rational* animal from other *non-rational* animals], and it does not pertain to either God or angels.

12. GA 3: 280.30–33 = 197.24–27.

13. Kant, *Critique of Pure Reason*, B 21.

To be thrown is to be a priori thrust into ex-sisting, into having to be as possibility without any reason why. It is to be "brought into one's openness but *not* of one's own accord."[14] It means being "delivered over" to one's ex-sistence as a "burden."[15] "The human being exists as an entity that has to be how it is and how it can be."[16] Ex-sistence is what Heidegger calls *Seinkönnen*, the *necessity* of our *ability* to know and do things in the free space of meaningfulness. Human being can and must live out of its concrete possibilities, all of this against the ever-impending possibility of death. Heidegger calls this state of affairs "facticity," the condition of being condemned to the original and ultimate *factum*: the radically finite meaning-giving clearing, which is "at once the earliest and the oldest of all," from which there is no escape.[17] And the basis of this necessary possibility is necessity itself in the form of our thrownness into possibility, back behind which we cannot go. We are the thrown basis of our own thrownness, *der nichtige Grund einer Nichtigkeit*, which is a way of saying that we are compelled to be an open hermeneutical space, but without a reason why.[18] Although we can *experience* this condition of thrownness, we can never *know* it in the sense of understanding its cause or origin.

Such groundlessness is what Augustine long ago described as *homo abyssus*, human ex-sistence as a bottom-less ocean (ἀ + βυσσός: ἡ ἄβυσσος).

> An abyss is an incomprehensible, unfathomable depth. We usually apply the word to a great mass of water. . . . If by "abyss" we understand a great depth, is not the human heart an abyss? For what is more profound than *that* abyss? . . . Don't you believe that there is in each of us a depth so profound that it is hidden even to ourselves in whom it is found?[19]

Augustine, of course, thought that God alone could fathom that human abyss.

---

14. SZ 284.12 = 329.36: "*nicht* von ihm selbst in seinem Da gebracht."

15. SZ 42.1 = 67.7–8: "seinem eigenen Sein überantwortet"; 135.34 = 174.34: "Lastcharakter des Daseins," and 284.23 = 330.12. Also Augustine, *Confessiones* IV, 7, 12, *Patrologia Latina* 32, 698.23–25: "portabam . . . animam meam . . . et ubi eam ponerem non inveniebam." "I carried my soul [as a burden] and knew not where I might lay it down."

16. SZ 276.17–18 = 321.11–12: "Es existiert als Seiendes, das, wie es ist und sein kann, zu sein hat." At GA 2: 56, note "d," Heidegger glosses the phrase *Zu-sein* with "daß es zu seyn hat" ("that it has to be").

17. GA 12: 246.28 = 127.8–9: "Das Früheste und Uralte zugleich."

18. The German phrase in the sentence above is usually translated as "the null basis of its own nullity": SZ 306.20 = 354.13. However, the word "null" means "thrown." See "das geworfene (d.h. nichtige)": ibid., 306.24–25 = 354.17; and "geworfener Grund der Nichtigkeit": ibid., 325.36 = 373.14.

19. *Enarratio in Psalmum XLI*, 13 [re verse 8], *Patrologia Latina* 36: 473.13–16, .21–23, and 45–47. See GA 29/30: 411.4 = 283.30: Dread reveals "der ganze Abgrund des Daseins."

> The good heart lies hidden, the evil heart lies hidden; there is an abyss in the good heart and in the bad. But these things are bare to God's sight, from whom nothing is hidden.[20]

Heidegger, however, does not (and arguably cannot) find any phenomenological basis for the fulfillment Augustine believed in. Rather, the experience of one's inexplicable groundlessness strikes dread in one's heart.

> Because of your faith you may be "sure" of where you are going; or thanks to rational enlightenment, you may think you know where you came from. But all of that counts for nothing against the experience of dread, which confronts you with the sheer fact that you are thrown open, a fact that now stares you in the face as an unfathomable enigma.[21]

What does one experience in dread?

> the naked "that it is and has to be" [of one's ex-sistence]. The pure "that it is" shows up, but the "whence" and the "whither" remain in darkness.[22]

> [one's] naked ex-sistence, as something that has been thrown into homelessness. Dread brings ex-sistence back to the pure "that-it-is" of its ownmost individualized thrownness.[23]

Homo abyssus: Heidegger leaves us afloat on a bottomless ocean without a harbor to which we might return—and without a corresponding divine abyss that might somehow encompass our own. Our *abyssus* is our homelessness, in which we are most often strangers to ourselves. In an imaginary dialogue written in 1944–1945, a companion says to Heidegger,

> I hardly know anymore who and where I am.

to which Heidegger answers:

> None of us knows that, as soon as we stop fooling ourselves.[24]

---

20. *Enarratio in Psalmum CXXXIV*, 16 [re verse 6], *Patrologia Latina* 37: 1749. 3–5: "Latet cor bonum, latet cor malum; abyssus est in corde bono et in corde malo: sed haec nuda sunt Deo, quem nihil latet." See *Confessiones* X, 2.3: "Domine, cuius oculis nuda est abyssus humanae conscientiae," ibid., 32: 779.23–24.

21. SZ 136.1–5 = 175.4–9, paraphrased.

22. SZ 134.39–40 = 173.28–30.

23. SZ 343.31–32 = 394.1–3.

24. GA 77: 110.14–17 = 71.22–24: "Das wissen wir alle nicht mehr, sobald wir davon ablassen, uns etwas vorzumachen." See GA 40: 31.20–21 = 32.15–16: "daß wir keinem Dinge ganz gehören können, sogar uns selber nicht." Plotinus, *Enneads* VI 4: 14.16:

We are most immediately aware of our factical thrown-openness through feelings or moods. Heidegger anchors these in the structural moment of ex-sistence that he calls *Befindlichkeit*, the condition of affective familiarity with a given context of meaning and its contents. Such affective attunement is the primordial way that a world of meaning is opened up to us. Heidegger further distinguishes between ordinary and extraordinary moods. Ordinary moods disclose to our embodied and affective understanding the meaning of individual things and the encompassing context (the "world") that bestows such meaning. For example, the mood of boredom colors our feelings not just about a specific thing—say, this or that television show—but more broadly about the whole world of watching television at all. Similarly, although in a very different emotional register, we may experience the mood of romantic love, which opens up an entirely new way of living *à deux* and transforms the significance of all that we encounter within that context.[25] Heidegger's analysis of these moods focuses on our attunement to the meaning-giving *whole* (i.e., the world) that lets things appear as this or that. In an ordinary mood we feel the power of the entire scenario, the tacit encompassing narrative that gives meaning to the individual things we meet within that world. Moods are a form of absorption not just in things but also and more basically in the meaning-giving world in which they are situated—absorption to the second power, as it were. And yet, writes Heidegger, "just when moods of this sort bring us face to face with things in a meaningful whole, these moods conceal from us the no-thing [*das Nichts*] that we are seeking."[26] Worlds give meaning to things, but the no-thing is what makes all such worlds possible. It is our non-entitative (not-a-thing) thrown-openness as the cleared space required for any and all meaning.

To experience that which is "not-a-thing" and yet is the most fundamental element of human being requires an extraordinary kind of mood, quite different from everyday moods and feelings in which we are affectively attuned to our worlds of meaning. Heidegger calls these special moods *Grundstimmungen*, "basic" or "foundational" moods that get to the foundation*lessness* of the meaning-

ἡμεῖς δέ—τίνες δὲ ἡμεῖς. Philosophers, Heidegger once said, "don't much talk about the despair that haunts them": GA 21: 97.27–30 = 81.6–8 (26 November 1925). Cf. http://www.dailymotion.com/video/x12spb_talking-heads-once-in-a-lifetime_music.

25. For both examples: GA 9: 110.15–17 and .23–25 = 87.21–23 and .27–29. For a more general treatment of boredom: GA 29/30: 117–159 = 78–105.

26. GA 9: 111.1–3 = 87.39–40. Nichts as no-thing: I hyphenate the English to show that the "nothing" Heidegger is seeking is not a nihil absolutum. Rather, it is the groundless clearing that one is as In-der-Welt-sein. See GA 9: 123.6–7 = 97.7–8, remarking on "What Is Metaphysics?": "Das Nichts ist das Nicht des Seienden [= the not-a-thing] und so das vom Seienden her erfahrene Sein [= and thus is being, as experienced from the viewpoint of things]."

process, the abyss of meaninglessness (*der Abgrund der Sinnlosigkeit*) that underlies and makes possible meaning at all.[27] Such basic moods attune us to the very basis of any given world of meaning—which is its baselessness: the groundlessness of the thrown-open clearing that lets us make sense at all. The encounter with this groundlessness of our engagement with meaning is a matter of awestruck wonder—θαυμάζειν—whether it takes the form of sobering dread (*Angst*) or unshakeable joy (*Freude*).[28] The early Heidegger is better known for his analyses of the experience of dread than of joy, and we may gain insight into that mood by revisiting his 1929 lecture "What Is Metaphysics?"[29]

The second and third parts of that lecture describe what a first-person experience of dread might feel like. Jean-Paul Sartre took up and transformed those pages in his early novel *Nausea* (1938) in describing the protagonist Antoine Roquentin's harrowing yet liberating experience of the absurd.[30] And whereas Heidegger employs the term *das Nichts*—that which is not-a-thing—to name the thrown-open clearing, we can emphasize the groundlessness of this not-a-thing by employing Sartre's term "the absurd," not in a strict Sartrean sense but rather as referring to that dimension of ourselves which escapes all reasoning and is deaf to any efforts to make sense of it. Therefore, let "the absurd" stand in for Heidegger's "no-thing," that which is utterly real and yet not-a-thing, that which we can indeed experience but can find no reason for. The groundlessness of our thrown-openness is the absurdity of it all: we can make no sense of it and yet must presuppose it as the basis for every act of thinking or doing.

As Heidegger presents it, dread is not fear in the face of any specific thing that threatens us—for example, that pit bull in your neighbor's front yard. Instead, it is overwhelming wonder in the face of the absurd thrown-open clearing-for-sense that we ourselves are. Dread is our response to discovering the yawning abyss that lurks beneath our discursive activity, making it both possible (I *can* take this as that) and necessary (I *must* take this as that if I am to make sense of it at all).

27. SZ 152.14–15 = 194.2–3.

28. SZ 310.14–15 = 358.5–7: die nüchterne Angst, die gerüstete Freude—the latter due to the sense of freedom that comes with authentic openness. Heidegger takes wonder as θαυμάζειν from Plato, *Theaetetus* 155d3, and Aristotle, *Metaphysics* I 2, 982b12. See GA 56/57: 67.2 = 56.17; GA 19: 125.22 = 86.23; and GA 11: 22.10 = 79.15.

29. GA 9:103–22 = 82–96. With Heidegger we may characterize this text as a "metaphysics of the [natural] metaphysics" that is human being: "Metaphysik der *Metaphysik*," GA 84, 1: 140.2–4.

30. Sartre, *La nausée*, 157–171 = 123–135.

Imagine, Heidegger suggests, that, regardless of the reason, in a deafening instant the world of meaning that you inhabit in such comfort and familiarity is thrown out of joint and collapses. In that terrifying moment everything around you is suddenly pitched into chaos and loses its significance. And not just this or that world of meaning—your job, your marriage—but your very reason for existing at all. As you lose touch with the overarching purposes and goals that gave meaning to your life, your world of sense implodes and significance is sucked out of all the things that got their meaning from it. Yes, those things are still *there*—but so what? Now they don't matter at all. Perhaps, like Sartre's Roquentin, you cannot say what exactly happened between one step and another on some grey February day, but in that dramatic instant all the things you once knew and were so sure of get detached from their predicates—practical, theoretical, or whatever—and begin to float free of their anchorage in the meaning-giving context that itself has abruptly disappeared. As they float away from their meanings, those things turn on you and press in upon you with a terrifying closeness: *horrent omnia*, as Augustine says: everything becomes terrifying.[31] No longer mediated by the now-lost world of significance, they become frighteningly *im*mediate, with no semantic framework to hold them at a safe distance and situate them in a meaningful relation to you.

In this instant of terror you, too, float away from the calm and self-assured self that you were only a second ago. In a flash of insight you realize that your world of meaning is based on nothing solid at all and has no final reason that can account for it. The thin wall that previously separated you from your groundless facticity collapses, and you have to face, for the first time, the absurdity of the burden you bear: the need to make sense of things, with no founding or final reason.[32] In confronting the ultimate meaninglessness of sense-making, you realize that whereas you once could make sense of everything, you now cannot make sense of anything, much less of sense-making itself, and least of all of your own self. You encounter the absurd—not just this or that puzzle or problem or mystery to be solved, but the very real fact that making sense is ultimately an ungroundable, futile task into which you are thrown by the sheer fact of being human. As Heidegger puts it, for that brief instant you hang suspended over the abyss of the absurd.[33]

But as absurd as it is, you also see, in a flash of insight, that your thrown-openness is *the only thing that separates you from your death*. It may be finite, groundless, and with no ultimate reason or outcome, but at least it is

31. *Confessiones* IV, 7, 12: "horrebant omnia." *Patrologia Latina* 32: 698.30.

32. SZ 278.19–20 = 323.18–20: "[die dünne] Wand, die gleichsam das Man von der Unheimlichkeit seines Seins trennt."

33. GA 9: 112.7 = 88.35, "schweben" with ibid., 115.5 = 91.7: "sich hineinhaltend in das Nichts."

not the *nihil absolutum*. This dreadful encounter with your absurd thrownness, right up to the point of death ("*bis zu seinem Ende*"),[34] is an encounter with the possibility of your own *im*possibility and thus with the awareness that the mortal ability to make sense of things is all that stands between you and complete obliteration.[35]

But surprisingly, the no-thing we encounter, this yawning abyss under our feet, is a *nihil* that is neither *absolutum* nor even *negativum*. It does not suck you into your death—it neither kills you nor encourages suicide—but rather in a "positive" way (and this is the wonder of it all) throws you back (*abweisen*)[36] upon your mortal self *as* a groundless engagement-with-meaning. You cannot make sense of the absurd—trying to do so would itself be absurd—but you can make sense of *everything else* as you stand there with your back pressed up against your death. You now see that, against the encompassing dark, you sustain a fragile bit of space within which things appear as meaningful. You realize that, despite its groundlessness, your mortal understanding of meaning is the thin line separating you from absolute nothingness. You understand that, even amidst your daily life of sense-making, you are at each moment already at the point of death—and therefore at the point of *life*, with the ability to make sense of everything you meet.

Although fundamental moods like dread confront you with the groundlessness of your engagement with meaning and leave you with nothing to hold on to, you still have the possibility of fleeing from this experience. You can retreat from this awareness of facticity and try to continue your life in the everyday ways that paper over mortality and the final absurdity of living—like the protagonist of T. S. Eliot's "The Love Song of J. Alfred Prufrock," who, once having seen the dreadful "thing itself," flees it.

> Though I have seen my head (grown slightly bald) brought in upon a platter
> I am no prophet—and here's no great matter;
> I have seen the moment of my greatness flicker,
> And I have seen the Eternal Footman hold my coat and snicker,
> And in short, I was afraid.

34. SZ 305.29 = 353.23. This Heidegger calls "die äußersten Grenzen des Möglichen," GA 16: 59.23 = 420.2–3.

35. SZ 250.38–39 = 294.25: the possibility of one's own impossibility.

36. GA 9: 114.8–11 = 90.18–19.

Prufrock has a riveting vision of his mortality—the Eternal Footman—but with his decisive "No!" he takes flight.

> And would it have been worth it after all . . .
> To have squeezed the universe into a ball,
> To roll it towards some overwhelming question,
> To say: "I am Lazarus, come back from the dead,
> Come back to tell you all"? . . .
> No! I am not Prince Hamlet, nor was meant to be.

Prufrock takes flight into a world of erotic fantasy, even though that "life" will prove to be only a suffocating death-in-life:

> We have lingered in the chambers of the sea
> By sea-girls wreathed with seaweed red and brown
> Till human voices wake us and we drown.[37]

(Note how subtly the poem begins with Prufrock, in the form of Guido da Montefeltro, the standard-bearer of bad faith, speaking to a distinct, even separate "you," the reader, from a safe distance—"*senza tema d'infamia ti rispondo*." The poem then progresses to your own side-by-side journey with him—"Let us go then, *you and I*"—and concludes with your virtual identification with him: "Till human voices wake *us* and *we* drown.")[38]

The alternative to Prufrock's flight would be to let yourself be held out into the no-thing for a cold, focused moment—to hang suspended, with nothing to hold on to, over the abyss of the utter absurdity that gapes at the heart of your life.[39] That would be to understand what is at stake in the seemingly innocent act of making sense of things. You could finally, despite the ultimate futility of it all, wake up to that absurdity, live through it, accept it as your personal condition, and then take responsibility, without appeal, for yourself and the life you create. In either case, whether you flee this awareness like Prufrock or live into the experience with faint hope and trembling courage, the outcome is the same. Experiencing the possibility of no-meaning-at-all—the possibility

---

37. T. S. Eliot, *The Complete Poems and Plays of T. S. Eliot*, 16–17.

38. The Italian lines from Dante's *Inferno* XXVII, 61–66 are not a detachable epigram but are the opening six lines of the poem, integral with it, and the key to understanding it.

39. GA 9: 115.4 = 91.6 and 118.25 = 93.25: "Hineingehaltenheit in das Nichts." See Heidegger's existential interpretation of the Catholic liturgical service of compline as a symbol "des Hineingehaltenseins der Existenz in die Nacht u. der inneren Notwendigkeit der Bereitschaft für sie": Letter of 12 September 1929 in *Martin Heidegger/Elisabeth Blochmann*, 32.23–24. (I correct the last word from "Sie" to "sie," referring to "die Nacht." A romantic lapsus on Heidegger's part?)

of your own impossibility as the groundless ground of meaning—throws you back upon yourself as a mortal engagement-with-meaning, but now with a choice. You may either flee and forget your experience of your groundlessness or hold on to that awareness and make it your own (*eigentlich*) as you return to the everyday business of living, but now as the author of your own life. This push-back from death—which is what mortality is and what the absurd does—will be the same for both the feckless Prufrock and the person of resolve, as they each face their facticity. What distinguishes them is their decision about living with that awareness.

In "What Is Metaphysics?" Heidegger employs a puzzling phrase that describes this push-back from the absurd. He writes, "*Das Nichts selbst nichtet*," usually and incomprehensibly translated as "The nothing itself nihilates."[40] The German phrase seems to defy translation. However, in the sentences that precede the phrase (as well as in his marginal notes to the lecture, published in GA 9), Heidegger tells us precisely what he means. That can be shown by the following paraphrase of his text, in which "the absurd," "groundlessness," and "the no-thing" all refer to one's thrown-openness as the clearing.

> In dread you "draw back" from the no-thing. This is not flight. It is the calmness of wonder. This movement "back from" is initiated by the no-thing, the groundlessness that you are experiencing. The no-thing does not suck you into absurdity; rather, by its very nature it pushes you back [*wesenhaft abweisend*]. This pushing-you-back [*Die Abweisung*] directs you to the very things that you experience as slipping out of meaning. This business of pushing you back from itself and directing you toward the things that are slipping out of meaning [*Diese im Ganzen abweisende Verweisung*] is how the no-thing presses in upon you during dread. This is *die Nichtung*, i.e., the way the groundless no-thing "is" and "acts" (*nichtet*). The no-thing does not annihilate things, nor does it result from acts of negation. Annihilation and negation cannot account for the action of the groundless, absurd no-thing. *Das Nichts selbst nichtet.* Of its own nature the no-thing pushes you back from itself.[41]

In dread the no-thing directs you back to things and to their possible meanings, for which *you* now are responsible, but with an awareness that your

40. GA 9: 114.15–16 = 90.24. More literally, and equally incomprehensible, "The nothing nothings," as if there were an intransitive or middle-voice verb "to nothing."

41. See GA 9: 114.1–16 = 90.15–24.

mortality—your being ever at the edge of death—underlies the entire meaning-process. Whatever you decide to do with this experience—to remain oblivious of it (like Prufrock's beloved), or to see and flee it (like Prufrock himself), or to embrace it in an act of resolve—in each case, dread in the face of the absurd will always be, as Heidegger says, "slumbering" within your experience, with the possibility of awaking at any moment.[42]

The exhortation to become what I already am comes not from Heidegger but from myself, from my own groundless ex-sistence as thrown-open possibility, always on the verge of death. This call of my existential (not moral) "conscience" is a summons directed to me as a crowd-self absorbed in the meaningful things of my concerns and forgetful of the finite and mortal thrown-aheadness that lets me have things meaningfully present at all. As Augustine might put it, the call of conscience is a call from "abyss to abyss" (*abyssus invocat abyssum*).[43] The abyss that does the calling is my ever-homeless, mortal ex-sistence; and the abyss that is called *to* is that same me, but as lost in my crowd-self's thing-orientation, oblivious of the no-thingness that is my true self. It is a call to return to myself as I really am. To understand and accept that call is to choose my aheadness and to resolutely *be* my mortal thrown-openness. It is to "anti-cipate" what I already am—to take my death on board (*capere*) before (*ante-*) I actually die, by living mortally *now*. Translating "*vorlaufen*" as "running towards [death]" dulls the resonance of "living mortally *now*" and perpetuates the notion of a "linear" relation to my death. Heidegger's *Sein zum Tode* is not about my future death but about my ever-present mortality. Authentic ex-sistence is "resolute anticipation" (*vorlaufende Entschlossenheit*), which in turn is the authentic form of ἀλήθεια-1: "dis-closedness as the *re-solvedness* of ex-sistence as being-in-the-world."[44]

---

42. GA 9: 117.31–32 = 93.10–11: "Sie schläft nur"; ibid., 118.12–13 = 93.21: "erwachen." See SZ 286.32 = 332.32: "das Schuld 'schläft.'" Heidegger declares that ex-sistence is "the place-holder of the no-thing": GA 9: 118.20 = 93.26. At GA 86: 508.20–21 Heidegger connects this designation with a later one: "der Mensch ist *als* 'Platzhalter des Nichts' nicht anderes als 'der Hirt des Seins.'"

43. Augustine, *Enarratio in Psalmum XLI*, *Patrologia Latina*, 36: 473.1.

44. GA 66: 168.26 = 146.23–24. "Wahrheit als *Ent-schlossenheit* des Da-seins als In-der-Welt-seins." Since "resolve/resolute" does not readily evoke the notion of "to un-close" oneself (ent + schließen) by choosing to live mortally, I translate Entschlossenheit as "authentic openedness."

Living mortally entails continually retrieving (*zurückholen*) my true self from its everyday absorption and learning to be at home in my homelessness.[45] The retrieved self now lives as personally responsible for its own engagement with meaning in light of its mortality and thus lives authentically as the "author" of its actions.[46] Heidegger describes the call of existential conscience as a *vorrufender Rückruf,* a summons *back* to our true self by summoning us *forward* to our thrown-aheadness (into mortality) and our thrown-openness (for meaning).[47]

Heidegger argues that if it we *can* choose resolute anticipation as our way of existing, it is because we *are structured* in such a way as to make that possible. An important methodological presupposition is again at work here. As noted above,[48] Heidegger's argument here reflects the medieval Scholastic axiom *operari sequitur esse*, that is: the way one acts follows from the way one is. In the present case, because we are structurally (existentially) stretched ahead as possibility into possibilities, right up to the possibility of our death, we can personally (existentielly) take over our thrownness in its finite, mortal wholeness (*Übernahme der Geworfenheit*).[49] We have seen that our engagement with meaning is structured as care (*Sorge*)—that is, as being already ahead in possibilities and returning from there to make sense of things in terms of those possibilities. We are an existential movement that is ever thrown-ahead-and-returning, stretched out (*erstreckt*) beyond ourselves while still remaining present to ourselves and the things we encounter. We have seen that Heidegger, in the tradition of Augustine's *distentio est vita mea*,[50] calls this kinetic stretched-out-ness of ex-sistence by the potentially misleading term "temporality."[51] The image that this phenomenon should evoke in our imagination is not that of a

---

45. SZ 287.12 = 333.13. Authentic openness (Entschlossenheit) is a matter of becoming at home in one's homelessness, "das Heimischwerden in Unheimischsein": GA 53: 151.26 = 121.26, where Heidegger is interpreting Sophocles' ὑψίπολις ἄπολις, *Antigone*, 370. Homelessness is one's essence: GA 4: 87. 10–11 = 112.1: "[das] Heimischwerden . . . im Eigenen"; ibid., 129.9–10 = 151.4–6: "das Unheimische . . . *zu Hauß*."

46. See αὐθέντης: the author of a deed and specifically the one responsible for a murder. Herodotus, *Histories* I, 117.3: The Median general Harpagos says he did not want to be "guilty of the murder"—[μὴ] εἴην αὐθέντης—of King Astyages' grandchild, Cyrus.

47. SZ 287.5–7 and .9 = 333.7 and .8–9. The "whence" of the call is "the uncanniness of thrown individualization": ibid., 280.27–28 = 325.29–30.

48. Chapter 3, note 164.

49. SZ 325.37 = 373.14–15. See GA 79: 70.13–14 = 66.13: "in die Weite seines Wesensraumes zurückfinden."

50. *Confessiones* XI 29, 39. *Patrologia Latina* 32, 825.6 ("My life is my extendedness").

51. GA 9: 173.29–30 = 134.1–2: "[das] Geschehen der Transzendenz als solcher (Zeitlichkeit)."

linear, chronological past-present-future but rather a stretched-open expanse, which is finite insofar as it is open and thus bound up with unrealized possibilities. This openness is contrasted with the "closure" upon itself of something like Aristotle's perfectly self-actualized God. The thrown-openedness of ex-sistence is what Heidegger finally means by the ill-termed "temporality." In 1969 he redefined "temporality" (*Zeitlichkeit*) as man's original disclosedness or openedness,ἀλήθεια-1.[52] We would do well, therefore, to retire the word "temporality" from Heidegger scholarship, or at least to put it under heavy erasure, when speaking of the thrown-open ("ex-static") dis-closedness of ex-sistence.

Heidegger presents the core of "temporality" in a mere two pages of *Being and Time* that contain some of the most condensed passages in the book and arguably not the clearest. Nonetheless, we can unpack those concentrated paragraphs fairly easily if we keep two things in mind: (1) the diagram of the movedness (*Bewegtheit*) of ex-sistence as thrown-open (chapter 5, figure 5.1) and (2) Heidegger's "methodological" principle that the way we *can act* follows from the way we *are.* Heidegger's procedure in SZ § 65 is to arrive at "temporality" as the "neutral" (neither authentic nor inauthentic) existential structure of ex-sistence (= the climactic sentence at 326.20–21 = 374.11–12) by first analyzing "*authentic* temporality" as manifest in existentiel resoluteness (325.14–326.18 = 372.20–374.8). He often conflates neutral and authentic "temporality," and we must carefully distinguish the two in what follows.

In the opening chapters of Division Two of *Being and Time* Heidegger showed that we can hear the call of existential conscience and accept it (SZ I.2, chapter 2)—that is, we can wake up to and take responsibility for our living at the point of death at every moment, and not just at the chronological end of our life (SZ I.2, chapter 1). Hearing the call of conscience (in *Being and Time*) is homologous with the experience of dread (in "What Is Metaphysics?"). Accepting that call, which is the same as choosing to live mortally, occurs when, by a personal decision, we make our structure (groundless, mortal thrown-openness) our own. Resolute anticipation is the same as authentic ex-sistence.

52. GA 16: 70.10–11 = 45.16–18: "im Sinne der ekstatischen Offenheit." GA 49: 54.28–29: "Innestehen in der ekstatischen Offenheit der 'Zeit.'" GA 9: 376.10–11 = 285.26–27: "die 'Zeit' als der Vorname für die Wahrheit des Seins" (also ibid., 159, note a = 123 note a; 377.4–5 = 286.12–14) with GA 65: 331.23–24 = 263.1–3: "ἀλήθεια—Offenheit und Lichtung des Sichverbergenden . . . verschiedene Namen für dasselbe." Likewise compare GA 88: 46.7–8, "(Zeitlichkeit und *Temporalität* als Anzeige der Da-heit des Da.)," with GA 68: 36.11–12, "Das Offene des Da (Da-heit)."

But what makes the personal embrace of our ex-sistence possible? Answer: That very ex-sistence itself. Under the rubric of "care" (*Sorge*), ex-sistence was shown to have "three" moments (aheadness, alreadiness, and presence-to) that in fact reduce to two: (1) already-ahead-ness and (2) rendering things meaningfully present. And now in SZ § 65 Heidegger argues that thrown-openness or "temporality" is structured by the very same three-reduced-to-two moments. This bivalent kinetic structure is existential and emphatically not a matter of chronology (past, present, and future). But before showing how resolute anticipation maps onto and is made possible by ex-sistence as thrown-openness, we must first clear up what the three-reduced-to-two moments of ex-sistence are in the present case. It is the so-called "second moment" (what-one-already-is) that will require the most attention.

ECSTATIC EXISTENCE ("TEMPORALITY")

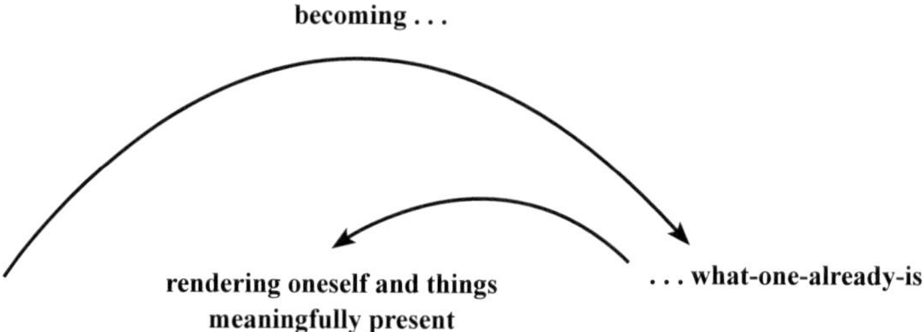

The "first" moment: Zu-kunft as becoming. To have to exist (*Zu-sein*) is an existential feature of human being: it is how we are built, not something that we personally do. It means that structurally we are ever becoming ourselves, ex-sisting as possibility. (Our essence is to ex-sist—simply *to be possible.*) Our very ex-sistence is "tasked"[53] with such *Zu-sein*, and that means structurally (and not yet as a personal act) sustaining ourselves as possibility while ex-sisting ever at the edge of our impossibility. This is the first of the so-called "three" moments of ex-sistence: becoming—in fact, *self*-becoming. Heidegger calls it "coming-to-oneself," *auf sich zu-kommen* or, as a noun, *Zu-kunft*, which we should translate not with the chronological term "future," but rather with the existential term "becoming."[54]

53. GA 29/30: 407.28 = 281.19: "aufgegeben."

54. SZ 325.34–326.8 = 372.20–373.11.

The "second" moment: das Gewesen as what one already is. Here things seem to get complicated, but really are not. The gist is this: That which ex-sistence is structurally becoming is its own "essence" (*Ge-wesen*)—that is, what and how it always already (a priori, essentially) is and must be. Understanding what Heidegger means here depends on realizing that with the word *das Gewesen* in SZ § 65 he is utilizing for his own purposes Aristotle's term for "essence," τὸ τί ἦν εἶναι.[55] If we were to translate that Greek phrase literally—and therefore wrongly—it would come out as "the what-it-*was*-to-be [such and such a thing]."[56] Why the "was" instead of "is"? Heidegger points out that the Greek verb εἶναι ("to be") has no present perfect tense (no "has been") and that Aristotle employed the imperfect tense (ἦν) as a stand-in for the present perfect.[57] But why would Aristotle want to define essence as "what it *has been* to be this-or-that"? We have here an example of what Heidegger calls the "ontological perfect."[58] This phrase does not refer to any tense at all, not even to the chronological "has been" (or "is-as-having been"). Instead, it designates the ontological status of Aristotelian essence as what "always was, is, and will be" (which may be a hold-over from Plato's notion of εἶδος as eternal and unchanging). The essence is what is always-already *priorly operative* in a thing in an ontological (not chronological) sense—as in Aristotle's notion of "the prior in terms of φύσις and οὐσία."[59] In a marginal note in *Being and Time* Heidegger writes:

> [That-which-is-always-already-operative] in this ontological sense is called *a priori* in Latin and πρότερον τῇ φύσει in Greek: Aristotle, *Physics* I, 1; or more clearly in *Metaphysics* VI [1] 1025b28–9 τὸ τί ἦν εἶναι, the "what it already was [for something] to be," "that which is always already operative before anything else," the already-is [*das Gewesen*], the perfect. . . . This is not an ontic past but that which is always earlier. . . . Instead of the a priori perfect it could also be called the ontological or transcendental perfect.[60]

55. For example, *Metaphysics* VI 1, 1025b28–9; VII 4, 1029b14. Heidegger first encountered the Greek construction in Braig, *Die Grundzüge der Philosophie*, 49.16–17.

56. As in the Latin "quod quid erat esse": Aquinas, *Sententia libri metaphysicae* VII, 3, 5 (no. 1310, commenting on *Metaphysics* VII 4, 1029b14): "[Aristotles] intelligit quod quid erat esse illius rei [e.g.,] quid est homo." Roughly: Aristotle understands ["essence"] as what something was to be—for example, what is man.

57. GA 2: 114, note a = Stambaugh 83, note ‡. See *Enneads* VI 9: 9.22: γίνεται αὐτὴ καὶ ὅσπερ ἦν: the soul becomes itself—that is, as it *was*.

58. See note 60.

59. *Metaphysics* V 11, 1019a2–3: [πρότερον] κατὰ φύσιν καὶ οὐσίαν. Also *Posterior Analytics* I 2, 71b34: πρότερον τῇ φύσει.

60. GA 2: 114, note a = Stambaugh 83, note ‡. The term "the perfect" does not refer to the present perfect tense but rather has the sense of *per* + *factum*, that which is "completely finished" and thus operative, as in the Greek τὸ τέλειον. *Physics* I, 1 does not actually speak of πρότερον τῇ φύσει but rather of σαφέστερα τῇ φύσει (184a17 and 20): things that are clearer by nature—that is, in themselves.

Heidegger signals that when he speaks of the *gewesen*-dimension of ex-sistence, what he means by *Gewesenheit* is "essence" in the form of "*wie es je schon war*." This is what his protreptic to authenticity urges us to take over as our own. He writes (the underlining is my own):

> *Übernahme der Geworfenheit aber bedeutet, das Dasein in dem, wie es je schon war, eigentlich sein.*[61]

In a close paraphrase:

> Taking over one's thrownness means authentically *being* one's ex-sistence *in the way that this ex-sistence always already* [i.e., essentially] *is*.

Translating "*wie es je schon war*" by "as it already was" (Macquarrie-Robinson) or "in the way that it always already was" (Stambaugh) entirely misses the crucial reference to Aristotle's non-chronological τὸ τί ἦν εἶναι: "what ex-sistence essentially is" (or, in Heidegger's implicit rewrite of Aristotle's Greek, τὸ ὥς ἦν εἶναι: "*in the way* that ex-sistence essentially is"). In turn, these errors in the English translations abet the mistaken notion that, in taking over its thrown-openness, ex-sistence is taking over its past (*das Vergangene*). That is certainly not what Heidegger means here: "The 'past,'" he writes, "is obviously different from *Gewesenheit*."[62] Nor does *das Gewesen* refer to the past insofar as it impinges on and is still operative in the present, as in the popular mistranslation of *das Gewesen* as one's "is-as-having-been."[63] It is important to note: The past in this present-perfect sense is not at all under discussion in SZ § 65. *That* first comes into play only in § 74, when Heidegger deals with historicity (see below in this chapter). Heidegger's analysis of ex-sistence in § 65 is entirely, and only, about thrown-*ahead*ness and return, and not at all about the past. The way we essentially-ontologically are does not follow along "behind" us ("*folgt das Dasein nicht nach*") and cannot be articulated with either the past tense or the present perfect tense. Rather, it lies "ahead" of us ("*geht ihm je schon vorweg*") as what we are always already becoming.[64] In

61. SZ 325.37–38 = 373.14–15, where the ET misses the point. Likewise the "était" in Martineau's French translation, *Être et Temps*, 229.38–39, is a misreading: "tel qu'il était à chaque fois déjà"; also online at http://t.m.p.free.fr/textes/Heidegger_etre_et_temps.pdf.

62. SZ 381.13–16 = 433.3–5: "'Vergangenheit' . . . unterscheidet sich offenbar von der *Gewesenheit*." Also GA 4: 84.6–8 = 109.7–8: "das fernher noch Wesende."

63. Heidegger describes the *proper* use of the phrase "is-as-having-been" as "[das] vormals Vorausgegangene und jetzt Zurückbleibende": "that which went before and yet now still remains behind": GA 2, 500 note a = 361 note *. On Greek past tenses, see appendix 3.

64. SZ 20.16–17 = 41.24–25, where Heidegger erroneously writes "Vergangenheit" when he means "Gewesenheit." He gets it right at ibid., 284.17–19 = 330.4–5: "Die Geworfenheit aber liegt nicht hinter ihm als ein sächlich vorgefallenes und von Dasein wieder losgefallen Ereignis . . . sondern *Dasein ist ständig*—solange es ist [etc.]." Also GA 11: 58.3 = 48.23: "[Das Gewesene] west ihr [= die Überlieferung] stets voraus."

taking over our thrown-aheadness, we personally become what we already essentially are: ourselves as mortal possibility.[65]

We may conclude this discussion of the so-called "second" moment of the allegedly "three" moments of thrown-openedness with Heidegger's summary of the existent*ial* structure that makes possible the existent*iel* act of resolve. (The numbering below is, of course, my own. I leave the German in Roman in order to manifest Heidegger's own italicizations.)

1. Die Übernahme der Geworfenheit ist aber nur so möglich, daß zukünftige Dasein sein eigenstes "wie es schon war," das heißt sein "Gewesen," *sein* kann.
2. Nur sofern Dasein überhaupt *ist* als ich *bin*-gewesen, kann es zukünftig auf sich selbst so zukommen, daß es *zurück*-kommt.
3. Eigentlich zukünftig *ist* das Dasein eigentlich *gewesen*.[66]

In a paraphrase:

1. I can personally take over my thrownness only insofar as I can *be* (in Aristotelian terms) "the-way-I-always-already-am"—that is, my "essence."
2. Only insofar as I always already *am* my essence (my τὸ τί ἦν εἶναι—that is, my "ich-*bin*-gewesen") can I personally become or "come to" my real self, in the sense of coming *back* to it.
3. When I authentically do become myself, I authentically *am my essence*—that is, my *Existenz*.

Each of these three consecutive sentences combines an existent*iel* possibility or actuality ("I can" or, in the third sentence, "I do") with the existent*ial* structure that makes it possible ("only insofar as"). That is, each sentence argues from a concrete *operatio* to its enabling *esse*[67]—which means: each sentence argues from a moment in the act of resolve to the structure that makes it possible. Granted, neither Heidegger's German in these sentences nor any English translation of them rolls off the tongue. In fact, this crucial text counts as one of the most compressed in *Being and Time*. Nonetheless, the "Aristotelian clue" which Heidegger offers—that *wie-es-je-schon-war* = τὸ τί ἦν εἶναι = the essence of ex-sistence = one's thrown-aheadness-as-thrown-openness—at least puts the reader in the ballpark of what Heidegger meant by this crucial passage.

The so-called "third" moment: Gegenwärtigen as the "return" to oneself. We are still discussing the "neutral" existential structure of thrown-openness (thrown-ahead-ness) and not yet the authentic personal assumption of that structure in resolve. Now that we have combined the first "two" structural moments

65. As what-is-always-already-operative, das Gewesene *in its concreteness* is one's finitude and mortality, its potential "goneness." That (and not "pastness" or "past"!) is what Heidegger means by "das Vorbei" at GA 64: 52.23–24 = 43.25 and 116.20 = 12E.2 (McNeill) = 207.9 (Kisiel).

66. SZ 325.38–326.4 = 373.16–21.

67. See chapter 3, note 164.

(self-becoming and alreadiness) into just one moment (ever-becoming-what-one-already-is), the so-called "third" moment of *Gegenwärtigung* is seen to be the *second* of the two moments that constitute the bivalence of ex-sistence. I have put the word "return" in scare quotes lest we think of it as coming "only after" the first moment. On the contrary, I am *always with* myself even as I transcend that self.[68] This is to say that *being* myself ("in the present," as it were) means being myself *as possibility*, ever stretched ahead, ever becoming, never at rest.

> This being-ahead-of-oneself as a returning [*Sich-vorweg-sein als Zurückkommen*] is, if I may put it this way, a peculiar kind of movement that ex-sistence *qua* "temporal" constantly makes.[69]

Hence, the so-called "return" to myself means that ex-sistence *always remains* with itself, but with itself *as possibility*. This is Heidegger's way of spelling out the structural fact that ex-sistence indeed *is*, but it always *is-as-possibility*.

Finally, the unity of the bivalence of already-ahead-and-return. Heidegger presents the unity of the "three" (which are now *two*) moments of thrown-open ex-sistence in the brief, compact, and difficult phrase that is his rock-bottom definition of "temporality" as the dynamic structure of thrown-openness: "*gewesend-gegenwärtigende Zukunft*."[70] Both Macquarrie-Robinson and Stambaugh mistranslate this crucial phrase as "a future that makes present in the process of having been," thereby privileging chronological terms (future, having been) and completely missing Heidegger's "Aristotelian" interpretation of *das Gewesen*.[71] The German phrase seems to defy translation, but in light of what has been said, the meaning can now become clear. The short paragraph in which this phrase is embedded[72] mixes together (and virtually blurs) two definitions of two distinct phenomena: (1) "temporality" in its *neutral* existential structure and (2) "temporality" in its *authentic* existentiel enactment.[73] The following English paraphrase, which proceeds phrase by phrase through the five sentences of the German paragraph, attempts to sort out the confusion.

---

68. Compare Aquinas, *Summa theologiae* I, 14, 2, ad 1: "inquantum vero [forma] in seipsa habet esse, in seipsam redit": "Insofar as, in itself, a form has being, it returns to itself." Aquinas' point is that "redire in seipsum" ("to return to oneself") means to *be* with oneself to one degree or another; and he uses the phrase analogously: God as a complete and perfect reditio in seipsum (= being as *pure* self-subsisting act), man as an imperfect reditio (= being as *possibility*). See chapter 3, note 166.

69. GA 21: 147.23–26 = 124.19–20. Here "Dasein" means "Existenz"; hence: ex-sistence. See chapter 3, note 167.

70. SZ 326.20–21 = 374.11–12.

71. Martineau's translation, *Être et temps*, 229.57, renders the phrase just as opaquely: "avenir étant-été-présentifiant." The obsolete verb "avenir" ("to come to pass") is nowadays used only as a noun: "future."

72. SZ 326.17–25 = 374.7–16.

73. The same goes for the previous three paragraphs, which mix together unhelpfully both the structurally neutral and the personally authentic moments of "temporality"—a sign, I believe, of the haste with which Heidegger composed SZ.

SZ 326.17–25 = 374.7–16

1. ***Existentiel act:***

Zukünftig auf sich zurückkommend,
bringt sich die Entschlossenheit
gegenwärtigend in die Situation.

Ex-sistence comes back to itself-as-becoming (i.e., it takes over its throw-ahead-ness)
in resolve, and in so doing
is meaningfully present in and as its own authentic situation.

---

2. ***Existential structure described*:**

Die Gewesenheit entspringt der Zukunft,
so zwar,
daß die gewesene (besser gewesende) Zukunft
die Gegenwart aus sich entläßt.

Ex-sistence is becoming what it always already is (i.e., its ἦν εἶναι),
such that
this becoming, as always-already (or better: as always-already-operative),
determines the self-presence of ex-sistence.

---

3. ***Existential structure defined*:**

Dies dergestalt einheitliche Phänomen als
[2] gewesend-
[3] gegenwärtigende
[1] Zukunft
nennen wir die Zeitlichkeit.

This unitary phenomenon of ex-sistence's
[1] becoming
[2] what-it-already-is,
[3] and thus being meaningful present to itself
is what I call "temporality" (i.e., meaning-giving thrown-ahead-ness).

---

4. ***This existential structure makes possible the existentiel act of resolve:***

Nur sofern das Dasein als Zeitlichkeit bestimmt ist,
ermöglicht es ihm selbst
das gekennzeichnete eigentliche Ganzseinkönnen
der vorlaufenden Entschlossenheit.

Ex-sistence (existential), insofar as it is "temporal,"
makes it possible for ex-sistence (existentiel)
to be authentically whole
by resolutely anticipating its death (= taking over its mortality).

---

5. ***Existential-existentiel conclusion:***

Zeitlichkeit
enthüllt sich als
der Sinn
der eigentlichen Sorge.

Thus the "temporality" of ex-sistence
is shown to be
what existentially accounts for and makes possible
one's existentiel authentic openness as care.

This brief (seventy words in five sentences) but complex paragraph is the hard core of *Being and Time*. It articulates both the existentiel process (the "protreptic" moment) and the existential grounding (the "analytic" moment) of authentic "temporality." We may reformulate the five sentences as follows:

1. The act of personally anticipating your death—that is, "taking over" yourself as the mortal possibility that you are (which is your *Gewesenheit*)—is the choice to existentielly become yourself: to "come back" (out of your fallenness) to your real self (*zu-kommen* as *zurückkommen*), with the result that you make yourself meaningfully present in your openness or *Da*, which is now called your "authentic situation."
2. But how is that existentiel act possible? Answer: because of your existential structure. Your essence or *Gewesenheit*—what you always already are—is yourself *as possibility*, your being-ahead (= your so-called "futurity"). This condition is always-already-operative. It *is* your way of being present to yourself, but present as always-already-ahead-as-possibility.
3. We may define this structure in "temporal" terms: Your essence is to be always-already-becoming what you always-already-are (namely, mortal possibility); and this *is* your ontological-existential mode of self-presence.
4. Given that dynamic existential structure, you *can* become yourself, *can* become that very structure and thus be your "whole self," by resolutely "anticipating" (choosing to be) the mortal possibility that you already are.
5. Conclusion: Your structural-existential thrown-openness as mortal possibility is what makes it possible for you to accept and become, personally-existentielly, your structural-existential thrown-ahead-ness as mortal possibility.

In short, the act of resolve is one's choice to "redouble" the structure of one's ex-sistence by choosing it. Moreover, Heidegger says that resolve, as the resolute anticipation of death, is an existentiel "interpretive process."[74] That is, it is the way we effectively understand ourselves in terms of the radical absurdity of our mortal thrown-ahead-ness, and decide to live from out of that. To do so, he implies, sheds a very different light on how we live and turns our everyday world into what he calls a "situation"—a sphere of meaningfulness insofar as it is "opened up in authentic resoluteness."[75] But Heidegger gives no concrete guidance on *how* the authentic person should live and think, and

74. GA 64: 52.16 = 43.17–18: "das Vorlaufen als auslegendes."

75. SZ 299.36–37 = 346.22–23: "Die Situation ist das je in der Entschlossenheit erschlossen Da."

on his own principles he cannot. "The only way to get clear on the question of ex-sistence is to ex-sist."[76]

One last and important note: The existential structure of ex-sistence as ahead-and-return makes possible not only the existentiel decision for authentic ex-sistence but also our everyday acts of making sense of things in whatever sphere of life.

> Factical ex-sistence, understanding itself and its world ex-statically in the unity of its openedness, comes back from these horizons to the things encountered within them. Coming back to these things understandingly is the existential meaning of letting them be encountered in making them [meaningfully] present.[77]

Thus, the neutral-existential structure of aheadness-and-return is what allows us to make sense of things in our everyday, ordinary (and mostly "fallen") way. But the *resolute assumption* of that structure allows us to make *authentic* sense of things. This is what Heidegger implies when he says that neutral-existential temporality, when authentically embraced, makes possible "authentic care."[78]

A brief review: At the beginning of this chapter we noted that Heidegger's task has both an analytic and a protreptic moment. In its analytic moment his thought is focused on what allows for meaningful presence at all, and his answer is: ex-sistence as the thrown-open clearing. First Heidegger analyzed the a priori engagement with the world of meaning that determines human being. He found that we make sense of things by relating them to our possibilities and concerns (SZ I.1, chapter 3) and that we *can* do so because of the two moments of our structure as care: (1) being always already ahead as possibility among possibilities and (2) returning from there to the things we encounter (SZ I.1, chapters 5 and 6). He then showed that this structure of care is grounded in the "kinetic" structure of (1) becoming-what-one-always-already-is, which determines (2) one's-way-of-being-present to oneself and things (SZ I.2, chapter 3: "temporality"). Because ex-sistence *is* this kinetic openedness, an individual *can* personally embrace it by resolutely "anticipating" death and living mortally. Thus, the analysis of ex-sistence—from the engagement with meaning

76. SZ 12.30–31 = 33.8–9. (Heidegger's rhetorical flourish about authentic ex-sistence at ibid., 384.1–11 = 435.22–33 is just that.)

77. SZ 366.14–19 = 417.30–34: gegenwärtiges Begegnenlassen.

78. SZ 326.24–25 = 374.15–16: "Zeitlichkeit enthüllt sich als der Sinn der eigentlichen Sorge," all italicized.

to the thrown-open structure that makes it possible—undergirds Heidegger's protreptic to become the mortal becoming that you already are.

All of this should ultimately bear upon the kind of choices that a resolute, authentic self might make in life. So, how are specific possibilities opened up to me? And how do I choose among them authentically? What standards or "measures" should guide my decisions if I want to conjugate my possible choices with personal responsibility for my mortality? Heidegger addresses these questions in SZ I.2, chapter 5, which shifts the discussion from ex-sistence as "temporal" (§ 65) to ex-sistence as historical (§ 74).

Heidegger notes the ambiguity of the word "history" (*Geschichte*): it can refer to either (1) the actual living of a life stretched out between birth and death ("living one's history") or (2) the *science* of history that investigates such living ("She teaches history.") Heidegger holds that the subject matter of history in the second sense (as a science) is history in the first sense—namely, human beings "living their history" between birth and death. He brackets out the second sense, the science of history (which he calls *Historie*), and uses the word *Geschichte* to refer only to what he calls "historical reality" (*geschichtliche Wirklichkeit*)[79]—that is, the very *living* of the events of one's life. (Nature does have its "history," but it is distinct from the existential history of humankind.) This movement of being stretched out existentially and stretching oneself out existentielly between birth and death—that is, living a connected life in and through this stretch—is what Heidegger calls man's *Geschehen* ("historical living"), a term that is virtually the same as *Geschichte* ("history") as the early Heidegger understands that term.[80] His interest in historical living is twofold: (1) to discover its a priori structure, which he calls the "historicity" or "historicalness" of ex-sistence (*Geschichtlichkeit*), and (2) to find out what it would mean to actually live one's history authentically. These two topics are the subject matter of *Being and Time* § 74.

Historical living is not a linear, chronological affair in which an unchanged self steps from one currently actual moment (this "now") to another, while the no-longer nows and not-yet nows stretch out to the horizon before and behind us. Human beings "make their history" as much as they are shaped and buffeted by it. As contingent and perhaps even unsuccessful as the outcome may turn out to be, we do choose our historical future and relate to our historical

79. SZ 378.12 = 430.8.

80. SZ 375.3 = 427.11. Macquarrie-Robinson translate Geschehen by the neologism "historizing"; Stambaugh by "occurring"; Richardson by "coming-to-pass."

past. The question now is how we are *able* to do so and whether we can do it *authentically*.

Heidegger wants to bring the *whole* of ex-sistence into his analysis. So far, however, his treatment of thrown-openness as a "movement" of already-ahead-and-returning has dealt with ex-sistence only in its "future" and "present" moments (ex-sistence as "facing forward"[81]) and has generally neglected to show how the past (*das Vergangene*) figures into authentic openedness. As we have seen, there is no mention of the past in Heidegger's discussion of the dynamic structure of ex-sistence in § 65, only an analysis of "ontological alreadiness" (*Gewesenheit*) as one's a priori thrownness into mortality. But as we live our own history, the past is always with us, even if only implicitly, in its "present-perfect" form—that is, not as a bygone time that has no impact on the present, but rather as that which *once was* and *still is* impacting the present. For example, one *still is* a bachelor of arts *as having been* awarded that degree in the past. Heidegger glosses this present-perfect sense of the past with "[*das*] *vormals Vorausgegangene und jetzt Zurückbleibende*," that which has gone before and yet still remains—what-is-as-having-been.[82] These possibilities are what Heidegger calls our "heritage" (*Erbe*), elements that have come down to us from the past and still weigh upon the present as possible ways of living. In Heidegger's view it is this dimension of the present-perfect that pushes the analysis of "temporality" in § 65 (which ignored the past altogether) into the analysis of historicity in § 74, which for the first time takes into consideration the past-as-still-present. However, Heidegger repeatedly insists that he can give no instruction on which possibilities we *should* choose from out of our past-yet-present heritage. He can only lay out the formal structure of how we might free up an inherited possibility and put it to work for ourselves.

> Our existential interpretation of what one is summoned to by the call [of conscience] cannot try to define any concrete individual possibility of ex-sistence.[83]

> In the existential analysis we cannot, on principle, discuss what ex-sistence *factically* decides in any particular case. Our investigation excludes even the existential sketch of the factical possibilities of ex-sistence. Nonetheless, we must ask *whence, in general*, ex-sistence can draw those possibilities in terms of which it understands itself.[84]

Heidegger approaches the question of authentic historical living by first spelling out more concretely what is entailed in authentic "temporality" as

81. SZ 373.9 = 425.12. "nach vorne."

82. GA 2, 500, note a = Stambaugh 361 note.

83. SZ 280.9–12 = 325.8–10.

84. SZ 383.1–6 = 434.24–28.

the resolute anticipation of death. Taken neutrally, apart from whether it is authentic or not, "temporality" is the movement of being ahead as possibility and returning to oneself (and to things) in order to interpret how they are meaningfully present. And *authentic* "temporality," as we have seen, redoubles that structure insofar as we choose to become what we already are and to render ourselves meaningfully present, but now *in light of our mortality*. In resolve, we follow out our structural aheadness and personally embrace it by "anticipating" our final possibility and living mortally. In so doing, Heidegger says, ex-sistence goes "right into the teeth of death"[85]—and in fact "shatters against death"[86]—"in order thus to take over, in its entirety, the thrownness that it is in itself."[87]

But this anticipatory confrontation with death, like the encounter with the groundless no-thing in dread, does not destroy ex-sistence but rather pushes it back into its now authentic openedness (the existential "situation") in what Heidegger calls the *Augenblick* or "moment of insight."[88] The insight that is operative in the act of resolve brings into view not only the a priori structure of ex-sistence as thrown possibility but also the *specific inherited possibilities* that populate the present situation of our lives. As inherited, these possibilities do indeed come from the past, but a past that still impacts us today. They are historical in a double sense, both insofar as they come from our own past-that-is-still-present (what-is-as-having-been) *and* insofar as they can be resolutely taken up into shaping our historical present and future. But freeing up inherited possibilities requires a struggle, because these possibilities are not existentielly neutral but are suffused with the interests of the crowd.

> For the most part, the self is lost in the crowd. It understands itself in terms of the possibilities of ex-sistence that "circulate" in the current "average" public interpretation of ex-sistence. Ambiguity has made most of these possibilities unrecognizable, but they are still familiar. Authentic personal understanding is far from extricating itself from traditional interpretations; in fact in each case we seize upon a possibility in terms of this interpretation, then against it, and yet again for it.[89]

---

85. More literally, ex-sistence goes "under the eyes of death." SZ 382.31–32 = 434.20: "es dem Tod unter die Augen geht." (But after all, under the eyes of death there are only its nose and its teeth.)

86. SZ 385.12 = 437.7–8: "an ihm zerschellend."

87. SZ 382.32–33 = 434.21–22. See ibid., 385.15–16 = 437.10: "die eigene Geworfenheit übernehmen."

88. Situation alone: SZ 326.18 = 374.7–8. Moment of vision into the dis-closed situation: ibid., 328.24 = 376.28–29: "'Augen*blick*' auf die erschlossene Situation."

89. SZ 383.22–30 = 435.6–14. The phrase "and then again for it" may refer to what he later describes as making a "rejoinder" to the inherited possibility; see "erwidert": ibid., 386.4 = 438.1.

The purpose of such an insight into the situation is to measure those possibilities against the stark fact of one's mortality, and then to choose from among them in light of that radical finitude. The task is to bring the choice of my existentiel-personal possibilities into line with what I now see as my existential structure. Doing so is a matter of choosing possibilities *for* my present and future *from out of* my inherited past insofar as that past is still operative in the present. Citing Goethe, Heidegger calls this "choosing one's hero."[90] The process is one of "freeing up," in the light of my mortality, elements of what I have "inherited," in order that, with them, I might try to live an authentic present and future.

> When we come back to ourselves in resoluteness, we disclose current factical possibilities of authentic existing *from out of the heritage* that we *take over* as thrown. Resolutely coming back to our thrownness involves *freeing ourselves up* [*Sichüberliefern*] with regard to the possibilities that have come down to us, although not necessarily *as* they have come down to us. If everything "good" is our heritage, and if the "good" makes authentic ex-sistence possible, then freeing up a heritage occurs in one's resoluteness.[91]

The word Heidegger uses for this process is *überliefern*, which both Macquarrie-Robinson and Stambaugh mistranslate as "to hand down," thereby completely blocking what Heidegger is getting at and destroying the sense of the text.[92] For example, the current translations of the previous passage (specifically, *Sichüberliefern*) would have it that our authentic openness "hands us down" to ourselves, which, of course, makes no sense at all. To begin with, the *liefern* that lies at the heart of *überliefern* comes from the Latin *liberare*, to set free.[93] Heidegger himself points the way to the correct translation of *überliefern*:

---

90. SZ 385.28–29 = 437.23: "sich seinen Helden wählt." Far from having to do with Heidegger's politics, as some have claimed, this phrase was a schoolboy's motto in late nineteenth-century Germany, taken from Goethe's *Iphigenie auf Tauris*, II, 1. Pylades, the cousin of Orestes (and co-murderer of Clytemnestra), encourages Orestes in prison: "Ein jeglicher muß seinen Helden wählen, / Dem er die Wege zum Olymp hinauf / Sich nacharbeiten." In Anna Swanwick's classical translation: "Each must select the hero after whom / To climb the steep and difficult ascent / Of high Olympus."

91. SZ 383.31–384.1 = 435.15–22, paraphrased.

92. See SZ 384.12–14: "sich überliefert" becomes "*hands itself down* to itself" (!) in both Macquarrie-Robinson at 435.34–35 and Stambaugh at 365.42–366.1. Martineau, however, has "il se *délivre* à lui-même" at 265.11.

93. Friedrich Kluge, *Etymologisches Wörterbuch*, 440, s.v. "liefern": "liefern Ztw. Lat. *liberare* 'befreien'."

> *Überlieferung* is a freeing-up in the sense of *liberare*, setting free. As such a freeing-up, *Überlieferung* brings to light the hidden treasures of what is already operative.[94]
>
> *Überliefern, délivrer*,[95] is a freeing-up, specifically unto the freedom of a conversation with the essential.[96]

Sichüberlieferung in the present context has nothing to do with "handing oneself down to oneself" (whatever that would mean). Rather, it means "freeing oneself up," and in this case, freeing up from our past-present possibilities for our present and future. The language of "handing down" (*tradere, traditio*) betrays the meaning of the text.

Although Heidegger insists that his analyses cannot help anyone choose among specific possibilities, he is sure of the effect of resolute anticipation. In what can be called the culminating *protreptic* paragraph of *Being and Time* he writes (I paraphrase):

> The more authentically I enact authentic openness—i.e., understand myself unambiguously in terms of my ownmost distinctive possibility by anticipating my death—the more unequivocally and the less haphazardly will I find and choose the possibility of my ex-sistence. Only the anticipation of death drives out every random and "provisional" possibility. Only freedom *for* death gives me my goal in its simplicity and drives me into my finitude. Once grasped, the finitude of my ex-sistence snatches me back from the endless series of possibilities that are offered up as most tangible—taking it easy, sluffing off, shirking responsibility—and brings me to the simplicity of my *fate*. This word designates my original, authentically open historical living, in which I am freed up for myself, free for death, in a possibility that I have *inherited* and yet have *chosen*.[97]

94. GA 10: 153.7–10 = 102.6–8: "weil die Überlieferung eigentlich, was ihr Name sagt, ein Liefern im Sinne des liberare, der Befreiung ist. Als ein Befreien hebt die Überlieferung verborgene Schätze des Gewesenen ans Licht."

95. This French word is derived from the Romanic or Vulgar (not classical) Latin *deliberare*, "to set free, liberate": *The Compact Edition of the Oxford English Dictionary*, I, 166, s.v. "deliver"; also Ernest Weekley, *An Etymological Dictionary of Modern English*, I, 427, s.v. "deliver."

96. GA 11: 10.34–35 = 35.1–2. See ibid., 20.2–5 = 71.7–11: "im Gespräch mit dem [= dem Gewesenen] bleiben, wohin uns die Überlieferung der Philosophie ausliefert, d.h. befreit."

97. SZ 384.1–14 = 435.22–36. See GA 36/37: 264.10–12 = 201.28–29.

The word "fate" (*Schicksal*) may be a bit too Wagnerian for what Heidegger means here. The word must be stripped of any notions of a fatalistically predetermined "destiny" that is "sent" to me. *Schicksal* as it is used here should be understood in terms of the German adjective *schicklich* (fitting, proper): it refers to my freeing up and embracing a concrete possibility that *befits* my thrownness into mortality. My "fate" (if we choose to use the word at all) is my freedom to make my own history in the light of my radical finitude.

Having worked out the relation between authentic openedness and the historical past, Heidegger takes one more step and spells out how, in and through such openness, one can explicitly "retrieve" an inherited possibility. The German word here is *wiederholen*, which has the sense of "hauling" something up from the past, as if from a well, so that it can be seen again and chosen in a new way.[98] In authentic openness I need not explicitly know the origin of the possibilities in terms of which I understand myself mortally. However, there is the possibility of such a thematic understanding—that is, of self-consciously freeing up from a past world of meaning a possibility that is still available in the present. This is what Heidegger means by retrieval: the act of *explicitly* freeing up a possibility from the historical present-perfect, "recovering what is always-already-operative, but in a more original way."[99] The workings of retrieval are perhaps most clearly seen in Heidegger's engagement with previous philosophers and his ferreting out from their texts the unsaid-but-sayable possibilities regarding being and, above all, its source. (See, for example, Heidegger's readings of Kant at GA 3.) Heidegger applies the term "retrieval" to the explicit freeing up and "disclosing of [ex-sistence's] original and heretofore hidden possibilities" such that the retrieval "has the effect of transforming" ex-sistence by keeping its possibilities "free and alive" and available for reappropriation in a present that reaches ahead into the future.[100]

98. Wiederholen: Macquarrie-Robinson unfortunately translate it as "to repeat"; Stambaugh as both "to repeat" and "to retrieve"; Martineau as "répétition"; Richardson renders it correctly as "re-trieve."

99. GA 12: 123.29–30 = 36.28: "das Gewesene ursprünglicher zurückzugewinnen" (via what Heidegger here calls an "anscheinend revolutionäre Wille"). See also GA 77:110.28–29 = 71.34: "Haben Sie vergessen, was ich über das Revolutionäre sagte?" He defines das Revolutionäre at GA 45: 37.10–11 = 35.19–20: "Der ursprüngliche und echte Bezug zum Anfang" (repeated at ibid., 41.1–2 = 38.28–29). This "revolution" would presumably lead to "eine Verwandlung der Metaphysik" (GA 9: 368.4–5 = 279.22) and perhaps even to "eine Wende des gegenwärtigen Weltzustandes," but not through "menschliches Rechnen und Machen": *Zollikoner Seminare* 332.21–23 = 266.6–8.

100. See GA 3: 204.3–9 = 143.4–9: "die Erschließung seiner ursprünglichen, bislang verborgenen Möglichkeiten, durch deren Ausarbeitung es verwandelt . . . wird"; "frei und wach halten."

At this point our study has taken us through some key portions of *Being and Time* as published in 1927, and only that far. And yet even at this early moment in Heidegger's career, it seems that he had already sketched out the response to his basic question. In 1936 Heidegger wrote:

> *Being and Time* has not become something past for me, I have still not "gotten any further" today because I know with every increasing clarity that I must not get any "further." But perhaps I have gotten closer in some things to what was attempted in *Being and Time*.[101]

What allows for intelligibility at all? Answer: thrown-openness, which will later be articulated as ap-propri-ation, the ever-operative "bringing" of ex-sistence into its proper state as the openedness that allows us to take this as that and so to make sense of it. In fact, as far as it goes, *Being and Time* had already laid out the basic pattern that would remain unchanged *in its essentials* for the remainder of Heidegger's career. As we shall see, not even his 1930s shift (*Wendung*) to what he called the *seinsgeschichtlich* approach (the analysis of how clearing is "sent" by appropriation) would change those essentials. Much remained to be done, of course, but with *Being and Time* the skeletal structure around which Heidegger would build the rest of his work was already in place. There would be no need for a so-called "turn" from Dominant Dasein to Big Being, from "ex-sistence-projects-the-clearing" to a "the-clearing-projects-ex-sistence"—for two reasons: first, because *Being and Time* never did hold to the Dominant Dasein myth; and second, because such a notion of "the turn" is based on a misunderstanding. (See chapter 8.)

Being and Time, as Heidegger frequently said, was a transitional work.[102] In 1926–1927, he based himself on thrown-open ex-sistence as horizon-forming insofar as it is "temporal"—that is, existentially present to itself by becoming what it already is. SZ I.3 was to show how the schema-forming moments in thrown-openness affect the whole range of intelligibility (the "being of things"), including its possible variations and different regions. But that approach soon fell by the wayside. In the 1930s Heidegger shifted his attention away from that systematic (and arguably somewhat lateral) development of his project in order to focus on the appropriated clearing as the *hidden source* of all meaningful presence. In the next chapter we will have to sort out why he did so.

To be sure, the "destruction of the history of ontology" (SZ II.1–3) was yet to be worked out. Heidegger would get to that over the next four decades of his

101. Heidegger, *Schellings Abhandlung* 229.14–18 = 189.6–9.

102. GA 65: 305.24 = 241.24: "Fundamentalontologie das Übergängliche." Ibid., 251.3 = 197.21: "Im übergänglichen Denken." Also GA 70: 194.28–30.

career, but he could have published Part II of *Being and Time* without having published SZ I.3. In fact, he took the first step in doing just that when he put out his *Kant and the Problem of Metaphysics* (now GA 3) in 1929. The still further step, beyond the destruction of onto-theology to the retrieval of appropriation as the unsaid of Western metaphysics, is already implicit in the resolute retrieval of thrownness from fallenness in *Being and Time*. So, yes, a good deal of fruitful work remained to be done, and without it Heidegger would not be the Heidegger we know today. But the Heidegger of the 1930s and thereafter (Heidegger II) is not a fundamental departure from the Heidegger of the 1920s (Heidegger I). Nor is the later Heidegger a retrieval of the earlier. I argue for the unity and continuity of Heidegger's thought—its laser-like focus on the same and abiding "thing itself"—through all the twists and turns, expansions and applications, advances and reversals of his thinking, from *Being and Time* until his death. He claimed to be the thinker of one thing only. Part Three endeavors to follow the course of that single thought in his later work.

PART THREE

The Later Heidegger

7

Transition

From *Being and Time* to the Hidden Clearing

By way of review: We have seen that Heidegger's main topic was not "being" (*Sein*) in its metaphysical sense of the objective whatness, thatness, and howness of things—and this for at least two reasons. First of all, as Heidegger reads it, classical metaphysics usually deals with things apart from and independent of their relation to human beings—Aristotle's ἔξω ὂν καὶ χωριστόν, things outside of and separate [from thinking]."[1] On the other hand, despite his confusing employment of the classical lexicon of *Sein*, Heidegger properly understands *Sein* phenomenologically as the meaningfulness of things. Underlying all of his work is a phenomenological reduction of things to their significance to human beings. *Being and Time* first focused on meaningfulness as the relation between what we encounter in everyday praxis, on the one hand, and our world-shaping interests and concerns on the other (SZ I.1, chapter 3).

The second reason why "being" was not Heidegger's main topic is the same reason why an investigation of the meaningfulness of things was not his final goal. To analyze meaningfulness merely as what makes things humanly present to us would produce only a phenomenologically transformed metaphysics; but Heidegger wanted to move beyond such meaningfulness to what makes it possible. Thus in SZ I.1, chapter 5, he analyzed ex-sistence as the thrown-open clearing, and in SZ I.2, chapters 1–3 he showed the basic structure of thrown-openness to be mortal self-becoming. He was after what *allows for* meaningfulness (*das Anwesen<u>lassen</u>*), the "whence" of significance (*die Herkunft von Anwesen*).[2] He called this "whence" the "realm of dis-closedness or

---

1. *Metaphysics* XI 8, 1065a24.

2. "Anwesen*lassen*": GA 14: 45.29–30 = 37.5–6. "Herkunft von Anwesen": GA 6:2, 304.11–12 = 201.13–15. See GA 2: 53 note a = Stambaugh 37 note †: "Das Anwesen aus dieser Herkunft"; GA 10: 131.19–20 and .28 = 88.27 and .34: "Wesensherkunft des Seins"; and GA 73, 2: 984.2: "nach ihrer Wesensherkunft (Ereignis)." GA 14: 29.15 = 24.3 speaks of this "whence" as "der Quell." Sometimes (but not consistently) he speaks of this source as "Seyn": GA 68: 51.5–6: "Seyn—als Grund und Zulassung der Seiendheit, die anfängliche φύσις." The "lassen" of "Anwesen*lassen*" is "Das Sein-lassen des Seins, nicht erst des Seienden": GA 70: 128.20.

the clearing (intelligibility)."[3] Here "dis-closedness" refers to the thrown-openness of ἀλήθεια-1; and "intelligibility" means that whereby things are *able* (cf. –ible) to be known and dealt with. This possibilizing element is the "space" that our thrown-open ex-sistence *is* and that lets us take things *as*—that is, in terms of their possible meanings. This *Lichtung* is always understood in terms of its *Lichten*: the opening-and-sustaining of the openness thanks to our ever-operative ap-propri-ation to our proper condition as thrown-open. The appropriated clearing is the core fact, *die Sache selbst*, of all Heidegger's work.

But if Heidegger had established that much by the end of *Being and Time*, what more remained to be done? In this chapter, after some opening remarks we will study the formidable obstacles that Heidegger confronted as he struggled to complete *Being and Time* in the years 1927 through 1930. The chapter proceeds as follows:

1. Preliminary remarks (pp. 190–195)
2. The projected contents of SZ I.3 (pp. 195–201)
3. A "new" working out of SZ I.3 in "Basic Problems of Phenomenology" (pp. 201–210)
4. The scope of fundamental ontology (pp. 210–218)
5. Overcoming transcendentalism and the horizon for being (pp. 218–223)
6. The crucial breakthrough (1930): the intrinsic hiddenness of the clearing (pp. 223–228)

Readers are forewarned: This makes for a very thick chapter, and much of the material (especially topics 2 through 4) may light the fire only of truly paid-up Heideggerians. That said, however, the distinction between the two kinds of ontological difference (in number 2) as well as the last two topics (5 and 6) are of more general interest, and number 6 is utterly important for understanding the later Heidegger.

1. PRELIMINARY REMARKS

Within the transcendental framework that governs *Being and Time*, at best only half of Heidegger's task had been carried out by the end of SZ I.2. To be sure, in good transcendental fashion he had begun by turning the inquiring subject into the subject of the inquiry. Insofar as ex-sistence is the only place where meaning shows up, the question about meaning and its source had been turned back on the questioner. The early Heidegger's wager was that if we understood

3. GA 16: 424.20–21 = 5.14–15: "der Bereich der Unverborgenheit oder Lichtung (Verstehbarkeit)." See GA 9, 199.21 = 152.24: "[das] Offene des Begreifens."

ourselves as the understanding of meaning (*Seinsverständnis*), we would come to understand, in a formal and general way, all that can be understood by that understanding. Our engagement with the clearing and with the meaning that it makes possible, when put under the microscope, would reveal how far that engagement extends, what kind of things fall within its scope, the various regions of meaningfulness, and the general ways in which things can be meaningful. In other words, as conducted within its early, transcendental framework, Heidegger's SZ I.1–2, published in February of 1927, needed to be rounded out by a further inquiry (the planned SZ I.3) into *what can be understood* (and in what way) by ex-sistence as a *Seinsverständnis* grounded in the groundless clearing. In the ontological language of *Being and Time*, the transcendental question about *ex-sistence* as the engagement with and understanding of being (= SZ I.1–2) must now become the question about the *clearing* that is ex-sistence itself, insofar as it makes possible all forms of meaningfulness (SZ I.3).

In other words, by spelling out the finitude and dynamism of openedness in SZ I.2, Heidegger had merely (and barely) accomplished the "laying free of the horizon for interpreting the intelligibility of being."[4] However, "this interpretation of ex-sistence as 'temporality' does not yet provide the *answer* to the guiding question [*die leitende Frage*] about the intelligibility of being."[5] Yes, much of *Being and Time*, especially SZ I.1, spells out the *fact that* being is the intelligibility of things. But Heidegger's *Grundfrage* went beyond that *Leitfrage*, or beneath it, to *what allows for* being-as-intelligible: the thrown-open clearing. This basic question about the "whence" of intelligibility was the task reserved for SZ I.3.

Of course, there is meaning only because of our innate discursivity, structured as a horizon-forming aheadness-and-return. Hence the unfinished task: man's existential dynamism and the horizon it shapes, riding under the early rubrics of, respectively, "temporality" and "time" (i.e., *Zeitlichkeit* and *Zeit*; or *Zeitlichkeit* and *Temporalität*), "must be brought to light, and genuinely conceived, as the horizon for all understanding of being and for any way of interpreting it."[6] SZ I.3 was to show how ex-sistence's finite movedness of aheadness-and-return unfolds (*sich zeitigt*) into a correlative and equally finite horizon. That is, "We need to explain primordially, from out of 'temporality' as the being of ex-sistence, that 'time' is the horizon for the understanding of being."[7] Translation: SZ I.3 would show that the thrown-open

4. SZ 15.9–11 = 36.4: "die Freilegung des Horizontes für eine Interpretations des Sinnes von Sein." The closest *Being and Time* comes to doing that is § 69c. See below, note 38: "A 'new' working out of SZ I.3."

5. SZ 17.24–26 = 38.25–27, my emphasis.

6. SZ 17.34–35 = 39.6–8.

7. SZ 17.36–38 = 39.8–10, italicized in the original.

clearing (= ἀλήθεια-1 = "time") is what lets us understand the being/meaningfulness of things.

The paradox of *Being and Time* as published is that the *finitude* of ex-sistence guarantees the *in*finitude of ex-sistence's reach. Our structural engagement with meaning is radically open-ended and in principle without closure. Yes, there is an intrinsic limit to that stretch: ex-sistence can encounter the meaning only of material things, for as embodied and thrown, ex-sistence is "submitted" exclusively to sensible things rather than being open to trans-sensible ("meta-physical") reality.[8] But that notwithstanding, the search for the meanings of spatio-temporal things meets no barrier inscribed "thus far and no farther," because we can always ask "Why no farther? What am I being excluded from?" and thus transcend the barrier, if only interrogatively. And secondly, yes, ex-sistence is thoroughly mortal and will certainly die, and its death will mark the definitive end to its search for meaning. But although it will surely end, perhaps even tragically, ex-sistence will nonetheless go out with its glory intact, insofar as it will die *as* an in-principle unbounded capacity for the meaning of everything it can sensibly encounter.

Being and Time as published shows that our ability to understand the meanings of natural, sensible things is unrestricted. In the Proemium to *Metaphysics* Aristotle had declared, "All human beings by nature desire to know," this in a passage that culminates in the possibility of human beings knowing the very highest entity. The object of the highest instance of knowledge would be the highest instance of being, and so Aristotle concludes, "This sure knowledge [ἐπιστήμη] either God alone can have, or God *above all others*"[9]—thereby implying that even human beings have a shot at fully knowing God. The soul is *capax omnium* because it is *capax Dei*, it is πάντα πῶς because it is θεὸς πῶς.[10] As Heidegger cites Aristotle in *Being and Time*, "The soul is somehow all things."[11] Heidegger follows up that sentence from Aristotle by citing Aquinas' statement that the soul is *ens quod natum est convenire cum omni ente*:

8. SZ 87.24–26 = 120.31–121.2: "Dasein hat sich, sofern es *ist*, je schon auf eine begegnende 'Welt' angewiesen." See ibid., 137.35–38 = 177.6–10; and 161.27 = 204.23, etc.

9. Respectively, *Metaphysics* I 1, 980a1 and I 2, 983a9–10.

10. πάντα πῶς: see the following footnote; θεὸς πῶς: Rousselot, *L'Intellectualisme*, 62 = 71. Augustine agrees with Aristotle, if for different reasons: *De trinitate*, XIV, 8, 11, *Patrologia Latina*, 42, 1044.39–42: "Eo quippe ipso [mens humana] imago eius est, quo eius capax est, eiusque particeps esse potest": The mind is the image of God in that it is capable of God and can be a partaker of him.

11. *De Anima* III 8, 431b21: ἡ ψυχὴ τὰ ὄντα πώς ἐστι πάντα. Heidegger translates, "Das Seele ist in gewisser Weise das Seiende alles." Heidegger, *Übungen im Lesen*, 13 February 1952, 45.14–15. (These words are omitted at GA 83: 654.8.) At SZ 14.6 = 34.23–24 Heidegger omitted the last Greek word by mistake: "Das πάντα ist in S.u.Z. aus Versehen herausgeblieben." *Übungen im Lesen*, 13 February 1952, 45.8–9, omitted at GA 83: 654.8.

"By its very nature this entity [= the soul] is suited to come together with all things."[12] In Heidegger's reading of these texts, Aristotle and Aquinas are not asserting that the soul (read: ex-sistence) is ontically the *same* as everything in the universe. Rather:

> Clearly the soul will be "all things" only with regard to their meaningful presence, and that is because the soul is determined by νοῦς, and νοῦς is determined by ἀληθεύειν. The soul is the place where things, of and by themselves, can come to appearance. In this way the soul is involved with and participates in the meaningful presence of what is meaningfully present.[13]

Such participation of the soul in meaningful presence (*Anwesen*) does not, of course, make *Anwesen*/*Sein* into something merely mental. At stake is always the meaningful presence of some thing in space and/or time.

Structurally and in principle we are *able* to know everything about everything, even though we never will. Such ever-unrealized omniscience comes with our very ex-sistence. (Husserl: "God is the '*infinitely distant man*.'")[14] This open-ended possibility is a "bad infinity," which in this context denotes the asymptosis of endless progress in knowledge and control.[15] Heidegger's philosophical critique of (as contrasted with his personal opinions about) the modern age of science and technology cannot, on principle, be leveled against our ability to endlessly understand the meanings of things and even to bring them under our control, because this possibility is given *with* human nature, as Aristotle intimated and as Heidegger accepts in principle. What troubles Heidegger, rather, is the generalized overlooking of one's mortal thrown-openness in today's Western, and increasingly global, world. The mystery of human being consists in both the endless comprehensibility of whatever we can meet and the incomprehensibility of why everything is comprehensible. Everything is knowable—except the reason why everything is knowable.[16]

---

12. SZ 14.20–21 = 34.37, citing Aquinas, *Quaestiones de veritate* I, 1, corpus.

13. Heidegger, Übungen *im Lesen*, 13 February 1952, 45.16–20: "Die Seele wird offensichtlich das Seiende alles nur sein hinsichtlich seines Anwesens, weil nämlich die Seele durch νοῦς bestimmt ist und dieser durch ἀληθεύειν. Die Seele ist der Ort, wo das Seiende von sich her zum Erscheinen kommen kann. So ist die Seele beteiligt am Anwesen des Anwesenden." GA 83: 654.8 omits this text.

14. Husserl, Husserliana VI, *Die Krisis*, 667.29 = 66.18–19: "Gott ist der '*unendlich ferne Mensch*.'"

15. Schlechte Unendlichkeit: see Hegel, *Wissenschaft der Logik*, *Gesammelte Werke*, XI, 81.14–15 and 83.11 = 13.14 and 120.21.

16. "[T]he eternal mystery of the world is its comprehensibility": Albert Einstein, *Physics and Reality*, 18.

The various reasons why Heidegger held back SZ I.3 are the subject of much commentary by scholars and very few words by Heidegger himself. In 1946 ("Letter on Humanism") he wrote famously that in this projected third division the plan was to be that "everything turns about" (*umkehrt*), both as regards *what* was to be thought and *how* it was to be thought.[17] He is referring here to the transition that had been planned from the very beginning of *Being and Time* and was to be carried out in SZ I.3 from *ex-sistence* as structurally opening up and sustaining the clearing to *the clearing itself* insofar as it makes possible the meaningfulness of things. In a lecture course at Freiburg in 1952 (on 13 February, precisely twenty-five years after *Being and Time* was published) Heidegger said:

> Soon after *Sein und Zeit* was printed I got a shock. As regards *In-der-Welt-Sein* (which I have labored over for quite a long time and which Sartre, for example, has completely misunderstood), *Sein* is certainly always touched upon along with other things and certainly is *there*, but in the formulation it sort of limps along behind.[18]

Here Heidegger (as he often and confusingly did) is using "*Sein*" to refer to the clearing. The clearing certainly *was* mentioned in *Being and Time*, where it was identified with ex-sistence itself as being-in-*the-world*; but it was to come into its own only in SZ I.3, where the transition would take place from ex-sistence as sustaining the clearing to the clearing that is sustained by ex-sistence. But we must avoid the subject-object mistake of thinking of ex-sistence as standing on one side and the clearing on the other as a phenomenon that is separate (or even distinct) from ex-sistence. "They," in fact, are the same phenomenon seen from two viewpoints—that of the sustaining and that of the sustained—but "both" are ex-sistence as thrown-open. The clearing is the οὗ ἕνεκα of ex-sistence, its very raison d'être, that for the sake of which ex-sistence ex-sists at all. The planned change of focus in SZ I.3 would concentrate on the same phenomenon as in SZ I.1–2, but now on the thrown-open clearing with regard to how it makes all forms of meaningfulness possible. But from SZ I.1–2 to SZ I.3 the same fundamental principle would hold: No ex-sistence, no clearing; no clearing, no ex-sistence.

---

17. GA 9: 328.1 with note = 250.1 with note.
18. GA 83: 650.30–651.3.

Already in the first pages of SZ Heidegger had left the human subject behind in favor of what he called the *subjectivity* of the subject,[19] the *essence* of human being as the thrown-open clearing for meaningfulness. But Heidegger was concerned to avoid any impression that the origin of meaningfulness as such "is determined from out of thought."[20] Soon enough after *Being and Time* was published, Heidegger came to see that the transcendental approach of the book at least risked leaving the false impression that the already-aheadness of ex-sistence existentielly thrusts open the horizon or "creates" it *sua sponte* as if by a Promethean act of will. The real insight came sometime before December of 1930 (the lecture "On the Essence of Truth") when Heidegger saw for the first time that the clearing—which is always already opened up whenever and wherever there is ex-sistence—is *intrinsically hidden.* As we shall see, this insight led to the change in Heidegger's approach in the 1930s, when he abandoned the transcendental framework and adopted his *seinsgeschichtlich* (i.e., the "giving-of-the-clearing") approach. This alteration of approach, which obviously was not programmed into the original project of *Being and Time*, is quite distinct from and not to be confused with the transition to SZ I.3, which had been already planned in 1926 as the change of focus from *Da-<u>sein</u>* to *<u>Da</u>-sein.* The scholarship has generally confused the two, a matter that we take up later in the next chapter when we study the *Kehre*.

We turn now to the issues that presented difficulties for Heidegger in the years 1927–1930 and prevented him from completing *Being and Time* in the form in which it was originally projected.

2. THE PROJECTED CONTENTS OF SZ I.3.

It could be argued that after writing *Being and Time* in Todtnauberg and Marburg in 1926, Heidegger spent the next fifty years formulating and reformulating, with varying degrees of clarity and success, what was to have been the subject matter of SZ I.3. Some evidence for that might be found in the title he chose for a public lecture in Freiburg as late as January of 1962: "Time and Being."[21] In any case it is clear that soon after the publication of *Being and Time* the project was in trouble. Heidegger had rushed his treatise into print prematurely under publish-or-perish conditions in an effort to win an appointment to

19. SZ 24.5–6 = 45.31 speaks of SZ I.1–2 as (in Kantian terms) an "Analytik der Subjektivität des Subjekts."

20. GA 44: 179.6 = 175.33.

21. GA 14: 5–30 = 1–24.

a chair of philosophy at Marburg University. In the event the effort failed, and Heidegger was left with a book project about which he would later write, "The fundamental flaw of the book *Being and Time* is perhaps that I ventured forth too far too soon."[22]

The hastiness with which *Being and Time* was written is evidenced by the laundry list of topics that the book merely mentions and then defers for treatment in SZ I.3. The main topic of that missing division was to be the working out of the clearing itself as the horizon for the "temporal" determination of all forms of being. But along with that central topic, Heidegger promised that the forthcoming division would also treat the following topics (all references are to SZ):

- the possibility of regional ontologies, based on the "non-deductive genealogy of the different possible modes of being" (11.10–14 = 31.18–21)
- the possibility of ontological conceptuality (39.18–19 = 63.22–24)
- the distinction between the "who" of ex-sistence and the "what" of objective presence in the broadest sense (45.6–9 = 71.3–7)
- why Parmenides and the rest of Western philosophy have overlooked the phenomenon of the world (100.27–30 = 133.29–32)
- why things-within-the-world intervene as an ontological theme rather than the phenomenon of the world[23] (100.31–32 = 133.33–34)
- why such things-within-the-world are found in the first instance in "nature" (100.33 = 133.35)
- why the phenomenon of value crops up whenever one needs to round out an ontology of the world (100.34–35 = 133.36–37)
- the full treatment of λόγος (160.10–13 = 202.39–203.2)
- what it means to say that "being *is*" (230.7–10 = 272.36–39)
- an interpretation of the kinds of things that require a regional division of the totality of things (241.21–22 = 285.21–22)
- the condition of notness and negativity (286.5–10 = 332.5–9; see GA 9: 173.16–8 = 133.30–31)
- the variations of "being" for everything of which we say "it is" (333.29–32 = 382.24–26)
- a repetition of the analysis of ex-sistence on the truly ontological level at which the concept of being will have reached (333.35–37 = 382.30–32)[24]

22. GA 12: 89.1–2 = 7.32–34: "zu früh zu weit."

23. This sentence foreshadows the question that concludes "Was ist Metaphysik?" at GA 9: 122.27–28 = 96.31–32: "Warum ist überhaupt Seiendes und nicht vielmehr Nichts?"

24. This is what Heidegger called "the *thematic* analysis of ex-sistence" (SZ 436.23–25 = 487.4–6) and the proper carrying out (*Durchführung*) of the analysis of ex-sistence (ibid., 13.8–10 = 33.24–25). See also GA 14: 40.13–15 = 32.12–14. This repetition of the analysis of ex-sistence should not be confused with the *first* repetition of ex-sistence in terms of

- the "temporal" constitution of discourse and the "temporal" characteristics of language patterns (349.25–29 = 400.36–40)
- how meaning arises (349.33–35 = 498.7 note xiii)
- the possibility of concept-formation (loc. cit.)
- the ontological meaning of the "is" of the copula (349.30 = 401.1)
- the existential interpretation of science (357.13–17 = 408.29–32)
- the full idea of phenomenology (357.17–20 = 408.32–36)
- the thematizing of the *as*-structure (360.20–24 = 411.36–412.2)
- how the intentionality of consciousness is grounded in the unity of ex-sistence's self-transcendence (363 note = 498.24–26 note xxiii)
- the concrete elaboration of the world-structure in general and its possible variations (366.35–39 = 418.9–13)
- how space and time are coupled together (368.25–27 = 420.3–4)
- an adequate conceptual interpretation of everydayness (372.2–5 = 423.24–27)
- the differentiation between the ontic and the historical (403.35–39 = 455.23–26)
- how time has its own mode of being (406.1–5 = 458.1–5)[25]

To justify such a litany of topics, it would seem that by the time he finished SZ I.1–2, Heidegger must have already had (or at least wants the reader to think he had) a virtually complete draft of SZ I.3, or at least a detailed outline. However, that eventuality is far from certain. Nonetheless, some bits of evidence attest that Heidegger had some elements of a draft of "Time and Being" by the time he submitted the final text of SZ I.1–2 to the printer. None of these reports, however, is very strong; at best they provide only hints and a few clues.

First of all: Heidegger informed Hans-Georg Gadamer that in early 1927 SZ I.3 was ready to be printed along with I.1 and I.2. Nevertheless, the third division was held back because Heidegger's SZ had to share the already oversized volume VIII of Husserl's *Jahrbuch für Philosophie und phänomenologische Forschung* with Oskar Becker's 370-page treatise *Mathematische Existenz: Untersuchungen zur Logik und Ontologie mathematischer Phänomene.*[26]

"temporality." That takes place at SZ I.2, chapter 4: see SZ 17.22–24 = 38.23–25; 234.36–38 = 277.33–38; 304.31–34 = 352.19–22; and 333.32–34 = 382.27–28.

25. Later, in GA 24: 319.23–24 = 224.7–8, Heidegger added another topic: the possible variations and different regions of being.

26. Oral communication to this writer from Gadamer, 12 April 1974. On the basis of Theodore Kisiel's research (see below) I find Heidegger's claim to be dubious. See also the elaboration at GA 66: 413.25–30 = 366.30–35.

Second: Ten weeks after publishing *Being and Time* Heidegger began his lecture course "The Basic Problems of Phenomenology" (30 April 1927), and a marginal note to his own manuscript of the text reads, "A new working out of Part I, Division 3, of *Being and Time*." In that regard, Professor Friedrich-Wilhelm von Herrmann, who edited the course for publication as GA 24, reports:

> The designation "*New* working out" means that an *older* one preceded it. The first working out of the Division "Time and Being" came about in the train of writing Divisions 1 and 2. As Martin Heidegger has communicated to me orally, he burned the first draft [*die erste Fassung*] soon after he wrote it.[27]

Third: A footnote in the first edition of SZ at p. 349 (but omitted from 1953 onwards—that is, in the seventh and following editions) refers the reader ahead to *chapter 2* of SZ I.3 for a clarification of the origin of meaning and the possibility of concept formation. This is the only reference to a specific chapter within SZ I.3, and it would seem to indicate that Heidegger had at least some kind of outline of "Time and Being," if not a full text, when he wrote the footnote.[28]

Fourth: What about the contents of this famous missing section? As Theodore Kisiel has reported, all that has survived in the Marbach archives is a large packet of notes ("some 200 pages"), thirty pages of which have been published.[29] But it is difficult to discern how "Time and Being" would have been organized as a whole, much less how it would have accommodated the list of twenty-plus topics provided above. Basing himself on the large packet of archived notes, Kisiel remarks:

> A summary of the classification of the notes indicates a division into about six chapters in the missing division. Chapter 1 would have probably borne a title such as "Phenomenology and the Positive Sciences" and would have treated the method of ontological (as opposed to ontic) thematization. "Temporality (*Zeitlichkeit*) and Worldliness" is the explicit title of Chapter 4, which would have taken its themes primarily from § 69c of *Being and Time*.[30]

Fifth: But we have a thicker sketch of some of the material from the first draft of SZ I.3, thanks to a post-war exchange between Heidegger and his former student, Professor Max Müller. Müller writes:

27. GA 2: 582.25–29 (Editor's Epilogue).

28. This early footnote is given in the Macquarrie-Robinson translation of *Being and Time* at 498.7 note xiii.

29. The published pages are in Heidegger, "Aufzeichnungen zur Temporalität," 11–23.

30. Kisiel, "The Demise of *Being and Time*," 211.10–15.

> According to a personal communication, in the first elaboration of *Sein und Zeit*, Part I, Division 3—which, as I mentioned above, was to bear the title "*Zeit und Sein*" and was to bring about a "turn" in the treatment of being itself [= the planned change of focus, from ex-sistence to the clearing]—Heidegger attempted to distinguish a threefold difference:
>
> 1. the "transcendental" ["*transzendentale*"] difference, or ontological difference in the *narrower* sense: the differentiation of things from their being.
> 2. the "transcendence-related" ["*transzendenzhafte*"] difference or ontological difference in the wider sense: the differentiation of things *and* their being from [the clearing].[31]
> 3. the "transcendent" ["*transzendente*"] difference, or the theological difference in the strict sense: the differentiation of God from things, being, and [the clearing].
>
> However, because it was not experienced but only set up speculatively, this attempt at a draft was given up as "onto-theological," because it ventures an assertion about God which even now in the experience of "essential thinking" is not immediately made.[32]

This report by Müller presents us with three kinds of "difference," each of which plays on the word "transcendence" in a different way. The first two kinds correspond to major elements of Heidegger's project as we know it, whereas the third is one that he let drop.

MÜLLER:
THREE KINDS OF "DIFFERENCE" IN HEIDEGGER

1. **things ← as differentiated from → their being: the transcend*ental* difference**
   This ontological difference (in the *narrow* sense) is related to acts of taking something *as* or *in terms of* its whatness and howness. This is the difference that metaphysics already knows about.
2. **the being of things ← as differentiated from → the clearing: the transcend*ence*-related difference**
   This ontological difference (in the *wider* sense) is a matter of the structure of ex-sistence as meta-metaphysical. As the thrown-open clearing, ex-sistence is always already beyond—and is the groundless ground for—things-in-their-being.
3. **things, their being, and the clearing ← differentiated from → God: the transcen*dent* difference**
   This is the classical onto-theological difference between non-divine being and divine being.

31. Müller uses the term "das Sein selbst" here, but to avoid the ambiguity in Heidegger's use of "das Sein," both here and in the next sentence I substitute "the clearing" for the merely formal indicative "das Sein selbst."

32. Müller, *Existenzphilosophie*, 73f.

Heidegger's remarks as reported by Müller tally at least in part with a marginal note in Heidegger's personal copy of SZ. At SZ § 8, where he presents the outline of his treatise, he glosses the title of SZ I.3, "*Zeit und Sein*," with an outline of how that division was to unfold (the numbering is mine):

1. *Die transzendenzhafte Differenz.*
2. *Die Überwindung des Horizonts als solchen.*
3. *Die Umkehr in die Herkunft.*[33]
4. *Das Anwesen aus dieser Herkunft.*[34]

1. The transcendence-related difference.
2. The overcoming of the horizon as such.
3. The turn into the origin.[35]
4. Meaningful presence from out of this origin.

Only apparently cryptic, this gloss gives us an important insight into how Heidegger envisioned his project early on and how he in fact carried it out in his later work. The following numbers refer to the list above.

1. "The transcendence-related difference" between things-in-their-being and the clearing maps onto the difference between traditional ontology and Heidegger's own work. In *Being and Time* he carried out his project in a transcendental framework where the clearing for being/meaningfulness was seen as a horizon that is projected open (existentially, not existentielly) by the very structure of ex-sistence.

2. "The overcoming of the horizon as such" references Heidegger's later insight into the inadequacy of viewing the clearing as a transcendental horizon. Whereas *Being and Time* argued that the clearing (here called "the horizon") is always already *thrown open structurally* rather than being projected open by a personal-existentiel act, Heidegger wanted to avoid any impression that the clearing is open only because of "the fact that we look into it,"[36] an impression that a transcendental approach might well give. So he abandoned the transcendental-horizonal approach and shifted to what he called a *seinsgeschichtlich* approach, one that discusses how various configurations of the clearing are "given" (or "sent": *geschickt*) in so-called "dispensations" (*Geschicke*), the

33. The next chapter will show that this Kehre-as-Umkehr is not the *primary and proper* meaning of die Kehre (namely, die Gegenschwung), but rather is only the long-planned change of focus between SZ I.1–2 (Da-*sein*) and SZ I.3 (*Da*-sein) that Heidegger mentions at GA 9: 328.1 and .3 = 250.1 and .3: "Hier kehrt sich das Ganze um." This is the "turn" to which Müller, too, refers in his report.

34. GA 2: 53 note a = Stambaugh 37 note †.

35. See note 33, above.

36. GA 77: 112.8 = 72.31–32: "daß wir hineinsehen."

concatenation of which Heidegger called his "history of the dispensations of the clearing" or *Seinsgeschichte*. (See chapter 9.)

3. "The turn into the origin" refers to the transition from SZ I.2 to SZ I.3 that was already foreseen and programmed into the original project of *Being and Time* in 1926: the progression from *ex-sistence* as sustaining the clearing (= SZ I.1–2) to *the sustained clearing* (which is the same as ex-sistence) insofar as it is responsible for all meaningfulness (= SZ I.3). This is not *die Kehre* in its primary and proper sense (see chapter 8).

4. "Meaningful presence from out of this origin" (which Heidegger elsewhere calls "being with regard to its essential origin")[37] refers to the core element of Heidegger's phenomenology: the search for "the thing itself"—that is, the *origin* of meaningfulness. The phrase implicitly affirms that the thrown-open clearing is the fundamental presupposition (*prae-sub-positum*) and groundless ground of our need and ability to make sense of everything we encounter.

3. A "NEW" WORKING OUT OF SZ I.3 IN "BASIC PROBLEMS OF PHENOMENOLOGY"

The fourfold list given just above provides something of a "diachronic" menu of how Heidegger planned to proceed in working out the material of SZ I.3. Just ten weeks after *Being and Time* was published, Heidegger began his Marburg course "Basic Problems of Phenomenology" (30 April–17 July 1927), which he envisioned as "a new elaboration of *Being and Time*, Part One, Division 3."[38] On the second day of the course Heidegger presented a more "synchronic" and topical plan of the core contents that he projected for SZ I.3:

1. the ontological difference
2. being as *essentia* and *existentia*
3. the possible modifications and unity of being
4. the "truth"-character of being [i.e., ἀλήθεια-1][39]

However, Heidegger spent most of that course providing background about being (in Kant, Aristotle, Descartes, and logic: 7 May to 2 July) and about time (Aristotle's *Physics* IV: 6 July), as well as briefly reviewing the core of *Being*

37. GA 12: 249 note 2 (carried over from the previous page) = 129 n.: "Sein hinsichtlich seiner Wesensherkunft."

38. GA 24: 1, note 1 = 1, note 1: "Neue Ausarbeitung."

39. GA 24: 33.5–11 = 24.12–17 (4 May 1927).

and Time (13 and 16 July). Thus it was only in the last half of the last day of the course (16 July 1927) that he left the material of SZ I.1–2 behind and made a brief sortie into the "new" material of what was to be SZ I.3, in what turned out to be a not very informative effort to elaborate the "temporal" horizon of "the present."

In *Being and Time*, the closest Heidegger had come to discussing the clearing as the "temporal" horizon for all forms of being was SZ § 69c, "The Temporal Problem of the Transcendence of the World." In § 65 Heidegger had already established that the structure of ex-sistence as aheadness-and-return (becoming-what-it-already-is *as* being-meaningfully-present-to-itself) is what in turn allows things to be meaningfully present to ex-sistence. At § 69c he had reiterated that same point, but in specifically transcendental-horizonal language:

> By tracing being-in-the-world back to the thrown-open horizonal unity of "temporality," we have made intelligible the existential and ontological possibility of this fundamental constitution of ex-sistence.[40]

> [Ex-sistence] already maintains itself in the *horizons of its ex-stases*, and, as it unfolds in that way, it returns to the things it encounters within the open.[41]

In § 69c he went on to assert, briefly and dogmatically, that correlative to the three-reducible-to-two "temporal" modes of self-transcendence or thrown-openness (the "ex-stases"), there is a unified horizon comprised of three-moments-reducible-to-two. That is to say: As "temporal," ex-sistence is thrown-open *as* empty horizonal formations (like "moments" or even "regions" of the clearing) that correspond to, respectively, its "becoming" (or aheadness), its "thrownness" (or its being *always-already* ahead in meaningful possibilities), and its "present" (as being-present-to-itself and making-other-things-present). These "temporal" moments of the opened-up horizon that provide a "temporal" shape or coloration to the meaningful presence of the things we meet. However, that is as far as Heidegger had gotten by February of 1927.

Now, in the course "Basic Problems of Phenomenology," he took a further stab at explaining how the transcendental-horizonal clearing determines two things: (1) the "directionality" of thrown-openness and, in turn, (2) the "temporal" meaningfulness of whatever we encounter.[42] In § 21a of "Basic

40. SZ 366.32–34 = 418.7–9

41. SZ 366.4–6 = 417.18–21. "Unfolds": sich zeitigend.

42. SZ 365.20–21 = 416.30–32: "Der Horizont der ganzen Zeitlichkeit bestimmt das, *woraufhin* das faktisch existierende Seiende wesenhaft *erschlossen* ist."

Problems,"[43] Heidegger argues that, correlative to the three (reducible-to-two) ways ex-sistence is thrown open as possibility, there are three specific and distinct "schemata," possible ways of "having" and shaping their meaningfulness both of ourselves and of possible objects.[44] Heidegger's treatment of horizonal schemata in "Basic Problems" is quite complex. The following diagram may at least help visualize matters.

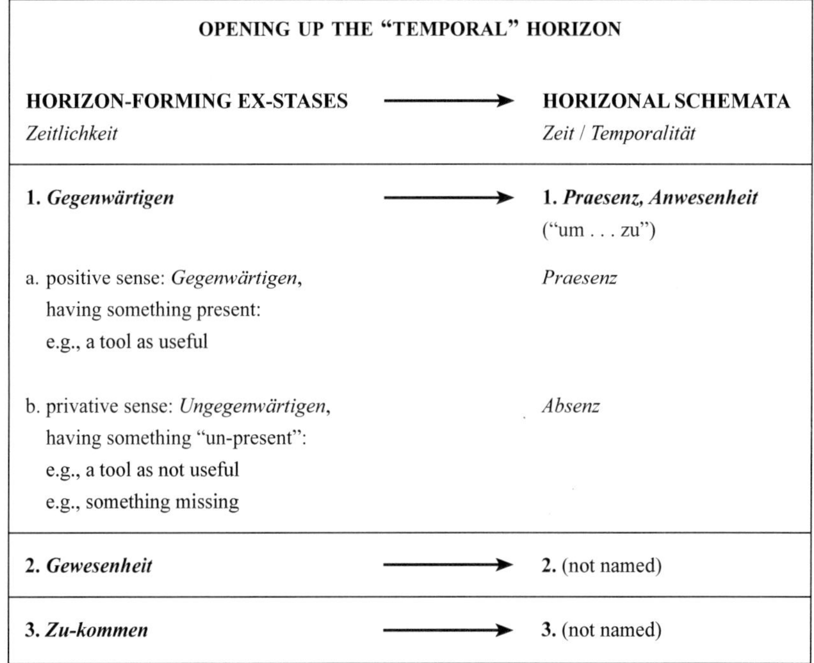

OPENING UP THE "TEMPORAL" HORIZON

HORIZON-FORMING EX-STASES *Zeitlichkeit*	→	**HORIZONAL SCHEMATA** *Zeit / Temporalität*
1. *Gegenwärtigen*	→	**1. *Praesenz, Anwesenheit*** ("um . . . zu")
a. positive sense: *Gegenwärtigen*, having something present: e.g., a tool as useful		*Praesenz*
b. privative sense: *Ungegenwärtigen*, having something "un-present": e.g., a tool as not useful e.g., something missing		*Absenz*
2. *Gewesenheit*	→	**2.** (not named)
3. *Zu-kommen*	→	**3.** (not named)

Heidegger describes a schema as the "whereunto" (*das Woraufhin*) of the directionality of ex-sistence as thrown-open or self-transcending; and the horizonal schema in turn determines how objects are "shaped" as "temporally" meaningful. He notes that "each ex-stasis as such has a horizon that is determined by it and that first of all completes that ex-stasis's own structure."[45] The ex-stasis of becoming (man's so-called "futurity" or *Zukünftigkeit*) opens

43. GA 24: 431–445 = 303–13.

44. The word "schema" (Greek: σχῆμα) is derived from the verb ἔχω, "to have," through the second aorist infinitive σχεῖν. The Latin for σχῆμα (as likewise for ἕξις) is "habitus": the way something has itself, bears itself. From that come the meanings "figure, shape, form" (as well as "looks, appearance").

45. GA 24: 435.10–12 = 306.21–22.

up the region of self-concern (ex-sistence is for the sake of itself), while the ex-stasis of thrownness opens up the arena of alreadiness (*das Gewesen*), and the ex-stasis of making things present opens up the field of the "in order to" (*um . . . zu*). Thus, at one pole, the three unified moments of thrown-openness; at the other pole, the three unified moments of the open region—the whole of this constituting a thrown-open correlation that is the articulated shape of our openness.

It is not entirely clear what Heidegger hoped to achieve by showing the symmetry between thrown-openness and the articulated horizon that it holds open. The pages that make up "Basic Problems" § 21a ("*Temporalität und Sein*") add very little to what he had already said in SZ § 69 about the thrown-open structure of ex-sistence; in fact, the few steps he takes into the supposedly new material are quite hesitant. "In order not to complicate too much our view of the phenomenon of 'temporality,'" he says, "which in any case is difficult to grasp,"[46] he imposes a double limit on his treatment. (1) He restricts himself to only *one* of the three horizonal schemata, the one corresponding to the ex-stasis of "the present" (having something meaningfully present), and he does not take up the schemata that correlate with becoming and alreadiness. (2) Within that one horizonal schema, he further restricts himself to dealing only with tools, to the exclusion of whatever else one can render meaningfully present.

Correlative to but distinct from the moment of having a tool present and useful in terms of a task, there is the horizonal schema whose thrown-open "time"-character is called presence (*Praesenz*).[47] Having-present, as an ex-static moment, has a schematic pre-indication (*Vorzeichnung*)[48] of that out-towards-which transcendence reaches in using a tool—namely, the horizon of *Praesenz* (also called *Anwesenheit*). *Praesenz* thus constitutes "the condition of the possibility of understanding usefulness as such."[49] Having-present, in fact, understands whatever it has-present in terms of this field of *Praesenz* and so understands those things as having a "presential sense" (*ein praesentialer Sinn*) and thus as "meaningfully present things" (*als Anwesendes*).[50]

As he had done earlier in SZ § 69c, so again in "Basic Problems" Heidegger analyzes the breakdown of a tool and finds therein a privative modifica-

46. GA 24: 435.32–33 = 306.37–38.

47. In order to show the distinctness of the thrown-open ("ex-static") pole and the horizonal pole in their correlativity, Heidegger generally, but not consistently, uses German-based words for the thrown-open pole (for example, *Zeitlichkeit, Zukunft, Gewesenheit, Gegenwart*) and Latin-based words for the horizonal pole (*Temporalität, Praesenz, Absenz*): GA 24: 433.25–29 = 305.20–23.

48. GA 24: 435.20 = 306.28.

49. GA 24: 434.9–10 = 305.35–36.

50. GA 24: 433.22 = 305.17 and 436.6 = 307.2, respectively.

tion of having-the-tool-present to having-it-un-present or, in other words, a modification of its being from usefulness to unavailability (from *Zuhandenheit* to *Abhandenheit*), from presentness to un-presentness (from *Anwesenheit* to *Abwesenheit*).[51] He uses the "un-" to indicate that the no-longer-useful tool is still *there* in the carpenter shop but no longer present *as useful*.

> Thus there is in general no horizon corresponding to "missing" as a determined [mode of] having-present, but rather a *specifically modified horizon . . . of presence*. Belonging to the ex-stasis of having-unpresent, which makes "missing" possible, there is the horizonal schema of *absence*.[52]
>
> This absential modification of the presence . . . which is given with [the experience of] missing, is precisely what allows the useful to become conspicuous [as lacking].[53]

At this point (GA 24: 443.24 = 312.4) Heidegger's advance into SZ I.3 stops, and it is a very meager advance at that. At bottom, all we have seen is that, correlative to the ex-stasis of "making-present," there is a horizonal schema of *Praesenz* or presentness, with un-presentness as its privative modification. But this has been shown in only the one horizonal schema corresponding to the one ex-stasis of having-present in the one area of tool-use. Left undiscussed are: the other "temporal" schemata (with their privative modifications) in which tools are experienced; all the "temporal" schemata of non-tools; and above all, the unified "temporal" meaning of the horizon-for-being as such. The course "Basic Problems of Phenomenology" hardly represents any notable progress into SZ I.3—a sign, perhaps, that the project of SZ as planned was already in trouble as soon as it was published.

Despite Heidegger's failure to make progress in working out SZ I.3 in the spring and summer of 1927, the same new, fourfold outline for SZ I.3 that he provided in "Basic Problems of Phenomenology" continued at least through the following summer. In his last semester at Marburg he repeated it at the very end of his course on "The Metaphysical Foundations of Logic" (10 July 1928), along with a slight and unremarkable rearrangement of the outline:

1. the ontological difference
2. the articulation of being into whatness and thatness
3. the truth-character of being
4. the regionality of being and the unity of the idea of being[54]

---

51. GA 24: 433.17 = 305.17 and 436.7–8 = 307.4–5, respectively.
52. GA 24: 442.1–4 = 311.3–6.
53. GA 24: 442.29–31 = 311.24–26.
54. GA 26: 191.29–194.2 = 151.24–153.4.

That fall (24 October 1928), during his first semester in Freiburg as Husserl's successor, Heidegger told the Australian philosopher (and translator of Husserl's *Ideen I*) W. R. Boyce Gibson that it would be "some little time"—not likely by the next issue of Husserl's *Jahrbuch*—before the rest of *Being and Time* appeared.[55] After that we hear nothing more about the completion of Heidegger's *magnum opus*. The project of SZ, which basically remains enclosed within the Marburg period, had apparently ground to a halt. In the 1953 Foreword to the seventh edition of SZ we read:

> While the previous editions have borne the designation "First Half" [= SZ I.1–2], this has now been deleted. After a quarter of a century, the second half [especially SZ I.3 but also II.1–3] could no longer be added unless the first were presented anew. Nonetheless, the road it has taken remains even today a necessary one, if our ex-sistence is to be stirred by the question of being.[56]

But back for a moment to SZ § 69c, where Heidegger adds an important proviso to his transcendental-horizonal treatment of the future material of SZ I.3. There he notes that, given our factical ex-sistence, whatever we might meet is already dis-covered within our own openedness—that is, it is a priori meaningful. However:

> The fact that such things get dis-covered along with the openedness of our own ex-sistence does not mean that this matter is under our control. Only *what*, in *which* direction, *to what extent, and how* we actually dis-cover and dis-close is a matter of our freedom, although always within the limits of our thrownness.[57]

"Not under our control." The major issue in the transition to SZ I.3 was the question of the clearing in itself and in relation to intelligibility at all. We noted above that Heidegger was at pains to avoid the impression that thought, or human will, makes the clearing come to pass.[58] "The meaning-giving relations that determine the structure of the world are not a network of forms that a worldless subject casts over things."[59] That having been said, however, the transcendental approach that Heidegger employed, along with the language of ex-sistence "projecting" the horizon, did risk the misunderstanding that

55. Gibson, "From Husserl to Heidegger," 72b.22–23.
56. SZ v.10–14 (Vorbemerkung) = 17.10–14.
57. SZ 366.7–11 = 417.22–27.
58. See note 64.
59. SZ 366.12–14 = 417.28–30: "Bedeutsamkeitsbezüge . . . kein Netzwerk . . . übergestülpt."

ex-sistence opens the clearing and grounds meaning by an existentiel act. Take the following sentence, for example: "We understand *Sein* from out of the original horizonal schema of the ex-stases of 'temporality'."[60] This could be misread as saying that we ourselves, existentielly, project open the horizon for being. But once we understand that the ex-stasies of "temporality" are merely specifications of the *thrown*-open-ness of ex-sistence, Heidegger's sentence provides not the least warrant for such a misunderstanding. In SZ Heidegger was clear about the fundamental and inescapable priority of the existential-structural thrownness of ex-sistence over any and all ways of existentielly understanding the being of things.

> Disclosing [things] is not the result of knowledge and thus does not have the same essential origin as knowledge. Whether a thing is hidden or disclosed, it has its home [i.e., its essential origin] in the clearing.[61]

Nonetheless he feared—rightly, in the event—that some readers might wrongly infer that ex-sistence projects open the meaning-giving horizon "subjectively," by an act of will. The verb "to project" might abet such a misunderstanding, and here, as with his use of the word *Sein*, Heidegger may have been his own worst enemy. Again, following Aristotle's διορίσωμεν,[62] let us make some distinctions. In *Being and Time*, the verb *entwerfen* has two very distinct meanings, existentiel and existential, although Heidegger does not always make that clear. In the existentiel sense, *entwerfen auf* means "to project some thing *in terms of* something else" (never "upon" something else), more specifically: to take X *as* or *as suitable for* Y. The image that comes with *ent-werfen* is: to "throw" X forward, as it were, in the direction of a task or a possible meaning so as to see whether it is suitable for that task, or whether it is the possible subject of a certain predicate. In these cases, "to project something" means to *understand* it by taking it in terms of something else: a rock in terms of hammering, Socrates in terms of being-a-philosopher. "Projection" here refers to the existentiel act of σύνθεσις-as-διαίρεσις:[63] synthesizing two things in thought or action while keeping them distinct.

But there is a second meaning of *entwerfen*, a structural-existential one. As we have seen, performing concrete acts of projecting and synthesizing requires the always-already-opened existential "space" for doing so, and for Heidegger, this space is not opened up by one's own will. Our ex-sistence is structurally

60. GA 24: 436.11–13 = 307.7–8.

61. GA 88: 311.7–10: keine Frucht der Erkenntnis; nicht gleichen Wesensursprungs; beheimatet im Sein.

62. *Metaphysics* X 6, 1048a26.

63. See GA 21: 135–161 = 114–135.

pro-jected (*geworfen*; even *als Entworfenes*) “before” we can existentielly project X in terms of Y.[64] Hence we have a second meaning of *entwerfen* or *Entwurf* as the essential structure of human being. Here the word *Entwurf* (cf. the homologous Latin word *pro-jectum*, something *thrown* forward) is not a matter of “project*ing* [something]” but rather of “being project*ed*.” The German *Wurf* can mean both the throwing (*jacere*) and the thrown (*jactum*).[65] Therefore, I will translate (1) *Entwurf* in its existentiel meaning as the “taking-as” (or “projection”) of something in terms of something else; and (2) *Entwurf* in its existential sense as man’s “being thrown” or “projected” open as the clearing.[66]

> Being projected means opening up and holding open the open region, opening up the clearing within which what we call and know by the name of being (not things) is *manifest* as *being*.[67]

The clearing is indeed projected open, but not by a subjective act of will. Heidegger establishes this a priori existential projectedness in the same way that he does in all his phenomenology: from a well-described *operatio* to its most probable form of *esse*, from actual human acts to what most likely explains how they are possible. We do in fact make sense of things by existentiel acts of projection. But if we *do* that, we must be *able* to do that. And Heidegger argues that our existentiel acts of projection are made possible by our existential projectedness as *thrown possibility*, a structural openedness within which we can understand the things in terms of *their* possibilities.

However, once Heidegger has established this argument about man’s a priori projectedness, he can and must affirm the obvious: that within the limits of our thrownness, we ourselves do indeed decide the meanings of things on our own initiative, whether practically or theoretically. (Does this squiggle on the computer screen represent a meson or a gluon? Is President So-and-So a beacon of democracy or a fascist?) Yes, we are structurally thrown-open; but nonetheless it is we ourselves, as existentiel actors, who decide the current whatness

---

64. GA 65: 239.17–18 = 188.36: “enthüllt sich, daß er selbst [= der Werfer], je entwerfender er wird, um so geworfener schon der Geworfene ist”; ibid. 45.21 = 37.21: “Der geworfene Werfer.” These later texts merely restate the fundamental position of SZ.

65. Wurf as “what gets thrown”: “Wurf” can mean the sketch that has been sketched; in baseball, the pitch that has been thrown; or, in dog breeding, the litter of pups that a bitch has thrown.

66. See GA 66: 325.30–32 = 289.19: Dasein “als Entworfenes eines Entwurfs.”

67. GA 49: 41.25–28: “Ent-wurf besagt: ‘Er-öffnung und Offenhalten des Offenen, Lichten der Lichtung, in der das, was wir Sein (nicht das Seiende) nennen und somit unter diesem Namen auch kennen, eben als *Sein offenkundig* ist.’”

and howness of things, their *jeweiliges Sein*. What is more, there is *in principle no limit* to what we can know about the knowable or do with the doable. There should be no shrinking back from the human will, no looking askance at the scientific and technological achievements of existentiel "subjects" in the modern world—with only one proviso: so long as such achievements do not hinder but rather promote the full humanization of human beings—that is, the co-existential (*mitdaseinsmäßig*) flourishing of what Heidegger called the *perfectio* of our shared ex-sistence: "becoming what we can be as free for our ownmost possibilities (our being projected)."[68]

Underlying the whole of Heidegger's philosophy is the fact that we cannot encounter anything outside the parameters that define us as human—as a thrown-open, socially and historically embodied λόγος. But granted that much, we also cannot *not* make sense of anything we meet, whether in practice or in theory.[69] In the theoretical order, we make sense of things in existentiel acts of λέγειν as ἀποφαίνεσθαι: showing things in the way we claim (rightly or wrongly) that they are. In the practical order we also make sense of things, but by changing them in some way. Heideggerians seem a bit anxious about the practical (not to mention technological) achievements of the existentiel subject—including socio-political projects for "changing the world."[70] However, as τὸ ζῷον τὸ λόγον ἔχον, we possess the power not only to make sense of things cognitively but also to remake the world as we see fit, for better or worse. But we possess that power only because we are *possessed by* the existential ability to make sense and change the world: ὁ λόγος τὸν ἄνθρωπον ἔχων.[71] Without the clearing we would be worse than blind: we would be dead. But without existentiel acts of λέγειν, the clearing would be empty—and we might as well be dead.

Pace Heideggerian nervousness about the matter, we certainly *are* conscious subjects and should not overlook, much less denigrate, that fact. Conscious subjectivity is a given for ex-sistence, whether we read that as

68. SZ 199.15–16 = 243.27–28: "Das perfectio des Menschen, das Werden zu dem, was er in seinem Freisein für seine eigensten Möglichkeiten (dem Entwurf) sein kann." (Note that "dem Entwurf" is in the dative as the object of "zu." I take it out of parentheses.) This seems to go against the grain of so many of Heidegger's followers. But why should it?

69. To make sense of something is in fact to change it—even to "humanize" it—if only by introducing it into a human world, whether practical or theoretical.

70. See Heidegger's own ambivalence (if we can call it that) expressed at GA 16: 702.33–703.25 = 81.27–33.

71. See GA 40: 184.11 = 195.11: φύσις = λόγος ἄνθρωπον ἔχων—the ever-hidden giving of the clearing means that the necessity to make discursive sense of things "possesses" man. See GA 9: 75.3 = 59.24: "die Sprache, die den Menschen 'hat.'" That is: λόγος/the clearing—as what makes possible acts of discursive sense-making, whether silently or in speech—defines human being.

psychological subjectivity à la Husserl, or existentiel subjectivity à la Heidegger, or social subjectivity à la Marx. Ex-sistence does have things intentionally present-to-mind and even "represents" them (*vorstellen*) and sometimes has to treat them as "objects" (*Gegenstände*)—otherwise, all its hammering and nailing and other practical activities could turn out to be quite a mess. But Heidegger's point is that the basis for such worldly intentional acts is the "essence" of the subject, "the subjectivity of the subject"[72] as always already "drawn out"[73] in such a way that existentiel subjects *can* be intentional and *can* change the world—as described, for example, in the first choral ode of Sophocles' *Antigone*.[74] Modern subjectivity, in and of itself, is a glorious fact that should be celebrated, along with all its humanizing achievements, including calculative thinking, scientific discoveries, and technological advances. Heidegger's grounding of such subjectivity in the finite and mortal clearing in no way puts the breaks on such achievements. The interplay between finite existential projectedness and open-ended existentiel projecting is not, on Heidegger's own principles, a zero-sum game.

4. THE SCOPE OF FUNDAMENTAL ONTOLOGY

In *Being and Time*, and in the first years after the book was published, Heidegger called his central question "the fundamental ontological question about the intelligibility of being in general," and he designated his enterprise as "fundamental ontology."[75] But soon thereafter he found this title misleading and dropped it from his lexicon.[76] Nonetheless, in dropping the term "fundamental ontology," Heidegger did not give up the *project* of SZ, although he did transform his approach to that project. That alteration in Heidegger's procedure in the 1930s, his change from a transcendental to a *seinsgeschichtlich* approach, has long been called the "turn" (*die Kehre*). (As we shall see in chapter 8, that is not the primary and proper meaning of *die Kehre* in Heidegger's work.) He insisted on calling the alteration of his procedure in the 1930s a *Wendung*

72. SZ 24.6 = 45.31.

73. Drawn out: GA 8: 11.6–8 = 9.13–15: "zieht uns" etc.

74. See GA 40: 155ff. = 163ff.; GA 13: 35–36; GA 53: 71ff. = 57ff.

75. SZ 436.9–10 = 486.27–28: "die fundamentalontologische Frage nach dem Sinn von Sein überhaupt."

76. GA 9: 380.15–16 = 288.34–5; GA 14: 39.19–21 = 31.19–20. Also GA 83: 222.19–21: "Die *Fundamentalontologie* macht die Ontologie als solche zum *Problem* und *darum selber keine Ontologie und keine Metaphysik mehr*."

or *Wandlung*, an alteration in his approach to his unchanging topic.[77] Moreover, this altered approach is distinct from the already planned transition from SZ I.1–2 (ex-sistence as sustaining the clearing) to SZ I.3 (the clearing as the source of all forms of meaningful presence). So we must distinguish (and we will take up these questions in the next chapter):

1. the transition from ex-sistence to the clearing (planned in 1926),
2. the change from a transcendental to a *seinsgeschichtlich* approach (carried out in the 1930s), and
3. *die Kehre* in the primary and proper sense of that term.

We begin now with a question: Before Heidegger dropped "fundamental ontology" as a description of his early work, what did the term refer to? In answering that question, *doctores scinduntur*—and in fact not only are the *scholars* divided on this matter. Heidegger himself in *Being and Time* and "Basic Problems of Phenomenology" (the lecture course of 1927) seems divided against himself in his declarations of what comprises fundamental ontology. There are three options for what fundamental ontology did cover, or was meant to.

Option one. Fundamental ontology encompasses only SZ I.1–2, that is, basically the existential analytic of ex-sistence as authentic care (*Sorge*) and thrown-openness (*Zeitlichkeit*).

Option two. Fundamental ontology was restricted to the unpublished SZ I.3 alone, the elaboration of the finitude of intelligibility and of all its modifications and regions.

Option three. Fundamental ontology comprises all of Part I of SZ as originally projected—that is, SZ I.1–3.

The least one can say is that in 1927 Heidegger himself seemed ambivalent on this question. Finally, however, he clearly affirmed the third option—namely, that fundamental ontology refers to the entire project outlined for Part I of *Being and Time* (although not Part II).[78]

But first the ambivalence: Throughout much of his magnum opus and in the lecture course that immediately followed its publication, Heidegger seems

77. See GA 11: 150.19 = xix.26–27 (Wendung im Denken); GA 9: 187.21–22 = 143.33 (Wandlung des Denkens) and ibid. 202.4–5 = 154.18 (Wandel des Fragens); GA 14: 35.14 = 27.24: "Wandel des Heideggerschen Denkens." Cf. GA 65: 84.32–85.1 = 67.34: "vom Grund aus wandeln."

78. Although fundamental ontology does not include SZ II *per se*, Heidegger does say, "The question of the intelligibility of being does not achieve its true concreteness until we have carried through the process of destroying the ontological tradition": SZ 26.29–30 = 49.8–9.

to hold to the *first* option—that is, he restricted fundamental ontology to the analytic of ex-sistence, which in turn he confined to SZ I.1–2. On this reading, fundamental ontology corresponds to *Being and Time* as published, which was to serve as merely a foundation for the new and radical ontology that was reserved for the unpublished SZ I.3. This new ontology would differ from the tradition by arguing for the inexorable finitude of all forms of meaningful presence, grounded as that is in the utterly finite, groundless clearing. Fundamental ontology *qua* analytic of ex-sistence would thus be only a *Vorbereitung*, a preparation for a new post-metaphysical, phenomenological vision of being.[79] This first option is still held by a number of Heidegger scholars, and indeed *Being and Time* contains enough texts that seem to support it.

> Ontologies that take as their theme things of a non-existential character of being have their foundation and motivation in the ontic structure of ex-sistence itself, which comprises and is characterized by a pre-ontological understanding of being.
>
> Therefore *fundamental ontology*, from which alone all other ontologies can take their rise, must be sought in the *existential analytic of ex-sistence.*[80]

> [I]t has been shown that the ontological analytic of ex-sistence in general is what makes up fundamental ontology.[81]

And most clearly in 1962:

> According to *Being and Time* fundamental ontology is the ontological analysis of ex-sistence.[82]

And this analytic of ex-sistence is restricted to the published divisions of *Being and Time*, which work out the unity and wholeness of ex-sistence.

> Exposition of the basic constitution of ex-sistence, its existential constitution, is the task of . . . the existential analytic of the structure of ex-sistence. It must

79. It is called "vorbereitend" (preparatory—i.e., *for SZ I.3*) at GA 24: 319.21, .25, and .26 = 224.5, .8, and .9; and at 322.21 = 227.19. This usage is to be distinguished from "the preparatory fundamental analysis of ex-sistence" (SZ 41.6 = 67.2–3) that makes up SZ I.1. In that *latter* case, SZ I.1 is preparatory for SZ I.2. Confusion is almost inevitable, and this is another sign of the hastiness with which Heidegger composed SZ I.1–2. That Heidegger considered SZ I.3 to be an ontology is beyond question: SZ 37.21–26 = 61.35–40; GA 24: 323.31–34 = 228.24–26.

80. SZ 13.17–23 = 33.31–34.2.

81. SZ 14.31–33 = 35.7–8: "daß die ontologische Analytik des Daseins überhaupt die Fundamentalontologie ausmacht."

82. GA 14: 39.24–25 = 31.23–24. Ibid., 40.1 = 31.35 speaks of "[die] Fundamentalontologie des Daseins."

> aim at bringing to light the ground of the basic structures of ex-sistence in their unity [*Sorge*] and wholeness [*Sein zum Tode*]. . . . Before we discuss the basic ontological problem [= SZ I.3], the existential analytic of ex-sistence needs to be developed.[83]

In this view, the meaning of the adjective "fundamental" in "fundamental ontology" is that SZ I.1–2 is a *foundation for* the radical ontology of SZ I.3, and thus is distinct from it.

> If the interpretation of the being of ex-sistence is to become primordial, *as a foundation for working out the basic question of ontology*, then it must first have brought to light existentially the being of ex-sistence in its possibilities of authenticity and wholeness.[84]
>
> Working out and answering [the question of the intelligibility of being in SZ I.3] requires a general analytic of ex-sistence. Ontology has for its *foundational disciple* the analytic of ex-sistence.[85]
>
> [The existential analytic] can only be preparatory because it aims merely to establish *the foundation for a radical ontology.*[86]

This first option—that fundamental ontology is reducible to the existential analytic in SZ I.1–2 and is only preparatory for "Time and Being"—seems to be confirmed by the fact that, after SZ I.3 had fully worked out the intelligibility of being, the existential analytic was to be "repeated" or "retrieved" in the light of the results of Division Three. "Therefore, following the exposition of the intelligibility of being and the horizon of ontology, [the existential analytic] has to be repeated at a higher level"[87]—in fact, "in a completely different way."[88]

But a *second* option on the scope of fundamental ontology is possible, one which would confine it to the never-published SZ I.3. Heidegger speaks,

83. GA 24: 322.19–25, 30–32 = 227.18–22, .26–27. The existential analytic brings out not only the unity and wholeness of ex-sistence, as above, but also its grounding the clearing in "temporality": ibid., 323.10 = 228.7. Note, moreover, that SZ 233.33 = 276.36 adds: its authenticity.

84. SZ 233.30–34 = 276.33–34. My emphasis.

85. GA 24: 26.21–24 = 19.32–34. My emphasis.

86. GA 24: 319.28–30 = 224.11–12. My emphasis.

87. GA 24: 319.30–32 = 224.12–14. See SZ 13.7–10 = 33.23–25; 333.35–37 = 382.30–32; 436.23–25 = 487.4–6.

88. GA 14: 40.13–15 = 32.12–14.

for example, of "the fundamental ontological question of the intelligibility of being in general"[89] and of "our fundamental analysis of being"[90]—all of which, of course, pertains to and presumably would be carried out only in the unpublished division "Time and Being." And most clearly:

> The problem of differentiating between the ontic and the historical cannot be worked out as a problem for research unless we have made sure in advance what is the clue to it: the fundamental ontological clarification of the question of the intelligibility of being in general.[91]

> The analytic of ex-sistence . . . is to prepare the way for the problematic of fundamental ontology—*the question of the intelligibility of being in general.*[92]

On this reading, SZ I.1–2—*Being and Time* as published—would *not* be fundamental ontology but only a preparation for a fundamental ontology that never got written. That is, SZ I.1–2 merely works out the structures of ex-sistence while leaving to SZ I.3 the fundamental-ontological analysis of the clearing and what it makes possible. Whereas the first option would hold that Heidegger's fundamental ontology did indeed get published, the second option would hold that none of it ever saw the light of day. Moreover, since the rubric "fundamental ontology" was dropped by Heidegger after 1927, the second option would maintain that Heidegger stopped at the threshold of fundamental ontology and never even ventured into the project except in the brief and meager attempt in "Basic Problems of Phenomenology" that we have already noted. Both the first and second options agree that nothing of Heidegger's radical new ontology was ever fully elaborated.

Finally, there is a *third* option, one that reconciles the first and the second options by combining (1) fundamental ontology = SZ I.1–2 *and* (2) fundamental ontology = SZ I.3. Speaking of SZ I.1–3 *as a whole*, Heidegger says that "its aim is one of fundamental ontology"[93] and that ex-sistence has a "function

89. SZ 436.9–10 = 486.27–28: title of § 83.

90. SZ 360.20 = 411.37: "Bei der Fundamentalanalyse des Seins."

91. SZ 403.35–39 = 455.23–26: "die fundamentalontologische Klärung der Frage nach dem Sinn von Sein überhaupt."

92. SZ 183.10–12 = 227.29–31.

93. SZ 131.27 = 170.4–5: "Ihre Absicht ist eine fundamentalontologische." Italicized in the original.

in fundamental ontology."[94] Moreover, in *Basic Problems of Phenomenology* he remarks that in SZ I.3 ex-sistence does not lose its "priority in the whole ontological problematic, thanks to the understanding of being that belongs to it."[95] In addition, everything that is said about ex-sistence in SZ I.1–2 is oriented to the question of the intelligibility of being in SZ I.3. To begin with, "The working out and answering of the fundamental question about the intelligibility of being in general *demands* a general analytic of ex-sistence."[96] But this existential analytic neither stands alone nor is carried out for its own sake. Rather, the "grounding of ex-sistence . . . is *guided by* the question [of the source of being].[97] Thus "the analytic of ex-sistence remains wholly *oriented towards* the guiding task of working out the question of being."[98] In his review of Cassirer's *Philosophy of Symbolic Forms* Heidegger speaks of the need for "a radical ontology of ex-sistence *in the light of* the problem of being in general."[99] In SZ itself Heidegger virtually equates the inquiry into "the meaning of existentiality itself" with the prior inquiry into "the intelligibility of being in general."[100] In marginal notes to SZ Heidegger constantly relates the analysis of ex-sistence to fundamental ontological issues. He says that to interpret something (in this case, understanding) as a "fundamental existential" is to interpret it "*fundamentalontologisch*, that is, in terms of its relation to the disclosedness of 'being.'"[101] Or again: Heidegger glosses the phrase "The existential problematic" with "indeed the fundamental ontological problematic, i.e., the one that aims at the question of being as such in general."[102] In his 1927–1928 lecture course on the *Critique of Pure Reason* Heidegger gathers the *whole* of SZ I.1–3 under the rubric of fundamental ontology (the bracketed numbers are mine):

---

94. SZ 182.11–12 = 226.35: "ihre fundamentalontologische Funktion." Ibid. 372.10–19 = 424.4–14.

95. GA 24: 319.18–20 = 224.3–4.

96. GA 24: 26.21–22 = 19.31–33: "fordert eine allgemeine Analytik des Daseins." Emphasis added.

97. GA 40: 183.23–24 = 194:24–25: "einer von dieser Frage ausgeleiteten Gründung des Daseins." My emphasis.

98. SZ 17.6–7 = 38.7–8: "orientiert." My emphasis.

99. GA 3: 265.30–32 = 187.17–18 (emphasis added): "eine radikale Ontologie des Daseins im Lichte des Seinsproblems überhaupt."

100. SZ 20.35–36 = 42.9–11: "dem Sinn der Existentialität selbst, d.h. vorgängig dem Sinn des Seins überhaupt nachzufragen." Note that existentiality gets clarified *after* the clarification of the clearing ("the intelligibility of being" in general).

101. GA 2: 190.7 and note, corresponding to SZ 143.1 = 182.17: "fundamentalontologische, d.h. aus dem Bezug der Wahrheit des Seins." (Stambaugh 138 and note.)

102. GA 2: 313, note 6, corresponding to SZ 235, note 1 = 494.30, note vi: "und zwar fundamentalontologische, d.h. auf die Seinsfrage als solche überhaupt zielende." (Stambaugh 225 note.)

> [1] All ontic research objectifies things. But ontic objectifying is possible only on the basis of and by way of [2] the ontological, i.e., *pre*-ontological understanding of the structure of being. But at the same time the ontological inquiry and the objectifying of being also requires [3] an original grounding, and this is carried out by the investigation that we call *fundamental ontology*.[103]

Translation: (1) The sciences objectify things, but this is possible only thanks to (2) a pre-thematic awareness of and objectifying of the being of those things—in short, an ontology. But in turn all such ontology—all understanding of things in terms of their being—requires (3) a "fundamental ontology," the investigation of the clearing which is thrown open and sustained by (in this text, "grounded" in) ex-sistence (= SZ I.1–3) and within which such understanding can take place at all.

Statements like these indicate that fundamental ontology encompasses both moments of the transcendental analysis: ex-sistence as the thrown-open clearing (SZ I.1–2), and the thrown-open clearing as what makes intelligibility possible and necessary (SZ I.3). The bracketed numbers are mine, whereas the parentheses are Heidegger's.

> Our results are that the basic problem of metaphysics demands in its radicalization and universalization [1] an interpretation of ex-sistence on the basis of "temporality." From this interpretation, [2] the intrinsic possibility of the understanding of being and thereby of ontology should become evident. . . . [This inner possibility] gets understood in carrying out, working out, the basic problematic itself (in the four main problems that we have presented). Fundamental ontology is this whole of the founding and the elaborating of ontology; fundamental ontology is (1) the analysis of ex-sistence [= SZ I.1–2] and (2) the analysis of the "time-character" of being [= SZ I.3].[104]

I understand these texts, when taken as a unity, to be affirming the following: (1) Fundamental ontology is already operative in, but not restricted to, SZ I.1–2 and finds its *culmination* in SZ I.3.[105] (2) SZ I.3 not only is "based" on SZ I.1–2 but also guides and orients those two earlier divisions to their natural conclusion.[106] (3) The "ontological analysis of ex-sistence" that Heidegger

103. GA 25: 36.29–37.1 = 25.35–40. "Understanding": Entwurf.

104. GA 26: 201.18–28 = 158.19–29. "Time-character": Temporalität.

105. See SZ 200.26–29 = 244.37–39: "Je angemessener und ursprünglicher die Explikation dieses Seienden [= Dasein] gelingen konnte, um so sicherer wird der weitere Gang der Ausarbeitung des fundamental-ontologischen Problems ans Ziel komme."

106. I place "based" in scare quotes because Heidegger states that SZ I.1–2 is "incompatible with any building upon it" ("kein Aufbauen darauf verträgt"): GA 14: 40.12–13 = 32.11–12. Nonetheless, von Herrmann speaks of it as a "basis" (Boden): see what immediately follows above.

identifies with fundamental ontology[107] was to extend *beyond* the published divisions of *Being and Time* into the unpublished third division. That is to say, (4) just as ex-sistence is inseparable from the clearing, so too the existential-analytical preparation (= SZ I.1–2) for a full-blown fundamental ontology (= SZ I.3) is *already part of that ontology*. Thus, Professor von Herrmann gets it right when he speaks of

> the fundamental-ontological question about the intelligibility of being in general that guides the analysis of ex-sistence . . . the working out of the question of being and of the existential analysis that belongs to it.[108]

And in his famous letter of 1962 to William J. Richardson, Heidegger indirectly affirmed this third option when he spoke of the strict unity of his lifelong project: "[The thought of] Heidegger I becomes possible only if it is contained in Heidegger II."[109]

This third option also helps us to understand why Heidegger dropped the term "fundamental ontology" as a designation of his work. He provides his reasons in two post-war texts: "Introduction to 'What Is Metaphysics?'" (1949) and "Summary of a Seminar" (1962).[110] These texts correct his earlier use of both terms, "ontology" and "fundamental." In the 1949 text, he says he dropped the title "fundamental ontology" in order to avoid the mistaken impression that SZ I.3 would be *any kind of ontology at all*—that is, any form of metaphysics. In 1927 he had wrongly taken over the traditional title for the study of the openness *of things* (*die Wahrheit des Seienden: Ontologie*)—for his own work, which in fact had left all that behind as it sought the openedness of the clearing itself (*die Wahrheit des Seins selbst*).

> What the title "fundamental ontology" suggests is that the thinking that attempts to think the openness of being—and not, like all ontology, the openness of things—is, as fundamental ontology, still a kind of ontology. But in fact, the attempt to recall the openness of being, insofar as it is a going back into the ground of metaphysics, has already left the realm of all ontology with its very first step.[111]

---

107. GA 14: 39.24–25 = 31.23–24: "Nach *Sein und Zeit* ist Fundamentalontologie die ontologische Analytik des Daseins."

108. Respectively, Editor's Epilogue, GA 24: 472.34–35 = 332.14–16 and 473.7–8 = 332.20–22. Heidegger later (GA 83: 9.26) equates "fundamentalontologisch" and "transcendental," which would seem to contradict what Müller reports that Heidegger said about the "transcendental difference" or ontological difference in the narrower sense (above, note 32).

109. GA 11: 152.18–19 = xxii.15–17.

110. Respectively: GA 9: 365–383 = 277–290 and GA 14: 33–66 = 25–54.

111. GA 9: 380.22–28 = 289.2–7.

(We note as well that in this text Heidegger does not confine fundamental ontology to SZ I.1–2 but includes all of SZ I.3 under that title.)

Likewise the 1962 "Summary of a Seminar" records Heidegger correcting possible misunderstandings of the word "fundamental." (Here Heidegger *does* seem to restrict fundamental ontology to SZ I.1–2.) He says:

> According to this [i.e., SZ 13.22–24 = 34.1–2] it looks as if fundamental ontology were the foundation for ontology itself, an ontology that is still lacking but that is to be built upon that foundation. . . . Thus the relation of fundamental ontology to the clarification of the intelligibility of being—which was not published—would be analogous to the relation between fundamental theology and systematic theology.
>
> This, however, was not the case, although it cannot be denied that this is not yet clearly expressed in *Being and Time* itself. Rather, *Being and Time* is on the way—beyond the "temporality" [*Zeitlichkeit*] of ex-sistence, in the interpretation of [the clearing] as "time-character"—toward finding a "time"-concept and what is most proper to the "time" [= the clearing] whence "being" is given as meaningful presence. But this means that what is fundamental in fundamental ontology is incompatible with any building on it.[112]

On both counts, then—"fundamental" and "ontological"—Heidegger found the early rubric for his work unsatisfying and misleading, and he saw fit to drop it in favor of "thinking the clearing" (*Seinsdenken*). Such thinking is not mere cogitating (thinking seriously about something), and it is not at all focused on *Sein*-as-being (the meaningful presence of things). Rather, it is a "*Vor-denken in den Anfang*"[113]—a thinking "ahead" to what is prior—namely, the *origin* of being. Such thinking searches out *die Wahrheit des Seins*, the opened clearing, which accounts for why there is meaningful presence at all.

5. OVERCOMING TRANSCENDENTALISM AND THE HORIZON FOR BEING

In a somewhat lapidary note from an unpublished manuscript written in 1940–1941 ("Der Weg durch Sein und Zeit") Heidegger observes:

> The relation of the clearing to man is the clearing itself, insofar as the clearing itself, in coming to pass, lets the essence of man come to pass as what is

112. GA 14: 39.28–40.13 = 31.27–32.12. Heidegger writes "Sein" in scare quotes to show that it means being as the Anwesen of things, not the clearing.

113. GA 86: 189.26.

> needed by the clearing and as what is detained and held by that need as such. In essence, man is man only as the one who is needed by the clearing for the sake of the clearing.[114]

This text might sound as if the clearing and the essence of man were two different phenomena, but "they" are not. As ex-sisting, man cannot *not* sustain—and in that sense "is"—the *Da* or *Lichtung*, the openedness that lets meaning occur.[115]

The problem, however, lay in the transcendental approach of Heidegger's early work, which contributed to the false impression that ex-sistence *qua* sustaining the clearing is merely self-projecting existentiel subjectivity. However, in that same 1940s manuscript Heidegger wrote concerning *Being and Time*, "Already at the very start, subjectivity was overcome and openness to [i.e., as] the clearing was preserved; nonetheless the kind of questioning and the way it was carried out still remain[ed] on the tracks of a transcendental form of questioning."[116] There was, however, an important difference that separated Heidegger's transcendentalism from Kant's. Kant sought the conditions of the possibility of the experience of *things* in their being-as-objectivity within a Newtonian scientific universe. Thus he remained caught within metaphysics' concern for being as the ἀρχή of things.[117] By contrast, Heidegger's early transcendentalism was after the conditions of the possibility of *being at all*: Why is it necessary and how it is possible for us to understand the *being* (the meaningful presence) of things? Hence Heidegger's early work was in transition (1) from metaphysical intentionality and its ontological difference in the "narrow" sense (2) through existential self-transcendence (3) to the structural appropriation of ex-sistence as the open space for being at all.[118] In that manuscript from the 1940s Heidegger distinguished his own transcendental inquiry

---

114. "Der Weg," ms. 20.18–22, paraphrased. I translate *Seyn* (understood as "being itself"—Heidegger's *Erfragtes*) as "the clearing." "Der Bezug des Seyns zum Menschen ist das Seyn selbst, insofern es selbst wesend das Wesen des Menschen wesen läßt als das vom Seyn Gebrauchte und in den Brauch als der Brauch einbehaltene. Der Mensch ist im Wesen nur Mensch als der vom Seyn zum Seyn Gebrauchte." Manuscript available on request.

115. In the fractured prose of "Der Weg": "[sofern der Mensch] stehen im Offenen des Seins bestimmt bleibt und das Da—die Lichtung des Seins 'ist'—ek-sistiert": ibid., 22.20–22.

116. "Der Weg," 19.16–19: "Obzwar schon im Ansatz die Subjektivität des Menschen überwunden und das Offene zum Sein selbst gewahrt war, bleibt doch die Art des Fragens noch in der Bahn der transzendentalen Fragestellung."

117. GA 65: 253.1–5 = 199.13–16

118. "Der Weg," 22.15–17: "'Sein und Zeit'—nur ein Übergang, der unentschieden zwischen 'Metaphysik' und E[reignis]. Auch 'Sein und Zeit' deshalb noch auf dem Weg über den Menschen zum Sein, freilich zum Sein als solchen."

in *Being and Time* from Kant's in the *Critique of Pure Reason* by calling his own a "potentiated" (*potenzierte*) transcendental approach—one that is "raised to a higher power" insofar as it seeks the condition of the possibility of *being* rather than of things.[119] Thus,

> traditional [*gewohnten*] ways of thinking offered themselves as way-stations that . . . could provide some help in laying out the question of being and in bringing it closer to contemporary eyes and ears. But in that way the inquiry again veered off the proper track that alone was adequate to what was to be thought, especially because in the origin [i.e., in the pre-Socratics] the basic experience of the clearing was not original or constant or clear enough to experience this relation [of being and time] originally and on its own terms and to lead it back to its ground and basis.[120]

Heidegger eventually came to see *Being and Time* as a "transitional" work that was on the way to a clearer vision and expression of the clearing as ex-sistence.[121] That transition entailed showing that even his "potentiated" transcendental approach was inadequate to the project of SZ I.3.

> The task is not to surpass things (transcendence) but, instead, to leap over this distinction [of things and being] and thus to leap over *transcendence* and to question from out of the clearing and its dis-closedness, i.e., from out of the origin [*anfänglich*].[122]

All Heidegger's intentions to the contrary notwithstanding, traces of subjectivity and Promethean self-transcendence still seemed to cling to this notion of the transcendental, and he found the entire framework of transcendentalism to be a roadblock on making the transition. "The division in question [SZ I.3] was held back because thinking failed in adequately saying and showing this [transition from SZ I.2 to I.3] and did not succeed with the help of the language of metaphysics."[123] So, as he had done with the title "fundamental ontology," Heidegger dropped the term "transcendental" from his lexicon along with any efforts to work out SZ I.3 within the parameters of transcendentalism.

119. "Der Weg," 9.2–3. But see his retraction: GA 73, 2: 1272.31–32.

120. "Der Weg," 8.1–9.1.

121. See GA 65: 305.24 = 241.24: "Fundamentalontologie das Übergängliche." Ibid., 251.3 = 197.21: "Im übergänglichen Denken."

122. GA 65: 250.32–251.2 = 197.28–30. See GA 10: 116.12–15 = 78.33–36.

123. GA 9: 328.1–4 = 250.1–4, incorporating note "a" ("Sichzeigenlassen") into the text.

How did the transcendentalism of *Being and Time* throw up obstacles to Heidegger's progress? Why did he find that approach inadequate to unfolding his insights into the clearing? In his 1945 "dialogue on a country path" titled Ἀγχιβασίη ("Approaching"), Heidegger provides one of his more discursive (if largely metaphorical) comments on overcoming the transcendental-horizonal approach of *Being and Time*. A horizon, he says, is the field of vision (*Gesichtskreis*) that "encircles" subject and object, making possible intentionality on the part of the subject and meaningful appearance on the part of the object.[124] In that sense, the horizon lies "beyond" the objects, "just as transcendence passes beyond the mere perception of the object" to the apprehension of the being of the object.[125] Heidegger emphasizes that in a transcendental approach, transcendence and its correlative horizon are defined and determined only relative to intentional objects and our presentation (*Vorstellung*) of them as meaningful—this, as a way of saying that the transcendental approach is inadequate for understanding what *opens up the horizon itself.* The horizonal field of vision is certainly open, but it "does not have its openness from the fact that we look into it."[126] It's the other way around. We *can* look into the horizon only because it is already opened up. In other words,

> What has the character of a horizon is thus only the side turned toward us of a surrounding openness, an openness that is filled up with [presentational] viewings of the meaningful appearances of what shows up as objects to our presenting of them [*Vorstellen*] as objects.[127]

But even if one were to stay within the early transcendental-horizonal approach of *Being and Time*, the openedness of the horizon would not be due to either presentational intentionality or Promethean projectivity. The open field that allows for transcendental, object-presentational thinking is prior to all that and cannot be accounted for by it.

The question then becomes: What is this open itself, if we disregard the fact that it (or "the side turned towards us") can also appear as the horizon of our presentational thinking? And how is it opened up? Heidegger's metaphorical answer to that question plays on the German preposition *gegen*, less in the sense of "over against" and more in the sense of the Latin *contra*, "in

124. GA 77: 111: 19–20 = 72.14–15. See GA 26: 269.4–10 = 208.12–18.

125. GA 77: 111.22–25 = 72.17–20. Here and in what immediately follows, I translate "vorstellend" as "presentational."

126. GA 77: 112.6–8 = 72.38–41.

127. GA 77: 112.13–16 = 72.30–32.

front of."[128] The open clearing is like the expansive *countryside* (*die Gegend*) that en-*counters* us (*ent-gegen-kommt*) as always already open.[129] The usual translation of *die Gegend* by the opaque "region-that-regions" (which says absolutely nothing) misses Heidegger's nuanced metaphorical sense of the clearing as the *countryside* that already lies open before us (*contra*) before we do anything within it (for example, picnicking on the grass or strolling through the fields). This countryside lies open *before* us without ever being an object (*Gegen-stand*) standing over "against" us as subjects. Heidegger's *Gegend*-metaphor evokes "the already open countryside" in which we find ourselves and within which particular things are meaningfully present.

We recognize here yet another formulation of that which makes possible the distinguishing-and-synthesizing discursivity in which we take this *as* that (or this as *for* that) and thus render those things meaningfully present. This clearing lies beyond (and in that sense makes possible) what Heidegger, according to the Müller report, called the ontological difference in the "narrow" sense: the distinction between things and their being. Therefore, let us reserve the adjective "transcendental" for the "narrow" sense of the ontological difference and for the movement that goes beyond things and mediates them to their meanings.[130] In contrast to that, we might denominate the openness that makes such movement possible as "*trans*-transcendental." This term indicates the progress of Heidegger's transitional thinking (1) *through* the "narrower" ontological difference that defines the problematic of metaphysics, and (2) *beyond* it to (3) the ontological difference in the "broader" sense: the difference between things-in-their-meaningfulness and the clearing that makes the "narrower" difference possible. Heidegger moves beyond transcendentalism to the a priori fact of the clearing. This move is what he is referring to when he writes about the ontological difference in the "narrow" sense in the following texts:

> "The question about being" in *Being and Time* [is] the abbreviated title for the question about the *origin* of the ontological difference.[131]
>
> From the perspective of appropriation it becomes necessary to free thinking from the ontological difference.[132]

---

128. Cf. "Contra Costa County," which lies in front of (and not over against) a San Franciscan who looks east across the Bay.

129. See GA 77: 113.17 = 73.23: entgegenkommt. See GA 83: 157.5 and .11–20: "Das Gegnende: die zu-kommend sich öffnende umgebende Weite" understood as the χώρα: "Von wo her etwas [here: a thing in its being] anwest" (both phrases italicized in the original).

130. See GA 9: 413.17–19 = 312.25–26: "Überall ist der auf das Seiende zurückkommende Überstieg, das 'transcendens schlechtin' (Sein und Zeit § 7), 'das Sein' des Seienden."

131. GA 14: 87, note "(27)" (which is not found in the ET): "'Seinsfrage' in *Sein und Zeit* [ist] der verkürzte Titel für die Frage nach der Herkunft der ontologischen Differenz."

132. GA 14: 46.22–23 = 37.30–32: "daß es vom Ereignis her nötig wird, dem Denken die ontologische Differenz zu erlassen." He means the ontological difference in the narrow sense.

> With the clearing, the ontological difference disappears.[133]
>
> . . . overcoming the difference by entering into the appropriation of world.[134]
>
> . . . the question about the overcoming of the ontological difference between being and things.[135]

Thus the transition from *Being and Time* to the later work entailed

> *first*, bringing this distinction [of things and their being] to an initial clarity, and *then* leaping over that very distinction. Yet such leaping-over occurs only . . . through the leap into the appropriation of ex-sistence.[136]

The transition from SZ I.2 to SZ I.3 that Heidegger had programmed into *Being and Time* lies at the heart of why that book remained a torso. (We take up that matter in the next chapter.) Why he failed to complete that text is the *crux interpretum*, the puzzle that continues to torment interpreters who seek to make sense of the apparent gap separating the early and later Heidegger and who argue for the continuity between the two. In trying to work out that change of direction in the years 1927–1930, Heidegger was struck by an insight that changed everything in how he approached his question.

6. THE CRUCIAL BREAKTHROUGH (1930): THE INTRINSIC HIDDENNESS OF THE CLEARING

As William J. Richardson pointed out over fifty years ago, Heidegger's lecture "On the Essence of Truth," delivered in December of 1930 but not published until 1943, is the "decisive point" in Heidegger's development and constitutes the "breakthrough" in which "Heidegger I becomes Heidegger II."[137] That

133. GA 15: 366.27–28 = 60.44–61.3: "Mit dem Sein verschwindet auch die ontologische Differenz."

134. A paraphrase of GA 81: 274.11: "Verwindung (der Differenz) in das Ereignis von Welt," where the last four words parallel "die ereignete Lichtung" at GA 71: 211.9. Is the note at GA 81: 274 intended for Hannah Arendt ("H.A." at ibid., 274.1)?

135. GA 81: 348.3–5: "die Frage nach der Überwindung der ontologischen Differenz zwischen Sein und Seiendem." See also GA 29/30: 521.32–522.18 = 359.12–28, and GA 15: 310.12–15 = 24.31–34.

136. GA 65: 251.4–9 = 197.31–36, Heidegger's emphasis.

137. Richardson, *Heidegger*, respectively 211.3; 243.17; and 254.12. The essay itself: GA 9: 177–202 = 136–54.

breakthrough consisted in Heidegger's insight into the *intrinsic hiddenness* of the appropriated clearing. *Being and Time* had spoken of the hiddenness of thrown-openness, but not in terms of the clearing as such.[138] The inaugural lecture at Freiburg, "What Is Metaphysics?" (1929), took a small step forward when it spoke, somewhat hesitantly, of "the essential impossibility of determining" the clearing, the no-thing encountered in dread.[139] However, it was not until a year later, in "On the Essence of Truth," that Heidegger began to articulate his dawning insight that the clearing is hidden *in and of itself* and not because of the limitations of our knowing powers. The lecture reaches its climax in section 6, where Heidegger declares for the first time in his career that, in contrast to ἀλήθεια-2 as the disclosedness of things, ἀλήθεια-1, as the openness of the clearing, is *un*-disclosed, and this un-disclosedness is the very essence of the clearing.[140]

Unfortunately, in that crucial passage Heidegger made two mistakes. First, contrary to his own principles, he used the misleading language of "truth" to translate both ἀλήθεια-1 and ἀλήθεια-2.[141] And secondly, he did not adequately distinguish between those two levels of disclosedness. A close paraphrase of the difficult German text may clarify the matter. (The bracketed numbers are mine.)

> [1] *Die Verborgenheit ist dann,*
> [2] *von der Wahrheit als Entborgenheit her gedacht,*
> [3] *die Un-entborgenheit und somit die dem Wahrheitswesen eigenste und eigentliche Un-wahrheit.*[142]

> [1] Ἀλήθεια-1,
> [2] when contrasted with ἀλήθεια-2 as the dis-closedness of things,
> [3] is the *un*-disclosedness that is the most proper and essential characteristic of the clearing as such.

138. SZ 348.26–30 = 399.32–400.3: Verschlossenheit, Geworfenheit, Faktizität.

139. GA 9: 111.29 = 88.23–24: "die wesenhafte Unmöglichkeit der Bestimmbarkeit" of das Nichts—that is, of the clearing; however, he did not thematize that in terms of intrinsic hiddenness.

140. See Heidegger's letter to Heinrich W. Petzet in "Afterthoughts on the Spiegel Interview" in Neske and Kettering, *Martin Heidegger and Nationalism Socialism*, 69.11–13: "the genuine Kehre was mentioned for the first time in 1930 in a lecture on 'The Essence of Truth.'"

141. He complicates matters even further by speaking of "non-truth proper" and "the proper non-presence of truth": GA 9: 194.13–14 = 148.28: "die eigentliche Un-wahrheit. Das eigentliche Un-wesen der Wahrheit."

142. GA 9: 193.24–27 = 148.12–14: "Die Verborgenheit [= ἀλήθεια-1] ist dann, von der Wahrheit als Entborgenheit [= ἀλήθεια-2] her gedacht, die Un-entborgenheit [*un*-disclosedness] und somit die dem Wahrheitswesen [= the clearing as such] eigenste und eigentliche Un-wahrheit [*un*-disclosedness]."

That is, while the clearing (ἀλήθεια-1) enables the meaningful presence of things (ἀλήθεια-2), it itself remains intrinsically undisclosed or "hidden"—unknowable in its why and wherefore. There is nothing mystical about this, and one is not talking about being "concealing *itself*" as if it possessed some weird kind of agency. We should avoid the hypostasization and quasi-personalization of the clearing that insinuates itself into Heideggerian discourse via the *faux* reflexive: "The clearing hides *itself*."[143] In this case, verb forms like *sich entziehen* and *sich verbergen* are to be read as "The clearing *is* withdrawn, *is* hidden" instead of "The clearing *ups and hides itself*." (Compare *etwas zeigt sich*: something shows up vs. "shows *itself*.")[144] In any case, this text from the 1930 lecture records Heidegger's breakthrough into his later work. We may mark it with the formula "ἀλήθεια-1 = λήθη-1": the clearing, as the basis for the disclosure of everything meaningful, is itself intrinsically hidden. This is the ur-insight, the founding vision that drove all Heidegger's work, early and late. To adapt the words of William J. Richardson, it is "the living center of Ur-Heidegger."[145]

From something he said in 1946, it would seem this insight dawned on Heidegger in the 1920s and yet took some years to mature. In his "Letter on Humanism" he calls this insight the "fundamental experience"[146] that he tried (but failed) to work out in *Being and Time*. In "Letter on Humanism" he calls it an experience of *Seinsvergessenheit*, a term that has two distinct meanings. (1) In its primary and proper sense *Seinsvergessenheit* refers to the intrinsic hiddenness of the clearing. (2) This hiddenness is the reason why the clearing is mostly overlooked and forgotten in metaphysics—and this latter is *Seinsvergessenheit* in its secondary and derived sense. However, in both of these senses, the term is a misnomer. Being is always the being of things, and such being is not intrinsically concealed; rather, it is quite knowable, and has long been the focus of metaphysics. Rather, what is intrinsically hidden, and therefore has been forgotten, is the *appropriated clearing*. In "Letter on Humanism" Heidegger is referring to the hiddenness of the clearing (λήθη-1) as his "fundamental experience," and he shows as much when he glosses that phrase with "*Vergessenheit*—Λήθη—concealment—withdrawal—non-appearance-of-appropriation = appropriation."[147] This was the insight that Heidegger's

143. Or even "the hiddenness hides itself" as at GA 6:2: 319.1–2 = 214.8: "diese Verborgenheit sich in sich selbst verbirgt." The meaning here is: the clearing is *intrinsically* hidden.

144. See also "sich ausnehmen" at: GA 66: 340.13–14 = 303.18–19.

145. Richardson, *Heidegger*, 640.28–29.

146. GA 9: 328.11 = 250.10: Grunderfahrung.

147. GA 9: 328.11 note d = 250.10 note d: "*Vergessenheit*—Λήθη—Verbergung—Entzug—Enteignis: Ereignis." The usual translation of the neologism "Enteignis" as "expropriation" makes no sense. The context shows that Enteignis is the hiddenness (or "withdrawal") of Ereignis and thus is equivalent to λήθη-1.

transcendental approach prevented him from articulating in *Being and Time*. It is also what finally motivated his 1930s change from a transcendental to the *seinsgeschichtlich* approach, which has to do with how the appropriation of ex-sistence "gives" (makes possible) various configurations of the clearing. Moreover, as the unthought of Western philosophy, the intrinsic hiddenness of the clearing is the core of Heidegger's history of the clearing-for-being and the reason why he sees a trajectory of decline in Western culture.

We can see that there is a two-sidedness about the clearing: it *remains hidden* while *disclosing things as meaningful*. "The origin does not show itself in what it has released."[148] Heidegger calls this two-sidedness the "hiding of the clearing as the 'releasing' of things [-in-their-being]," and he glosses that two-sidedness as "the differentiation"—that is, the ontological difference in its "broad" and proper sense.[149] Moreover, Heidegger calls the intrinsic hiddenness of the clearing *das Geheimnis*, "the mystery," but not as some dark, supra-human realm of "Being Itself," inaccessible to human beings. The mystery consists in our inability to get behind appropriation, back behind our own thrownness, to its "cause." In *Being and Time* Heidegger called this state of affairs "facticity." In 1930 he rewrites that as the mystery of the hiddenness of the clearing—which is in fact the (mostly overlooked) mystery of *ourselves*, of ex-sistence itself. Thus in the lecture in which he first introduced this intrinsic hiddenness, Heidegger speaks of it as *das Geheimnis des Daseins*,[150] as the "singular mystery" that "thoroughly dominates our ex-sistence,"[151] and he calls it *das vergessene Geheimnis des Daseins*: the overlooked mystery that is ex-sistence itself.[152] Likewise, at the height of his shift to the *seinsgeschichtlich* approach, he speaks of this mystery of λήθη-1 as the "withdrawal" of the clearing and declares that "*Der Entzug aber ist des Da-seins*": the withdrawal is of the very nature of ex-sistence.[153] And again in the late 1930s:

---

148. GA 4: 92.21–22 = 116.15: "daß [der Ursprung] sich in diesem Entsprungenen selbst nicht zeigt." And GA 5: 336.3–4 = 253.30–31: "Verbergen seines Wesens und der Wesensherkunft." Yet elsewhere he seems to say the opposite: GA 5: 337.3–4 = 253.35: "Das Sein entzieht sich, indem es sich in das Seiende entbirgt." He means that at best the clearing is *indirectly* manifest in the meaningful appearance of entities. Cf. GA 29/30: 431.14–15 = 298.1–2: "Das Weltphänomen können wir nie direkt in den Blick bekommen."

149. GA 70: 98.28–29: "Verbergung des Seins als Entlassung des Seienden; (die Unterscheidung)."

150. GA 9: 197.26 = 151.9.

151. GA 9: 194.6–9 = 148.22–24: "das Eine"; "das Geheimnis . . . das Da-sein des Menschen durchwaltet."

152. GA 9: 195.23 = 149.28.

153. GA 65: 293.9 = 231.8–9.

> In this withdrawal (or *intrinsic hiddenness*), the clearing's utmost closeness consists in the *Da*, the open, insofar as it ap-*propri*-ates [brings into its proper condition] our *being*-the-open.[154]

Heidegger says the clearing is what is "hidden in the first and primary sense."[155] He is arguing that the clearing is intrinsically *unknowable*, if "knowing" means discerning the reason for something, what Aristotle would call "knowing the αἰτία of something."[156] The open space that makes possible the distinguishing-and-synthesizing whereby we understand things as meaningfully present is not available to the discursive intellect. It can be *experienced* in the non-discursive immediacy of dread or wonder (Heidegger's rewriting of the function of Aristotelian νοῦς).[157] However, such an encounter with the clearing robs us of speech[158] because

> [t]he clearing is itself "the immediate." Therefore nothing mediate [such as discursive speech] . . . can ever attain the immediate immediately.[159]

Heidegger's point: Insofar as our appropriation is what lets us make sense of things at all, it is the προϋποκείμενον πρῶτον, the *praesuppositum primum*, of everything human and thus of all knowing and doing.[160] As the ultimate presupposition, the clearing must always be presupposed in any attempt to know it. It always lies "behind" us, so to speak, and it will always remain behind us (i.e., unknowable) even when we turn around to take a look at it. Consequently, we cannot go "beyond" or "behind" it without contradicting ourselves. We cannot (without moving in a vicious circle) seek the presupposition of this ultimate presupposition of all our seeking. "There is nothing else to which appropriation could be led back or in terms of which it could be explained."[161]

---

154. GA 65: 249.15–18 = 196.21–24: "Aber in diesem Sichentziehen (*Sichverbergen*) hat das Seyn seine nächste Nähe in der Lichtung des Da, indem es das Da-*sein* er-eignet."

155. GA 9: 194.11–12 = 148.26–27: "das erstlich Verborgene."

156. *Posterior Analytics* I 2, 71b10–11: τὴν αἰτίαν γιγνώσκειν. See "rerum cognoscere causas": Virgil, *Georgics* II, 490, repeated in the tondo of Rafael's "School of Athens" in the papal apartments in the Vatican, La Stanza della Segnatura.

157. See *Metaphysics* IX 10, 1051b24. Heidegger retrieves the unmediated θιγεῖν performed by νοῦς as the θαυμάζειν that is dread or wonder. Cf. GA 11: 22.11 and .14 = 85.1 and 85.4–5: "θαυμάζειν, das Erstaunen" and "Zurücktreten vor dem Sein"—that is, vor der Lichtung.

158. GA 9: 112.14 = 89.5: "Der Angst verschlächt uns das Wort."

159. GA 4: 61.21–23 = 83.27–29: "Das Offene selbst ist das Unmittelbare. Kein Mittelbares . . . vermag deshalb je das Unmittelbare unmittelbar zu erreichen."

160. On προϋποκείμενον as that which is always already (πρό) under (ὑπό) lying (κείμενον) see Damascius, *De Principiis* III, 153.2 = *Dubitationes et solutions* I, 312.21.

161. GA 12: 247.12–13 = 127.28–30. GA 10: 169.6 = 113.18 (referring to Heraclitus, fragment 52): "Das 'Weil' versinkt im Spiel. Das Spiel ist ohne 'Warum.'"

Rather, it is "what originally *makes everything possible*," analogous to the Good in Plato.[162]

We will never get an answer to the question "What possibilizes that which possibilizes everything?" Even to ask that question is a fool's errand insofar as it traps us in a *petitio principii*, a begging of the question—in this case, not realizing that we are already wrapped up from the outset in what we are attempting to find.[163] Heidegger does say that "the *petere principium*, the reaching out to the supporting ground, is the only move that philosophy ever makes."[164] But what he means is that true philosophical thinking *actively presupposes* the presupposition by electing to leave it in its unknowability rather than trying to question behind it. Thus, to seek the ultimate basis for intelligibility already presupposes the ultimate basis for intelligibility and thus is caught in circular reasoning.[165] Everything is knowable except the reason why everything is knowable.[166] The unknowability of the why and wherefore of our thrown-openness as the clearing is what Heidegger finally means by "facticity," now reread as the mystery.

With Heidegger's lecture "On the Essence of Truth" the door opens on to the later Heidegger. By December of 1930 he had the wherewithal to begin working out what he had projected for SZ I.3 but had been unable to finish. He could now take up "the thing itself" outside the Procrustean bed of transcendentalism. It would take him a few more years to settle into the new approach that would shape his work for the next four decades, but at last the way was clear. The transition to the clearing, which he had originally programmed into *Being and Time*, would henceforth be absorbed into the changed perspective of the 1930s that issued in his *seinsgeschichtlich* approach.

The issues we have discussed in this chapter were among the many obstacles that hindered Heidegger's efforts to complete SZ I within a transcen-

162. GA 22: 106.32 = 87.32: "Alles ursprünglich *ermöglichend*." Thus, too, Plotinus, *Enneads* VI 9: 11.2–3, οὐκ ἔκφορον ἐκεῖνο ὄν: The Good cannot be "brought out" or disclosed. Ibid., VI 7: 40.51–52: ᾧ δὲ μήτε τι ἄλλο πρὸ αὐτοῦ: that before which there is nothing. GA 34: 78.6 = 57.22: "daß das Wesentliche immer unbeweisbar bleibt."

163. Begging the question: Aristotle, *Prior Analytics* II 16, 64b28–65a9: τὸ ἐν ἀρχῇ αἰτεισθαι καὶ λαμβαίνειν ("Petere et sumere quod ab initio quaesitum fuit," Bekker III, 35a32.)

164. GA 9: 244.32–33 = 187.28–29.

165. Circular reasoning, τὸ κύκλῳ δείκνυσθαι: *Prior Analytics* II 5, 57b18–59b1.

166. See above, note 16.

dental framework. But with or without such obstacles, the promised content of SZ I.1–3—and the content of his work over the following fifty years—still entailed the long-planned transition from ex-sistence as the clearing to the clearing as the source of the meaningful presence of things. This change of perspective was necessary to articulate Heidegger's fundamental conviction that the clearing is the οὗ ἕνεκα of ex-sistence, its very reason-for-being-at-all. But this does not mean that the clearing—which is the *content* of the provisional, heuristic, and merely formally indicative phrase "*das Sein selbst*"—is some super-phenomenon that is "other" and "higher" than ex-sistence and endowed with a more elevated ontological status. That is, the clearing that cashes out the meaning of "being itself" is not the hypostasized Super-*Sein* of Heideggerian fiction, which somehow "gives itself to" and "withholds itself from" ex-sistence at will.[167] Any alleged "priority" of the clearing to ex-sistence can only come down to the fact that the clearing is the very raison d'être of ex-sistence. It is the *proprium* of ex-sistence, its very essence. Spelling out this fact remained Heidegger's lodestar throughout the half-century following the publication of *Being and Time*, and it led to the change in approach that shaped Heidegger's philosophical work in the 1930s and 1940s. We now turn to those issues in his later thought.

167. See GA 66: 340.13–14 = 303.18–19, where Heidegger distances himself from the following error: "Das Sein nimmt sich aus wie 'Etwas', auf das der Mensch zugeht oder nicht."

8

Appropriation and the Turn

After the Second World War, Heidegger noted that his work from 1936 on was an attempt "to say the openness of being in a simple manner."[1] Thus his effort, which he now called "essential thinking,"[2] remained the straightforward one of showing how the clearing occurs at all and makes it necessary and possible for us to understand the meaningfulness of things. Likewise the sole arena of this inquiry remained the same: ex-sistence in its fullness, neither more nor less. Insofar as ex-sistence itself *is* the clearing, the subject matter of Heidegger's work was always the human, the realm of the existential in its proper breadth, depth, and scope. He was after the a priori of human being, that which is always already operative wherever, and as long as, there are human beings. We may say, therefore, that over the half-century of his career he did nothing but pursue the mandate inscribed on the Temple of Apollo at Delphi: γνῶθι σεαυτόν, "Know yourself!"[3]

In this chapter we take up two crucial and usually misunderstood issues: *das Ereignis* and *die Kehre*. We will see that, properly understood, these two terms actually name the same thing, in fact the "thing itself," that guided all of Heidegger's work. Showing this to be the case will require rewriting the dominant scholarship on the *Kehre*, which reads the primary and proper sense of that term incorrectly as Heidegger's change in the 1930s from a transcendental to a *seinsgeschichtlich* model, or even more inaccurately, as his supposed turn from ex-sistence-projecting-the-clearing to the-clearing-projecting-ex-sistence.

1. GA 9: 313 note a = 239 note a: "die Wahrheit des Seins einfach zu sagen."

2. GA 65: 47.13 = 38.34; GA 66: 49.23–24 = 41.6 (where it is mistakenly translated as "foundational thinking").

3. Plato, *Protagoras* 343b3. GA 31: 123.11–12 = 85.34–36: "Die recht gefragte Seinsfrage als solche drängt ihrem Fragegehalt nach in die Frage nach dem Menschen"—in fact, "Mensch aus dem tiefsten Grunde seines Wesens": GA 88: 7.13–14. GA 66: 414.22–23 = 367.24–25: "*weil* die Frage nach dem Sein zuinnerst gegründet ist in die nach dem Da-sein und umgekehrt."

Ten years after writing *Being and Time*, Heidegger came up with the term "*Ereignis*," which he would later call "the word that has guided my thinking since 1936."[4] In normal German usage the word *Ereignis* means "event," and in Anglophone Heidegger scholarship it is usually translated either as "the event" or "the event of appropriation." However—and it is a big "however"—in establishing the technical meaning of the word in his own work, Heidegger explicitly rejected the understanding of *Ereignis* as any kind of event. That would include translating it as "the event of appropriation."

> What the term *Ereignis* names can no longer be represented by way of the current meaning of the word, for in that meaning *Ereignis* is understood as an event and a happening.[5]
>
> *Ereignis* . . . cannot be represented as either an event or a happening. Here the word *Ereignis* no longer means what we would otherwise call a happening or event.[6]
>
> *Ereignis* does not mean here something that happens [*ein Vorkommnis*].[7]

Instead, Heidegger understands *Ereignis* in terms of its etymological roots, which go back to the German word for "eye." The brothers Grimm had demonstrated that the original etymon of *Ereignis* is the Old High German *ouga*, "eye" (see the modern German *Auge*). *Ouga* underlies the Old High German verb *ir-ougen* and the Middle High German *er-öugen* and *er-äugen,* as well as the obsolete High German verb *er-eigen*, all of which mean "to place before the eyes, to show," parallel to the Latin verbs *monstrare* and *ostendere*. Over the centuries, however, the etymology shifted significantly as the entirely unrelated adjective *eigen* ("one's own") and its cognate verb *an-eigen* ("to appropriate") came to be associated with *sich er-eigen*. Eventually the two meanings—on the one hand, "to eye something," and on the other, "to own it"—got commingled. Furthermore, by the early 1600s the letter *n* crept in (as in *sich er-eig<u>n</u>en*).

4. GA 9: 316 note a = 241 note b: "seit 1936 das Leitwort meines Denkens." See GA 11: 45.15–17 = 36.15–16: "Leitwort im Dienst des Denkens."

5. GA 14: 25.33–26.1 = 20.29–33.

6. GA 11: 45.19–20 = 36.18–19, where in the German note 76, Heidegger glosses "Geschehnis" and "Vorkommnis" with "eine Begebenheit," an incident or occurrence.

7. GA 70: 17.19.

In short, the noun *Ereignis* is heir to a complex history that offers up two etymons: "to see" and "to own." Heidegger draws on the first meaning when he hears in *Ereignis* echoes of "*in den Augen fallen . . . erscheinen*" (to come into view, to appear),[8] whereas he has the second meaning in mind when he speaks of *Ereignis* as "appropriation" (from the Latin *proprius*, "one's own") and even calls man the "property" (*Eigentum*) of the clearing.[9] As we will see, this usage is quite misleading, not least of all because of the overtones of hypostatization and agency (the clearing as "something" that can "own" something else). We take up each of these two meanings in turn.

First, as regards "appear": Even though Heidegger explicitly disallows translations of *Ereignis* as "event" in a temporal sense, it might nonetheless be legitimate to understand it as an "occurrence"—but only if one means that in the *non-temporal* sense of "to occur" as in "to come to mind" and thus, in the phenomenological-intentional sense of "to appear." At the root of our word "occur" is the Latin verb *occurrere*, which describes something as "running towards us" (*ob-currere*), such that it comes into view, presents itself, and is given—as in the phrase "It occurs to me that . . . " or "It appears to me that . . ." In Latin literature there are abundant examples of *occurrere* in the sense of "to appear" rather than "to happen." At *Aeneid* V, 8–9, for example, Virgil speaks of Aeneas' ship as having sailed so far from the shores of Carthage that "land was no more to be seen" (*nec iam amplius ulla / occurrit tellus*: historical present).[10] And Cicero says, "Nothing reasonable occurs to me as to why Pythagoras' and Plato's opinion should not be true."[11] In the case of Heidegger's use of *Ereignis*, what "occurs" in this sense—or, more accurately, always already *has* "occurred"—is the thrown-openness of ex-sistence.

Second, as regards "appropriate": The second branch of the etymology of *Ereignis* ("own") can be combined with the first ("appear") if we think of the word "appropriation" in terms of its own etymology. The Latin *proprius* refers to what belongs to something as its very own. Thus the Latin *proprietas* does not first mean someone's "property" in the sense of what he or she has acquired

8. GA 71: 184.17–19 = 156.20–24.

9. GA 65: 263.14 = 207.16: "Die Er-eignung bestimmt den Menschen zum Eigentum des Seyns." I say "unfortunately" because this usage can, and in fact does, lead to the reification of the clearing/Seyn and the objectification of ex-sistence.

10. Virgil, at http://www.thelatinlibrary.com/vergil/aen5.shtml. In Fagles' translation: "no land in sight," *The Aeneid*, 153 (although he gets the line number wrong).

11. *Tusculanae disputationes* 1, 21 (49) (ET, 58): "Nec tamen mihi sane quidquam occurrit cur non Pythagorae sit et Platonis vera sententia"; see also *De natura deorum*, 1, 14 (36) (ET, 38): "si intelligi potest nihil sentiens deus [= aether], qui nunquam nobis occurit necque in precibus neque in optatis neque in votis": "If something insensate [= the ether] can be understood to be a god even though it never 'occurs' [= appears, shows up] to us in our prayers, petitions, or devotion."

and owns: land, for example, or a house. Rather, a *proprietas* first and foremost is a quality that belongs to a thing, a special property or characteristic that is appropriate to that thing and *makes it be what it is,* as in the philosophical sense of the "properties" of something.[12] Heidegger's meaning of *Er-eignis*/ap-*pro-pri*-ation is less about "owning" something and more about bringing something *ad proprium*, into its *own proper state* such that it comes into its own, into its *proprietas* as the essential "something" that it is. In Heidegger's specific sense of bringing-into-its-own, *Ereignis* means that ex-sistence has *always already* been brought into its own as the thrown-open clearing, and "occurs" precisely *as* that.[13] In another formulation, appropriation is the "opening of the clearing" as an always-already operative fact.[14]

Right at the start, the ordinary everyday German meaning of *Ereignis* presents a problem. So, Heidegger's objections notwithstanding, let us ask: Is appropriation an event? Is it a unique moment in a temporal continuum, with a before and an after? Does it happen at a certain distinguishable time, so that we can say "*Now* it is in effect, whereas before it was not"? No, appropriation is much more than an event: it is a *fact*, that which is always already done (*factum*) and thus always already operative.[15] And what is more, it is *the* fact, "the thing itself," without which there are no other facts, events, or happenings in the human realm.[16] This ur-fact both determines ex-sistence and is coterminous with it without being supervenient to or separable from it.

Thus when Heidegger allows himself to say that ap-propri-ation (*Er-eignung*) determines man as the *Eigentum* (usually "property") of the clearing, what he means is that human being, in its essence, has always already been brought into its "own" *as* the open space for meaningfulness. And as ever open, it "sustains" (*aussteht*) the clearing. We must be more careful than Heidegger himself was to avoid the reifying language that presents *Ereignis* or *Sein selbst* or *Seyn*

---

12. *Oxford Latin Dictionary*, 1495 b and c, s.v. "proprietās." See also *The Stanford Encyclopedia of Philosophy*, "properties": http://plato.stanford.edu/entries/properties/.

13. GA 65: 262.2–3 = 206.10–11: "die Gründung der Wahrheit des Seins im Dasein." That is: as appropriated, ex-sistence comes into its own as the groundless ground of the opened clearing. See ibid. 293.4–5 = 231.4–5: "[N]ur auf dem Grunde des Da-seins kommt das Seyn zur Wahrheit." Also ibid. 294.9 = 232.9.

14. GA 49: 41.26, GA 4: 56.27 = 79.12, etc.: "Lichten der Lichtung." This is also the meaning of Austrag ("drawing out"): GA 66: 84.33–34 = 70.37–38: "Der *Austrag* meint . . . Eröffnung, *Lichten der Lichtung—Er-eignis* als Austrag."

15. Appropriation is "das Unzugangbare," the inaccessible fact to which "wir Sterbliche / anfänglich ge-eignet sind": GA 13: 242.7–9. It is always already operative: GA 11: 20.23–26 = 73.10–14. Appropriation is that which "eh wir waren, schon bei uns gewesen und deshalb in der Rückkehr auf uns zukommt und unser Wesen in diese Zukunft ruft": "Der Weg," 26.5–7.

16. See GA 26: 270.10 = 209.7, where the unfolding of the clearing ("die Zeitigung der Zeitlichkeit") is not a "temporal" event but the always already operative "Urfaktum."

as if it were a quasi-something that "catches sight" of human being, calls it into its presence, and makes it its own, as in such unfortunate sentences as

> *Er-eignen heißt ursprünglich: er-äugen, d.h. erblicken, im Blicken zu sich rufen, an-eignen.*[17]

> *Er-eignen* originally means: to bring something into view, that is, to catch sight of it, to call it into view, to ap-propriate it.

The "something" that is allegedly "brought into view" is ex-sistence; and this hypostatizing language makes it seem that something separate from ex-sistence "sees" ex-sistence and makes it its own property. Instead of that, we may preserve both of the etymological stems of *Ereignis*—"occur" and "own"—by translating the word as "appropriation" (but never as "the *event* of appropriation") in the sense that ex-sistence has always already been "brought into its own essence" (*ad proprium*) and "come into view" as the clearing.[18] As such, *Ereignis* names "the thing itself" of Heidegger's philosophy: the ever-open "space" or *Da* that makes it possible and necessary for us to know things discursively in terms of their meaningfulness.

The danger that constantly lurks in Heidegger's rich and suggestive lexicon is that his technical terms will take on a life of their own as words and then get substituted for what they are trying to indicate, the way some scholarship treats the clearing (or *das Sein selbst*) "as if it were something present 'over against' us as an object."[19] Thus Heidegger's key term *Ereignis*—especially when English scholarship leaves it in the German—risks becoming a reified thing in its own right, a supra-human Cosmic Something that enters into relations with ex-sistence, dominates it, and sends *Sein* to it while withholding itself in a preternatural realm of mystery. To avoid such traps and to appreciate what Heidegger means by *Ereignis*, we must always remember that the term bespeaks our thrown-openness as the groundless no-thing of being-in-the-world, which we can experience in dread or wonder. Above all we should apply Heidegger's

---

17. GA 11: 45.13–15 (omitted without explanation in the English translation at 36.14). A marginal note in the German glosses the last word, an-eignen, with "in die Lichtung," "into the clearing." Other such hypostasizing examples abound: GA 12: 249.1–2 = 129.9: "Das Ereignis . . . in seinem Er-äugen des Menschenwesen."

18. In his clearer moments Heidegger says as much. Cf. GA 12: 249.5–6 = 129.13: "daß sie [= die Vereignung] das Menschenwesen in sein Eigenes entläßt"; ibid., 248.6–7 = 128.19–20: "Das Ereignis verleiht den Sterblichen den Aufenthalt in ihrem Wesen, daß sie vermögen, die Sprechenden zu sein"; ibid., 248.15–16 = 128.29–129.1: "Das Ereignis ist *das* Gesetz, insofern es die Sterblichen in das Ereignen zu ihrem Wesen versammelt und darin hält."

19. GA 65: 256.2–4 = 201.28–30: "als wese das Seyn für den Menschen wie ein *Gegenüber* und Gegenstand."

strict phenomenological rule to appropriation itself: "avoid any ways of characterizing it that do not arise out of the personal claims it makes on you."[20]

But why such a strange philosophical recasting of the common word *Ereignis*? Why does Heidegger use it at all? The new language of *Ereignis* should not lead us to think that in 1936 Heidegger stumbled upon a heretofore unnoticed phenomenon that required him to rewrite his philosophy. On the contrary, the key to understanding *Ereignis* is to realize that it is the later Heidegger's re-inscription of what he had earlier called *Geworfenheit*, "thrownness," and more fully *der geworfene Entwurf*, "thrown-openness."[21]

We have seen that Heidegger's basic and abiding question is this: What makes intelligibility-at-all—*Sein*, which is always the *Sein* of things—necessary and possible? The early Heidegger's response was: our a priori thrown-openness as the clearing, and the later Heidegger's answer was the same: our structural appropriation to being the open space for discursive intelligibility. Thrownness and appropriation are identical, simply earlier and later names for the same existential structure. We can see this identity of *Ereignis* and *Geworfenheit* from the way the later Heidegger equates the two by placing them in apposition to each another.

> *die Er-eignung, das Geworfenwerden*
>
> "being ap-propri-ated, becoming thrown"[22]
>
> *geworfener . . . d.h. er-eignet*
>
> "thrown . . . that is, ap-propri-ated"[23]
>
> *Das Dasein ist geworfen, ereignet*
>
> "Ex-sistence is thrown, [i.e.,] appropriated."[24]

We see it again in the equivalence of Heidegger's earlier and later formulations for what ex-sistence is called to "take over":

20. GA 9:113.8–10 = 89.24–26.

21. See GA 66: 108.20–21 = 90.22–23: "Geworfenheit und Entwurf sind bereits aus der Wahrheit des Seyns begriffene Züge der Lichtung."

22. GA 65: 34.9 = 29.7.

23. GA 65: 239.5 = 188.25.

24. GA 65: 304.8 = 240.16. See ibid., 252.23–25 = 199.3–4. Also GA 9: 377, note d = 286, note d: "Geworfenheit und Ereignis."

SZ: *die Übernahme der Geworfenheit*

"taking over one's thrownness."[25]

GA 65: *die Über-nahme der Er-eignung*

"taking over one's being appropriated."[26]

In appropriation, what gets appropriated (*geworfen, ereignet*) is human being itself.[27] However, we must be careful not to hypostatize appropriation or "Being Itself" into an ontological Super-Something—possessed of a life of its own with agency to boot—that does the appropriating and the throwing.[28] There is no "reason why" ex-sistence is thrown-open or appropriated: it is *ohne Warum*. We should drop all talk of man being "thrown or appropriated *by*," if only to purge, once and for all, the crypto-metaphysics that has colonized Heidegger scholarship in recent years (with quite a bit of help from Heidegger himself). Such fatal hypostatizations and personalizations of Being Itself, whether by the Master or his disciples, turns Heidegger's work into a parody of itself. Think of the pathos of "Being is still waiting for the time when It Itself will become thought-provoking to the human being."[29] Or the silliness of "Being *as such* is not yet awake enough to catch sight of us from out of its awakened essence."[30] This is less *dormitat Homerus* and more *inebriatus est Noe*, and it has understandably (one might even say: rightly) brought scorn upon Heidegger's head.

The "one thought"[31] that guided Heidegger's work—the answer to his basic and abiding question about why there is meaningful presence at all—is quite simply the thrown-openness or appropriation of ex-sistence. These "two" are existentially the same and constitute the very possibility of intelligibility.[32]

---

25. SZ 325.37 = 373.14–15.

26. GA 65: 322.7–8 = 254.36–37. GA 94: 337.7–8: resolve as "ein Zurückwachsen in das Tragende der Geworfenheit."

27. GA 12: 249.1–2 = 129.9. GA 94: 448.31: "das Er-eignis des Daseins, wodurch dieses dann geeignet wird." GA 65: 407, note = 322 note 1: "Hier ist das Ereignis auf den Menschen zu gesehen, der aus ihm als Dasein bestimmt wird." Also GA 14: 28.18–19 = 23.15–17.

28. GA 9: 442.22 = 334.21: "zu einem phantastischen Weltwesen hypostasieren." Cf. GA 73, 2: 975.22–23: "als Etwas für sich Vorhandenes." GA 66: 340.13–14 = 303.18–19: "Das Sein nimmt sich aus wie 'Etwas', auf das der Mensch zugeht oder nicht."

29. GA 9: 322.30–31 = 246.15–16.

30. GA 10: 80.29–30 = 54.11–13.

31. GA 13: 76.9–10 = 4.10.

32. GA 16: 424.20–21 = 5.14–15: "der Bereich der Unverborgenheit oder Lichtung (Verstehbarkeit)."

In turn, *actual* intelligibility occurs when I existentielly take up this particular tool as suitable for that particular task (using the primary or hermeneutical "as" of praxis) or understand this subject in terms of that predicate (employing the apophantic "as" of declarative sentences).[33] Such simple existentiel acts disclose *das jeweilige Sein* of things—that is, how and as what those things are present to us in their current meaning, whether correctly or not.[34]

In 1936 Heidegger not only began using *Ereignis* to name the core element of his thinking but also introduced the term *Kehre* ("turn") with a new technical meaning that is intimately bound up with appropriation. In GA 65 he speaks frequently of

die Kehre im Ereignis: the turn [at work] in appropriation[35]
die im Ereignis wesende Kehre: the turn that is operative in appropriation[36]
die Kehre des Ereignisses (subj. gen.): the turn that goes with appropriation[37]
das Ereignis der Kehre (subj. gen.): the appropriation that goes with the turn[38]
das Ereignis und dessen Kehre: appropriation and its turn[39]
die Er-eignung in ihrer Kehre: ap-propri-ating in its capacity as the turn[40]

Heidegger notes that section 6 of "On the Essence of Truth" is the point where his thinking first addresses "the *Kehre* that is at work in appropriation."[41] That section is also the first place where his work takes up—at least inchoately—the intrinsic hiddenness of the appropriated clearing, and this provides a clue to

33. Both uses of the "as" are hermeneutical in the broad sense, but that broad sense in turn divides into the primary hermeneutical "as" of praxis and the secondary "as" of declarative sentences.

34. See *Nicomachean Ethics* VI 3, 1139b15: ἀληθεύει ἡ ψυχή: ex-sistence dis-closes things in their current ἀλήϑεια-2.

35. GA 65: 34.10–11 = 29.8; 57.10 = 46.15; 262.3–4 = 206.11; 267.12 = 210.17–18; 320.19 = 235.27; 407.6 = 322.31. See ibid., 325.9–10 = 257.17–18: die Kehre im Wesen des Seins selbst.

36. GA 65: 407.8 = 322.33. See "die (im Ereignis wesende) Kehre": GA 9: 193, note "a" = 148, note "a."

37. GA 65: 311.5 = 246.18–19; 342.25 = 271.18–19; 351.22 = 277.40; 354.9–10 = 279.34–35.

38. GA 65: 311.13–14 = 246.27–28.

39. GA 65: 31.18–19 = 27.4–5.

40. GA 65: 342.22 = 271.15.

41. GA 9: 193, note a = 148, note a: "der Sprung in die (im Ereignis wesende) Kehre."

the togetherness, even the sameness, of appropriation, clearing, and "the turn." What, then, is the *Kehre* that Heidegger has in mind here?

To begin with, "the turn" definitely is not the 1930s change in Heidegger's approach to his topic (*die Wendung im Denken*). Heidegger writes to Father Richardson, "[My] thinking *about* the *Kehre is* an alteration in my thinking"[42]—thereby distinguishing between the *Kehre* and his philosophizing about the *Kehre*. (1) "The turn" in its primary and proper sense is only another name for Heidegger's abiding topic; and (2) Heidegger's thinking *about* that unchanged topic underwent a change from a transcendental to a *seinsgeschichtlich* model in the 1930s. Furthermore, Heidegger is clear that, first, the *Kehre* in its primary and proper sense is what it at work in appropriation; and second, as such, it is the basis of such derivative "turns" as the *Wendung im Denken* and the hermeneutic circle:

> *Ereignis* has its innermost occurrence and its furthest scope in the *Kehre*. The *Kehre* that is operative in *Ereignis* is the hidden basis of all the other, subordinate turns, circles, and circlings, which remain obscure and unquestioned as regards their origin, even though people are happy to take them as if they were "ultimate"—as, for example, the turn in the structure of the guiding questions [= the altered approach of the 1930s]; or the [hermeneutical] circle in understanding.[43]

It is not entirely clear why Heidegger chose the particular word *Kehre* to name the inner workings of appropriation. In fact, given the widespread misunderstanding of this term, it would be best to shelve it and instead to use the word he places in apposition to *Kehre*—namely, *Gegenschwung* or "oscillation." "Oscillation" says much more clearly what Heidegger meant.[44] What he had in mind with the *Kehre*-as-*Gegenschwung* is the *dynamic sameness* of ex-sistence/clearing, of *Da-<u>sein</u>* and *<u>Da</u>-sein*: a unique "back-and-forth-ness" (*reci-proci-tas*) as a single unified phenomenon. However, the later Heidegger often and unfortunately uses hypostatizing and objectifying language to express this oscillating reci-proci-ty. For example, he speaks of "the oscillating

42. GA 11: 149.21–22 = xviii.25–26: "Das Denken der Kehre *ist* eine Wendung in meinem Denken." I have added the emphasis on "about."

43. GA 65: 407.7–12 = 322.32–37.

44. Gegenschwung, a neologism Heidegger formed from gegenschwingen, appears in his notes beginning in 1936 and disappears (unfortunately, in my opinion) after 1946. In 1928 he spoke importantly of the "Schwingen" of the ex-stases as forming the world. "Das Ekstematische zeitigt sich schwingend als ein Welten": GA 26: 270.4–5 = 209.2–3. For Gegenschwung see GA 65: 29.15 = 25.18 et passim; also GA 70: 126.18; GA 75: 59.15; GA 78: 335.13; etc. On Gegenschwung and Ereignis (unfortunately translated as "event") see, for example, GA 65: 251.24f. = 198.14; 261.26 = 206.3; 262.7–8 = 206.15–16; 286.31f. = 225.19–21; 351.22 = 277.39–40; and 381.26–27 = 301.29–30.

relation of the clearing to man"[45] as entailing, on the one hand, the clearing's "claim on" and "need of" man (*Anspruch*, *Brauch*) and, on the other, man's belonging to and sustaining the clearing (*Zugehörigkeit*, *Ausstehen*).[46] But what he means is: no ex-sistence, no clearing; and no clearing, no ex-sistence.[47]

> *Das Seyn braucht den Menschen damit es wese, und der Mensch gehört dem Seyn.*[48]
>
> The clearing needs man in order to occur, and man belongs to the clearing.

But there are not "two things" here, the first needing the second, and the second belonging to the first. Heidegger clarifies:

> The relation [man-clearing] is not a bond stretched between the clearing and man. . . . The relation *is* the clearing itself, and man's essence *is* that same relation.[49]

Likewise Heidegger says that that man stands "in relation to" the clearing as "to that which is not man"—but he immediately explains that by saying "insofar as man *receives his determination from the clearing*."[50] That is, the clearing

---

45. GA 73, 1: 795.19–20: "das kehrige Verhältnis des Seyns zum Menschenwesen." One might also translate "kehrige" as "reci-proc-al," but there are limits to hyphenitus, and as William J. Richardson put it, "pur-ists may find it an-noy-ing": *Heidegger*, xxviii.12.

46. GA 79: 69.21–23 = 65.25–28. GA 65: 32.7 = 27.22; 251.24–25 = 198.14. In this pairing, the clearing's "need" of ex-sistence is sometimes unhelpfully (because anthropomorphically) described as the clearing's "call" to ex-sistence (Zuruf): GA 65: 233.23 = 184.15; 342.22 = 271.16; 372.15 = 294.14; 380.16 = 300.28; 384.2–3 = 303.17–18: 407.30 = 323.17. GA 6, 2: 443.4 = 78.4–5; GA 51: 89.3 and .5 = 75.6 and .8; GA 66: 224.13 = 198.20; GA 70: 106.1; etc.

47. See GA 45: 212.10–11 = 179.29–30: "Wäre der Mensch nicht seiend, dann könnte auch diese Lichtung nicht geschehen" and ibid., 212.11–14 = 179.30–32: The clearing "ist der tragende Grund für das Menschsein, und dieses geschieht nur, indem es [= das Menschsein] den tragenden Grund als solchen gründet und aussteht."

48. GA 65: 251.11–12 = 198.2–3. (With "need" I am translating the German "Not" and focusing on its primary Heideggerian sense of "neediness" rather than the derived sense of "emergency.") GA 65: 447.19–20 = 352.30: "Der Entwurf des Seyns kann nur vom Seyn selbst geworfen werden." GA 15: 370.18–19 = 63.16–17: "Das Sein aber braucht, um sich zu öffnen, den Menschen als das Da seiner Offenbarkeit."

49. GA 73, 1: 790.5–8, my emphasis: "Der Bezug ist jedoch nicht zwischen das Seyn und den Menschen eingespannt. . . . Der Bezug ist das Seyn selbst, und das Menschenwesen ist der selbe Bezug." "Einspannen" has the sense of yoking together, harnessing, as well as stretching between. Also "Der Weg," ms. 20.18–22.

50. GA 15: 390.9–11 = 75.4–5: "zu dem . . . was nicht der Mensch ist" followed by "indem er doch von dort seine Bestimmung empfängt." (My emphasis in the ET.) See chapter 1, note 133.

is not different from ex-sistence but is the reason why ex-sistence ex-sists at all. It is the existential essence of existentiel man. There are not two separate things, ex-sistence over here, the clearing over there, with "needing" and "belonging" as the glue that binds them together. The "two" are actually the same phenomenon considered from distinct viewpoints: either *ex-sistence* as the clearing or that same *clearing* as what makes possible all meaningfulness. As thrown-open, ex-sistence always already *is* the existential space in which the existentiel understanding of things-in-their-being takes place. Strictly speaking, therefore, it is incorrect to speak of ex-sistence as "open *to*" the clearing, as if the clearing were a space that ex-sistence could possibly enter, the way someone might, or might not, walk into a room.[51] This oscillating sameness was first designated as *In-der-Welt-sein*: the being of ex-sistence is to-sustain-and-be-the-world; and the ever-open world is the very being of ex-sistence.[52] Heidegger never loses sight of this structural sameness as a "*unitary* phenomenon [which] must be seen as a whole."[53] Meaningful presence is possible only because of this oscillating sameness (*reci-proci-tas*, *Gegen-schwung*) of "being-in" and "the world of meaning."[54]

Once the *Kehre* is understood in its primary and proper sense as the oscillation of ex-sistence/clearing, we readily see that *Ereignis* and the *Kehre* both name "the thing itself": the appropriation of human being to its dynamic thrown-openness. Without it, nothing human happens; and yet in itself it is not a happening but the presupposition of all happenings. Moreover, this oscillating reci-proci-ty is finite insofar as it is necessarily bound up with ex-sistence as possibility, the privation of full self-presence. If ex-sistence as privative self-absence (= possibility) were converted into full self-coincidence and actuality, we would not be able to (and we would not need to) make discursive sense of anything. Making sense of things requires the imperfection and incompleteness of possibility, along with the resultant space for mediation. Heidegger sets this particular notion of the human finitude over against the traditional one, which measures finitude against the infinity of the divine.

---

51. Nonetheless Heidegger himself abets the wrong impression when, for example, he speaks of "Geworfenheit in die Lichtung": GA 69: 21.16, et passim.

52. GA 9: 154.18–19 = 120.24–25: "Welt ist . . . die Bezeichnung für das menschliche Dasein im Kern seines Wesens." Also SZ 64.19–20 = 92.32; 365.38 = 417.11; 380.28–30 = 432.17–18. Also GA 24: 237.8–10 = 166.33–35. On world and clearing: GA 9: 326.15–16 = 248.36–37: "Die Lichtung des Seins, und nur sie, ist Welt."

53. SZ 53.12–13 = 78.22–23: "ein *einheitliches* Phänomen. . . . Dieser primäre Befund muß im Ganzen gesehen werden."

54. In a somewhat hypostasizing formulation: GA 78: 335.10–12: "Geworfen—nicht aus sich. / Woher anders denn aus Seyn selber? / *Ereignis*." Roughly: Ex-sistence is thrown-open, but not of its own accord. / What else explains this thrown-openness if not the appropriated clearing? / that is, *appropriation*.

> The finitude of appropriation . . . is nevertheless different from the finitude spoken of in the book on Kant, in that it is no longer thought in terms of the relation to infinity, but rather as *finitude in itself*: finitude, end, limit, one's own—to be secure in one's own.[55]

Once again we must invoke Aristotle's διορίσωμεν: we need to make some distinctions. We have established the meaning of the *Kehre* in its primary and proper sense. However, Heidegger himself, as well as his followers, use the term loosely and somewhat indiscriminately to cover a number of other "derivative turns"[56]—for example:

1. the transition that from 1926 on was programmed to take place between SZ I.2 and SZ I.3—namely, from *ex-sistence* as the clearing to the *clearing* as making possible meaningful presence. This is often and incorrectly taken to be the primary and proper meaning of the *Kehre*.
2. the 1930s change of approach (*die Wendung im Denken*) from a transcendental to a *seinsgeschichtlich* model, which is also frequently and incorrectly taken to be the primary and proper meaning of the *Kehre*.
3. the alleged future "turn in being," described in the 1949 essay "*Die Kehre*," that will supposedly lead to the utopia of "an altogether different age of the world."[57]
4. the "turn" that in 1928 Heidegger said would take place between a future, completed fundamental ontology (in the never-published SZ I.3) and a subsequent ontic investigation called "metontology."[58]

I will save the "utopic turn" (number 3 above) for treatment in the following chapters, and I will let footnote 58 cover the "metontological turn" (which gets

55. GA 14: 64.20–25 = 54.22–27 (my emphasis): that is, to be secure in one's appropriation or thrownness. (The internal reference is to GA 3.) See GA 66: 88.15–17 = 73.32–34: "Die 'Endlichkeit' des Da-seins . . . ist eine Wesensfolge seiner wesenhaften Er-eignung durch das Seyn."

56. GA 65: 407.9 and .11 = 322.34: "nachgeordenen . . . Kehren."

57. GA 5: 326.14–15 = 246.1–2: "eines ganz anderen Weltalters."

58. Metonology: In 1928 Heidegger mentioned the possibility of a post–SZ I.3 "turn" (Kehre: GA 26: 201.30 = 158.30) to a *regional ontology* or "metaphysiche Ontik" (GA 26: 201.29 = 158.31) dealing with such issues as philosophical anthropology and even ethics. "This new investigation resides in the essence of ontology itself and results from the transformation of [traditional] ontology: its μεταβολή [which SZ I.3 would have carried out]. I designate this set of questions as *metontology* [= 'that which follows ontology']": GA 26: 199.24–28 = 157.4–8 (cf. GA 9: 249.21–29 = 191.8–17; GA 22: 106.26–28 = 87.26–28). (It is not impossible that Heidegger's 1935–1936 essay on the artwork might have fallen within the parameters of metontology.)

mentioned only once in Heidegger's work). In this chapter I will take up the remaining two: the transition that was planned to take place between SZ 1.2 and SZ 1.3 (= number 1 above); and Heidegger's change in his approach during the 1930s (= number 2 above). These two—neither of which is the primary and proper meaning of the *Kehre*—are usually mixed together and called "the turn in Heidegger's thinking." Our task, therefore, is:

- to distinguish the two;
- to explain why neither of them is "the turn" in Heidegger's sense of that term;
- to show what the primary and proper sense of *die* Kehre is; and
- to show that the long-planned transition from ex-sistence to the clearing got absorbed into the unplanned change of approach in the 1930s.

Heidegger's confusion of the various meanings of *Kehre* is another of those hair-pulling moments for the scholarship; but sorting out these minute issues is hardly of earth-shaking philosophical importance. Rather than contributing very much to a *general* understanding of his work, it may be of concern only to Heidegger wonks. Non-wonks might well want to skip the following sections, or simply breeze through them on their way to chapter 9.

1. THE TRANSITION THAT WAS TO TAKE PLACE WITHIN *BEING AND TIME*

The program that Heidegger announced for *Being and Time* in 1927 divided Part I of the book into

SZ I.1–2: the analysis of thrown-open (= "ex-static") ex-sistence.
SZ I.3: the analysis of the horizon that is correlative to thrown-open ex-sistence and that determines the unity as well as various modes of meaningful presence.

These two moments are announced in the title that Heidegger gave to Part I of *Being and Time*:

SZ I.1–2: The interpretation of ex-sistence in terms of "temporality."
SZ I.3: The explanation of "time" as the transcendental horizon for the question about being.[59]

59. SZ 39.30–32 = 63.35–37, paraphrased.

In a course he gave in the summer of 1928, one year after publishing *Being and Time*, Heidegger expressed this same twofold division of labor as:

SZ I.1–2: the interpretation of ex-sistence in terms of "temporality."
SZ I.3: the understanding of the "time-character" of being; and the possibility of ontology.[60]

Eight years later he described this as:

SZ I.1–2: human being in its relation to the clearing.
SZ I.3: the clearing and its openness in relation to human being.[61]

In making this move from transcendence (SZ I.1–2) to the transcendent (SZ I.3) there was to be a transition from focusing on ex-sistence in its horizon-*forming* function to focusing on that transcendentally shaped horizon itself. In 1928 Heidegger for the first time called this transition the *Kehre* (but not in what would turn out to be its primary and proper sense).[62] The specific task of SZ I.3 was to show that the clearing is the thrown-open domain (*der Entwurfbereich*) that allows us to go beyond things to their being.[63] But in 1943 he said that this goal remained "intentionally undeveloped" in *Being and Time* because the transcendental approach of the book, saddled as it was with "the language of metaphysics," prevented him from carrying out this transition and completing his fundamental ontology.[64] In the 1930s Heidegger finally did carry out this "*Kehre*" (transition to SZ I.3), but he did so within his new *seinsgeschichtlich* model. With this long-planned and now achieved focus on the clearing, he wrote in 1946, "my thinking arrives for the first time at the place, the dimension, from out of which *Being and Time* is experienced in the fundamental experience of *Seinsvergessenheit*."[65] Here, as in the lecture "On the Essence of Truth," *Seinsvergessenheit* is a misnomer for the *intrinsic hiddenness* of the clearing (which, in turn, is responsible for the overlooking of the clearing in metaphysics).[66]

60. See GA 26: 201.19–28 = 158.20–29.

61. GA 45: 214.23–25 = 181.12–14 (paraphrased): "der Mensch in seinem Bezug zum Sein, d.h. in der Kehre: das Seyn und dessen Wahrheit im Bezug zum Menschen."

62. GA 26: 201.29 = 158.30, with "Kehre" italicized.

63. Entwurfbereich: GA 9: 201.31–32 = 154.13–14; GA 14: 35.23–24 = 27.31–33; Heidegger, *Schelling* 229.4 = 188.38; etc.

64. Respectively: GA 9: 201.33 = 154.14–15: "absichtlich unentfaltet"; and 328.3–4 = 250.3–4: "[die] Sprache der Metaphysik" with 201.33–202.1 = 154.15–16: "Das Denken hält sich dem Anschein nach in der Bahn der Metaphysik."

65. GA 9: 328.9–11 = 250.9–10.

66. Intrinsic hiddenness: GA 9: 328, note d = 250, note d: Vergessenheit = Λήθη = Verbergung = Entzug = Enteignis.

Here things get a bit messy, and distinctions need to be made. As we pointed out, in 1928 and 1937–1938 Heidegger called this transition from the material of SZ I.1–2 to that of SZ I.3 "*die Kehre*," and he repeated this usage ten years later.[67] In 1946 he further described it as a "turn-around" (*Umkehr*) in the direction of his project. (This latter text is often, and incorrectly, interpreted as Heidegger's change to the *seinsgeschichtlich* model of the 1930s.)[68] But in any case, that "turn" *was never carried out as it had originally been planned*—namely, within the transcendental framework of *Being and Time*. Rather, the transition from ex-sistence to the clearing got absorbed into and carried out within the new non-transcendental paradigm. Meanwhile, Heidegger's focal topic, *die Sache selbst*, remained the appropriated clearing. And another name for that topic is *die Kehre*, but now in its primary and proper sense: the a priori, always-operative oscillation (*Gegenschwung*) of ex-sistence/clearing as the groundless ground of the possibility and necessity of meaningful-presence-at-all. Therefore, the relevant distinction in this present case is between

1. the *Kehre* in its *proper* sense as yet another name for "the thing itself" of Heidegger's thought, and
2. the "*Kehre*" in a *derivative* sense as a name for the long-planned transition from *Da-<u>sein</u>* to *<u>Da</u>-sein*.

Could Heidegger have been a bit clearer and less confusing on this issue? Unquestionably. One way out of the confusion is to substitute Heidegger's term "oscillation" (*Gegenschwung*) for the word *Kehre* when that term is used in its primary and proper sense.

2. THE 1930S CHANGE OF APPROACH (*DIE WENDUNG IM DENKEN*)

Heidegger scholarship usually mixes together two very different things—on the one hand, *Being and Time*'s long-planned progression from ex-sistence to the clearing, and, on the other hand, the changed approach of the 1930s—and it then takes this mismatched combination to be *die Kehre* in its primary and proper sense.

67. In 1928: GA 26: 201.29 = 158.30. In 1937–1938: GA 45: 47.18 and .20 = 44.10 and .16; and ibid., 214.23–24 = 181.13: "in der Kehre."

68. "Turning around" of direction: umkehren. See GA 9: 328.1 and note a = 250.1 and note a: "Hier kerht sich das Ganze um," glossed with "im Was und Wie des Denwürdigen und des Denkens." Perhaps this is also alluded to at GA 2: 53, note a = 37, note †.

To sort this out, we should first decide how to translate Heidegger's neologism "*seinsgeschichtlich*." When that adjective is used in conjunction with *Denken* (*seinsgeschichtliches Denken*), the phrase is often translated by the barbaric "being-historical thinking," which, of course, says nothing because it misses what is meant by *Seinsgeschichte*. An alternate translation (in the ET of GA 65) is no better: "the thinking of being in its historicality." The problem with both these translations is that they wrongly assume that *geschichtlich* and *Geschichtlichkeit* centrally have something to do with history. Heidegger, however, plays on the etymological rootedness of *Geschichte* in the German verb *schicken*, "to send."[69] What he has in mind with *Seinsgeschichte* is his view that appropriation is responsible for (has "sent" or "given") various configurations of the clearing in metaphysics. Hence, as a pro-tem stand-in, I will interpret "*seinsgeschichtliches Denken*" by a periphrasis that may be more barbaric than "being-historical thinking," but nonetheless is closer to Heidegger's intentions—namely, the kind of philosophizing that thinks about how appropriation opens up (or "gives") various clearings-for-being. It hardly rolls off the tongue. But some such periphrasis is necessary to express what Heidegger is getting at.[70]

Heidegger usually calls his change to a *seinsgeschichtliches Denken* an alteration (*Wendung, Wandlung*) in how he worked his central and abiding question.[71] Thus, in a crucial but often misunderstood passage in his letter to William J. Richardson (1962), Heidegger famously distinguishes the *Kehre* in its proper sense (the oscillating sameness of ex-sistence/clearing) from his changed way of thinking about that core topic. In a close paraphrase:

> My thinking about the *Kehre* [beginning in the 1930s] is indeed a change in my thought. But this change is not a matter of altering the standpoint of *Being and Time*, much less of abandoning its fundamental topic. This change in thinking about the *Kehre* [the ex-sistence/clearing oscillation] results from the fact that I stayed with what *Being and Time* took as the subject matter to be thought through. That is, I continued to question in the direction of what *Being and Time* had already designated as "Time and Being" [= SZ I.3]. Most importantly the *Kehre* [in its proper sense] is not some way of carrying out thinking-as-questioning; rather, the *Kehre* is inherent in the very subject matter

69. GA 10: 90.24–28 = 61.35–38.

70. It's a matter of what William J. Richardson called choosing "the lesser of two barbarisms" (*Heidegger*, 50, note 64), if only because the lesser barbarism is closer to Heidegger's intentions. But finally, as Richardson also says (ibid., 579, note 6), "a man must live with himself."

71. See chapter 7, note 76.

> designated by the headings "being and time," "time and being." . . . The *Kehre* is operative in the very subject matter [designated by those headings]. It is not something that I came up with, and it does not pertain merely to my thinking.[72]

And later on in that same letter:

> The so-called "happening" of the *Kehre* "is" the clearing as such.[73]

We have seen that *Ereignis* and the *Kehre*, when properly understood, converge: they are only further ways of articulating the "thing itself" of all Heidegger's work. But much of what he has to say about these key terms, and especially about appropriation, is embedded in his meta-history of Western culture as read through what he calls "*die Geschichte des Seins*," an ambiguous term at best. In the next chapter we sort out what he means by that.

72. GA 11: 149.21–150.1 = xvi.25–xviii.8. The translation above, while superficially different from the current one, accurately captures the meaning of this passage: the proper meaning of the Kehre is neither the transition from ex-sistence to the clearing nor Heidegger's change in approach in the 1930s.

73. GA 11: 151.14–15 = xx.17–18: "Das 'Geschehen' der Kehre, wonach Sie fragen, 'ist' das Seyn als solches."

9

The History of Being

According to the original plan of *Being and Time*, Part II was to carry out a phenomenological "dismantling" of the history of ontology, running in reverse chronological order from Kant (SZ II.1) through Descartes (SZ II.2) to Aristotle (SZ II.3).[1] In Heidegger's formulation (before he had redefined "time" as the clearing),[2] the purpose of Part II would have been to establish that Western metaphysics had always, if unthematically, understood being in terms of some notion of "time," but had overlooked that fact and even blocked access to it.[3] Had it been completed, Part I of *Being and Time* would have shown that the transcendental horizon correlative to ex-sistence has a "time-character" (*Temporalität*, or equally *Zeit*). Heidegger claimed that by "dismantling" or "destructuring" the ontologies of Kant, Descartes, and Aristotle, he would discover in them an operative but unrecognized "time-character." However, establishing that fact would be as far as Heidegger would go in deconstructing these giants of Western ontology.

We note that *Being and Time*'s planned dismantling of ontology may have been on the way to, but was not yet, the full-blown retrieval of the most important "unsaid" element of metaphysics. Heidegger took up *that* task only after his breakthrough of 1930, when he first clearly understood that the clearing is intrinsically hidden. "*Destruktion ist nicht Wiederholung*," he said. "Destructuring is not retrieval."[4] Uncovering and articulating this hiddenness was the objective not of SZ II but only of Heidegger's later interpretations of metaphysics from the pre-Socratics through Nietzsche. Those re-readings tried to cash out diachronically what *Being and Time* had already demonstrated synchronically: the fact that, although we mostly overlook it, appropriation is what opens up and sustains the clearing. The "fallenness" of ex-sistence in its

1. SZ 39.33–35; 40.2–9 = 63.38–39; 64.6–12.
2. See chapter 3, notes 137–142.
3. SZ 21.21–22 = 43.7–8: Traditional ontology, "verlegt den Zugang zu den ursprünglichen 'Quellen.'"
4. In a personal conversation with the author, 12 May 1971, at his home in Freiburg (Zähringen).

everyday living—its overlooking of its own mortal thrown-openness—finds its diachronic parallel in the overlooking of the appropriated clearing in the history of Western metaphysics. The foundation of Heidegger's reading of history lay in what he had already established phenomenologically apart from that history—namely, ἀλήθεια-1 = λήθη-1.

A word on Heidegger's two terms, *Seinsgeschichte* and *Seinsvergessenheit*, the first usually translated as the "history of being" and the second as the "forgottenness of being." Neither translation is on the mark. Heidegger's *Seinsgeschichte* is not a "history" of being the way Frederick Copleston's books are a "history" of philosophy. Rather, it is a highly theorized argument about appropriation "giving" or "sending" (cf. *geben, schicken*) the clearing-for-meaning (ἀλήθεια-1) in various configurations throughout Western metaphysics.[5] In other words, it is a very idiosyncratic history of ontology, one that both presupposes and argues for Heidegger's unique view of the appropriated clearing. If he were to string those various "sendings" into a diachronic narrative, he would have written a work of scientific *Historie*: a history of philosophy about how appropriation "gives" the clearing-for-being and so is responsible for the various formations of being over the last twenty-four centuries—in short, a history of the metaphysical "dispensations" of being (*Seinsgeschicke*). And in a sense he did, not in a single book but in a series of monographs, lectures and essays that, as a whole, is called his *Seinsgeschichte*. But that would be quite a different book from a history of ontology that does not entertain those assumptions.

Coupled with, and in fact inseparable from, Heidegger's "history of dispensations" is his history of *Seinsvergessenheit*, the so-called "forgottenness of being" in Western metaphysics. But that's a misnomer: both the German and the English phrases obscure more than they convey. Being (*Sein, Seiendheit*, οὐσία, εἶναι, etc.) has certainly *never* been forgotten by Western metaphysics, any more than living organisms have been forgotten by biologists or money has been forgotten by capitalists. Whole libraries have been written on being since the Greeks, and Thomists rightly point out that *Sein* in the form of *esse* is the very heart of Aquinas' metaphysics. How, then, can Heidegger say that being is "forgotten" in metaphysics? Once again, *distinguo*. The *Sein* of Heidegger's *Seinsvergessenheit* does not refer to the being of things but rather to *what makes that possible*: the thrown-open clearing. The εἶδος and ἐνέργεια that Plato and Aristotle spoke about, like the *esse* that Aquinas articulated, are specific historical names for the essence and existence of entities within meta-

---

5. GA 10: 90.24–28 = 61.35–38. By "gives" Heidegger intends "enables, occasions, is responsible for" as at GA 22: 106. 32 = 87.32: "ursprünglich ermöglichend." GA 7: 10.18 = 7.20–21: verschulden; ibid., 12.10–11 = 10.2: veranlassen.

physics. When it comes to being, metaphysics has certainly covered the waterfront; but by its very structure it has been unaware of the clearing that makes being possible and necessary. Heidegger's history of *Seinsvergessenheit*, therefore, is more properly a history of *Lichtungsvergessenheit* or *Ereignissesvergessenheit*: the overlooking of appropriation as the opening up and sustaining of the intrinsically hidden clearing that underlies all historical formations of the being of things.

Heidegger's purpose in working through this history was not simply to restate what onto-theology had said about the being of things.[6] Rather, he was after what onto-theology had left *un*said. But in order to find that out, he first had to articulate what the metaphysicians *did* say. Much of his effort, therefore, consisted in doing metaphysics' homework for it in the form of brilliant interpretations of what certain ancient and modern thinkers had to say about being. And for all his efforts at deconstructing these onto-theologies in order to find the forgotten clearing, his respect for metaphysics remained unsurpassed. He also realized that a complete break with metaphysics was impossible insofar as ontology, in its most natural *lived* form, is a matter of our necessarily going "beyond" things to their meaningful presence/being. Ex-sistence *qua* intentional has present not just things but things as meaningful (as "having being"). By our very nature, we are meta-physical, and to break free of that would be to break free of being human. Heidegger simply wanted to find the reason for the inevitability of metaphysics, whether natural or scientific, whether in one's personal life or in the history of Western philosophy.

The clearing's intrinsic hiddenness virtually guarantees that it will be overlooked and forgotten. And indeed, as Heidegger tells the story, it was lost from sight for over two thousand years and remained unseen until Heidegger's fortuitous discovery of finite and mortal ex-sistence. This occurred just in the nick of time as the modern world, with all its technical and scientific achievements, was going to hell in a handbasket[7] because of philosophy's—and more generally humankind's—oblivion of the clearing. After we spell out how Heidegger reads the history of Western philosophy and culture, from the pre-Socratics through the modern era, we will have to ask how much of this sweeping meta-metaphysical narrative about the downfall of the West one must take on board in order to responsibly and fruitfully appropriate the core of Heidegger's thought.

Heidegger's story about the fateful devolution of the West unfolds in four chapters, and we will take up each in turn:

6. Onto-theology = "general metaphysics" (ontology) + "special metaphysics" (philosophical theology).

7. GA 16: 117.6–7 = 13.18–19: "in seinem Fugen kracht . . . in sich zusammenstürtz."

1. The pre-Socratics: The hidden clearing is discovered but not questioned.
2. Metaphysics: From Plato through Nietzsche the clearing gets increasingly overlooked.
3. Today: The overlooking of the clearing is itself overlooked.
4. Tomorrow: Heidegger holds out the possibility of rescue from oblivion of the clearing.

1. THE PRE-SOCRATICS: THE HIDDEN CLEARING IS DISCOVERED BUT NOT QUESTIONED

In its briefest formulation, Heidegger argues that the pre-Socratics (we will limit the discussion to Parmenides and Heraclitus) discovered the hidden clearing, ἀλήθεια-1, but failed to see that the appropriation of ex-sistence is the reason why there is a clearing at all.[8]

Heidegger thought the ancient Greeks, or at least their artists and thinkers, were gifted with a sense of the excess of meaningful presence: he thought this was the heart of Greek experience in the sixth and fifth centuries BCE.[9] But what about the *origin* of such presence? Heidegger argued that Parmenides and Heraclitus were indeed aware of what accounts for the presence of things. Parmenides called it ἀλήθεια, Heraclitus called it φύσις (two names for the same thing),[10] and for Heidegger this was the height of Greek thinking. But overwhelmed by the immediacy of the hidden source of presence, Parmenides and Heraclitus did not ask about the origin or "whence" of ἀλήθεια-1.[11] Hence the "first beginning" of awareness of the clearing stands in need of "another beginning," which happened when Heidegger saw that the appropriation of ex-sistence is why there is a clearing at all. This discovery went one step further back than the pre-Socratics had gone (not to mention Plato and Aristotle), and in that regard Heidegger says, "When one thinks about appropriation, one is no longer thinking with the Greeks at all."[12]

---

8. To keep the argument succinct I pass over Heidegger's 1942 retrieval of the "unsaid" of Anaximander's τὸ χρεόν (fragment 1), but *mutatis mutandis* the outcome is the same. See GA 78 and, taken from that ms., GA 5: 321–373 = 242–281.

9. See GA 4: 88.6–7 = 112.29–30: "angesichts des Übermaßes des Geschickes und seiner Schickungen." The Greeks also had an awareness of human being as the place where the power of this saturating presence was creatively at work.

10. GA 40: 109.26–27 = 112.12–14; GA 66: 111.18–19 = 93.6–7; GA 15: 344.5 = 46.30.

11. Sophocles, too. GA 40: 159.4 = 166.27: "das Überwältigende."

12. GA 15: 366.31–32 = 61.4: "Mit Ereignis wird überhaupt nicht mehr griechisch gedacht." GA 12: 127. 19–20 = 39.32: "nicht mehr, nie mehr griechisch." GA 66: 315.8–10 = 280.22–24.

Where—that is, in what texts—do we find a record of this first discovery of the clearing among the Greeks? Heidegger claims that in fragment 1.28–30, Parmenides conveys such an insight when he writes

> χρεὼ δέ σε πάντα πυθέσθαι
> ἠμέν Ἀληθείης εὐκυκλέος ἀτρεμὲς ἦτορ
> ἠδὲ βροτῶν δόξας[13]

> It is necessary that you learn all things,
> both the untrembling heart of well-rounded ἀλήθεια
> and the opinions of mortals.

Heidegger also finds this discovery of the clearing in Parmenides' fragment 6.1: ἔστι γὰρ εἶναι, which he translates as: the clearing is given (i.e., is present and operative precisely in its hiddenness).[14] In short, he retrieved from Parmenides the insight that, along with experiencing πάντα—that is, everything in its being (ἀλήθεια-2)—one should also experience the well-rounded openness that allows for that (ἀλήθεια-1). Heidegger claims that ἀλήθεια in Parmenides and φύσις in Heraclitus both refer to the ever-hidden clearing; and from Heraclitus' φύσις κρύπτεσθαι φιλεῖ (fragment 123: "φύσις loves to hide")[15] Heidegger retrieved the insight that this φύσις bespeaks the hidden *opening* of the clearing.[16] Nonetheless, Heidegger argues that Parmenides and Heraclitus missed two phenomenological dimensions of ἀλήθεια/φύσις: (1) the fact that things are encountered *only as meaningful*; and (2) the more basic fact that thrown-open ex-sistence is why there is a clearing at all. They did not work thematically as phenomenologists, and they did not ask about the *essence* (i.e., the "whence") of ἀλήθεια-1: appropriated ex-sistence.[17] That notwithstanding, Parmenides did announce the clearing, and Heraclitus did articulate its

13. Diels-Kranz, *Fragmente der Vorsokratiker*, I, 230.10–12 = 42.12–13. GA 14: 115.7–9; 83.11–13 = 67.22–24; 83.27–84.1 = 68.6–7: The clearing (see ibid., note 20: "d.h. die Lichtung") is "[das,] was erst Unverborgenheit [= ἀλήθεια-1] gewährt."

14. Diels-Kranz, *Fragmente der Vorsokratiker*, I, 232.21 = 43.1–2. GA 70: 53.23: "Das Sein *ist*."

15. Diels-Kranz, *Fragmente der Vorsokratiker*, I, 178.8–9 = 33.9. See GA 15: 343.24–25 = 46.18–19: "das Sichverbergen ist das innerste Wesen der Bewegung des Erscheinens [eines Seienden]" as well as other paraphrases at GA 15: 343.23–31 = 46.17–26.

16. GA 4: 56.26–27 = 79.11–12.

17. GA 15: 261.26–27 = 161. 23–24: "Über die ἀλήθεια als ἀλήθεια [= das Wesen der ἀλήθεια] steht in der ganzen griechischen Philosophie nichts." GA 75: 232.20 = 32.21–22: Among the Greeks "Ἀλήθεια ist erblickt, aber nicht in ihrem Eigenen eigens gedacht." See also GA 15: 366.31–32 = 61.4. On ex-sistence *qua* appropriated as the "es" that "gives" all forms of being: GA 73, 1: 642.27–29: "das Dasein ist das je vereinzelte 'es,' das gibt; das ermöglicht und ist das 'es gibt.'"

hiddenness, and for that reason they constitute the glorious "first beginning" of the thinking of the clearing, defined as the act of consciously corresponding to it.[18]

Heidegger's idealization and romanticization of archaic and classical Greece is well known and may be quite as harmless as the celebration of Hellas by Heidegger's idol, Jacob Burckhardt.[19] Nonetheless, as regards philology and historical science (*Historie*), his hyper-valorization of the pre-Socratics on the basis of a heavily theorized construal of a handful of fragments is highly questionable. He himself even called into doubt the historical (*historisch*) correctness of his own interpretations of archaic Greek thought. For example, after some twenty-five pages of dense philosophical elucidation of Heraclitus' fragment 16 ("How can anyone hide from that which never sets?"),[20] Heidegger asks:

> Did Heraclitus intend his question the way we have been discussing it? Does what we have been saying even fall within the range of his concepts? Who knows? Who can say?[21]

Yet Heidegger based much of his sweeping meta-history of the virtually inevitable decline of Western thought and culture on his idiosyncratic readings of a few cherry-picked fragments from the pre-Socratics that often lack sufficient hermeneutical context to support his interpretations. This is especially the case for Heraclitus' fragments, but the same can apply to Parmenides.[22] What to make, then, of a *Seinsgeschichte* that, at least as applies to the "first beginning" of thinking, is so dubiously grounded in *Historie*?[23]

---

18. GA 79: 71.13–14 = 67.11–12: "Dieses anfängliche Entsprechen [der Lichtung], eigens vollzogen [i.e., as an existentiel activity] ist das Denken." Such thinking is not a form of cogitation but rather "[d]as ekstatische Innestehen im Offenen der Ortschaft [= die Lichtung] des Seins": GA 6:2: 323.28 = 218.17 (italicized in the German).

19. Heidegger was a great admirer of Burckhardt's *Griechische Kulturgeschichtes* (1898–1902).

20. Diels-Kranz, *Die Fragmente der Vorsokratiker* I, 155.5 = 26.1.

21. GA 7: 286.34–286.1 = 120.21–23. Likewise Heidegger declares at GA 65: 253.14–15 = 199.25 that his interpretation of Kant in GA 3 is "*'historisch'* unrichtig, gewiß, aber sie ist *geschichtlich* . . . wesentlich," insofar as it is, as he says, "a preparation for future thinking."

22. One of the sources for Parmenides' remark about "being" as a "well-rounded sphere" (εὐκύκλου σφαίρης, VIII, 43) is Boethius' *Consolatio philosophiae*, III, Prosa XII, 37, which applies Parmenides' phrase to the divine substance, which "rerum orbem mobilem rotat dum se immobilem ipsa conseruat" (roughly: "rotates around the moving orb of things while keeping itself immovable"). *Patrologia Latina* 63, 781.20–21.

23. One might be reminded of the apocryphal statement attributed to Hegel: "Umso schlimmer für die Tatsachen." Or, for that matter, the Italian "Se non è vero, è ben trovato."

2. METAPHYSICS: FROM PLATO THROUGH NIETZSCHE, THE CLEARING GETS INCREASINGLY OVERLOOKED

Heidegger's history of metaphysics can be confusing insofar as he often fails to make clear to the reader some utterly important distinctions. We might briefly outline his view in this diagram.

HEIDEGGER'S "HISTORY OF BEING"

PARMENIDES, HERACLITUS **The first beginning**	**METAPHYSICS** **Various epochés from Plato to today**	**HEIDEGGER** **The other/second beginning**
The hidden clearing (= ἐποχή-1) is recognized.	The hidden appropriated clearing (= ἐποχή-1) is overlooked and forgotten (= ἐποχή-2).	The hidden appropriated clearing (= ἐποχή-1) is recalled and embraced in its hiddenness.
Appropriation, the opening of the clearing, is missed.	Various forms of being are articulated (e.g., εἶδος, ἐνέργεια, etc., right up to *Gestell*).	Freedom from metaphysics/ἐποχή-2.

Heidegger's history of metaphysics is a history of the overlooking of the appropriated clearing from Plato to today. Parmenides and Heraclitus are not included in this history because they were at least aware of the hidden clearing, even if they did not know how it comes about. They constitute the first (and imperfect) beginning of thinking about the clearing, just as Heidegger, who is also not included in this history of ἐποχή-2, constitutes the "other" or "second" beginning of thinking about the clearing, now in terms of appropriation. In brief:

1. Appropriation is the reason why there is the clearing at all. But appropriation and the clearing are not two different things. Ex-sistence, precisely *as* appropriated, is the dis-closed clearing. Heidegger expresses this sameness in the phrase "the appropriated clearing."[24]

24. GA 71: 211.9 = 180.1–2. Heidegger does not always distinguish between (1) appropriation as giving the clearing and (2) the appropriated clearing as "giving" or "sending" being (cf. number 5 in this list). See GA 73, 1: 642.27–28.

2. Appropriation "dispenses" the various configurations of being[25]—and thus it makes it possible and necessary that we know things only by taking them in terms of something. It is in this way that meaningful presence ("being") shows up in our everyday lives and can be thematized in metaphysics.
3. As the presupposition for everything human, the thrown-open clearing is intrinsically and necessarily hidden or, as Heidegger sometimes puts it, "under ἐποχή" (or "bracketed").[26] He also expresses this state of affairs as *Seinsvergessenheit*. But as we have seen, (a) this term refers first of all to the *intrinsic hiddenness* of the clearing and not to its "forgottenness"; and (b) it would be better expressed as *Ereignissesvergessenheit*, the hiddenness of the appropriated clearing. We may call this intrinsic hiddenness ἐποχή-1, another name for the earlier λήθη-1.
4. Because it is intrinsically hidden, the appropriated clearing gets overlooked both in everyday life and in metaphysics—that is, the bracketed clearing (= ἐποχή-1) gets *further* bracketed by being unwittingly forgotten (= ἐποχή-2).[27]
5. Even as it is intrinsically hidden (ἐποχή-1) and therefore overlooked by metaphysics (ἐποχή-2), the clearing nonetheless makes possible all forms of the being of things that metaphysicians have articulated or that persons have come up with in their everyday lives. In Western philosophy, the combination of (a) the overlooking of the clearing plus (b) the awareness of a specific formation of being, constitutes a particular "epoch" in metaphysics. But Heidegger understands an "epoch" *not* as a period of time but rather as a philosopher's articulation of the being of things while overlooking the clearing that makes that possible.[28] (The same applies analogously to one's "fallenness" in everyday living.) To avoid the mistake of thinking of a Heideggerian "epoch" in

25. Re schicken: see GA 71: 47.15 = 37.4, where it is unfortunately translated as "ordinance." Heidegger even speaks of schenken (giving-as-a-gift): for example, GA 66: 200.34 = 176.37. See GA 73, 1: 642.28–29.

26. GA 6:2: 347.19–22 = 239.7–8: "Das Ansichhalten . . . bestimmt als die ἐποχή des Seins selbst je eine Epoche der Geschichte des Seins."

27. In a rare moment of humor Heidegger says that the *hiddenness* and thus the *forgottenness* of the clearing is not like an umbrella that a philosophy professor forgot and left behind somewhere: GA 9: 415.22–25 = 314.10–12—with perhaps a nod in the direction of Nietzsche's "ich habe meinen Regenschirm vergessen" (fragment, autumn 1881), *Sämtliche Werke*, IX [Nachgelassene Fragmente], 587.

28. See GA 6:2: 347.19–22 = 239.7–8: "Das Ansichhalten . . . bestimmt als die ἐποχή [= ἐποχή-1] des Seinsselbst je eine Epoche [= ἐποχή-2] der Geschichte des Seins."

chronological terms, and to emphasize that it is a matter of "blocking out" the clearing, I will henceforth write the word as "epoché."

6. The concatenation of those historical "epochés" taken as a whole is what Heidegger means by the history of metaphysics: various formations of being along with the overlooking of the clearing—in fact, an ever-increasing forgetting of the clearing, with disastrous results in today's world.
7. When one becomes aware of the clearing and embraces one's appropriation in an act of resolve, metaphysics and its epochés (= all the instances of ἐποχή-2) are at an end.[29] But the end of metaphysics does not mean that the hidden clearing gets "un-bracketed"—that is, comes forth from its condition of ἐποχή-1 and "reveals itself." Rather, the point of resolve (*Entschluss*) or releasement (*Gelassenheit*) is to recognize the intrinsic hiddenness of one's appropriation, to *actively leave* it in its hiddenness, and to live, finitely and mortally, from out of it.

3. TODAY: THE OVERLOOKING OF THE CLEARING IS ITSELF OVERLOOKED

The "epochés" in Heidegger's history of metaphysics obtain not only in past philosophical history but also in one's own everyday life. In fact, ἐποχή-2 is our normal state, and in *Being and Time* it goes under the rubric of "fallenness" or "absorption." But Heidegger sees fit to generalize on the current *global* reach of such fallenness when he undertakes his analysis of the modern world in terms of *its* dispensation. As far as this writer can see, Heidegger did not give names to any of the dispensations of the clearing over the last three millennia except for two: "the age of the world picture," which he links with Descartes, and the present one, which he calls *das Gestell* (sometimes: *Ge-Stell*) and which he sees as the calamitous culmination of the millennia-long forgottenness of the clearing.

How to translate *Gestell*? Usually, and unfortunately, it comes out as "the enframing" (perhaps because *Gestell* can mean a "framework"—even a rack for holding wine bottles—neither of which images Heidegger has in mind). More recently it has been translated as "positionality," perhaps to convey a sense of "compulsion" (cf. *Gestellung*: one's "reporting for duty" upon having been drafted).[30] As always, however, it is best to look for the Greek words underlying Heidegger's terms, and in this case that word is μορφή. In commenting on Aristotle's

29. GA 14: 50.1–4 = 41.2–4.

30. See the translation of the Latin *positio* by Gestelle: *Deutsches Wörterbuch*, s.v. "Gestelle, Gestell," IV, 1.2, 4221.65.

Physics II 1, 193a30–31 Heidegger translates μορφή as *die Gestellung in das Aussehen*, a natural thing's "placing itself into appearance."[31] Heidegger understands μορφή as a self-pro-duction, literally a thing's "leading itself forth" into its intelligible appearance. It is true that Heidegger wants us to hear tones of *stellen* ("to place" or "posit") in the word *Gestell* when he defines that term as "the totality of all the forms of positing that are imposed on human beings insofar as they ex-sist today."[32] But the "positing" and "imposition" that Heidegger has in mind with *Gestell* is the particular dispensation that is imposed on us today and that compels us to posit and treat nature and people in terms of *extractable resources*. Hence, in keeping with the Greek word underlying Heidegger's *Gestellung*, and applying that to what he thinks is the ethos of the contemporary world, I will interpret *Gestell* (and I emphasize *interpret*) as "the world of exploitation."[33] The reason: Heidegger reads the current dispensation as one that provokes and even compels us to treat everything in terms of its exploitability-for-consumption: the being of things is now their ability to be turned into products for use and enjoyment.

For Heidegger *Gestell* is coterminous with the epoché of *Technik*, which is the specific way of disclosing the being of things as exploitability while overlooking the clearing. I will translate *Technik* by the forgivable neologism "technik" in order to distinguish it from both "technology" and "technique." *Gestell* and *Technik* go together as, in the one case, today's "world of meaning" and, in the other, the contemporary way of "being-in" that world by disclosing everything as exploitable-for-use. Heidegger claims that in the modern world of calculative rationality, the instruments of technology and the mind-set of technik dominate the way we understand and relate to everything. Earth is now seen as a vast storehouse of resources, both human and natural; and the value and realness of those resources, their being, is measured exclusively by their availability for consumption.[34] Things are viewed, at least tacitly, as first and foremost *producenda et consumenda*, stuff to be exploited for commercialization and use. Their significance is measured by the degree to which they

---

31. GA 9: 276.5–6 = 211.4–5. In Latin μορφή comes out as "forma," and Meister Eckhart translated forma as Gestellnis: GA 81:286.6–10. ("Gestellnis" does not appear in the *Deutsches Wörterbuch*, which covers only from the year 1450 on. Eckhart died in 1327.)

32. GA 15: 388.19–21 = 74.2–4: "die Gesamtheit aller Weisen des Stellens, die sich dem Menschenwesen in dem Maße auferlegen in dem es gegenwärtig ek-sistiert."

33. "Ex-ploit" from Latin ex-plicare, to unfold, unroll, extricate, through the French "-ployer" (cf. employer and exploiter). Here it has the sense of practical ἀληθεύειν: to dis-close-for-use, to bring from non-usability to usability. An outrageous interpretation? In light of Heidegger's view of the contemporary world, I think not. And to cite William J. Richardson's plea for one of his own translations, "What true disciple of the master will begrudge us this modest comfort?" *Heidegger*, 40 note 35.

34. See GA 7: 16.10–20 = 15.12–23.

can be owned, stockpiled, marketed, sold, and consumed. And in a perverse phenomenological correlation, human beings are valued only for their ability to extract, work, shop, and consume. Exploitability for production and consumption has become the "truth" (the ἀλήθεια-2) of things, the dominant way they are now disclosed and will continue to be disclosed for the foreseeable future. And as exploitability for production and consumption becomes the ἀλήθεια-2 of things, ἀλήθεια-1 as the origin of such "truth" has fallen into complete oblivion. Both ontology as a vision of reality and philosophical anthropology as an understanding of man are now in the thrall of an ideology that views everything as raw material for rationalization by techno-think and cybernization by techno-do.

Ex-sistence today has lost its grounding in the groundless clearing and runs amuck by first quantifying everything and then reducing it to the correlation of instrumental rationality and commodification. The clearing, that ur-phenomenon, does not show up on the radar screen of modern technology and finance, and given the global spread of Western culture, hardly at all (if at all) in the consciousness of most denizens of the globe. Over the past five centuries, the ethos of exploitation has colonized the world, and today it is not only Europe and North America but the whole planet that is in crisis. In Heidegger's catastrophic view of modernity, "the entire globe is shifting out of joint."[35]

Heidegger's nightmare vision of a world dominated by the techno-mentality of exploit-produce-consume may well resonate with some of his readers—although not necessarily for the reasons he gives. The conviction that drives Heidegger's own analysis is that all of this is the result of metaphysics. That is, while all epochés in his history of metaphysics are characterized by the overlooking of the appropriated clearing, what makes the current epoché of technik different from all the others, and dangerous in the extreme, is the fact that the overlooking has reached such a pitch that today we overlook the fact that the clearing has been overlooked at all. The epoché of technik not only omits the clearing but "omits even the omission of its own act"[36] and is characterized by "the *forgetting of the forgottenness*."[37] Together with the increasing oblivion of the thrown-open clearing, the powers of productive subjectivity have grown to such a degree that everything is taken to be within our current or eventual control. With that, the true essence of human being—mortal ex-sistence as the site of finite yet endless intelligibility—has devolved into nil-status. Hence the age of nihilism: the no-thing that is the clearing has become . . . simply nothing.[38]

---

35. GA 9: 242.4 = 185.23: "der Erdkreis geht aus den Fugen."

36. GA 6, 2: 325.22–23 = 219.30–31: "auch dieses Auslassen . . . ausläßt."

37. GA 79: 75.19–20 = 71.11–12: "so wie das Vergessen von etwas sich selber vergißt." My emphasis.

38. See GA 9: 106.11–12 = 84.22: "die Wissenschaft will vom Nichts nichts wissen."

It is at this point that Heidegger's profound social and political conservatism and cultural anti-modernism kick in and begin to hemorrhage into his "philosophical" analysis of the contemporary world, such that revanchist social, cultural, and political prejudices, including racism, come to expression in his philosophy the same way they did in his personal life. It is not the intent of this book to study and evaluate Heidegger's personal and political ideology, including the supinely stupid anti-Semitism that he laundered through his devolutionary history of modernity. (All of this, by the way, comes from a philosopher who called for rigorous "self-examination" at the very moment he was cravenly placing his own philosophy at the service of Nazi ideology.)[39] Extreme caution and a robust skepticism are in order when evaluating Heidegger's interpretations of modern cultural history and especially his opinions on the social, political, scientific, and technological achievements of the last two centuries. Liberalism and democracy, however they might be defined—let alone "the Jews"—were not Heidegger's favorite friends.[40] And cultural modernity—everything from radio and cinema to "modern art"—did not sit comfortably in the world of this socially blinkered, culturally narrow, and profoundly conservative man.[41] When it comes to Heidegger's far-right-wing ideas about society, politics, and culture, one might choose to follow Virgil's advice in the *Divina Commedia*, with its dripping irony: "*Non ragioniam di lor, ma guarda e passa*."[42] But one *has* to reason about Heidegger and these issues in order to see whether—and if so, how—they infect his

39. GA 16: 108.1–2 = 6.8–9 (Selbstbesinnung); 104 = 48 (Entschlossenheit); and at its most blatant, ibid., 190–93 = 49–52.

40. An investigation of Heidegger's anti-Semitism would have to take into account such texts as GA 95: 96.33–97.6 (the "Bodenlosigkeit" of "das Judentum": 97.1–2); GA 96: 46.22–28 ("Die zeitweilige Machtsteigerung des Judentums": .22–23), 56.16–19 ("Die Juden 'leben' *bei ihrer betont rechnerischen Begabung* am längsten schon nach dem Rasseprinzip [etc.]": .16–18); 133.15–19 ("das 'internationale Judentum'": .16); 243.1–14 ("Weltjudentum": .10 and .11); and 262.8–12, written in 1941? ("Weltjudentum" never takes part in war, whereas it falls to the Germans "das beste Blut der Besten des eigenen Volkes zu opfern"). Also Heidegger, "Über Wesen und Begriff von Natur, Geschichte und Staat," 82.26–29 = 56.13–16 ("den Semitischen wird sie [= 'die Natur unseres deutschen Raumes'] vielleicht überhaupt nie offenbar"). See further Petzet, *Auf einen Stern zugehen*, 40 = 34: "If Heidegger lacked a certain 'urbanity' and was estranged from everything pertaining to city life, this was especially true of the urbane spirit of the Jewish circles in the large cities of the West. But this attitude should not be misconstrued as anti-Semitism [*sic*], although Heidegger's attitude has often been interpreted that way."

41. Modern literature and art: GA 16: 670.30–31 = 64.17–35; also 682.6–24 = 57.10–11. (If only Heidegger had read Meyer Schapiro before Meyer Schapiro read Heidegger. See Schapiro, "Nature of Abstract Art," 1936.) Radio and film: GA 79: 77.2 = 72.27–28. Big cities: GA 16: 521.24–25 = 48.13. American tourists: GA 75: 221.15 = 12.18. Tourism in general: GA 15: 389.23–25 = 74.33–34. And so on.

42. *Inferno* Canto III, 51 (http://www.danteonline.it/english/opere.asp?idope=1).

devolutionary history of the West. I take up some of that in chapter 10. But given the limits of the present volume, a more thorough examination must remain a task for the future.

4. TOMORROW: THE POSSIBILITY OF RESCUE FROM THE OBLIVION OF THE CLEARING

Heidegger's utter pessimism about the contemporary world goes back earlier than the twentieth-century catastrophe that was Nazism, World War II, and the Holocaust. It may well grow out of his early, deeply conservative Catholicism and his revanchist nationalism, compounded by the tragedy of World War I, the collapse of the German Empire, and the economic depression that followed. But World War II and the defeat of Nazism seemed to confirm him in his despair over the present age. In the dark days after the war Heidegger spoke of an "eschatology of being." He meant this not as some future apocalypse in which Being would manifest Itself, but rather as the gathering up of the forgottenness of the clearing into its ἔσχατον, its most extreme and terrifying form, in the epoché of technik.[43] Nonetheless, Heideggerian folklore (with a little help from Heidegger himself) would have us await a future day when at long last Being will arrive and initiate a global millennium—"a change in the world's present condition" leading to "an altogether different age of the world" "in which 'the god of gods' perhaps appears"[44]—when there will be no more *Seinsvergessenheit* and, as the poet promises, "no more mourning or crying or pain."[45] But according to Heidegger, even if there *were* to be such a "rescue" (*Retten*), the clearing by its very nature would still remain hidden. Alas, if Heideggerians hope that someday Being will finally emerge from concealment and reveal Itself, they are in for a very long wait indeed.[46]

We have been pointing to the homology between Heidegger's "synchronic" and "diachronic" discussions of the overlooking of the clearing. (1) In *Being and Time* this overlooking is called "fallenness" and "absorption," and what

---

43. Eschatologie des Seins; ἔσχατον: GA 5: 327.17ff. = 246.33ff. For his quasi-apocalyptic language, see ibid., 325.33ff. = 245.27ff.

44. Respectively: *Zollikoner Seminare* 332.22–23 = 266.7–8; GA 5: 326.14–15 = 246.1–2; and *Zollikoner Seminare* 332.19–20 = 266.4–5. See Müller, "A Philosopher and Politics," in Neske and Kettering, *Martin Heidegger and National Socialism*, 181: "Heidegger speaks of the *Gestell* that cannot be rejected but must be carried through to the end. Then—and this is the missionary-romantic aspect of it—comes the new world."

45. *Revelation*, 21:4: οὔτε πένθος οὔτε κραυγὴ οὔτε πόνος.

46. In their more perfervid fantasies, paid-up Heideggerians relish the shock that analytic philosophers will feel when they wake up one morning to banner headlines in the *New York Times*: "*BEING REVEALS ITSELF! Heideggerians finally proven right!*"

the fallen/absorbed self overlooks is not being (otherwise one could make no sense of anything) but rather its own mortal thrown-openness as the source of all meaningful presence. (2) The same holds for Heidegger's history of metaphysics: *Seinsvergessenheit* is the overlooking not of being but of the clearing that accounts for all forms of being. The homology holds as well for the *overcoming* of the forgetting of the clearing. In the first case, in *Being and Time* that overcoming takes place when one responds to the "call of conscience" (or equally, wakes up to the no-thing in dread) by resolving to accept one's finite thrown-openness and to live mortally. In Heidegger's later work, it is still resolve—now in the form of taking "the turn into appropriation"[47]—that is our way of effectively acknowledging the ever-hidden clearing. In the first case (the early Heidegger), one turns *from* one's domination by the crowd-self *to* taking over one's mortal ex-sistence and becoming the author of one's own life-narrative. The world opens up afresh, making possible καινότης ζωῆς, a new way of living, in what Heidegger calls "the situation," the domain of meaningfulness insofar as it is informed by one's resoluteness.[48] In the second case (the later Heidegger), one turns from the oblivion of the clearing that characterizes the whole of metaphysics and especially the epoché of technik, and takes up one's home in appropriation,[49] such that the world of meaning opens up afresh (*das Welten von Welt*).[50] Thrown-openness as one's existential structure in the early Heidegger is the same as the appropriated clearing in the later Heidegger. And likewise the way of taking over one's essence[51] and thus "becoming what one already is"[52] is the same in both the early "diachronic" analysis and the later "synchronic" narrative.

However, when it comes to a possible "rescue" from the epoché of technik, the later Heidegger seems to go cosmic. In his 1949 lecture "*Die Kehre*"[53] Heidegger discusses what the end of the world of exploitation might look

47. GA 14: 51.33–34 = 42.30–31: "[die] Einkehr in das Ereignis"; see ibid., 50.23 = 41.24 and GA 15: 390.12 = 75.6.

48. SZ 328.22–25 = 376.26–29.

49. GA 79: 70.19 = 66.18–19: "darin Wohnen nimmt." One then lives in the existentiel condition of "releasement" (Gelassenheit: GA 77: 117.25 = 76.27), which is the later parallel of the earlier "authenticity."

50. GA 79: 74.21–22 = 70.17–18.

51. SZ 325.37 = 373.14–15 (with ibid. 325.38–326.4 = 373.16–21) and GA 65: 322.7–8 = 254.36–37.

52. SZ 145.41 = 186.4.

53. GA 79: 68–77 = 64–73.

like, and the scenario would seem to be a very public and almost apocalyptic affair. The lecture is not an easy read, and much of its difficulty lies in the perverse rhetoric of hypostasization and reification that Heidegger employs, as if Being Itself, after centuries of "refusing Itself" to humankind, suddenly chooses to turn and show Itself to us. This "self-refusal" is Heidegger's unhelpful way of speaking about the intrinsic hiddenness of the clearing and the centuries-long history of overlooking of it. We must avoid such language and the crypto-metaphysics that it harbors, as we lay out the substance of the lecture "*Die Kehre*."

Despite his over-wrought rhetoric, Heidegger is not talking about an event in future history, when the authentic among us will "enter *Ereignis*" as if crossing the bridge into a post-metaphysical Valhalla. Such confabulations are the stuff of Heideggerian fantasy. There will be no cosmic revelation of Being, no societal embrace of *Ereignis* (regardless of Heidegger's effort to present "resolve" as a corporate possibility for the German *Volk* in 1933).[54] True, the over-heated rhetoric of "*Die Kehre*" seems to promise drama on a cosmic scale when, if not everyone, at least an elite group that Heidegger calls "the few, the rare ones"[55] will suddenly be liberated from the world of exploitation and enter an ontological utopia. But on Heidegger's own terms that cannot be the case. In his clearer moments he holds out no possibility of a societal release from the current dispensation, only a personal transformation in understanding one's own ex-sistence.[56] The release from the oblivion of appropriation cannot happen *ab extra* either by a "return of the gods" à la Hölderlin or redemption by a preternatural "last god" or some supra-existential "turn in Being Itself." The release can happen only *ab intra* by embracing one's existential fate as thrown-open. This occurs in a paradoxical twofold awakening—namely, "from *Seinsvergessenheit* to *Seinsvergessenheit*."[57] Heidegger means: waking up from ἐποχή-2 (the overlooking of appropriation) and actively accepting ἐποχή-1 (the intrinsic hiddenness of appropriation).

One's personal "entrance into appropriation" is, Heidegger says, equivalent to (*gleichtbedeutend mit*) the end of metaphysics.

54. See Heidegger's speeches on 10 and especially 11 November 1933, the eve of the plebiscite on Germany's withdrawal from the League of Nations, effective 18 November 1933: GA 16: 188–193 = 47–52.

55. GA 65: 11.21 = 11.38 et passim. (Would these "rare few" have to have read and understood Heidegger?)

56. GA 45: 214.18 = 181.7–8.

57. GA 14: 63: 22 = 53.25–26: "Entwachen in das Ereignis" with 63.24–25 = 53.28–29: "Erwachen aus der Seinsvergessenheit zu ihr." One can imagine Heidegger channeling Stephen Dedalus: "The history of being is a nightmare from which I am trying to awake," *Ulysses*, Episode 2 (Nestor), 35.19–20.

> For the thinking *in* appropriation, that is, for the thinking that has entered into appropriation . . . the "history of being" is at an end. Thinking now stands in and before that which has sent the differing forms of epochal being.[58]

> This means that for the thinking that enters appropriation, the history in which being is the object of thought is at an end—even if metaphysics should continue to go on, something that we cannot determine.[59]

The transformation that Heidegger holds out as a possibility is a personal liberation from one's "fallenness" (= Heidegger I) and from technik as the current way of being-in-the-world (= Heidegger II). "Making [the hidden clearing] your own," he says, "is itself the transformation of your openedness."[60]

> What this means is that the essence of man must first open itself up to the essence of technik [i.e., appropriation]. . . . [To overcome ἐποχή-2] humankind today must first and foremost find its way back to the breadth of its essential space [the thrown-open clearing].[61]

> Unless we first establish ourselves beforehand in the space proper to our essence and take up our dwelling there, we will not be capable of anything essential within the current prevailing dispensation.[62]

The world of exploitation is not going to go away, even when an individual gets free from the epoché of technik. Rather, Heidegger's protreptic is to a new relation of the concrete human being to his or her thrown-openness, precisely *within* the world of exploitation. This requires an act of resolve, yes, but seen less as a Promethean act on one's own part and more as "being called" by one's appropriation to accept that appropriation, just as *Being and Time* had spoken of the "call" from one's existential essence *to* one's everyday self to embrace one's mortal thrown-openness. Heidegger argues that we are structurally "held in a relation" (*Ver-hältnis*) to our essence (i.e., we are "fated" to being thrown-open), and the point is to personally become what we already are.[63] But this

58. GA 14: 50.1–6 = 41.3–7: "dann ist für das Denken *in* Ereignis . . . die Seinsgeschichte zu Ende." My scare quotes around "history of being."

59. GA 14: 50.31–51.3 = 41.32–42.2: "die Seinsgeschichte als das zu Denkende zu Ende ist."

60. GA 88: 261.16 (my paraphrase): "*Aneignung der Wahrheit* ist in sich *Wandlung des Daseins*." In another iteration, entering appropriation is "die Wandlung des Menschenwesens aus dem Bezug zum Sein durch dieses and für dieses in den Bezug zu ihm": GA 70: 93.22–24.

61. GA 79: 70.4–14 = 66.3–13, emphasis added. This would constitute the end of metaphysics. GA 83: 220.17–18: "Mit der Verwindung der Metaphysik ist das Geschick des Seyns vollendet."

62. GA 79: 70.18–21 = 66.17–20.

63. GA 79: 70.16 = 66.15 with SZ 145.41 = 186.4.

is less a matter of "seizing" our thrown-openness and more a "releasedness" into it (*Gelassenheit*). He speaks of this as "being let free for what is always already operative (that is, letting it 'arrive')"[64] or "liberation into freedom for the openness of the clearing."[65] Doing that much entails first of all recognizing the "danger" (*Gefahr*) of the epoché of technik for what it is: the obliteration of the hidden source of meaningful presence.

> [O]nly when the danger . . . first comes expressly to light as the danger that it is, will this turn—from the forgottenness of appropriation to the protection of its essence—properly occur.[66]

That entails actively leaving appropriation in its hiddenness while recognizing and acknowledging it as the reason why there is intelligibility at all. That would be a "thoughtful encounter with the appropriated clearing in its absence."[67] Heidegger calls this "the glimpse into the mystery" of appropriation (*das Ausblick in das Geheimnis*).[68] Resoluteness, as the effective awareness of the danger *as* danger, is the same as the "entrance into appropriation."

This transformation is not some planetary shift in how human beings will view meaningfulness and its source. It will be no more dramatic than (or rather, only as dramatic as) the existentielly effective insight into one's own mortality and finitude. Heidegger describes this moment in a series of metaphors that risk being read as "cosmic" events but that in fact come down to only one thing. When the danger of the complete overlooking of appropriation is seen for what it is, "world occurs" (*ereignet sich Welt*)[69]—that is, for the one who has taken the turn into appropriation, the clearing is finally seen as embedded in thrown-openness. Heidegger says that this occurrence of a "new" world of meaning (*das Welten von Welt*) occurs "suddenly" and without mediation in what he compares to a flash of lightning (*das Blitzen*), not unlike the shock of the experience of dread.[70] In that rare and brief moment the groundless ground of life is illuminated in a gleam of light, a brief epiphany without discursive

64. GA 86: 508.2: "Freilassen ins Gewesen (Kommenlassen)."

65. GA 69: 24.5: It is "Die Befreiung in die Freiheit für die Wahrheit des Seyns."

66. GA 79: 71.26–28 = 67.24–26. Here "turn" (Kehre) names resolve or releasement.

67. GA 6:2: 332.23–24 = 225.20–21: "dem Sein in dessen Ausbleiben als solchen entgegendenk[en]." Ibid., 352.27 = 243.19–20.

68. GA 9. 198.21–22 = 151.36. Heidegger notes that this glimpse is one that comes "out of errancy" (ibid.)—that is, out of our absorption in meaningful things (in the present case, within the world of exploitation).

69. GA 79: 73.13 = 69.11. Further on Welt: ibid., 77.3–28 = 72.28–73.17.

70. GA 79: 74.1 = 69.31–32: "Das jähe Sichlichten ist das Blitzen." Ibid., 75.24–25 = 71.17–18: "in allem Verstellen des Ge-Stells lichtet sich noch der Lichtblick von Welt, blitzt Wahrheit des Seyns."

mediation, and one experiences the presence (as non-presence) of the ever-hidden clearing. But at this point in his lecture "*Die Kehre*" Heidegger reverts to his unhelpful hypostasizing language. Drawing on his interpretation of *Ereignis* as *ereigen/eräugen*, he says that man is "caught sight of" by a "look" (*Einblick*) on the part of *Ereignis*: "*Die Menschen sind die im Einblick Erblickten.*"[71] The outcome is a transformation in human being:

> Only when, having been caught sight of in appropriation-*qua*-insight, we disavow our self-will and project ourselves towards this "look" and away from ourselves, do we correspond in our essence to the claim of that "look."[72]

Heidegger's reifying language notwithstanding, the meaning is clear. Already "claimed" by appropriation, we become what we essentially are by understanding ourselves in terms of ("projecting ourselves towards") our mortal finitude as the source of all meaning.[73]

But what does all this come down to in one's daily life? What guidance can Heidegger's work provide regarding concrete choices and decisions? Where is the philosophical ethics that Heidegger might have worked out in the metontology that was projected as a sequel to *Being and Time*? Heidegger has no answer to such questions. The best he can say, and it's not much, is this: "The question of ex-sistence gets straightened out only by ex-sisting."[74]

In light of this brief outline of Heidegger's vision of "history," we may ask, as we did at the beginning of this chapter: How much of this sweeping meta-metaphysical narrative does one have to take on board in order to responsibly and fruitfully appropriate the core of Heidegger's thought? To speak for myself, I find his interpretations of individual philosophers in the Western canon to be always engaging and often quite brilliant. I also find quite convincing his thesis that metaphysics has consistently overlooked the appropriation of ex-sistence. What I find entirely unconvincing is his philosophical history of the devolution of the Western civilization, along with the reason he gives for the terrible state of the contemporary world: appropriation has been forgotten. The retrievable core of Heidegger's philosophy is quite substantial. It is found not only in his lectures and publications of the 1920s but also in some of his philosophical work in the 1930s and after World War II. This core stands on

71. GA 79: 75.34–35 = 71.27–28. Cf. GA 11: 45.13–15 (omitted without explanation in the English translation at 36.14).

72. GA 79: 76.1–5 = 71.29–33.

73. This is the same as authentic philosophizing understood as a way of existing "im Sinne der wesenhaften Zugehörigkeit des geschichtlichen Menschen ('Da-sein') in die Wahrheit des Seins": GA 71: 47.2–4 = 36.26–28.

74. SZ 12.30–31 = 33.8–9: "Die Frage der Existenz ist immer nur durch das Existieren selbst ins Reine zu bringen."

its own as a solid contribution to philosophy quite apart from the historically dicey *seinsvergesslich* superstructure that Heidegger perched precariously (and finally unsuccessfully) on top of it. The retrievable core includes, among other things, a phenomenological rereading of traditional being as the meaningfulness of things; a persuasive explanation of how we make sense of things, both in praxis and in apophantic discourse; the grounding of all sense-making in the a priori structure of human being as a mortal dynamism of aheadness-and-return; and, based on all of that, a strong philosophical exhortation, in the tradition of Greek philosophical protreptic, to become what we already are and to live our lives accordingly. But his meta-history of the decline of the West? It might be best to take a pass on that.

Over the half-century of his philosophical career, Heidegger's project went through two major developments: (1) the transition from ex-sistence as the openedness of the clearing to the *clearing itself* as the source of all meaning; and (2) the decisive insight into the hiddenness of the appropriated clearing and, with that, his 1930s change from the earlier transcendental paradigm to the later "giving-of-the-clearing" model. Nonetheless, in spite of such internal adjustments and readjustments, the work of the later Heidegger keeps continuity with the earlier project and its single goal. The later work carries out the "overcoming" of metaphysics by grounding the phenomenological correlation (which Heidegger takes to be the core of Western philosophy from Parmenides to Husserl) in appropriation: the groundless oscillating sameness of thrown-openness and the clearing—that is, our essence as "placeholder of the no-thing."[75] But Heidegger does all that only as a preparation for (*Vorbereitung*) and a protreptic to embracing the *proprium* of oneself, one's "ownness" as the mortal space for mediation and meaning.

The principle that guided the project, early and late, was Heidegger's reinterpretation of Aristotelian κίνησις, an insight that he articulated at the very beginning of *Being and Time* in the mantra "Higher than actuality stands *possibility*."[76] For Heidegger, ex-sistence is that kind of κίνησις. Our essence is thrownness as possibility into possibilities, and first of all into the possibility of our impossibility. In *Being and Time* he spelled out this insight in various ways: for example, in terms of our ineluctable engagement with the clearing-for-meaning (*In-der-Welt-sein*); or care (*Sorge*) as the structure of primal

75. GA 9: 118.20 = 93.26, where "Platzhalter" is translated unfortunately (if pseudo-literally in a Frenchish sort of way) as "lieutenant."

76. SZ 38.29–30 = 63.2.

openness (ἀλήθεια-1); or thrown-open-ness (*Zeitlichkeit*) as shaping the horizon for being. Running through all those articulations of ex-sistence is the archi-existential of *Geworfenheit*, the ne plus ultra of life and thought. The later discourse of appropriation rearticulates that most basic of human structures along with the new insight (1930) into the intrinsic hiddenness of the clearing. All of this, in turn, drives Heidegger's engagement with key figures in the history of metaphysics, where he sorts out various visions of the being of things and tries to retrieve the unspoken, hidden clearing from their texts.

Heidegger's work is situated decisively after the "death of God," and it is written in the name of what he calls "the last god": the finite, mortal, hidden, and inexplicable clearing *as* which we are thrown open. This god alone, he declares, can save us.[77]

> The essence of ex-sistence . . . consists in safeguarding and preserving the openedness of the appropriated clearing—that is, of the last god—in things.[78]

Once Heidegger had worked his way through and out of the limitations of transcendental thinking and had clearly seen the intrinsic hiddenness of the thrown-open clearing, he went on to re-articulate this in terms of our appropriation to being the clearing, which went unseen in the entire history of Western metaphysics. As a history of individual philosophers, Heidegger's *Seinsgeschichte* can be judged on its own merits. The same goes for his attempt to discover and articulate the unspoken secret of metaphysics. But whether Heidegger succeeds in demonstrating his further claim—that the forgottenness of appropriation adequately explains the current state of the entire world—is a matter of no little debate. I argue against this claim. But that is an issue for the final chapter.

77. GA 16: 671.26 = 57.31.

78. GA 65: 35.1–2 = 29.33–35: "Dasein . . . hat sein Wesen in der Bergung der Wahrheit des Seyns, d.h. des letzten Gottes in das *Seiende*." Also ibid., 308.24–26 = 244.23–25: "Das Wesen des Da-seins . . . ist die Bergung der Wahrheit des Seins, des letzten Gottes, in das Seiende." "Bergen" is early German translation of the Latin servare and tueri.

Conclusion

10

Critical Reflections

We return once more to the issue that occupied much of Heidegger's attention after World War II: the analysis of the contemporary world that he carried out under the rubric of *das Gestell* (the world of exploitation dispensed to us today) and *Technik* (the current way of disclosing things in unintended oblivion of the hidden clearing).[1] This chapter offers a critical commentary on the text that brings to a head Heidegger's views on the forgottenness of appropriation and that takes us to the heart of his later philosophy: his 1953 lecture *Die Frage nach der Technik* ("The Question of Technik").[2] In speaking of his "later philosophy" I now use the phrase more narrowly than before and specifically in a topical rather than a chronological sense. "Heidegger's later philosophy" now refers not to all of his philosophical work after 1932 but only to his claim—the driving force of the later thought—that the overlooking of appropriation explains the tragic condition of the contemporary world. A century ago Bergson wrote that a philosopher thinks only a single thought, "something simple, so infinitely and extraordinarily simple that he has never succeeded in saying it. That is why he has kept on speaking for his whole life."[3] "The Question of Technik" gives us Heidegger at the core of his own "single thought"[4] from which all the rest of his work flowed: the hiddenness of appropriation and the tragic consequences of overlooking it. The 1953 lecture, along with the other essays and lectures that bear on this topic, give us what Heidegger apparently thought was the contemporary import of his philosophical

1. See page 258 above.

2. GA 7: 7–36 = 3–35. The lecture was delivered on 18 November 1953 and published in 1954. The separate publication of the essay in Heidegger, *Die Technik und die Kehre*, claims incorrectly at 3.10 that it was first delivered in 1955.

3. Bergson, *Le Pensée et le mouvant*, 119 = 128: "quelque chose de simple, d'infiniment simple, de si extraordinairement simple que le philosophe n'a jamais réussi à le dire. Et c'est pourquoi il a parlé toute sa vie"—from a lecture Bergson gave in 1911. Compare Plato, *Seventh Letter* (ἐπιστολή Z) 341c5: ῥητὸν γὰρ οὐδαμῶς ἐστιν (roughly: there is no way "the thing itself" can be put into words).

4. GA 13: 76.9–10 = 4.10.

work.[5] However, the lecture also reveals the severe limitations of his entire philosophical project and thus is a fitting site around which to gather some concluding reflections on Heidegger's work.

We have already touched on *Gestell* and *Technik* in the previous chapter, but these topics deserve greater attention from a critical perspective. "The Question of Technik" was delivered just three years after the German government had lifted the ban on Heidegger's teaching, and arguably the lecture can be read, at least in part, as an *apologia pro sodalitate sua*, his offering of the "philosophical" reasons for why he supported the Nazis in the 1930s. During 1953, the same year in which he delivered this lecture, Heidegger was also editing for publication his 1935 summer semester course *Einführung in die Metaphysik* ("Introduction to Metaphysics"), which eventually became GA 40. Towards the end of that course in July of 1935, as the Nazis' anti-Jewish campaign was reaching a fever pitch and just weeks before the racist Nuremberg Laws were published, Heidegger lambasted the then current "philosophy of values" that (he said) "calls itself philosophy." He continued:

> In particular, what is peddled about nowadays as the philosophy of National Socialism has not the least thing to do with the inner truth and greatness of N. S.[6]

The "peddlers" Heidegger had in mind were probably such worthies as Alfred Rosenberg (1893–1946), Ernst Kreick (1882–1947), and Alfred Baeumler (1887–1968). But in contrast to *their* philosophies, what exactly constituted the "inner truth and greatness of National Socialism"? Heidegger didn't say in 1935. But years later, when he was editing his manuscript for publication, he saw fit to clarify the earlier statement by glossing it as follows:

> (namely, the encounter between global technology and modern man).[7]

Precisely what did Heidegger mean by that? In providing this bizarre reading of the "inner truth and greatness" of Nazism, was Heidegger offering *ex post*

---

5. "It was this work and its slowly attained products that were most important to him during his old age": Petzet, "Afterthoughts on the Spiegel Interview," in Neske and Kettering, *Martin Heidegger and National Socialism*, 72.

6. GA 40: 208.2–5 = 222.5–8. See the ET by Fried and Polt, xiv–xvii. Apparently the abbreviation "N.S." (= "Nationalsozialismus") in his hand-written text from 1935 was changed by Heidegger in 1953 to "diese Bewegung"—"this *movement*"—perhaps to put some distance between himself and the Nazi *party*, which in fact he had ardently supported in the early 1930s.

7. GA 40: 208.5–6 = 222.8–9; in the original *Einführung in die Metaphysik*, at 152.8 ("inneren Wahrheit und Größe") and .9–10 ("nämlich mit der Begegung [etc.]"). In their ET of GA 40, at 222, note 115, Fried and Polt remark that this parenthesis "was almost certainly added when Heidegger prepared this text for publication."

facto his "philosophical" reason for joining the Nazi party and shilling for it as rector of Freiburg University? Or was it a post-war fabrication, a pathetic effort at retrospective self-justification?[8] Given what is now known about Heidegger's social and political views in the 1920s and 1930s (not to mention what Hannah Arendt said about him),[9] one could be forgiven for leaning towards the fabrication-hypothesis. But even if one thinks Heidegger's adherence to Nazi ideology and politics had little or nothing to do with technology, it is true that from the 1920s on, he was deeply troubled by the increasing rationalizing and technologizing of life and culture that threatened his fantasy of halcyon village life in early twentieth-century Germany.[10]

Heidegger's post-war reflections on technology are neither an afterthought in his philosophical career nor an application of his philosophy to the modern world, nor simply a socio-cultural aside. They are the culmination of his later thought and may even provide a window onto what drove his earlier thinking as well.[11] When Heidegger in 1953 mentioned the "encounter between global technology and *modern man*," he may well have had himself in mind. Technology was the dark shadow haunting his romanticized vision of the peaceful simplicity of rural life in southwest Germany. He had witnessed firsthand the devastation that technology had wrought in World War I; but what troubled him more was the mind-set he thought lay behind it: the will to dominate the world by re-fashioning it in man's image and likeness. In modernity's rush to rationalize and control everything, what was quickly fading from the horizon was Heidegger's lifelong concern: man's incalculable, mysterious finitude—the very core of human being—which lies prior to and deeper than reason, science, and technology and is the final source of all meaning. In his early

8. See Petzet, "Afterthoughts on the Spiegel Interview," in Neske and Kettering, *Martin Heidegger and National Socialism*, 71: "He had a clear conscience and saw no reason to go on a humiliating penitential pilgrimage that would be a retrospective apology for his activities, especially for his thinking, and therefore an acknowledgment that they were wrong. . . . In his opinion he had made it clear that he had never been a National Socialist [*sic*] through his resignation of the rectorate in February 1934."

9. Heidegger, she said, was "notorious for lying about everything": in Elisabeth Young-Bruehl, *Hannah Arendt*, 247. See GA 16: 247.16–17, where Heidegger's wartime labors as a weatherman in the Ardennes Forest (helping prepare gas attacks on American soldiers advancing towards Sedan) got rewritten as service "at Verdun." See Sheehan, "'Everyone Has to Tell the Truth,'" 30 and note 2.

10. See GA 13: 9–13 = 27–30, especially 12.8–28 = 29.11–28, including his remarks on skiers in Todnauberg. For a less halcyon view see Michael Haneke's film "Die weiße Band" 2009 (originally "Kindergeschichte").

11. See Petzet, "Afterthoughts on the Spiegel Interview," in Neske and Kettering, *Martin Heidegger and National Socialism*, 72: "It was this work ['the work he had taken up again after 1949'], and its slowly attained products, that were most important to him during his old age."

Freiburg years he first analyzed that mysterious realm in terms of mysticism and a radicalized Christian eschatology (GA 60). But in 1921–1922 he shifted from this religiously motivated phenomenology to his famous reinterpretations of Aristotle (GA 61–63) in an effort to work out a religiously neutral phenomenology of everyday ex-sistence. As the culmination of that early work, *Being and Time* probed the mysterious dimension of ex-sistence under the rubric of the self as a mortal, thrown-open abyss, which, if accepted as one's own, might change how one decides to live.

But could it change society? This question came into sharp focus for Heidegger with the appointment of Hitler as the chancellor of Germany in January 1933. When Hitler dissolved the Reichstag and seized power a month later, did Heidegger really think this solidification of a fascist state would help "modern man" recover a sense of finitude and temper the onslaught of technology? And even if we postulate that this *was*, in fact, Heidegger's sincere view in 1933 and that he continued in his conviction even after the establishment of the concentration camps (Dachau: March 1933) and the Roehm murders (30 June 1934), what can one say about his stunning blindness not only as an intellectual and a philosopher but also as a rational and responsible citizen? What planet was Heidegger living on between 1933 and 1945? Karl Jaspers reports asking Heidegger in 1933, "How is such an uneducated man as Hitler supposed to rule Germany?" to which Heidegger replied, "Education isn't everything. Just look at his wonderful hands!"[12]—not to mention Heidegger's scandalous actions during and after 1933 (informing for the Gestapo, blackballing colleagues, refusing to direct PhD students who were Jews),[13] all of which, to say the least, contradicted what he had taught in *Being and Time*.

The present book is about Heidegger the philosopher, not Heidegger the man or the political actor, and the pages that follow focus specifically on his philosophical views of technology, history, and modern culture. A detailed study of his complex personal and political life lies beyond the scope of the present text. Presumably such an account would have to take into account not only all of his philosophical production as well as his actions both public and private during the Third Reich, but also his vast correspondence, only some of which is now published. It would also have to go beyond his writings and public actions into more personal issues—including, perhaps, his nervous breakdown in 1945–1946 and whatever else it was that underlay his private remark

12. "'Bildung ist ganz gleichgültig,' anwortete er, 'sehen Sie nur seine wunderbaren Hände an!'" Jaspers, *Philosophische Autobiographie*, 101.22–25.

13. See Sheehan, "Heidegger and the Nazis," passim. Also Max Müller, "A Philosopher and Politics," in Neske and Kettering, *Martin Heidegger and National Socialism*, passim; especially187: "But ever since the moment when Heidegger became rector, no Jewish student who had started a dissertation with him got a doctorate from him. [. . .] Heidegger still wanted his Jewish students to receive a doctorate after 1933, but not with him as an advisor."

to Richard Wisser in September 1969, a few days before his eightieth birthday: "Loneliness is bound up with the relation of man and God. . . . Yes, that's the problem. . . . I am lonely. Just how lonely you will never know."[14]

Heidegger had been concerned about technology at least since his experience in World War I, and his interest intensified in the 1930s thanks to his close study of Ernst Jünger's *Der Arbeiter* (cf. GA 90). Occasional remarks on modern technology appear in his 1936–1938 *Contributions to Philosophy* (GA 65) and elsewhere, but his signature text remains the 1953 lecture "The Question of Technik." His friend, the Bavarian senator Emil Preetorius, who was then president of the Bavarian Academy of Fine Arts in Munich, called Heidegger out of retirement to address a conference on "Art in a Technological Age." Heidegger opted to focus on technology rather than art (although he touched briefly on art at the end of his address), and he chose to do so, of course, from a philosophical point of view. For Heidegger, as we have noted, philosophy is "knowledge of the essence of things."[15] Thus his lecture quickly blows past technology understood as merely a means to an end (which he calls an "instrumental" or even "anthropological" approach)[16] in order to get to its *essence*. To sort out what he means by *die Technik* and how he discerns its essence, I will divide my remarks on his lecture into three topical sections corresponding to the three elements of any question: its *Befragtes*, *Gefragtes*, and *Erfragtes*:

1. The *field* of Heidegger's analysis (at some length);
2. His *focus* on that field (more briefly); and
3. The *final outcome* of his reflections.

1. THE FIELD

What is the state of affairs of which Heidegger is seeking the essence? That is, how (and how adequately) does he delineate the subject matter of his inquiry? What does the word "*Technik*" in the title of his lecture refer to? Is it technology? or τέχνη as one of Aristotle's "intellectual virtues"? or technical thinking as a certain kind of "logic"?[17] These are questions that we may gather under

14. In Neske, *Ereinnerung an Martin Heidegger*, 271.21–26.

15. "Philosophie [ist] das Wissen vom Wesen der Dinge": GA 45: 29.28–29 = 29.18–19. See chapter 2, note 1.

16. GA 7: 8.5–6 = 5.5–6.

17. Husserl designates normal logic (as contrasted with his own early ideal of a "pure logic") as a "Kunstlehre von der Wissenschaft," a "technology of [= for doing] science": "Über psychologische Begründung der Logik," 346.20–21.

the rubric of Heidegger's *phenomenological description* of the subject matter of his lecture.

Heidegger seems to presume that his audience knows what he means by *die Technik*. But do we? His examples are few and quite thin, and they are usually set against his idyll of pre-modern rural Germany. "Mechanized agriculture" is contrasted with peasants working their fields. A hydroelectric plant in the middle of the Rhine is set over against a wooden bridge crossing the river. The present-day timber industry is compared to a woodsman (one's "grandfather") who trudges through the Black Forest.[18] The unspoken assumption is that the first half of each of those contrasts reflects the devolution of Western culture. What exactly is Heidegger's point? By *die Technik* does he mean all those newfangled machines out there, including the digital gadgets that now fill our purses, pockets, and desktops—indeed, our lives? Or does he mean the *programs* that make those gadgets work? Or the *thinking* of those who design the programs? Or the digital *machines* that use the programs to produce the digital gadgets we own? Or the skills we ourselves need in order to use those gadgets? In a lecture that he gave (18 July 1962) nine years after *Die Frage nach der Technik*, Heidegger distinguished between machines, the products of these machines, and the calculative logic that generates and guides the production. But he said that all of those, singularly and together, do not help us understand what *Technik* really is.[19] That's not much of a help. If *die Technik* refers not to machines but to a mind-set that produces them, what are the differences between the mentalities that produced Archimedes' screw pump, roughly 200 BCE, James Watts' steam engine in 1756, and William Shockley's transistor in 1947? Is there any difference between the kinds of calculative thinking that produced the Sumerian abacus around 2500 BCE and today's circuit boards that use computational neuroscience and work nine thousand times faster than a typical PC?[20]

In *Die Frage nach der Technik* Heidegger employs three terms: *das Technische*, *die Technik*, and *das Wesen der Technik*.[21] By *das Technische*, he seems to mean the instruments (the machines) that do the production, and not just any machines but only modern-day ones. But then how is *das Technische* different from *die Technik*? Does *die Technik* refer to "technology" as in the title of the current English translation? In fact, Heidegger often seems to lump together

18. GA 7:15.34–16.6; 16.28–30; 18.29–32 = 15.1–7; 16.9–11; 18.17–20.

19. Heidegger, *Überlieferte Sprache und technische Sprache*, 10.15–26.

20. B. V. Benjamin et al., "Neurogrid: A Mixed-Analog-Digital Multichip System for Large-Scale Neural Simulations," 699–717. https://ieeexplore.ieee.org/stamp/stamp.jsp?tp=&arnumber=6807554.

21. GA 7: 7.11 and .16–17 = 4.3 and .7–8: "Die Technik ist nicht das gleiche wie das Wesen der Technik. . . . So ist denn auch das Wesen der Technik ganz und gar nichts Technisches."

technology as a "means to an end" (the machines as the means for generating products) and technology as a "human activity" (i.e., the skill for carrying our production as well as the skilled productive activity itself).[22] In that case the ambiguous and all-too-Protean word "technology" covers everything (the skills, programs, instruments, processes, and products of production) as caught up in what Michel Foucault might call an "economy" of technology. It is more probable, however, that Heidegger's *Technik* is the modern incarnation of Aristotle's τέχνη, which refers to a knowing-how-to, rather than to the products of such know-how, even if those products, as machines, produce even more machines. *Technik* names what Aristotle would call an "intellectual virtue" in the order of praxis, specifically the "habitual" practical cognition that creates the programs and manages the machines. Hence I reserve the word "technology" for the machines while translating *Technik* by "technik" in the broadly construed sense of practical know-how—that is, τέχνη as techno-think in conjunction with ποίησις as techno-do. Despite superficial appearances, therefore, the subject matter or *Befragtes* that Heidegger bears down on in his lecture is not all that "technological stuff" (*das Technische*) or the programs and machines that churn it out (*die modern Technologie*). His topic is instead τέχνη itself as a way of *disclosing* things, specifically in its contemporary form.

"The Question of Technik" traces the current mode of disclosure back to Aristotle's notion of τέχνη, the human capacity to bring things into meaningful presence by producing or constructing them, as contrasted with φύσις, whereby natural things emerge of and by themselves. Heidegger declares that, whether in Aristotelian τέχνη or in its modern version as technik, one is talking about ἀληθεύειν, the human *disclosure* of things by bringing them into their ἀλήθεια-2, their pre-theoretical intelligible availability, not by thinking or speaking about them but by working on them, shaping and transforming them into something that they were not before. Much of what Heidegger says about technik is heavily indebted to Aristotle's *Nicomachean Ethics* VI, and specifically to its doctrine of the intellectual virtues. Crucial elements of Heidegger's argument might escape readers who are unfamiliar with that text of Aristotle's, so it is worth taking a minute to review it. However, those who are already familiar with how Heidegger reads Aristotle (or who have had enough Aristotle for one book, thank you) may want to skip the present section after simply perusing the following diagram.

22. That is, Technik as "ein Mittel für Zwecke" and as "ein Tun des Menschens": GA 7: 7.28–31 = 4.19–21.

THE SOUL AND ITS POWERS

<table>
<tr><td colspan="7">τὸ ἔμψυχον
ψυχή / ζωή[1]
animatum
anima / vita</td></tr>
<tr><td colspan="2">τὸ ἄλογον[2]
irrationale
anima irrationale

(ἀρεταί ἠθικαί)[3]
(virtutes morales)</td><td colspan="5">τὸ λόγον ἔχον[4]
rationale / intellectivum.
anima rationalis

(ἀρεταί διανοητικαί)[5]
(virtutes intellectuales)</td></tr>
<tr><td>τὸ θρεπτικόν[6]
τὸ φυτικόν[11]
vegetativum
nutritivum

anima
vegetabilia

(τὸ φυτόν)
planta</td><td>τὸ αἰσθητικόν,[7]
ὀρεκικόν, ἐπιθυμητικόν[12]
sensitivum
appetitivum/concuscibile

anima sensibilis

(τὸ ζῷον ἄλογον)
animal irrationale</td><td colspan="2">τὸ λογιστικόν,[8] λογισμός[9]
opinativum
rationativum

anima rationalis

(τὸ ζῷον τὸ λόγον ἔχον)
animal rationale</td><td colspan="3">τὸ ἐπιστημονικόν[10]
scientificum
speculativum

anima rationalis

(τὸ ζῷον τὸ λόγον ἔχον)
animal rationale</td></tr>
<tr><td>τὸ τρέφεσθαι[13]
τὸ αὔξεσθαι[20]
nutrimentum
augmentum</td><td>αἴσθησις[14]
ὄρεξις[21]
sensus
appetitus</td><td>τέχνη[15]
ars

(ποίησις)[22]
productio</td><td>φρόνησις[16]
prudentia

(πρᾶξις)[23]
actio</td><td>νοῦς[17]
intellectus</td><td>ἐπιστήμη[18]
scientia</td><td>σοφία[19]
sapientia</td></tr>
</table>

1. *De anima* II 2, 413a21. Here Aristotle mentions the τὸ ἄψυχον, that which is without soul or life Latin, inanimatum).
2. *Nicomachean Ethics* I 13, 1102a28; 1102b29; VI 1, 1139a4–5.
3. *Nicomachean Ethics* I 13, 1103a5.
4. *Nicomachean Ethics* I 13, 1102a28; VI 1, 1139a5.
5. *Nicomachean Ethics* I 13, 1103a5–6.
6. *De anima* II 3, 414a31 and 33.
7. *De anima* II 3, 415a1–2.
8. *Nicomachean Ethics* VI 1,1139a12 (13 = λογίσθαι). This deals with what can change, τὰ ἐνδεχόμενα: VI 6, 1141a1.
9. *Metaphysics* I 1, 980b28.
10. *Nicomachean Ethics* VI 1,1139a12. This deals with what cannot change, τὰ μὴ ἐνδεχόμενα: VI 6, 1141a4.
11. *Nicomachean Ethics* I 13, 1102a32–33.
12. *Nicomachean Ethics* I 13, 1102b30.
13. *Nicomachean Ethics* I 13, 1102a33.
14. *Nicomachean Ethics* VI 2, 1139a18.
15. *Nicomachean Ethics* VI 4, 1140a7.
16. *Nicomachean Ethics* VI 4, 1142a23.
17. *Nicomachean Ethics* VI 6, 1141a5.
18. *Nicomachean Ethics* VI 3, 1139b18. This deals with demonstration, ἀπόδειξις: VI 6, 1141a2–3.
19. *Nicomachean Ethics* VI 7, 1141a9.
20. *Nicomachean Ethics* I 13, 1102a33.
21. *Nicomachean Ethics* VI 2, 1139a18.
22. *Nicomachean Ethics* VI 4, 1140a16.
23. *Nicomachean Ethics* VI 4, 1140a16.

Aristotle divides life (ζωή) into life-without-λόγος (τὸ ἄλογον) and life-with-λόγος (τὸ λόγον ἔχον), the latter usually and ambiguously called "intellectual" life.[23] Life-with-λόγος has the ability to *know correctly* (as well as incorrectly), whether in theory or practice; and when Heidegger reads *Nicomachean Ethics* VI, he interprets such life-with-λόγος as ex-sistence. Aristotle further divides knowing into two kinds: knowing-*that* (τὸ ἐπιστημονικόν) and "knowing-*how* (τὸ λογιστικόν), the latter also being called λογισμός or "calculative thinking."[24] Both these ways of knowing disclose things within their proper range[25]—that is, render them meaningfully present in their ἀλήθεια-2. Knowing-that, insofar as it functions correctly, discloses things by taking them as what and how they actually are. Knowing-how, insofar as it functions properly, successfully discloses how to change something into the meaningful appearance one wants it to have.[26]

Corresponding to these two distinct ways of knowing, there are two distinct kinds of "virtues" (ἀρεταί) that are oriented to helping one achieve what is best (ἄριστον) for that particular kind of knowing.[27] In Aristotle a virtue is "good habit" whereby one is competent at doing something.[28] We may call it a "habitual capability." Aristotle divides these intellectual capabilities into (1) the three capabilities of knowing-that: intellectual intuition of first principles (νοῦς), discursive knowledge of the unchanging (ἐπιστήμη), and wisdom (σοφία); and (2) the two capabilities of knowing-how: φρόνησις and τέχνη. In

23. *Nicomachean Ethics* VI 1, 1139a4–6; ibid., I 13, 1102b17 and 24.

24. *Metaphysics* I 1, 980b28. "Calculative thinking" is virtually a swearword on some Heideggerian lips even though Heidegger himself employed such thinking throughout his life: for example, in everything he wrote.

25. *Nicomachean Ethics* VI 3, 1139b15: ἀληθεύει ἡ ψυχή.

26. A philosophy student may *think* that he understands Ἀγχιβασίη (Heraclitus, fragment 122) but in fact be mistaken. A carpenter may *think* she knows how to do the job, but likewise be mistaken, as the botched outcome shows. In both cases, knowing-that and knowing-how did not flourish. The student flunked the exam, and the carpenter got fired. Both ways of knowing are by "affirmation and denial," τῷ καταφάναι ἢ ἀποφάναι: *Nicomachean Ethics* VI 3, 1139b15.

27. Cf. *Nicomachean Ethics* I 13, 1103a5–6. There are, respectively ἀρεταί διανοητικαί or "intellectual virtues," which assist in both knowing-that and knowing-how; and ἀρεταί ἠθικαί or "moral virtues," that assist in matters of character. The intellectual virtues help us attain what is best for our "reason" (λόγος/διάνοια) in both of its functions: knowing-that and knowing-how. The moral virtues do the same for our character (ἦθος), helping it attain the best of whatever-benefits-it (= τὸ ἀγαθόν: the good). In human beings the character function can participate in, and ideally be guided by, the knowing function (ibid., 1102b26), when the former is "attentive" (κατήκοον) and "obedient" (πειθαρχικόν) to the latter: ibid., 1102b26 and 31.

28. Cf. ἔχειν = Latin habere, "to have"; ἕξις = habitus, a way of "having oneself" (i.e., a way of being oneself). Cf. GA 18: 172–80 = 116–22, commenting on *Metaphysics* V 20 and 23 and *Nicomachean Ethics* II 1–5.

"The Question of Technik" Heidegger is focused only on knowing-how: calculative thinking or instrumental/means-ends rationality. Calculative thinking is all about *fore*sight, knowing ahead of time what one wants to achieve and how to achieve it. The habitual capabilities of foresightful knowing-how are distinguished as follows.

The first instance, φρόνησις, is the capability to act well in *human* affairs both individual and social—for example, in ethical, political, or economic matters.[29] In this case, one can fore-see the goal to be achieved as well as the best means for achieving it. In human affairs the goal is some kind of human good, τὸ ἀνθρώπινον ἀγαθόν,[30] and such goals can be as different as founding a city state or losing weight.[31] This capability to fore-see in human affairs is called "practical wisdom," whereby one sees ahead to, and thus discloses, the specific human good that one wants to achieve, as well as seeing ahead to and disclosing, the *ways* to achieve it. This calculative virtue of φρόνησις is what *Being and Time* calls *Umsicht*, the existential capability to look *ahead* to both an existentiel goal and the means to attain it. (*Umsicht* looks *ahead* rather than "looking around cautiously" as the current translation "circumspection" would have it.)[32] That which is guided by fore-sightful φρόνησις is the kind of activity that Aristotle calls πρᾶξις, not just any action but only rational action (μετὰ λόγου),[33] action that has to do with achieving, for ourselves or others, some perceived form of the human good.

In the second instance (and this is Heidegger's specific focus here), foresightful or calculative thinking is directed at changing not persons but *things*—for example, converting a pile of wood into a bookcase, or transforming a mountain into a strip mine: in short, producing a product. In this kind of calculative thinking, the foresightful know-how—the skill or practical cognition that guides the production process—is called τέχνη (Latin *ars*), whereas the actual pro-duction or bringing forth of the product is called ποίησις. While clearly connected with the τέχνη, ποίησις is distinct from and guided by it. (The artist's τέχνη may remain unimpeachable even when the execution fails: for example, the sculptor expertly designs a statue and selects the perfect marble, but his ποίησις makes a hash of it.) Τέχνη is a form of knowledge and thus a way of disclosing. It is the a-lethic skill of (1) envisioning beforehand the desired product, and (2) knowing the right means for completing the production. What

29. *Nicomachean Ethics* I 5, 1097b11: φύσει πολιτικὸς ἄνθρωπος.

30. *Nicomachean Ethics* I 1, 1094b7. And for Aristotle, that good is socio-political: ibid., 1094a26–28.

31. For the first, cf. obviously *Politics*. Re losing weight: *Metaphysics* IX 6, 1048b19–20.

32. Seeing ahead vs. looking around: cf. Latin "pro-videre"; hence "pro-videntia," condensed into "prudentia," which is the Latin translation of φρόνησις.

33. *Nicomachean Ethics* VI 4, 1140a7.

the τέχνη/skill envisions and discloses is first of all the planned outcome: the "looks" of the product that are "chosen beforehand" (εἶδος προαιρετόν)—that is, imagined and planned before it gets produced.[34] This is what Marx meant when he contrasted the lousiest architect with the busiest honeybee: "What distinguishes the worst architect from the best of bees is that the architect has first built his structure in his head before building it in reality."[35]

If the τέχνη that is analyzed and celebrated in the *Nicomachean Ethics* produced the glories of classical Greece, for Heidegger it has long since soured into a witches' brew that is poisoning the modern world. Today's *Technik* is no longer the simple τέχνη practiced in 1920s Todtnauberg by Heidegger's storied farmer in his shed, puffing on his pipe as he saws away at the log he has chopped down in the Black Forest and dragged to his farmhouse. For Heidegger the technik of today is τέχνη on steroids, colonizing the bodies, minds, and lives of everyone on the planet, sucking them out of their peaceful villages into the frantic, alienating rush of cosmopolitan "life" that demands techno-think and techno-do as the only way to survive. This dehumanized way of being-in-the-world and disclosing things has deformed all that was once bucolic and beautiful into little more than commodities: products for consumption. The world of exploitation compels us to understand whatever we meet, people as well as things, solely in terms of their extractable usefulness as natural or human "resources," raw material to be exploited, manufactured, warehoused, sold, and consumed—and then recycled, refashioned, redistributed, and sold again. Heidegger's own description of this downward spiral of disclosure speaks of "provocation" (*Herausforderung*). Modern man is "provoked" by an invisible and mysterious power to (in turn) "provoke" everything else to yield up something that can be processed, circulated, and consumed.

Such a reading of modern industrial society is hardly new, but what is unique about Heidegger's approach is that he knows *how and why* this dreadful situation came about. He understands the *essence* of modern technik, the reason why the world today is in such a terrible state. Heidegger found that out not by studying the last twenty-five centuries from an economic, social, or political point of view, but rather by means of philosophy, viewing the entire history of the West since the Greeks *sub specie metaphysicae*. Already by 1935 he saw clearly the deadly trap into which metaphysics had led us:

---

34. For Heidegger's treatment of εἶδος προαιρετόν (this exact phrase does not appear as such in Aristotle), see GA 9: 251.13–252.2 = 192.23–193.6.

35. See chapter 2, note 98.

> the hopeless frenzy of unchained technology and the rootless organization of the average man . . . spiritual decline . . . the darkening of the world, the flight of the gods . . . the destruction of the earth, the reduction of human beings to a mass, the preeminence of the mediocre . . . the disempowering of spirit, its dissolution, diminution, suppression, and misinterpretation . . . all things sinking to the same depths, to a flat surface resembling a dark mirror that no longer reflects anything and gives nothing back . . . the boundless etcetera of the indifferent, the ever-the-same . . . the onslaught of what aggressively destroys all rank, every world-creating impulse of the spirit . . . the regulation and mastery of the material relations of production . . . the instrumentalization and misinterpretation of spirit.[36]

Already by 1935 he had seen that all of this devastation was ultimately due to one thing only: the West's long and disastrous overlooking of the hidden clearing, the very essence of human being and the source of all meaning. He saw that the century's economic, social, and spiritual ruination was the consequence of our forgetting

> that depth from which the essential always comes and returns to human beings, compelling them into superiority and allowing them to act on the basis of rank . . . [as against] the onslaught of what aggressively destroys all rank and all that is world-spiritual.[37]

The result is the catastrophe that we are living today:

> The spiritual strength of the West fails, its structure crumbles, this moribund semblance of a culture caves in upon itself and drags all powers into confusion, suffocating them in madness.[38]

And all of this, he had discerned, was due to nothing human and can be traced to no human causality. In fact, it ultimately has nothing to do with what we call human history as the drama of personal and social decisions, successes, and failures. Rather, the contemporary dehumanized and dehumanizing way of disclosing the world was *given* to us as our *destiny* by the incomprehensible "it" (*es*) that gives (*gibt*) or sends (*schickt*) all meaning-giving worlds, including the one we are stuck with today. In the world of exploitation, "being" is

---

36. These lines are excerpted from GA 40: 40.32–51.10 = 41.26–52.19.

37. GA 40: 49.17–21 and .34–35 = 50.23–25 with 51.6–7.

38. GA 16: 117.5–8 = 13.18–20. That was in 1933. See Petzet, "Afterthoughts on the Spiegel Interview," in Neske and Kettering, *Martin Heidegger and National Socialism*, 70: "In September 1961 he [Heidegger] wrote to me from Todtnauberg that the whole hollow essence of the West was now coming to light. In the mean time, however, people did not yet notice it."

the producibility and consumability of whatever we meet. This goes hand-in-hand with a virtually complete blindness to the mortal thrown-openness that makes everything possible, including this bankrupt mode of disclosure and its alienating way of being human. All of this is accounted for by the intrinsic hiddenness of that which has dispensed to us this destiny of *Gestell*, the world of exploitation and the epoché of technik.

How did Heidegger arrive at such an insight into the essence of the modern condition? What was the *method* that guided him in his analysis of *Gestell*? Heidegger does not like to use the term "method" and prefers to speak, with Aristotle, of μέθοδος, the "pursuit" of a subject matter. Glossing *Physics* III 1, 200b13, Heidegger writes:

> μέθοδος: the step-by-step inquiry that pursues the subject matter, not our later "method" in the sense of a certain kind and manner of μέθοδος.[39]

But how to go about such a step-by-step inquiry into the state of the modern world? Socrates in the *Phaedrus* offers some guidelines:

> In reflecting about the nature of anything, we should first decide whether the object that we want to know and communicate to others is simple or complex . . . and if it is complex, to enumerate its parts.[40]

Modern "technology," whether in the form of the machines, the mind-set, or the world of meaning that those two inhabit, is indeed quite complex, and it seems Heidegger's rough and ready description of the matter in "The Question of Technik" hardly does justice to the intricacies of the subject matter whose "essence" he purports to reveal. The lecture elides the multifaceted elements of this vast global phenomenon and reduces the issue to a Solzhenitsyn-like jeremiad against modernity *au large* and its intrusions on rural life. Can Heidegger the phenomenologist get away that easily? If nothing else, phenomenology is the promise of a rich and convincing description of the lived sensorium within which we relate to and are impacted by the phenomenon in question. Phenomenology challenges the natural attitude's presumption that we simply have to "take a look" at things to know what's going on, or that we are endowed with an intellectual X-ray vision for intuiting the essence of a phenomenon before its complexity has even been broached. Surely phenomenology, especially Heidegger's own, knows that states of affairs are historical and come in contexts—not just personal but also economic, social, political, and cultural—that cannot be captured in thinned-out anecdotal "descriptions."

---

39. GA 9: 271.10–12 = 207.19–21.

40. *Phaedrus* 270c10–d6. Note that what is translated as "to know" in this passage is the Greek εἶναι τεχνικοί, literally "to be skilful at," hence "to be knowledgeable of."

But Heidegger's impressionist limning of modern "technology" and technik lacks anything like historical context. There is nothing at all about the multilayered historical conditions that generated modern "technology" (whether machines, mentalities, or meanings). What we get instead are vignettes about peasant farming and mechanized agriculture, or about modern forestry in contrast to one's German grandfather's trekking through the woods. It's all very local and intensely personal, and we may wonder whether such passing allusions to Heidegger's own quite limited world of experience cuts very deeply into the substance of the matter. Surely he need not have been an expert in economics or sociology or political science to have at least alluded to how modern technology is embedded in such configurations of power.[41] True, the lecture does reference the economic principle of "maximum yield at minimum expense."[42] And in GA 65 Heidegger did make a passing reference to the social uprooting and economic exploitation of "industrial workers, torn from homeland and history, exploited for profit"—although the point quickly gets lost in an elitist trivialization: "Training in mechanics: machination and business. What sort of transformation of the human being is setting in here?"[43] Should we assume that Heidegger was fully aware of the historical decisions and indecisions that had led to modern technology, and that he simply presupposed them in the lecture? But if he *was* aware of all that, such awareness does no work in the lecture, whether in his descriptions of modern "technology" or in his analysis of its essence. What are the specific contexts, the historical "worlds" that are operative in the new relations of contemporary technik? What political and economic forces have brought about these worlds and continue to dominate the way they operate? Questions like those would have issued in a richer and more robust phenomenological description of modern "technology" and would have set the parameters for a more adequate philosophical articulation of its "essence."

2. THE FOCUS

Heidegger's contribution to this important topic is his analysis of the *essence* of technik and thus, indirectly, of the programs, machines, products, and even

41. On Heidegger's "absolute rejection of sociology and psychology as big-city, decadent ways of thinking," see Müller, "A Philosopher and Politics," in Neske and Kettering, *Martin Heidegger and National Socialism*, 178.

42. GA 7: 16.13–14 = 15.16–17: "die größtmögliche Nutzung bei geringstem Aufwand." No great insight here. Even Stephen Dedalus knew the game is about buying cheap and selling dear: Joyce, *Ulysses*, Episode 2 (Nestor), 39.36.

43. GA 65: 392.20–24 = 310.8–11: "Exploited for profit." The German "auf Verdienst gesetzt" is translated by Rojcewicz and Vallega-Neu as "resettled as wage earners." Here I follow the translation by Parvis Emad and Kenneth Maly (274.13–16).

the lifestyle that he thinks characterize *Gestell*. But in fact, one might be forgiven for thinking that, long before he embarked on his analyses of the contemporary situation, Heidegger *already* knew what had brought about *Gestell*. We might even say (as we hinted above) that *all* of Heidegger's philosophy, both early and late, was devoted to showing that the West's overlooking of appropriation as the source of meaningful presence was responsible for the sorry state of affairs he encountered when he left Meßkirch in the fall of 1909 for big-city life in Freiburg. In Heidegger's case, Minerva's owl took to wing as the peaceful afternoon of late nineteenth-century Germany was folding into the troubled night of the Great War. That's when Heidegger began to see the reason why the "darkening of the world" was coming about. And, as Bergson said, "*that* is why he kept on speaking for his whole life."[44]

We have said that the epoché of technik refers not to a span of time but to one's *oblivion*, one's unconscious bracketing out (= ἐποχή-2) of the source of all meaningfulness, which itself is "bracketed out" by its very essence (= ἐποχή-1). Thus, ἐποχή-1, the hiddenness of appropriation, is ultimately responsible for ἐποχή-2, our oblivion of that hidden source. In this sense, the forgottenness of the *es-gibt*-ness of the clearing—including the current world of produce-for-use—is not brought about by any concrete actions or attitudes of human beings. Rather, it is "sent" to us, even "destined" to us from beyond our powers. Thus, modern technik, this drive to "provoke" everything into yielding something useful for accumulation and commodification, does not come from us or through us *qua* existentiel persons ("it happens neither exclusively *in* man nor definitively *through* man"),[45] but rather comes from an ontological source that we do not control, one that *obliges* us to disclose nature as nothing but the source of extractable and marketable use-values.

> Man does not have control over the disclosedness itself in which at any given time an actual thing shows up or withdraws.[46]
>
> The disclosedness itself within which the ordering [of nature and persons] unfolds is never a human handiwork, any more than is the realm we traverse every time we as subjects relate to an object.[47]
>
> Only to the extent that we, for our part, are *already* challenged to exploit the energies of nature can this disclosure that orders [nature and persons] take place.[48]

---

44. See above, note 3.
45. GA 7: 24.31–32 = 24.2–3.
46. GA 7: 18.18–20 = 18.5–7.
47. GA 7: 19.9–13 = 18.30–33.
48. GA 7: 18.23–25 = 18.11–13, my emphasis.

In other words, what is finally in charge here is *Ereignis* and its dispensations. Hence the *specific form* of the disclosing of nature that appropriation currently gives us—technik as a turbocharged and totalizing form of τέχνη—is also beyond our control. For reasons that have nothing to do with human agency, we find ourselves trapped in a world of exploitation that is visited upon us by something that compels us into relations of exploitation.

With that, Heidegger has arrived at the core of his analysis: his philosophical etiology of the depredations of modernity. His argument about the essence of technik, and thus of modern "technology," has three moments to it:

1. *Ereignis* is what "dispenses" *all* meaning-giving worlds in phenomenological correlation with man's way of being "in" those worlds.
2. Thus *Ereignis* also dispenses the *current* world (*Gestell*) and "destines" modern man to disclose everything in those terms (*Technik*).
3. *Ereignis* does so precisely because the West has grown increasingly oblivious of it; and in direct proportion to that, man has come to dominate nature and transform it into mere objects for consumption.[49]

By the "essence" of technik Heidegger does not mean the traditional notion of the "whatness" of a thing, Aristotle's τὸ τί ἦν εἶναι or the medieval *quid erat esse*, that which something "ever-enduringly" is. He means, rather, what "holds forth" in a thing, what is responsible for how the thing in question maintains its presence—even (via a very dubious reference to Goethe's word *fortgewähren*) "that which continually grants something."[50] This allows Heidegger to interpret the "essence" of technik in terms of his theory of dispensations, now read as the "grantings" of such worlds: "Every granting of a [world of] disclosure occurs from out of a granting and as a granting."[51]

How adequate is this highly theorized, strictly "philosophical" view of what is ultimately responsible for the modern way of being-in-the-world? Has Heidegger's phenomenological analysis moved a bit too fast? Without providing anything like a thick description, Heidegger declares that the epoch of technik—disclosing things as usable while ignoring appropriation—applies everywhere and to everyone, to the exclusion of all other worlds of disclosure. But do the millions of evangelical Christians, orthodox Jews, and Wahabi Muslims who make their living writing code, see everything (their families

---

49. GA 14: 62.14–15 = 52.18–19: "die Seinsgeschichte [ist] die Geschichte der sich steigernden Seinsvergessenheit [= Ereignissesvergessenheit]."

50. "Fortgewähren" is Goethe's hapax legomenon from *Die Wahlverwandtschaften, Sämtliche Werke* IX, 476.26 ("man ließ eben von beiden Seiten alles so fortgewähren") = *Elective Affinities*, trans. Constantine, 187.36–37: "[to let things] carry on." Also *Elective Affinities*, trans. Hollingdale, 238.25–26: "[to let things] go on as before." GA 7: 32.19 = 31.6.

51. GA 7: 33.7–8 = 32.2–3.

and friends included) as "resources" to be exploited and utilized? Heidegger seems to say that if they do not *now*, they soon will. Or to broaden the scope: Can Heidegger actually tell us how an entire culture—the Greeks, for example—viewed reality? Does he think that fourth-century Greece as a whole was dominated by Plato's epoché of εἶδος, even when it overlapped with Aristotle's epoché of ἐνέργεια? Isn't an epoché simply the way a "fallen" or "absorbed" individual is in-the-world? When and how does such an epoché expand to include entire populations and whole cultures, not to mention the whole world?

Moreover, what does the "essence" of technik and "technology" have to do with concrete historical (*historisch*) events that have transpired over the last five hundred years? The word "history" is normally taken to mean what the early Heidegger called *Geschehen*, actual living among the materialities, forces, and accidents which direct our lives and to which we respond with various degrees and kinds of agency—history as "a chapter of accidents." The problem, of course, is that the narrative Heidegger lays out is a *meta*-history that makes no contact with what is usually called history except through the texts of a dozen metaphysicians. His "deep history" of the West has nothing to say about lived history as the medium and the product of human action in nature and society. Rather, ever since Anaximander, Parmenides, and Heraclitus failed to inquire into what is responsible for φύσις and ἀλήθεια, history has been tumbling toward disaster. Heidegger takes his individual "synchronic" analyses of those dozen or so philosophers and strings them together diachronically to chart how the West ended up, almost inevitably, in the dark Satanic mills of technology.

Yes, the structure of onto-theology can certainly be parsed out in specific metaphysicians, and Heidegger does so, often brilliantly. But how any moment in that philosophical narrative is embedded in and reflects the social and political history of its times holds no interest for Heidegger. What he offers instead is a meta-historical "explanation" of how the West devolved into the nightmare of modernity. What else would we expect from a philosopher who says that "metaphysics is the *essential ground* of Western history"?[52] This vision verges on an idealist illusion that metaphysics drives the history of the world and that we merely have to discern how great philosophers viewed the being of things in order to understand why we are where we are—all of this without reference to the invention of gun powder, the stirrup, or the printing press, not to mention the "voyages of discovery" that led to the enslavement of so much of Africa and the Americas. To give a concrete example: Professors François Jaran and Christophe Perrin's three-volume *Heidegger Concordance* references the volume number and page of every one of the seven thousand major terms appear-

52. GA 76: 56.18: "Die Metaphysik ist der *Wesensgrund* der abendländischen Geschichte."

ing in the thirty thousand pages of Heidegger's *Gesamtausgabe* as currently available. A search through volume two of the *Concordance* reveals that the list of terms jumps from "*Kampf um Dasein*" to "*kategorial*."[53] Which is to say that in all of Heidegger's publications (some ninety-six volumes as of this writing) there is not a single mention of *Kapitalismus*.[54] Heidegger's narrative of decline remains resolutely uncontaminated by such "ontic" history, and as a result has about as much explanatory power as does the Christian story of original sin.

3. THE SOUGHT-FOR OUTCOME

Heidegger's 1953 lecture holds out the hope of a certain "overcoming" (or at least a remaining free) of modern technology by awaking to and resonating with the concealed power that "sends" us the *Gestell* in correlation with *Technik*. But first he must identify the danger that he would have us get free of.

> The threat to man does not come in the first instance from the potentially lethal machines and apparatus of technology. The actual threat has already afflicted us in our essence. The dominance of the age of exploitation threatens us with the possibility that we could be denied entrance into a more original disclosing and thus into the experience of the call of a more primal disclosure.[55]

The real threat is not "ontic" and historical but "ontological"—our being destined to disclose the being of things as their exploitability. Sometime in the nineteenth or twentieth century, appropriation "suddenly and inexplicably" (i.e., without *historisch* reasons) "sent" us *Gestell* and *Technik* as "a dispensed way of disclosing things, which takes the form of a provocation"[56]—and we are stuck with it. But there's hope! If only we could *get over* all of that by a spiritual or internal change of mind, by acknowledging and embracing *Ereignis*, we just might be rescued from this nightmare. (This might remind one of the fabled German professor who worked diligently all his life to put an end to drowning by trying to banish the idea of gravity from people's minds. But,

---

53. Jaran and Perrin, *The Heidegger Concordance* I, 781.

54. Professor Jaran has since informed me that there are two passing references to capitalism, at GA 16: 321.11 ("die Geschichte des Kapitalismus") and GA 90: 118.4 ("Maschine und Industrie in 'Kapitalismus'") as well as two uses of "kapitalistisch": GA 90.115, note 1 (kapitalistische Wirtschaft); and 157.19 ("das kapitalistische Kräftespiel"). Because of their insignificance in all four cases, none of these references is included in *The Heidegger Concordance*.

55. GA 7: 29.9–15 = 28.9–14.

56. GA 7: 30.34–35 = 29.31–32, and 32.28–29 = 3.17–18. "Suddenly and inexplicably": ibid. 31.4–5 = 29: 36: "je und jäh und allem Denken unerklärbar."

alas, they continued to drown.)[57] Citing Hölderlin, Heidegger sees within the current dispensation the possibility of a "saving power":

> But where danger is, there grows
> The saving power as well.[58]

> [Appropriation, i.e.,] the granting that dispenses the various forms of disclosure—precisely as such a dispensing—is the saving power . . . that lets us see and enter into the highest dignity of our essence.[59]

That dignity consists in our vocation to safeguard ἀλήθεια-1 in its intrinsic hiddenness or λήθη-1. And if we see and embrace this hidden source of *Gestell* itself, then "precisely in this most extreme danger there comes to light our innermost, indestructible belonging within that which does the granting."[60] For Heidegger *Gestell* is ambiguous. It imposes on us the task of challenging nature to yield the useful; and yet paradoxically it also allows us to experience (if not right now, then "perhaps more in the future")[61] that our vocation and highest possibility is to safeguard *Ereignis*. By way of conclusion, Heidegger says we can see this most fully in another kind of τέχνη—namely, art, the very disclosure of dis-closure-at-all (i.e., of ἀλήθεια-1) within the "materiality" of the work of art: words, movement, stone, color, and so on. Adapting Plato to his own ends, Heidegger calls this disclosure-at-all τὸ ἐκφανέστατον,[62] that which "shines forth most brightly—*precisely in its hiddenness*. The sheer thrown-openness of ἀλήθεια-1 is ever present in its absence,[63] the astonishing, question-provoking source of everything human, of all beauty, goodness, and meaning. The questioning of *that*, Heidegger says, is "the piety of thinking."[64] With that his lecture ends.

Given Heidegger's view that the *Gestell* and *Technik* are dispensed to us from beyond our control, there is little Heidegger can offer as a prescription for "overcoming" technology, or even an exhortation about how to act. At best:

57. Marx and Engels, *Die deutsche Ideologie*, 3.30–37. See GA 11: 158.28–160.35.

58. "Wo aber Gefahr ist, wächst / Das Rettende auch": *Patmos*, 3–4, Hölderlin, *Selected Poems and Fragments*, 230.

59. GA 7: 33.11–14 = 32.6–9.

60. GA 7: 33.19–21 = 32.14–16: "gerade in dieser äußersten Gefahr kommt die innigste, unzerstörbare Zugehörigkeit des Menschen in das Gewährende zum Vorschein."

61. GA 7: 34.11 = 33.8–9: "unerfahren bislang, aber erfahrener vielleicht künftig."

62. *Phaedrus* 250d7.

63. GA 14: 23.35 = 18.30: "ein Anwesen von Abwesen." See GA 54: 176.19–23 = 119.4–9.

64. GA 7: 36.35 = 35.30.

> "Cells" of resistance will be formed everywhere against technology's unchecked power. They will keep reflection alive inconspicuously and will prepare the turn-around for which people will clamor when the general desolation becomes unbearable.
>
> From all corners of the world, I now hear voices calling for such a reflection and for ways to find it—voices that are renouncing the easily attainable effects of the power of technik.[65]

It seems that all we can do to free ourselves from the domination of "technology" is to enact an interiorized resistance, a philosophical quietism in which we maintain a certain distance from techno-think and techno-do as we tune into our nature as guardians of *Ereignis*. "Entering into appropriation"—what *Being and Time* had called "resolve"—may give us a sense of being "free" of history and technology, even as their ravages continue. Perhaps someday there will be a new dawn, perhaps not. In any case Heidegger has nothing more to say about that. Here his discourse reaches its limits.

In the "The Question of Technik" the severe limitations of Heidegger's thought are on full display. First of all, on the perhaps impossible assumption that one *could* get to the essence of such a complex, multilayered phenomenon as modern "technology"—whether as machines or mind-set or the world of meaning that goes with them—one would first need a much more granular and precise description of *what the subject matter is*, including at least a brief account of the historical origins and current socio-economic forms of the exploitation of man and nature. Absent that, Heidegger's delineation of his topic (*das Befragte*) risks devolving into a curmudgeon's lament against the ravages of modern industry. Heidegger once said that no one can jump over his own shadow.[66] And he liked to cite Hölderlin's verse, *Wie du anfiengst, wirst du bleiben*—"As you began, so will you remain."[67] These may provide clues to Heidegger's own approach to modern history and technology. We may wonder whether his own shadow—his limited personal and cultural experience, his pinched worldview, his deep anti-modern conservatism—restricted his ability to understand and properly engage the facts of modern history. In fact, we may wonder what Heidegger thought history was all about. On 11 December

65. *Zollikoner Seminare* 352.18–24 = 283.3–10. "Turn around": Umkehr. Here that word is a synonym of the "Einkehr ins Ereignis" rather than pertaining to the shift in focus of SZ I.3. See chapter 7, note 17. My thanks to Richard Polt for calling this text to my attention.

66. GA 41: 153.24 = 150.28–29.

67. GA 12: 88. 25 = 7.24–25. The text is from "Der Rhein," line 48, in *Selected Poems and Fragments*, 198.

1941, three days after Japan attacked Pearl Harbor, Hitler declared war on the United States, thus bringing that then neutral nation into the European conflict. That same day the American Congress reciprocated with a declaration of war against Germany—at which point Heidegger told his students, as if Hitler had done nothing:

> We know today that the Anglo-Saxon world of Americanism has resolved to annihilate Europe, the homeland [*Heimat*], which means: the origin [*Anfang*] of the Western world. But what is bound up with this origin is indestructible. America's entry into this planetary war is not an entry into history [*Geschichte*]. No, it is already the last American act of its own lack of history and its self-destruction. This [declaration of war] is the renunciation of the origin, it is America's decision to be without that origin.[68]

Likewise, as Hitler's Panzers were rolling into Paris in June of 1940, Heidegger suggested to his students that the defeat of France was actually an event in the collapse of Western metaphysics and specifically of Cartesian subjectivity.

> In these days we are witnesses to a mysterious law of history which states that one day a people [= the French] no longer measures up to the metaphysics that arose from its own history. That day arrives precisely when such metaphysics has been transformed into the absolute.[69]

Heidegger broached everything, even World War II and the Holocaust, from the standpoint of his idiosyncratic meta-metaphysical view of history. As illuminating as his interpretations of various philosophers from Parmenides to Nietzsche may be, he far exceeded his competence when he conjured up his philosophical narrative of how the West devolved from the glories of sixth-century Greece to the depredations of modern technology, all because it had forgotten *Ereignis*.

---

68. GA 53: 68.8–16 = 54.38–55.3. Heidegger certainly had a thing about Americans. Cf. ibid., 179.18–20 = 143.29–31: "Ungeschichtlich [in contrast to nature as merely 'geschichtlos'] und daher katastrophenhaft, wie es keine Natur je sein kann, ist z.B. der Amerikanismus." A few lines earlier (179.13–14, .17 = 143.24–26, .28) such un-historicalness is defined as breaking off from the very essence of one's human being (an "Abbruch," from one's "Wesensart" as one's "Eigenstes"). For Heidegger's earlier (summer 1941) remarks on "amerikanische Scheinphilosophie," see GA 51: 84.1–2 = 70.33–34. Since Heidegger's knowledge of English was quite limited, it is not clear which American philosophers he had in mind. On the "durcheinander gewirbelter rein amerikanischer Mensch," see ibid., 14.3–4 = 11.24–27.

69. GA 6, 2: 146.11–15 (= GA 48: 205.2–6) = 116.27–30. A few weeks later he said Germany could never justify (and presumably would never undertake) an action like the British destruction of the French fleet at Oran, Algeria (3 July 1940)—this less than a year after the Wehrmacht had leveled Warsaw on 25–26 September 1939: GA 6, 2: 176.12–17 (= GA 48: 264.32–265.3) = 144.24–145.2.

Of such a narrative one feels compelled to say, as Pieter Geyl did of Arnold Toynbee's work, "*C'est magnifique, mais ce n'est pas l'histoire.*"[70]

In order for Heidegger's etiology of *die Technik* to earn its right to any serious philosophical attention, he (or his followers) would need to conjugate this meta-metaphysical account with something more than the texts of a few select metaphysicians. This would require rethinking the relation between his ontological history of being and the ontic course of lived history in its concrete material manifestations. Is Heidegger arguing that the forgottenness of appropriation is the driving force of Western history or only a reflection of such forces in philosophical terms? Or is it something in between? Heidegger is notoriously vague about all of this. He seems to agree with Hegel that philosophy, his own included, arrives too late to direct the course of history. But he does claim to have found the ultimate reason for why "the world is shifting out of joint," and he purports to offer a "glimpse into what is the case today."[71] Is it philosophically responsible to pontificate on the current state of the world—and in fact the whole trajectory of Western history—by engaging in yet one more, and in fact quite idiosyncratic, "labor of the concept" while refusing to take up the labor of history?

Richard Rorty has claimed that "[t]he whole force of Heidegger's position lies in his account of the history of philosophy."[72] If that refers to Heidegger's devolutionary vision of how metaphysics has unfolded in the West, along with the technological consequences of that, I think the statement is dead wrong. With his history of philosophy, especially as he worked that out in the 1930s and 1940s, Heidegger overplayed his hand. The enduring core of Heidegger's work is his demonstration that, overlooked as it might be, radical human finitude—with no need for a supervenient God or some preternatural "Being"—is the ultimate source of meaning-at-all and thus of culture in all its historical configurations. He laid the foundations for this argument in his masterwork as well as in his subsequent readings of individual philosophers in the Western tradition. After that, full stop.

Heidegger had originally planned *Being and Time* in two parts: first, to trace meaningful presence back to finite, mortal thrown-openness ("temporality") in its horizon-forming and presence-defining function; and then

70. Pieter Geyl, "Toynbee's System of Civilizations" in Pieter Geyl, et al., *The Pattern of the Past*, 43.9, reprinted from *Journal of the History of Ideas* IX (1948) 1, 93–125 (at 111.3–4).

71. GA 9: 242.4 = 185.23: "Der Erdball geht aus den Fugen." "What is": GA 79: 74.29 = 70.27.

72. Richard Rorty, *The Consequences of Pragmatism*, 52.

> to destroy the traditional content of [Kantian, Cartesian, and] ancient philosophy until we arrive at those primordial experiences in which we achieved our first ways of determining the nature of being—the ways that have guided us ever since.[73]

Clearly, if Part I of the project had been carried out in 1927, it would not have moved beyond a transcendental framework and into what Heidegger later worked out as the "givenness of the clearing." Given that limitation, we may be fairly sure that Part II of the project would not have pressed back behind Aristotle into the pre-Socratics' awareness of the hidden clearing. Nonetheless, Heidegger's phrase "our first ways of determining the nature of being" remains vague. Does he mean our first ways *within metaphysics*? Or is he referring to the pre-metaphysical determination of being in the pre-Socratics?

In either case, whether the reference is to classical Greek philosophy (Plato, Aristotle) or to its origins in pre-Socratic thinking, the project of *Being and Time* as presented in 1927 did not yet entail the quasi-deterministic *Seinsgeschichte* stretching from ancient Greece to modern technology. The project would have been better off without that story (and Heidegger's personal fortunes might have fared better without his application of it to politics). His efforts to draw a straight line from Anaximander to the atom bomb are a failure, and necessarily so, given his self-imposed restrictions on the scope of philosophical reflection. His hyper-metaphysical story about the ultimate source of modernity unfolds without any focused discussion of such events as the French revolution and the emancipation of the Jews, nineteenth-century colonialism and racism, twentieth-century ideologies of the left and the right, liberal and neo-liberal economics, and the like. On his own terms this failure puts his top-down philosophical history of the West outside the pale of serious discussion. Back in his early years, Heidegger said, "We cannot separate metaphysics [which at that time meant his own philosophy] from positive research."[74] It would seem he forgot that principle when it came to his later "philosophizing" about the contemporary world. A truly productive philosophical interpretation of the contemporary situation, including the growth and dominance of technology, requires a story quite different from the history of being, and it demands competence in matters other than the "thinking of appropriation." Heidegger's philosophy demonstrates no such competence.

73. SZ 22.28–31 = 44.14–17.

74. GA 29/30 279.9–10 = 189.24.

Heidegger's philosophical work stands, and may endure for a while, as the text in which radical human finitude was shown to be the ungroundable ground of the phenomenal world we inhabit. It is also the text in which Western metaphysics, with the God-pretensions of its onto-theology, found a proper and respectful burial. A certain Western valorization of stability over flux, of eternity over time and history, of the imperialism of the one over the dispersion of the many, met its end in *Being and Time* and the subsequent writings. Those texts purport to chart the demise of a certain kind of thinking in the West in a way analogous to Ludwig Feuerbach's efforts in the nineteenth century. Just when Hegel had brought metaphysics, both Greek and Christian, to a great onto-theological culmination, Feuerbach appeared with his mission of "transforming theology into anthropology."[75] In the twentieth century, standing on this side of Nietzsche, whom he called the last of the onto-theologians, Heidegger took as his mission the destruction of metaphysics and all forms of subjectivity (including Feuerbachian anthropology) in the name of the inexplicably finite source of meaning as such.

Two cheers for Heidegger *and* for Feuerbach. We all stand in their debt. From Feuerbach we have learned to live without a certain kind of deep metaphysical backup. From Heidegger we have learned to shoulder the burden of our μοίρα, our fatedness to making sense of the world with our backs pressed up against mortality. With his final exhortation to "become what you already are," Heidegger—having deconstructed onto-theology and turned us over to our radical finitude—felt that his work was done. Be that as it may, it is not enough. As with Feuerbach before him, so, too, with Heidegger the point holds true: "He overlooks the fact that after completing this work, the chief thing still remains to be done."[76]

---

75. Feuerbach, *Grundsätze der Philosophie der Zukunft* in *Gesammelte Werke*, IX, 265 = 5: "Der Aufgabe der neueren Zeit war die Verwirklichung und Vermenschlichung Gottes—die *Verwandlung* und Auflösung der Theologie in die Anthropologie."

76. "Er übersieht, daß nach Vollbringung dieser Arbeit die Hauptsache noch zu tun bleibt." Fourth Thesis on Feuerbach, *Marx Engels Gesamtausgabe*, Abt. I, Bd. 30, no. 2, 793.45–46; cf. ibid., Abt. IV, Bd. 3, no. 1 (1998), 20.18–20; and *Die deutsche Ideologie*, 534.22–33. See *Nicomachean Ethics* VI 7, 1141b3–8.

APPENDICES

1. The Existential Components of Openness and Care
2. ψυχή, νοῦς ποιητικός, and *lumen naturale* in Aristotle and Aquinas
3. Greek Grammar and "Is-as-Having-Been"

APPENDIX 1

The Existential Components of Openness and Care

The haste with which *Being and Time* was written is perhaps nowhere more obvious than in Heidegger's various lists of the existential components of *Erschlossenheit* (disclosedness), *das Da* (the open, or openness), *In-der-Welt-sein* (engagement with meaning), and *Sorge* (care). In the later pages of the book Heidegger clearly states that *Rede* (his tentative rendering of λόγος in *Being and Time*) names the whole of ex-sistence when he writes, "Only in terms of the temporality of *Rede*—that is, of *Dasein* in general—can we clarify how 'meaning' 'arises.'"[1] Earlier he had argued that ex-sistence, as open, is structured by *Befindlichkeit* and *Verstehen*, and that this bivalent openness is determined by *Rede*/λόγος (see below, nos. 1.1 through 2.3), and this would seem to be a correct statement of the structure of openness.

However, this clear view begins to fog up whenever Heidegger runs together *Befindlichkeit*, *Verstehen*, and *Rede* as if they were three co-equal *components* of the open (see nos. 2.4–2.7).

Heidegger gets back on sure ground when he defines *Sorge* in terms of the bivalence of (1) *Existentialität*-and-*Faktizität* on the one hand and (2) *Sein bei* (which is *Verfallenheit* in everydayness) on the other, and when he says that this unitary bivalent structure is "articulated" by *Rede*. (See 3.1 through 4.1.)

But things get wobbly again when Heidegger runs together *Befindlichkeit*, *Verstehen*, *Verfallen*, and *Rede* as if they were four co-equal components of disclosedness (nos. 4.2 and 4.3).

1. Only *Befindlichkeit* and *Verstehen*[2]

1.1: "In *Befindlichkeit* and *Verstehen* we see the two equiprimordially constitutive ways of being the open [*das Da*]." SZ 133.22–23 = 171.38–172.1.

1. SZ 349.32–33 = 401.2–4.

2. See SZ 181.4–5 = 225.18–20: "Gefragt wird nach der ontologischen Einheit von Existenzialität und Faktizität, bzw. der wesenhaften Zugehörigkeit dieser zu jener."

1.2: "The basic existentials that constitute the being of the open—that is, the disclosedness of the engagement-with-meaning—are *Befindlichkeit* and *Verstehen*." SZ 160.27–29 = 203.17–19.
1.3: "In its being, [ex-sistence] is disclosed to itself. *Befindlichkeit* and *Verstehen* constitute the kind of being of this disclosedness." SZ 182.7–8 = 226.29–31.
1.4: "Ex-sistence is constituted by disclosedness, that is, by a *befindliches Verstehen*." SZ 260.31–32 = 304.36–37.

2. *Rede* mentioned in conjunction with *Befindlichkeit* and *Verstehen*

2.1 "*Befindlichkeit* and *Verstehen* are determined equiprimordially by *Rede*." SZ 133.26–27 = 172.4–5.
2.2: "*Rede* is existentially equiprimordial with *Befindlichkeit* and *Verstehen*." SZ 161.5–6 = 203.34. Italicized in the German.
2.3: "*Rede* is constitutive for the being of the open, that is, for *Befindlichkeit* and *Verstehen*." SZ 165.12–13 = 208.29–30.
2.4: "The theme [of this chapter] has been the ontological constitution of the disclosedness that essentially belongs to ex-sistence. The being [of that disclosedness] is constituted in *Befindlichkeit*, *Verstehen*, and *Rede*." SZ 180.12–14 = 224.28–30.
2.5: "Disclosedness is the basic character of ex-sistence according to which it *is* its openness [*sein Da*]. Disclosedness is constituted by *Befindlichkeit*, *Verstehen*, and *Rede*." SZ 220.31–34 = 263.19–21.
2.6: "[Disclosedness] is constituted by *Befindlichkeit* and *Rede* along with *Verstehen*." SZ 295.32–33 = 342.13–14.
2.7: "The third essential moment of disclosedness is *Rede*." SZ 296.6 = 342.26.

3. *Existentialität, Faktizität,* and *Sein bei* (or *Verfallen*)[3]

3.1: "The basic ontological characteristics of [ex-sistence] are *Existentialität*, *Faktizität*, and *Verfallensein*." SZ 191.21–22 = 235.36–38.
3.2: "Being-already-ahead-of-itself-in-the-world essentially includes one's *verfallende Sein bei* [things]." SZ 192.31–33 = 237.5–7.
3.3: "[Care] means being-ahead-of-itself-already-in-(the-world) as *Sein bei* (things encountered within the world)." SZ 192.36–37 = 237.11–12.[4]
3.4: "The unity of the constitutive moments of care—*Existentialität*, *Faktizität*, and *Verfallenheit* . . ." SZ 316.33–34 = 364.28–29.

3. In some of these texts *Existentialität* and *Faktizität* are understood when Heidegger speaks of "being-already-ahead-of-itself-in-the-world."

4. Also at SZ 317.1–3 = 364.31–33; and 327.13–14 = 375.8–10. Cf. 322.17–19 = 369.5–7.

4. *Verstehen, Befindlichkeit, Verfallen,* and *Rede*

4.1: "The full disclosedness of the open, which is constituted by *Verstehen*, *Befindlichkeit*, and *Verfallen*, achieves articulation through *Rede*." SZ 349.5–6 = 400.16–18.[5]

4.2: "This disclosedness, as a basic state of that entity which we ourselves are, is constituted by *Befindlichkeit*, *Verstehen*, *Verfallen*, and *Rede*." SZ 269.26–28 = 314.10–12.

4.3: "Conscience discloses, and thus belongs within the range of, those existential phenomena that constitute the *being of the open* [*das Da*] as disclosedness. We have analyzed the most universal structures of *Befindlichkeit*, *Verstehen*, *Rede*, and *Verfallen*." SZ 270.14–18 = 315.10–13.

5. Heidegger goes on to say that Rede does not have a determined ex-stasis: "Daher zeitigt sich die Rede nicht primär in einer bestimmten Ekstase": ibid., 349.7–8 = 400.18–19.

APPENDIX 2

ψυχή, νοῦς ποιητικός, and *lumen naturale* in Aristotle and Aquinas

Unless otherwise noted, the references are to Aristotle's *De anima*.

1. ψυχή *qua* νοῦς is bivalent:

1.1: passively able to receive all things and thus somehow capable of becoming all things.

III 4, 429a15–16:

δεκτικόν τοῦ εἶδους καὶ δυνάμει τοιοῦτον ἀλλὰ μὴ τοῦτο

receptive of the intelligible appearance and potentially the same as it, but not identical with it

III 4 429a21–22:

φύσιν μηδεμίαν ἀλλ᾽ ἢ ταύτην, ὅτι δυνατόν

[ψυχή] can have no other nature than this: to be in potency [to receive intelligible appearances]

III 4, 429b24–25:

τὸ νοεῖν πάσχειν τί ἐστιν

thinking is a way of being acted upon

III 5, 430a14–15:

ὁ [νοῦς] τῷ πάντα γίνεσθαι

intellect insofar as it becomes all things

III 8, 431b21:

ἡ ψυχὴ τὰ ὄντα πώς ἐστι πάντα

the soul is somehow all things

1.2: actively pro-ductive of the knowability of things.

III 5, 430a15:

ὁ [νοῦς] τῷ πάντα ποιεῖν [νοητά]

intellect insofar as it makes all things [intelligible]

(This ever-in-act [ἐνεργείᾳ] and actively productive [ποιητικός] function of the intellect is the "activating intellect.")

2. The activating intellect activates intelligibles.

2.1: The light analogy.

Aristotle compares the function of the activating intellect to the action of light on colors. The analogy proceeds as follows (III 5, 430a16–17):

2.1.1: What we see is color (τὸ ὁρατόν ἐστι χρῶμα: II 7, 418a29).

2.1.2: In the dark, when the space between colors and the eye is not transparent, colors are unseeable ("hidden"). They have merely the possibility to be seen (δυνάμει: III 5, 430a16; ἔχει τὸ αἴτιον τοῦ εἶναι ὁρατόν: II 7, 418a31).

2.1.3: When the spatial medium is lit up and becomes transparent, the colors become *actually-able-to-be-seen* (ἐνεργείᾳ: III 5, 430a 18; κατ᾽ ἐνέργειαν: II 7, 418b1).

2.1.4: But the colors get *actually seen* only when the viewer's eyes actually do see them.

2.2: Intelligibles.

2.2.1: What the νοῦς apprehends is τὸ νοητόν.

2.2.2: When things are considered as unrelated to ("hidden from") the intellect—that is, when they are not taken κατὰ τὸν λόγον, they are merely-able-to-be-known.

2.2.3: The activating intellect (ὁ νοῦς ποιητικός: cf. III 5, 430a15) is analogous to the light (οἷον τὸ φῶς: III 5, 430a15) that illuminates the spatial medium so that colors can be seen. The activating intellect makes things *actually-able-to-be-known*. In one metaphor, it "abs-tracts" (draws out) the intelligible characteristics of things—that is, distinguishes the "intelligibles" (Latin, *intelligibiles*) from the particular things that are instantiations of them.

2.2.4: But the intelligibles get *actually known* (*intellecta*) only when the intellect (νοῦς, *intellectus*) actually knows them.

2.3: Source of this position.

This triad of merely-able-to-be-known, actually-able-to-be-known, and actually known, is implied in the controversial passage at III 5, 430a17–22 (οὗτος ὁ νοῦς χωριστός . . . οὐχ ὁτὲ μὲν νοεῖ ὁτὲ δ› οὐ νοεῖ), which is interpreted by Aquinas in the sense that Heidegger accepts (namely, the activating intellect is a *human* capacity) at Thomas Aquinas, *In Aristotelis librum De anima commentarium*, liber III, lectio X, nn. 732–41: http://www.dhspriory.org/thomas/DeAnima.htm#310.

3. The activating intellect activates the possible intellect.

3.1: For Aristotle "knowledge" means that the knower actually *is* the known (III 5, 430a 19–20). Therefore, it can be said that, in activating *things* (= making them actually knowable), the activating intellect equally activates the *possible intellect* (see above under 1.1: III, 5, 14–15 and III 4 429a21–22).

3.2: The activating intellect does so by producing (ποιεῖν), via "abstraction" or distinction (see 2.2.3 above), the knowable appearance (Latin, *species intelligibilis*) which,

3.3: when "received by" (cf. δεκτικόν: III 4, 429a15–16) or "impressed on" the possible intellect,

3.4: determines and activates the possible intellect and makes it produce the "expressed intelligible species"—the *intentio* or *verbum mentale*—(thus Aquinas)

3.5: in and by means of which the intellect is made to be actually knowing (ἡ κατ' ἐνέργειαν ἐπιστήμη: III 5, 430a20 and III 7, 431 a 1).

4. The "natural" light and other lights.

4.1: Aquinas accepts Aristotle's comparison of the activating intellect to light but, for theological reasons, describes the *intellectus agens* as only the *natural* light of reason (*lumen naturale rationis*, which Heidegger mentions at SZ 133.1 = 171.17)

4.2: in contrast to the divine light (*lumen dei* vs. *lumen naturale rationis* at *Summa theologiae* I, 12, 11, ad 3; cf. I, 12, 13, corpus),

4.3: the light of faith (*lumen fidei* or *lumen gratiae*) and

4.4: the light of prophesy (*lumen prophetiae*) (both of these last two at *Quaestiones disputatae de anima*, quaestio unica, art. 5, ad 6), as well as

4.5: the light of glory (*lumen gloriae* at *Summa theologiae* I, 12, 5, ad 3).

APPENDIX 3

Greek Grammar and "Is-as-Having-Been"

1. In Greek antiquity the noun χρόνος meant both "time" and, when used in a grammatical sense, "tense."
2. Grammarians spoke of the past tense in general as either ὁ χρόνος παρελθών or ὁ χρόνος παρεληλυθώς.
   - παρελθών is the masculine singular second aorist participle of παρέρχομαι (παρά + ἔρχομαι), to go by, to pass by.
   - παρεληλυθώς is the masculine singular perfect participle of the same verb.
   - Thus the generalized past tense was understood as referring to "time that has gone by."
3. What we call the present-perfect tense is first alluded to by the Greek grammarian Dionysius Thrax (ca. 170–90 BCE) in his immensely influential Τέχνη γραμματική. There he spoke of ὁ [χρόνος] παρακείμενος, the tense that refers to "[the time that is] lying close by/alongside"—that is, time that has passed by and yet still is near.
4. Sometime between 400 and 700 CE the Byzantine grammarian Stephanus, in his commentary on Dionysius' Τέχνη γραμματική, wrote, "ὁ δὲ παρακείμενος καλεῖται ἐνεστὼς συντελικός." Roughly, "The [tense that refers to time that is] past-but-near is called ἐνεστὼς συντελικός."
   - ἐνεστώς is the masculine singular perfect participle of the causative verb ἐνίστημι (to put or place *in*, in the sense of to make something stand *present*).
   - συντελικός (from συντελέω, to bring to an end, to complete) means "completed" or "brought to perfection."
   - Hence ἐνεστὼς συντελικός refers to the form of time that "stands [as having been made to stand] in the present, but as completed or per-fected [thoroughly done, finished]"—time that is-present-as-having-been-completed, time that "is-as-having-been" in the sense of being completed but still present.

SOME TEXTS

Dionysius Thrax, *Dionysii Thracis Ars Grammatica* / Τέχνη Διονυσίου γραμμτικοῦ, ed. Gustav Uhlig, in *Grammatici Graeci*, I, i (Leipzig: B.G. Teubner, 1883; reprinted, Hildesheim: Georg Olms, 1965), 5–100.

"The TEKHNÉ GRAMMATIKÉ of Dionysius Thrax," translated by Alan Kemp, in Daniel J. Taylor, ed., *The History of Linguistics in the Classical Period* (Amsterdam and Philadelphia: John Benjamins Publishing Company, 1987), 170–89. (This replaces T. Davidson's 1874 translation, which first appeared in the *Journal of Speculative Philosophy*.)

Stephanus' commentaries on the Τέχνη γραμματική are preserved only in fragments in *Scholia in Dionysii Thracis Artem Grammaticam*, ed. Alfred Hilgard, in *Grammatici Graeci*, I, iii (Leipzig: B.G. Teubner, 1901; reprinted, Hildesheim: Georg Olms, 1965), 251.4.

On Stephanus see:

Pauly-Wissowa, *Real-Encyclopädie der classischen Altertumswissenschaft*, III/A, ii, 2401a and b, s.v. "Stephanos," no. 13.

J. R. Martindale, *The Prosopography of the Later Roman Empire* (Cambridge: Cambridge University Press, 1980), II (A.D. 395–527), 1030, s.v. "Stephanus 16."

Note the anomaly of the absence of any mention of Stephanus in Robert A. Kaster, *Guardians of Language: The Grammarian and Society in Late Antiquity* (Berkeley: University of California Press, 1988), 361–63 and 464–65.

See further *Scholia in Dionysii Thracis Artem Grammaticam* (as above): *Scholia Marciana*, 405.14–15: πεπληρωμένος: "[is as] having been fulfilled" (cf. Mark 1:15).

Bibliographies

HEIDEGGER'S GERMAN TEXTS AND THEIR ENGLISH TRANSLATIONS (AS OF OCTOBER 2014)

A. Texts within the *Gesamtausgabe*

I. Texts Already Published between 1910 and 1976

- GA 1: *Frühe Schriften*. Edited by Friedrich-Wilhelm von Herrmann, 1978; first edition 1972; texts from 1912–1916.
  - GA 1: 1–15, "Das Realitätsproblem in der modernen Philosophie (1912)" = "The Problem of Reality in Modern Philosophy," translated by Philip J. Bossert, revised by Aaron Bunch. In *Becoming Heidegger: On the Trail of His Early Occasional Writings, 1910–1927*, edited by Theodore Kisiel and Thomas Sheehan, 20–29. Evanston, IL: Northwestern University Press, 2007.
    [Earlier] "The Problem of Reality in Modern Philosophy (1912)," translated by Philip J. Bossert and John van Buren. In *Supplements: From the Earliest Essays to Being and Time and Beyond*, edited by John van Buren, 39–48. Albany: State University of New York Press, 2002.
  - GA 1: 17–43, "Neuere Forschungen über Logik (1912)" = "Recent Research in Logic, translated in part by Theodore Kisiel." In *Becoming Heidegger*, 31–44. (See above.)
  - GA 1: 55.23–57.14 ["Antrittsrede, Heidelberger Akademie der Wissenschaften" (1957)]" = "A Recollective 'Vita' (1957)," translated by Hans Seigfried. In *Becoming Heidegger*, 9–10. (See above.)
  - GA 1: 189–411, *Die Kategorien- und Bedeutungslehre des Duns Scotus (1915)* = *The Doctrine of Categories and Meaning of Duns Scotus*. Translated by Joydeep Bagchee. Bloomington: Indiana University Press, forthcoming.
  - GA 1: 399–411, "Schluß. Das Kategorienproblem" = "Conclusion [to *Die Kategorien- und Bedeutungslehre des Duns Scotus*: The Problem of Categories (1916)," translated by Roderick M. Stewart and John van Buren. In *Supplements*, 62–68. (See above.)
  - GA 1: 412, "Selbstanzeige (1917)" = "Author's Notice," translated by Aaron Bunch. In *Becoming Heidegger*, 77–78. (See above.)
    [Earlier] "Author's Book Notice [on *Die Kategorien- und Bedeutungslehre*]," translated by John van Buren. In *Supplements*, 61–62. (See above.)

- GA 1: 413–433, "Der Zeitbegriff in der Geschichtswissenschaft (1916)" = "The Concept of Time in the Science of History," translated by Thomas Sheehan. In *Becoming Heidegger*, 61–72. (See above.)
  [Earlier] "The Concept of Time in the Science of History (1915)," translated by Harry S. Taylor, Hans W. Uffelmann, and John van Buren. In *Supplements*, 49–60. (See above.)

- GA 2: *Sein und Zeit*. Edited by Friedrich-Wilhelm von Herrmann, 1977; first edition 1927.
  - *Being and Time*. Translated by John Macquarrie and Edward Robinson. New York: Harper & Row, 1962.
  - *Being and Time: A Translation of Sein und Zeit*. Translated by Joan Stambaugh, revised by Dennis J. Schmidt. Albany. New York: State University of New York Press, 2010.

- GA 3: *Kant und das Problem der Metaphysik*. Edited by Friedrich-Wilhelm von Herrmann, 1991; first edition 1929.
  - *Kant and the Problem of Metaphysics*, 5th, enlarged ed. Translated by Richard Taft. Bloomington: Indiana University Press, 1997.

- GA 4: *Erlaüterungen zu Hölderlins Dichtung*. Edited by Friedrich-Wilhelm von Herrmann, 1981, 1996; first edition 1944. Texts from 1936–1968.
  - *Elucidations of Hölderlin's Poetry*. Translated by Keith Hoeller. Amherst, MA: Humanity Books, 2000.

- GA 5: *Holzwege*. Edited by Friedrich-Wilhelm von Herrmann, 1977, 2003; first edition 1950. Texts from 1935–1946.
  - *Off the Beaten Track*. Translated by Julian Young and Kenneth Haynes. New York: Cambridge University Press, 2002.
    [Earlier in the following:]
  - GA 5: 1–74, "Der Ursprung des Kunstwerkes (1935/36)" = "The Origin of the Work of Art," translated by David Farrell Krell. In *Basic Writings: From Being and Time (1927) to The Task of Thinking (1964)*, rev. and exp. ed., edited by David Farrell Krell, 143–212. San Francisco: HarperSanFrancisco, 1992.
  - GA 5: 75–113, "Die Zeit des Weltbildes (1938)" = "The Age of the World Picture." In *The Question Concerning Technology and Other Essays*, edited and translated by William Lovitt, 115–154. New York: Harper & Row.
    [Earlier: "The Age of the World View." Translated by Marjorie Grene, *Measure: A Critical Journal* 2 (1951): 269–284.]
  - GA 5: 115–208, "Hegels Begriff der Erfahrung (1942/43)" = *Hegel's Concept of Experience*. Translated by J. Glenn Gray and Fred D. Wieck. New York: Harper & Row, 1970.
  - GA 5: 209–267, "Nietzsches Wort 'Gott ist tot' (1943)" = "The Word of Nietzsche: 'God Is Dead,'" In *The Question Concerning Technology and Other Essays*, 53–112. (See above.)

- GA 5: 269–320, "Wozu Dichter? (1946)" = "What Are Poets For?," translated by Albert Hofstadter. In *Poetry, Language, Thought*, 91–142. New York: Harper & Row, 1971.
- GA 5: 321–373, "Der Spruch des Anaximander (1946)" = "The Anaximander Fragment," translated by David Farrell Krell. In *Early Greek Thinking*, translated by David Farrell Krell and Frank A. Capuzzi, 13–58. New York: Harper & Row, 1975.)

- GA 6.1: *Nietzsche* vol. I. Edited by Brigitte Schillbach, 1996; first edition 1961. Texts from 1936–1939.
  - GA 6.1: 1–224 (= GA 43: 3–274.8), "Der Wille zur Macht als Kunst" (1936–1937) = "The Will to Power as Art," translated by David Farrell Krell. In *Nietzsche, Volume One: The Will to Power as Art*, edited by David Farrell Krell, 1–220. New York: Harper & Row, 1979.
  - GA 6.1: 225–423 (= GA 44: 1–233), "Die ewige Wiederkehr des Gleichen" (1937) = "The Eternal Recurrence of the Same," translated by David Farrell Krell. In *Nietzsche, Volume Two: The Eternal Recurrence of the Same*, edited by David Farrell Krell, 1–208. New York: Harper & Row, 1984.
  - GA 6.1: 425–594 (= GA 47: 1–295), "Der Wille zur Macht als Erkenntnis" (1939) = "The Will to Power as Knowledge," translated by Joan Stambaugh and David Farrell Krell. In *Nietzsche, Volume Three: The Will to Power as Knowledge and as Metaphysics*, edited by David Farrell Krell, 1–158. New York: Harper & Row, 1987.
- GA 6, 2: *Nietzsche* vol II. Edited by Brigitte Schillbach, 1997; first edition 1961. Texts from 1939–1946.
  - GA 6, 2: 1–22, "Die ewige Wiederkehr des Gleichen und der Wille zur Macht" (1939) = "The Eternal Recurrence of the Same and the Will to Power," translated by David Farrell Krell. In *Nietzsche, Volume Three: The Will to Power as Knowledge and as Metaphysics*, edited by David Farrell Krell, 159–183. New York: Harper & Row, 1987.
  - GA 6, 2: 23–229 (= GA 48: 1–332.32), "Der europäische Nihilismus" (1940) = "European Nihilism," translated by Frank A. Capuzzi. In *Nietzsche, Volume Four: Nihilism*, edited by David Farrell Krell. New York: Harper & Row, 1982.
  - GA 6, 2: 231–300, "Nietzsches Metaphysik" (1940) = "Nietzsche's Metaphysics" In *Nietzsche, Volume Three*, 187–251. (See above.)
  - GA 6, 2: 301–361, "Die seinsgeschichtliche Bestimmung des Nihilismus" (1944–1946) = "Nihilism as Determined by the History of Being," translated by Frank A. Capuzzi. In *Nietzsche, Volume Four: Nihilism*, 199–250. (See above.)
  - GA 6, 2: 363–416, "Die Metaphysik als Geschichte des Seins" (1941) = "Metaphysics as History of Being," translated by Joan Stambaugh. In *The End of Philosophy*, edited by Joan Stambaugh, 1–54. Chicago: University of Chicago Press, 2003; originally New York: Harper & Row, 1973.
  - GA 6, 2: 417–438, "Entwürfe zu Geschichte des Seins als Metaphysik" (1941) = "Sketches for a History of Being as Metaphysics," translated by Joan Stambaugh. In *The End of Philosophy*, edited by Joan Stambaugh, 55–74. (See above.)

◦ GA 6, 2: 439–448, "Die Erinnerung in die Metaphysik" (1941) = "Recollection in Metaphysics," translated by Joan Stambaugh. In *The End of Philosophy*, edited by Joan Stambaugh, 75–83. (See above.)

• GA 7: *Vortäge und Aufsätze*. Edited by Friedrich-Wilhelm von Herrmann, 2000; first edition 1954. Texts from 1936–1953.

PART ONE:

◦ GA 7: 7–36, "Die Frage nach der Technik" (1953) = "The Question Concerning Technology," translated by William Lovitt. In *The Question Concerning Technology and Other Essays*, 3–35. New York: Harper and Row, 1982.

◦ GA 7: 39–65, "Wissenschaft und Besinnung" (1953) = "Science and Reflection," translated by William Lovitt. In *The Question Concerning Technology and Other Essays*, 155–182. (See above.)

◦ GA 7: 69–98, "Überwindung der Metaphysik" (1936–1946) = "Overcoming Metaphysics," translated by Joan Stambaugh. In *The End of Philosophy*, 84–110. Chicago: University of Chicago Press, 2003; originally New York: Harper & Row, 1973.

◦ GA 7: 101–124. "Wer Ist Nietzsches Zarathustra?" = "Who Is Nietzsche's Zarathustra?" translated by David Farrell Krell. In *Nietzsche, Volume Two: The Eternal Recurrence of the Same*, 211–233. New York: Harper & Row, 1984.

PART TWO:

◦ GA 7: 129–143, "Was heißt Denken?" [not translated].

◦ GA 7: 147–164, "Bauen Wohnen Denken" = "Building Dwelling Thinking." In *Poetry, Language, Thought*, translated by Albert Hofstadter, 145–161. New York: Harper and Row, 1975. (Also in *Basic Writings*, rev. and expanded ed., edited by David Farrell Krell, 343–363. San Francisco: HarperSanFrancisco, 1993. (See also GA 79.)

◦ GA 7: 167–187. "Das Ding" = "The Thing." In *Poetry, Language, Thought*, 165–186. (See above.)

◦ GA 7: 191–208, ". . . dichterisch wohnet der Mensch . . ." = ". . . Poetically Man Dwells. . . " In *Poetry, Language, Thought*, 213–229. (See above.)

PART THREE:

◦ GA 7: 213–234, "*Logos* (Heraklit, Fragment 50)" = "*Logos* (Heraclitus, Fragment B 50)," translated by David Farrell Krell and Frank Capuzzi. In *Early Greek Thinking*, 59–78. New York: Harper and Row, 1985.

◦ GA 7: 237–261, "*Moira* (Parmenides VIII, 34–41)" = "Moira (Parmenides VIII, 34–41)," translated by Frank Capuzzi. In *Early Greek Thinking*, 79–101. (See previous entry.)

◦ GA 7: 265–288, "*Aletheia* (Heraklit Fragment 16) = "*Aletheia* (Heraclitus, Fragment B 16)," translated by Frank Capuzzi. In *Early Greek Thinking*, 102–123. (See previous entry.)

• GA 8: *Was heißt Denken?* ed., Paola-Ludovika Coriando, 2002; first edition 1954. Lecture course 1951–1952.

◦ *What Is Called Thinking?* Translated by Fred D. Wieck and J. Glenn Gray. New York: Harper and Row, 1968.

• GA 9: *Wegmarken*. Edited by Friedrich-Wilhelm von Herrmann, 1976; first edition 1967. Texts from 1919–1958.
  ◦ *Pathmarks*. Edited by William McNeill. New York: Cambridge University Press, 1998.
  ◦ GA 9: 1–44, "Anmerkungen zu Karl Jaspers *Psychologie der Weltanschauungen* (1919/21)" = "Comments on Karl Jasper's *Psychology of Worldviews* (1919/21)," translated by John van Buren, 1–38.
  [Also, "Critical Comments on Karl Jasper's *Psychology of Worldviews*," translated by Theodore Kisiel. In *Becoming Heidegger*, edited by Theodore Kisiel and Thomas Sheehan, 111–149. Evanston, IL: Northwestern University Press, 2007.]
  ◦ GA 9: 45–67, "Phänomenologie und Theologie (1927)" = "Phenomenology and Theology (1927)," translated by James G. Hart and John C. Maraldo, 39–54.17. (See GA 80.)
  ◦ GA 9: 68–77, "Einige Hinweise auf Hauptgesichtpunke für das theologische Gespräch über 'Das Problem eines nichtobjektivierenden Denkens und Sprechens in her heutigen Theologie" (11 March 1964) = "The Theological Discussion of 'The Problem of a Nonobjectifying Thinking and Speaking in Today's Theology'—Some Pointers to Its Major Aspects," translated by James G. Hart and John C. Maraldo, 54–62.
  ◦ GA 9: 79–101, "Aus der letzten Marburger Vorlesung (1928)" = "From the Last Marburg Lecture Course (1928)," translated by Michael Heim, 63–81.
  ◦ GA 9: 103–122, "Was ist Metaphysik? (1929)" = "What Is Metaphysics?," translated by David Farrell Krell, 82–96.
  ◦ GA 9: 123–175, "Vom Wesen des Grundes (1929)" = "On the Essence of Ground (1929)," translated by William McNeill, 97–135.
  ◦ GA 9: 177–202, "Vom Wesen der Wahrheit (1930)" = "On the Essence of Truth (1930)," translated by John Sallis, 136–154.
  ◦ GA 9: 203–238, "Platons Lehre von der Wahrheit (1931/32, 1940)" = "Plato's Doctrine of Truth (1931/32, 1940)," translated by Thomas Sheehan, 155–182.
  ◦ GA 9: 239–301: "Vom Wesen und Begriff der Φύσις. Aristoteles, Physik B, 1 (1939)" = "On the Essence and Concept of Φύσις in Aristotle's *Physics* B, 1 (1939)," translated by Thomas Sheehan, 183–230.
  ◦ GA 9: 303–312, "Nachwort zu 'Was ist Metaphysik?' (1943)" = "Postscript to 'What Is Metaphysics?' (1949)," 231–238.
  ◦ GA 9: 313–364, "Brief über den Humanismus (1946)" = "Letter on 'Humanism,' (1946)," translated by Frank A. Capuzzi, 239–276.
  ◦ GA 9: 365–383, "Einleitung zu 'Was ist Metaphysik?' (1949)" = "Introduction to 'What Is Metaphysics?' (1949)," translated by Walter Kaufmann, 177–290.
  ◦ GA 9: 385–426, "Zur Seinsfrage (1955)" = "On the Question of Being," translated by William McNeill, 291–322.
  ◦ GA 9: 427–444, "Hegel und die Griechen (1958)" = "Hegel and the Greeks (1958)," translated by Robert Metcalf, 323–336.

- GA 9: 445–480, "Kants These über das Sein (1961)" = "Kant's Thesis about Being (1961)," translated by Ted E. Klein Jr. and William E. Pohl, 337–363.

- GA 10: *Der Satz vom Grund*. Edited by Petra Jaeger, 1997; first edition 1957. Lecture course 1955–1956.
  - *The Principle of Reason*. Translated by Reginald Lilly. Bloomington: Indiana University Press, 1991.

- GA 11: *Identität und Differenz*. Edited by Friedrich-Wilhelm von Herrmann, 2006.
  - GA 11: 3–26, "Was ist das—die Philosophie? (1955)" = *What Is Philosophy?* Translated by Jean T. Wilde and William Kluback. London: Rowman and Littlefield, 2003; originally New York: Twayne, 1958.
  - GA 11: 27–50, "Identität und Differenz" = "Identity and Difference." In *Identity and Difference*, translated by Joan Stambaugh, 21–41. Chicago: University of Chicago, 2002; originally New York: Harper & Row, 1969. (See GA 79.)
    [Also GA 11: 31–50, "Der Satz der Identität (1957)" without GA 11: 29, "Vorwort" = "The Principle of Identity," revised by Jerome Veith. In *The Heidegger Reader*, edited by Günter Figal, 284–294. Bloomington: Indiana University Press, 2009.]
  - GA 11: 113–124, "Die Kehre (1949)" = "The Turning," translated by William Lovitt. In *The Question Concerning Technology and Other Essays*, edited by William Lovitt, 36–49. New York: Harper & Row, 1977. (See GA 79.)
  - GA 11: 125–140 (= GA 79: 81–96), "Grundsätze des Denkens (1957)" = "Basic Principles of Thinking: Freiburg Lectures 1957. Lecture I," translated by Andrew J. Mitchell. In *Bremen and Freiburg Lectures*, 77–91. Bloomington: Indiana University Press, 2012. (See GA 79.)
    [Earlier: "Principles of Thinking," translated by James G. Hart and John C. Maraldo. In *The Piety of Thinking*, 46–58. Bloomington: Indiana University Press, 1976.]
  - GA 11: 143–152, "Ein Vorwort. Brief an Pater William J. Richardson (1962)" = "Preface," translated by William J. Richardson, in his *Heidegger: Through Phenomenology to Thought*, viii–xxii. The Hague: Martinus Nijhoff, 1963; fourth expanded edition. New York: Fordham University Press, 2003.
  - GA 11: 153–161, "Brief an Takehiko Kojima (1963)" (not translated).

- GA 12: *Unterwegs zur Sprache*. Edited by Friedrich-Wilhelm von Herrmann, 1985; first edition 1959.
  - GA 12: 7–30, "Die Sprache" (1950) = "Language." In *Poetry, Language, Thought*, translated by Albert Hofstadter, 189–210. New York: Harper and Row, 1975.
  - GA 12: 33–78, "Die "Sprache im Gedicht. Ein Erörterung von Georg Trakls Gedicht" (1952) = "Language in the Poem: A Discussion on Georg Trakl's Poetic Work," translated by Peter D. Hertz. In *On the Way to Language*, 159–198. New York: Harper and Row, 1971.

- ◦ GA 12: 81–146, "Aus einem Gespräch von der Sprache. Zwischen einem Japaner und einem Fragenden" (1953/54) = "A Dialogue on Language," translated by Peter Hertz. In *On the Way to Language*, 1–54. (See above.)
- ◦ GA 12: 149–204, "Das Wesen der Sprache" (1957–1958) = "The Nature of Language," translated by Peter Hertz. In *On the Way to Language*, 57–108. (See above.)
- ◦ GA 12: 207–225, "Das Wort" (1958) = "Words," translated by Joan Stambaugh. In *On the Way to Language*, 139–156. (See above.)
- ◦ GA 12: 229–257, "Der Weg zur Sprache" (1959) = "The Way to Language," translated by Peter Hertz. In *On the Way to Language*, 111–136. [Also in *Basic Writings*, rev. and exp. ed. by David Farrell Krell, 397–426. San Francisco: HarperSanFrancisco, 1993.]

- GA 13: *Aus der Erfahrung des Denkens*. Edited by Hermann Heidegger. Texts from 1910–1976.
  - ◦ GA 13: 7, "Abendgang auf der Reichenau" (1916) = "Eventide on Reichenau," translated by William J. Richardson. In *Heidegger: Through Phenomenology to Thought*, by William J. Richardson, 1. The Hague: Martinus Nijhoff, 1963; fourth exp. ed. New York: Fordham University Press, 2003.
  - ◦ GA 13: 9–13, "Schöpferische Landschaft: Warum bleiben wir in der Provinz? (1933)" = "Why Do I Stay in the Provinces?" translated by Thomas Sheehan. In *Heidegger: The Man and the Thinker*, edited by Thomas Sheehan, 27–30. Chicago: Precedent Publishing, 1981.
  - ◦ GA 13: 35–36, "Chorlied aus der Antigone des Sophocles (1943)" = [The First Choral Ode from Sophocles' *Antigone*, lines 279–330]. In *Introduction to Metaphysics*, translated by Gregory Fried and Richard Polt. New Haven, CT: Yale University Press, 2000; 2nd revised and expanded edition, 2014, 156.6–158.3.
  - ◦ GA 13: 37–74 (which mostly correspond to GA 77: 105.18–123.25; 138.16–153.19; and 156.13–157.10) = "Zur Erörterung der Gelassenheit. Aus einem Feldweggespräch über das Denken (1944/45)" = "Ἀγχιβασίη: A Triadic Conversation on a Country Path between a Scientist, a Scholar, and a Guide." In *Country Path Conversations*, translated by Bret W. Davis, 68.5–80.24; 90.1–100.25; 102.26–103.4. Bloomington: Indiana University Press, 2010. [Earlier: "Conversation on a Country Path about Thinking," translated by John M. Anderson and E. Hans Freund. In *Discourse on Thinking: A Translation of Gelassenheit*, edited by, John M. Anderson and E. Hans Freund, 58–90. New York: Harper & Row, 1966.]
  - ◦ GA 13: 75–86, "Aus der Erfahrung des Denkens (1947)" = "The Thinker as Poet". In *Poetry, Language, Thought*, translated by Albert Hofstadter, 1–14. New York: Harper and Row, 1975.
  - ◦ GA 13: 87–90, "Der Feldweg (1949)" = "The Pathway," translated by Thomas F. O'Meara, revised by Thomas Sheehan. In *Heidegger: The Man and the Thinker*, 45–67. (See above.)
  - ◦ GA 13: 93–109, "Zu einem Vers von Mörike. Ein Briefwechsel mit Martin Heidegger von Emil Staiger (1951)" = "The Staiger-Heidegger Correspondence," translated by Arthur A. Grugan. *Man and World* 14 (1981): 291–307.

- GA 13: 111, "Was heißt Lesen? (1954)" = "What Is Reading?" translated by John Sallis. In *Reading Heidegger: Commemorations*, 2. Bloomington: Indiana University Press, 1993.
- GA 13: 123–125, "Die Sprache Johann Peter Hebels (1955)" = "The Language of Johann Peter Hebel," translated by Jerome Veith. In *The Heidegger Reader*, edited by Günter Figal, 295–297. Bloomington: Indiana University Press, 2009.
- GA 13: 133–150, "Hebel—der Hausfreund (1957)" = "Hebel—Friend of the House," translated by Bruce V. Foltz and Michael Heim. In *Contemporary German Philosophy*, edited by Darrel E. Christensen, 3:89–101. University Park: Pennsylvania State University Press, 1983.
- GA 13: 185–198, "Adalbert Stifters 'Eisengeschichte' (1964)" = *Adalbert Stifter's "Ice Tale," by Martin Heidegger*. Translated by Miles Groth. New York: Nino Press, 1993.
- GA 13: 203–210, "Die Kunst und der Raum (1969)" = "Art and Space," translated by Jerome Veith. In *The Heidegger Reader*, edited by Günter Figal, 305–309. Bloomington: Indiana University Press, 2009.
  [Earlier, "Art and Space," translated by Charles Seibert, *Man and World* 6 (1973): 3–8.]
- GA 13: 221–224, "Gedachtes (1970)" = "Thoughts," translated by Keith Hoeller. *Philosophy Today* 20, no. 4 (1976): 286–290.
- GA 13: 229 (see GA 81: 289.1–14), "Sprache (1972)" = "Language," translated by Thomas Sheehan. *Philosophy Today* 20, no. 4 (1976): 291.
- GA 13: 231–235, "Der Fehl heilger Namen (1974)" = "The Want of Holy Names," translated by Bernhard Radloff. *Man and World* 18 (1985): 261–267.

- GA 14: *Zur Sache des Denkens*. Edited by Friedrich-Wilhelm von Herrmann, 2007; first edition 1962.
  - GA 14: 3–104 = *On Time and Being*. Translated by Joan Stambaugh, Chicago: University of Chicago Press, 2002; originally New York: Harper & Row, 1972.
  - GA 14: 105–119, "Beilagen" [not translated].
  - GA 14: 129–132: "Brief an Edmund Husserl vom 22. Oktober 1927" = "Heidegger's Letter and Appendices," translated by Thomas Sheehan. In *Psychological and Transcendental Phenomenology and The Confrontation with Heidegger (1927–1931)*, by Edmund Husserl, edited and translated by Thomas Sheehan and Richard E. Palmer, 136–139. Dordrecht: Kluwer Academic Publishers, 1997.
  - GA 14: 145–148: "Über das Zeitverständnis in der Phänomenologie und im Denken der Seinsfrage (1968)" = "The Understanding of Time in Phenomenology and in the Thinking of the Being-Question," translated by Thomas Sheehan and Frederick Elliston. *The Southwestern Journal of Philosophy* 10, no. 2 (Summer, 1979): 199–200.

- GA 15: *Seminare*. Edited by Curd Ochwadt, 1986. Parts of this were first published as *Heraclitus* (1970) and *Vier Seminare* (1977).
  - GA 15: 9–263 = *Heraclitus Seminar, 1966/67 with Eugen Fink*. Translated by Charles H. Seibert. Tuscaloosa: University of Alabama Press, 1979.

- ◦ GA 15: 270–400 = *Four Seminars*. Translated by Andrew Mitchell and François Raffoul. Bloomington: Indiana University Press, 2003.
- ◦ GA 15: 425–429: "Zürcher Seminar" (6 November 1951): not translated.

- GA 16: *Reden und andere Zeugnisse eines Lebens, 1910–1976*. Edited by Hermann Heidegger, 2000. Texts from 1910–1976.
  - ◦ GA 16: 3–6 (no. 1), "*Per mortem ad vitam*" = "*Per mortem ad vitam*," translated by John Protevi and John van Buren. In *Supplements*, edited by John van Buren, 35–37. Albany: State University of New York Press, 2002.
  - ◦ GA 16: 7–8 (no. 2), review of Fr. W. Förster, *Autorität und Freiheit*, translated by John Protevi. In *Becoming Heidegger*, edited by Theodore Kisiel and Thomas Sheehan, 13–14. Evanston, IL: Northwestern University Press, 2007.
  - ◦ GA 16: 9 (no. 3), review of Ad. Jos. Cüppers, *Versiegelte Lippen*, translated by John Protevi. *Graduate Faculty Philosophy Journal* 14–15 (1991): 495.
  - ◦ GA 16: 10 (no. 4), review of Johannes Jörgensen, *Das Reisebuch*, translated by John Protevi. *Graduate Faculty Philosophy Journal* 14–15 (1991): 495.
  - ◦ GA 16: 11–14 (no. 5), "Zur philosophischen Orientierung für Akademiker" = "On a Philosophical Orientation for Academics (*Der Akademiker* 3, No. 5 [March 1911]: 66–67)," translated by John Protevi. In *Becoming Heidegger*, 14–16. (See no. 2 above.)
  - ◦ GA 16: 16 (no. 7), "Auf stillen Pfaden (Juli 1911)" = "On Still Paths," translated by Allan Blunden. In *Martin Heidegger: A Political Life*, by Hugo Ott, translated by Allan Blunden, 68. London: Basic Books, 1993.
  - ◦ GA 16: 18–28 (no. 9), "Religionspsychologie und Unterbewusstsein" = "Psychology of Religion and the Subconscious," translated by John Protevi. *Graduate Faculty Philosophy Journal* 14–15 (1991): 503–517.
  - ◦ GA 16: 29–30 (no. 10), review of Jos. Gredt, *Elementa philosophiae aristotelico-thomisticae*, translated by John Protevi. *Graduate Faculty Philosophy Journal* 14–15 (1991): 517–519.
  - ◦ GA 16: 31 (no. 11), review of *Bibliothek wertvoller Novellen und Erzählungen*, edited by D. Hellinghaus, translated by John Protevi. *Graduate Faculty Philosophy Journal* 14–15 (1991): 519.
  - ◦ GA 16: 32 (no. 12), "Lebenslauf (Zur Promotion 1913)" = "Curriculum Vitae 1913," translated by Thomas Sheehan. In *Becoming Heidegger*, 6–7. (See no. 2 above.)
  - ◦ GA 16: 36 (no. 14), "Trost (1915)" = "Consolation," translated by Allan Blunden. In *Martin Heidegger: A Political Life*, by Hugo Ott, 88–89. (See no. 7 above.)
  - ◦ GA 16: 37–39 (no. 15), "Lebenslauf (Zur Habilitation 1915)" = "Curriculum Vitae 1915," translated by Thomas Sheehan. In *Becoming Heidegger*, 7–9. (See no. 2 above.)
  - ◦ GA 16: 41–45 (no. 17), "Vita (1922)" = "Vita," translated by Theodore Kisiel. In *Becoming Heidegger*, 106–109. (See no. 2 above.)
  - ◦ GA 16: 49–51 (no. 18), "Wilhelm Diltheys Forschungsarbeit und der Kampf um eine historische Weltanschauung" (Kasseler Vorträge, 16–25 April 1925) = "Wilhelm Dilthey's Research and the Current Struggle for a Historical Worldview,

(1925)," translated by Charles Bambach. In *Supplements*, edited by John Van Buren, 147–176. Albany: State University of New York Press, 2002. See GA 80.

- GA 16: 56–60 (no. 21), "Edmund Husserl zum siebenzigsten Geburtstag (8. April 1929)" = "For Edmund Husserl on his Seventieth Birthday (April 8, 1929)," translated by Thomas Sheehan. In *Psychological and Transcendental Phenomenology and the Confrontation with Heidegger*, by Edmund Husserl, edited and translated by Thomas Sheehan and Richard E. Palmer, 475–477. Dordrecht: Kluwer Academic Publishers, 1997.
- GA 16: 104 (no. 48), "Nach der Rede des Führers am 17. Mai 1933" = "Announcement from the University." In *German Existentialism*, edited and translated by Dagobert D. Runes, 48. New York: Philosophical Library, 1965.
- GA 16: 107–117 (no. 51), "Die Selbstbehauptung der deutschen Universität" = "The Self-Assertion of the German University," translated by Lisa Harries. In *Martin Heidegger and National Socialism: Questions and Answers*, edited by Günter Neske and Emil Kettering, 5–13. New York: Paragon House, 1990.
- GA 16: 125–126 (no. 59), "Arbeitsdienst und Universität" (14 June 1933) = "Labor Service and the University." In *German Existentialism*, edited and translated by Dagobert D. Runes, 21–22. (See no. 48 above.)
- GA 16: 156 (no. 80), "Hier ist es leider sehr trostlos (22. August 1933)" = "Letter to Carl Schmitt," no translator listed, *Telos* 72 (summer 1987): 132.
- GA 16: 184–185 (no. 101), "Zum Semesterbeginn vgl. Universitätsführer Wintersemester 1933/34) = "German Students," translated by William S. Lewis. In *The Heidegger Controversy*, edited by Richard Wolin, 46–47. New York: Columbia University Press, 1991.
- GA 16: 188–189 (no. 103), "Aufruf zur Wahl (10. November 1933)" = "German Men and Women!" translated by William S. Lewis. In *The Heidegger Controversy*, 47–49. (See no. 101 above.)
- GA 16: 190–193 (no. 104), "Ansprache am 11. November 1933 in Leipzig" = "Declaration of Support for Adolf Hitler and the National Socialist State (November 11, 1933)," translated by William S. Lewis. In *The Heidegger Controversy*, 49–52. (See no. 101 above.)
- GA 16: 227 (no. 121), "Das Geleitwort der Universität (6. January 1934)" = "A Word from the University," translated by William S. Lewis. In *The Heidegger Controversy*, 52–53. (See no. 101 above.)
- GA 16: 232–237 (no. 124), "Zur Eröffnung der Schulungskurse für die Notstandsarbeiter der Stadt an der Universität (22. January 1934)" = "National Socialist Education (January 22, 1934)," translated by William S. Lewis. In *The Heidegger Controversy*, 55–60. (See no. 101 above.)
- GA 16: 238–239 (no. 125), "Der Ruf zum Arbeitsdienst (23. Januar 1934)" = "The Call to the Labor Service (January 23, 1934)," translated by William S. Lewis. In *The Heidegger Controversy*, 53–55. (See no. 101 above.)
- GA 16: 372–394 (no. 180), "Das Rektorat 1933/34—Tatsachen und Gedanken (1945)" = "The Rectorate 1933/34: Facts and Thoughts," translated by Lisa Harries. In *Martin Heidegger and National Socialism*, 15–32. (See no. 51 above.)

◦ GA 16: 397–404 (no. 182), "Antrag auf die Wiedereinstellung in die Lehrtätigkeit (Reintegrierung—4. November 1945)" = "Letter to the Rector of Freiburg University, November 4, 1945," translated by William S. Lewis. In *The Heidegger Controversy*, 61–66. (See no. 101 above.)
◦ GA 16: 423–425 (no. 189) "Was ist das Sein selbst? (12. September 1946)" = "The Basic Question of Being as Such," translated by Parvis Emad and Kenneth Maly. *Heidegger Studies* 2 (1986): 4–6.
◦ GA 16: 430–431.24 (no. 192), "Zu 1933–1945 (Brief an Marcuse, 20 Januar 1948)" = "Letter from Heidegger to Marcuse of January 20, 1948," translated by Richard Wolin. In *The Heidegger Controversy*, edited by Richard Wolin, 162–163. (See no. 101 above.)
◦ GA 16: 452–453 (no. 204), "Betr. die Notiz 'Hanfstaengl contra Heidegger' in der Münchner Süddeutschen Zeitung von Mittwoch, den 14. Juni 1950" = "On My Relation to National Socialism," translated by Frank Meklenberg. *Semiotext(e)* 4, no. 2 (1982): 253–254.
◦ GA 16: 517–529 (no. 224), "Gelassenheit (30. Oktober 1955)" = "Memorial Address," translated by John M. Anderson and E. Hans Freund. In *Discourse on Thinking*, edited by John M. Anderson and E. Hans Freund, 43–57. New York: Harper and Row, 1966.
◦ GA 16: 552–557 (no. 230), "Die Kunst und das Denken (18. Mai 1958)" = "Art and Thinking," translated by Hannah Arendt. In *Listening to Heidegger and Hisamatsu*, by Alfred L. Copley, 48–78. Kyoto: Bokubi Press.
◦ GA 16: 565–567 (no. 234), "Dank bei der Verleihung des staatlichen Hebelgedenkpreises (10. Mai 1960)" = "Acknowledgment on the Conferment of the National Hebel Memorial Prize," translated by Miles Groth. *Delos* 19/20, April 1997 (Summer-Winter 1994): 30–34.
◦ GA 16: 574–582 (no. 236), "700 Jahre Meßkirch (Ansprache zum Heimatabend am 22. Juli 1961)" = "Messkirch's Seventh Centennial," translated by Thomas Sheehan. *Listening: Journal of Religion and Culture* 1–3 (1973): 40–57.
◦ GA 16: 620–633 (no. 246) "Zur Frage nach der Bestimmung der Sache des Denkens (30. Oktober 1965)" = "On the Question Concerning the Determination of the Matter for Thinking," translated by Richard Capobianco and Marie Göbel. *Epoché: A Journal for the History of Philosophy* 14, no. 2 (Spring 2010): 213–223.
◦ GA 16: 650–651 (no. 252), "Grußwort an das Symposium über Heideggers Philosophie an der Duquesne-Universität in Pittsburgh 15./16. Oktober 1966 (20. September 1966)" = "A Letter from Martin Heidegger," translated by Arthur H. Schrynemakers. In *Heidegger and the Path of Thinking*, edited by John Sallis, 9–10. Pittsburgh: Duquesne University Press, 1970.
◦ GA 16: 652–683 (no. 253) "Spiegel-Gespräch mit Martin Heidegger (23. September 1966)" = "'Only a God Can Save Us': The *Spiegel* Interview (1966)," translated by William J. Richardson. In *Heidegger: The Man and the Thinker*, edited by Thomas Sheehan, 45–67. Chicago: Precedent Publishing, 1981.
[Also "*Der Spiegel* Interview with Martin Heidegger," translated by Jerome Veith. In *The Heidegger Reader*, edited by Günter Figal, 313–333. Bloomington: Indiana University Press, 2009.]

- GA 16: 684–686 (no. 254), "Grußwort an das Heidegger-Symposium Chicago 11./12. November 1966 (20. Oktober 1966)" = "A Letter from Heidegger," translated by William J. Richardson. In *Heidegger and the Quest for Truth*, edited by Manfred S. Frings, 19–21. Chicago: Quadrangle.
- GA 16: 702–710 (no. 262) "Martin Heidegger im Gespräch" = "Martin Heidegger in Conversation," translated by Lisa Harries. In *Martin Heidegger and National Socialism*, 81–87. (See no. 51 above.)
- GA 16: 721–722 (269), "Gruß und Dank an die Teilnehmer der Heidegger-Konferenz in Honolulu auf Hawai 17.–21. November 1969" = "Letter from Heidegger," translated by Albert Borgmann. In "Introduction to the Symposium and Reading of a Letter from Martin Heidegger," edited by Winfield E. Nagley. *Philosophy East and West* 20 (1970): 221.
- GA 16: 744–745 (no. 279), "Ein Grußwort für das Symposium in Beirut November 1974" = "A Greeting to the Symposium in Beirut in November 1974," translated by Lisa Harries. In *Martin Heidegger and National Socialism*, 253–254. (See no. 51 above.)
- GA 16: 747–748 (282), "Neuzeitliche Naturwissenschaft und moderne Technik—Grußwort an die Teilnehmer des zehnten Colloquiums von 14.–16. Mai 1976 in Chicago (11. April 1976)" = "Modern Natural Science and Technology," translated by John Sallis. In *Radical Phenomenology*, edited by John Sallis, 1–2. Englewood Cliffs, NJ: Humanities Press, 1978.
- GA 16: 759–760 (no. 285) "Gedenkworte zu Schlageter (26. Mai 1933 vor der Universität)" = "Schlageter (May 26, 1933)," translated by William S. Lewis. In *The Heidegger Controversy*, 40–42. (See no. 101 above.)
- GA 16: 761–763 (no. 286), "Die Universität im Neuen Reich (30. Juni 1933)" = "The University in the New Reich," translated by William S. Lewis. In *The Heidegger Controversy*, 43–45. (See no. 101 above.)

II. Lecture Courses 1919–1944

At Marburg University, 1923–1928

- GA 17: *Einführung in die phänomenologische Forschung*. Edited by Friedrich-Wilhelm von Herrmann, 1994; lecture course, winter 1923–1924.
  - *Introduction to Phenomenological Research*. Translated by Daniel O. Dahlstrom. Bloomington, Indiana University Press, 2005.

- GA 18: *Grundbegriffe der aristotelischen Philosophie*. Edited by Mark Michalski, 2002; lecture course, summer 1924.
  - *Basic Concepts of Aristotelian Philosophy*. Translated by Robert D. Metcalf and Mark B. Tanzer. Bloomington: Indiana University Press, 2009.

- GA 19: *Platon: Sophistes*. Edited by Ingeborg Schüßler, 1992; lecture course, winter 1924–1925.
  - *Plato's Sophist*. Translated by Richard Rojcewicz and André Schuwer. Bloomington: Indiana University Press, 1997.

• GA 20: *Prolegomena zur Geschichte des Zeitbegriffs*. Edited by Petra Jaeger, 1979; lecture course, summer 1925.
  ◦ *History of the Concept of Time: Prolegomena*. Translated by Theodore Kisiel. Bloomington, Indiana: Indiana University Press, 1985.

• GA 21: *Logik. Die Frage nach der Wahrheit*. Edited by Walter Biemel, 1976; lecture course, winter 1925–1926.
  ◦ *Logic: The Question of Truth*. Edited and translated by Thomas Sheehan. Bloomington: Indiana University Press, 2010.

• GA 22: *Die Grundbegriffe der antiken Philosophie*. Edited by Franz-Karl Blust, 1993; lecture course, summer 1926.
  ◦ *Basic Concepts of Ancient Philosophy*. Translated by Richard Rojcewiz. Bloomington: Indiana University Press, 2008.

• GA 23: *Geschichte der Philosophie von Thomas v. Aquin bis Kant*. Edited by Helmut Vetter, 2006; lecture course, winter 1926–1927.

• GA 24: *Die Grundprobleme der Phänomenologie*. Edited by Friedrich-Wilhelm von Herrmann, 1975; lecture course, summer 1927.
  ◦ *The Basic Problems of Phenomenology*. Translated by A. Hofstadter. Bloomington: Indiana University Press, 1982.

• GA 25: *Phänomenologische Interpretation der Kants Kritik der reinen Vernunft*. Edited by Ingtraud Görland, 1977; lecture course, winter 1927–1928.
  ◦ *Phenomenological Interpretation of Kant's Critique of Pure Reason*. Translated by Parvis Emad and Kenneth Maly. Bloomington: Indiana University Press, 1997.

• GA 26: *Metaphysiche Anfangsgründe der Logik im Ausgang von Leibniz*. Edited by Klaus Held, 1978; lecture course, summer 1928.
  ◦ *The Metaphysical Foundations of Logic*. Translated by Michael Heim. Bloomington: Indiana University Press, 1984.

At Freiburg University, 1928–1944

• GA 27: *Einleitung in die Philosophie*. Edited by Otto Saame and Ina Saame-Speidel, 1996; lecture course, winter 1928–1929.
  ◦ *Introduction to Philosophy*. Translated by Eric Sean Nelson and Virginia Lyle Jennings. Bloomington: Indiana University Press, forthcoming.

• GA 28: *Der deutsche Idealismus (Fichte, Schelling, Hegel) und die philosophische Problemlage der Gegenwart*. Edited by Claudius Strube, 1997; lecture course, summer 1929.
  ◦ *German Idealism*. Translated by Peter Warnek. Bloomington: Indiana University Press, forthcoming.

- GA 29/30: *Die Grundbegriffe der Metaphysik. Welt—Endlichkeit—Einsamkeit.* Edited by Friedrich-Wilhelm von Herrmann, 1983; lecture course, winter 1929–1930.
    - *The Fundamental Concepts of Metaphysics: World, Finitude, Solitude.* Translated by William McNeill and Nicholas Walker. Bloomington: Indiana University Press, 1995.

- GA 31: *Vom Wesen der menschlichen Freiheit. Einleitung in die Philosophie.* Edited by Hartmut Tietjen, 1982; lecture course, summer 1930.
    - *The Essence of Human Freedom: An Introduction to Philosophy.* Translated by Ted Sadler. London: Bloomsbury (Continuum), 2002.

- GA 32: *Hegels Phänomenologie des Geistes.* Edited by Ingtraud Görland, 1980; lecture course, winter 1930–1931.
    - *Hegel's Phenomenology of Spirit.* Translated by Parvis Emad and Kenneth Maly Bloomington: Indiana University Press, 1988.

- GA 33: *Aristoteles, Metaphysik Θ 1–3. Vom Wesen und Wirklichkeit der Kraft.* Edited by Heinrich Hüni, 1981; lecture course, summer, 1931.
    - *Aristotle's Metaphysics Θ 1–3: On the Essence and Actuality of Force.* Translated by Walter Brogan and Peter Warnek. Bloomington: Indiana University Press, 1995.

- GA 34: *Vom Wesen der Wahrheit. Zu Platons Höhlengleichnis und Theätet.* Edited by Hermann Mörchen, 1988; lecture course, winter 1931–1932.
    - *The Essence of Truth: On Plato's Cave Allegory and the Theaetetus.* Translated by Ted Sadler. London: Bloomsbury (Continuum), 2002.

- GA 35: *Der Anfang der abendländischen Philosophie: Auslegung des Anaximander und Parmenides.* Edited by Peter Trawny, 2011; lecture course, summer 1931.
    - *The Beginning of Western Philosophy: Anaximander and Parmenides.* Translated by Richard Rojcewiz. Bloomington: Indiana University Press, 2015, forthcoming.

- GA 36/37: *Sein und Wahrheit: 1. Die Grundfrage der Philosophie* (lecture course, summer 1933), *2. Vom Wesen der Wahrheit* (lecture course, winter 1933/34). Edited by Hartmut Tietjen, 2001.
    - *Being and Truth.* Translated by Gregory Fried and Richard Polt. Bloomington: Indiana University Press, 2010.

- GA 38: *Logik als die Frage nach dem Wesen der Sprache.* Edited by Günter Seubold, 1998; lecture course summer 1934.
    - *Logic as the Question Concerning the Essence of Language.* Translated by Wanda Torres Gregory and Yvonne Unna. Albany: State University of New York Press, 2009.

- GA 39: *Hölderlins Hymnen "Germanien" und "Der Rhein,"* ed. Susanne Ziegler, 1980; lecture course, winter 1934–1935.
    - *Hölderlin's Hymns "Germanien" and "Der Rhein,"* trans. William McNeill and Julia Ireland. Bloomington: Indiana University Press, 2014.

- GA 40: *Einführung in die Metaphysik*. Edited by Petra Jaeger, 1983; lecture course, summer, 1935; first edition 1953.
    - *Introduction to Metaphysics*. Translated by Gregory Fried and Richard Polt. New Haven, CT: Yale University Press, 2000; 2nd revised and expanded edition, 2014.

- GA 41: *Die Frage nach dem Ding. Zu Kants Lehre von den transzendentalen Grundsätzen*. Edited by Petra Jaeger, 1984; lecture course, winter 1935–1936; first edition 1962.
    - *What Is a Thing?* Translated by W. B. Barton and Vera Deutsch. Chicago: Henry Regnery, 1967.

- GA 42: *Schelling: Vom Wesen der menschlichen Freiheit (1809)*. Edited by Ingrid Schüßler, 1988; lecture course, summer 1936; first edition 1971.
    - *Schelling's Treatise on the Essence of Human Freedom*. Translated by Joan Stambaugh. Athens: Ohio University Press, 1985.

- GA 43: *Nietzsche: Der Wille zur Macht als Kunst*. Edited by Bernd Heimbüchel, 1985; lecture course, winter 1936–1937; first edition 1961: see GA 6.1.
    - GA 43: 3–274.8 (= GA 6.1: 1–224.10) = *Nietzsche, Volume One: The Will to Power as Art*. Edited and translated by David Farrell Krell. New York: Harper & Row, 1979.

- GA 44: *Nietzsches metaphysische Grundstellung im abendländischen Denken: Die ewige Wiederkehr des Gleichen*. Edited by Marion Heinz, 1986; lecture course, summer 1937; first edition 1961: see GA 6.1.
    - GA 44: 1–233 (= GA 6.1: 225–423) = *Nietzsche, Volume Two: The Eternal Recurrence of the Same*. Edited and translated by David Farrell Krell. New York: Harper & Row, 1984.

- GA 45: *Grundfragen der Philosophie. Ausgewählte "Probleme" der "Logik."* Edited by Friedrich-Wilhelm von Herrmann, 1984; lecture course, winter 1937–1938.
    - *Basic Questions of Philosophy: Selected "Problems" of "Logic."* Translated by Richard Rojcewicz and André Schuwer. Bloomington: Indiana University Press, 1994.

- GA 46: *Zur Auslegung von Nietzsches II. Unzeitgemäßer Betrachtung "Vom Nutzen und Nachteil der Historie für das Leben."* Edited by Hans-Joachim Friedrich, 2003; lecture course, winter 1938–1939.

- GA 47: *Nietzsches Lehre vom Willen zur Macht als Erkenntnis*. Edited by Eberhard Hanser,1989; lecture course, summer 1939; first edition 1961.
    - GA 47: 1–295 (= GA 6.1: 425–594) = "The Will to Power as Knowledge," translated by Joan Stambaugh and David Farrell Krell. In *Nietzsche, Volume Three: The Will to Power as Knowledge and as Metaphysics*, edited by David Farrell Krell, 1–183. New York: Harper & Row, 1987.

- GA 48: *Nietzsche: Der europäische Nihilismus* (1986); lecture course, second trimester 1940; first edition 1961.
    - GA 48: 1–332.32 (= GA 6, 2: 23–229) = "European Nihilism," translated by Frank A. Capuzzi. In *Nietzsche, Volume Four: Nihilism*, edited by David Farrell Krell, 1–196. New York: Harper & Row, 1982.

- GA 49: *Die Metaphysik des deutschen Idealismus. Zur erneuten Auslegung von Schelling: Philosophische Untersuchungen über das Wesen der menschlichen Freiheit und die damit zusammenhängenden Gegenstände (1809)*. Edited by Günter Seubold, 1991.

- GA 50: *1. Nietzsches Metaphysik (1941–42); 2. Einleitung in die Philosophie—Denken und Dichten (1944–45)*. Edited by Petra Jaeger, 1990; lecture course preparations for courses never given; first edition of the first course, 1961.
    - GA 50: 1–87 (= GA 6, 2: 231–300), "Die fünf Grundworte der Metaphysik Nietzsches" (1940) = "Nietzsche's Metaphysics," translated by Frank A. Capuzzi and David Farrell Krell. In *Nietzsche, Volume Three: The Will to Power as Knowledge and as Metaphysics*, edited by David Farrell Krell, 185–251. New York: Harper & Row, 1987.
    - GA 50: 90–160 *Einleitung in die Philosophie—Denken und Dichten = Introduction to Philosophy—Thinking and Poetizing*. Translated by Phillip Jacques Braunstein. Bloomington: Indiana University Press, 2011.

- GA 51: *Grundbegriffe*. Edited by Petra Jaeger, 1981; lecture course, summer 1941.
    - *Basic Concepts*. Translated by Gary Aylesworth. Bloomington: Indiana University Press, 1993.

- GA 52: *Hölderlins Hymne "Andenken."* Edited by Walter Biemel, 1982; lecture course, 1941–1942.
    - *Hölderlin's Hymn "Andenken."* Translated by William McNeill and Julia Ireland. Bloomington: Indiana University Press, forthcoming.

- GA 53: *Hölderlins Hymne "Der Ister."* Edited by Walter Biemel, 1984; lecture course, summer, 1942.
    - *Hölderlin's Hymn "The Ister."* Translated by William McNeill and Julia Davis. Bloomington: Indiana University Press, 1996.

- GA 54: *Parmenides*. Edited by Manfred S. Frings, 1982; lecture course, winter, 1942–1943.

- *Parmenides*. Translated by André Schuwer and Richard Rojcewicz. Bloomington: Indiana University Press, 1992.

- GA 55: *Heraklit. 1. Der Anfang des abendländischen Denkens* (lecture course, summer 1943), *2. Logik. Heraklits Lehre vom Logos* (lecture course, summer 1944). Edited by Manfred S. Frings, 1979.
  - GA 55: 252.28–270.13 = "*Logos* and Language" , translated by Jerome Veith. In *The Heidegger Reader*, edited by Günter Figal, 239–252. Bloomington: Indiana University Press, 2009.

At Freiburg University, 1919–1923

- GA 56/57: *Zur Bestimmung der Philosophie. 1. Die Idee der Philosophie und das Weltanschauungsproblem* (lecture course, War Emergency Semester, winter 1919); *2. Phänomenologie und transzendentale Wertphilosophie* (lecture course, summer 1919); *3. Anhang: Über das Wesen der Universität und des akademischen Studiums* (lecture course, summer, 1919). Edited by Bernd Heimbüchel, 1987.
  - *Towards the Definition of Philosophy: 1. The Idea of Philosophy and the Problem of Worldview; 2. Phenomenology and Transcendental Philosophy of Value; with a transcript of the lecture course "On the Nature of the University and Academic Study (Freiburg Lecture-courses 1919)*. Translated by Ted Sadler. New Brunswick, NJ: Bloomsbury (Athlone), 2000.

- GA 58: *Grundprobleme der Phänomenologie*. Edited by Hans-Helmut Gander, 1992; lecture course, winter 1919–1920.
  - *Basic Problems of Phenomenology: Winter Semester 1919/20*. Translated by Scott M. Campbell. London: Bloomsbury, 2013.

- GA 59: *Phänomenologie der Anschauung und des Ausdrucks*. Edited by Claudius Strube, 1993; lecture course, summer 1920.
  - *Phenomenology of Intuition and Expression*. Translated by Tracy Colony. London: Bloomsbury (Continuum), 2010.

- GA 60: *Phänomenologie des religiösen Lebens. 1. Einleitung in die Phänomenologie der Religion* (ed. Matthias Jung and Thomas Regehly; lecture course, winter 1920–1921); *2. Augustinus und der Neuplatonismus* (ed. Claudius Strube; lecture course, summer 1921); *3. Die philosophischen Grundlagen der mittelalterlichen Mystik* (ed. Claudius Strube; preparation for a course not given), 1995.
  - *Phenomenology of Religious Life: 1. Introduction to the Phenomenology of Religion; 2. Augustine and Neo-Platonism; 3. The Philosophical Foundations of Medieval Mysticism*. Translated by Matthias Fritsch and Jennifer Anna Gosetti-Ferencei. Bloomington: Indiana University Press, 2004.

- GA 61: *Phänomenologische Interpretationen zu Aristoteles. Einführung in die phänomenologische Forschung*. Edited by Walter Bröcker and Käte Bröcker-Oltmanns, 1985; lecture course, winter, 1921–1922.

- *Phenomenological Interpretations of Aristotle: Initiation into Phenomenological Research*. Translated by Richard Rojcewicz. Bloomington: Indiana University Press, 2001.

- GA 62: *Phänomenologische Interpretationen ausgewählter Abhandlungen des Aristoteles zur Ontologie und Logik*. Edited by Günther Neumann, 2005; lecture course, summer 1922.
  - GA 62: 345–375, "Phänomenologische Interpretationen zu Aristoteles (Anzeige der hermeneutischen Situation). Ausarbeitung für die Marburger und die Göttinger Philosophische Fakultät (Herbst 1922)" = "Indication of the Hermeneutical Situation," translated by Michael Baur, revised Jerome Veith. In *The Heidegger Reader*, edited by Günter Figal, 38–61. Bloomington: Indiana University Press, 2009. [Also "Phenomenological Interpretations with Respect to Aristotle: Indication of the Hermeneutical Situation," edited and translated by Theodore Kisiel. In *Becoming Heidegger*, edited by Theodore Kisiel and Thomas Sheehan, 155–174. Evanston, IL: Northwestern University Press, 2007.]

- GA 63: *Ontologie. Hermeneutik der Faktizität*. Edited by Käte Bröcker-Oltmanns, 1988; lecture course, summer 1923.
  - *Ontology: The Hermeneutics of Facticity*. Translated by John van Buren. Bloomington: Indiana University Press, 1999.

III. Papers, Conferences, and Thoughts Not Published during Heidegger's Lifetime

- GA 64: *Der Begriff der Zeit*. Edited by Friedrich-Wilhelm von Herrmann, 2004.
  - GA 64: 3–103, "Der Begriff der Zeit (1924)" = *The Concept of Time: The First Draft of Being and Time*. Translated by Ingo Farin with Alex Skinner. London: Bloomsbury (Continuum), 2011.
  - GA 64: 107–125, "Der Begriff der Zeit (Vortrag 1924)" = *The Concept of Time*. Translated by William McNeill. Oxford: Blackwell, 1992. [Also "The Concept of Time," translated by Theodore Kisiel. In *Becoming Heidegger*, edited by Theodore Kisiel and Thomas Sheehan, 200–213. Evanston, IL: Northwestern University Press, 2006.]

- GA 65: *Beiträge zur Philosophie (Vom Ereignis)*. Edited by Friedrich-Wilhelm von Herrmann, 1989; notes from 1936–1938.
  - *Contributions to Philosophy: Of the Event*. Translated by Richard Rojcewicz and Daniela Vallega-Neu. Bloomington: Indiana University Press, 2012. [Earlier: *Contributions to Philosophy: (From Enowning)*. Translated by Parvis Emad and Kenneth Maly. Bloomington: Indiana University Press, 1999.]

- GA 66: *Besinnung*. Edited by Friedrich-Wilhelm von Herrmann, 1997; notes, 1938–1939.
  - *Mindfulness*. Translated by Parvis Emad and Thomas Kalary. London: Bloomsbury (Continuum), 2006.

- GA 67: *Metaphysik und Nihilism: 1. Die Überwindung der Metaphysik; 2. Das Wesen des Nihilismus*. Edited by Hans-Joachim Friedrich, 1999.

- GA 68: *Hegel*. Edited by Ingrid Schüßler, 1993.
    - *Hegel*. Translated by Joseph Arel and Niels Feuerhahn. Bloomington: Indiana University Press, 2015, forthcoming.

- GA 69: *Die Geschichte des Seyns*. Edited by Peter Trawny, 1998.
    - *History of Beyng*. Translated by Jeffrey Powell and William McNeill. Bloomington: Indiana University Press, forthcoming.

- GA 70: *Über den Anfang. 1. Die Geschichte des Seyns (1938/40); 2. KOINON. Aus der Geschichte des Seyns (1939/40)*. Edited by Paola-Ludovika Coriando, 2005.

- GA 71: *Das Ereignis*. Edited by Friedrich-Wilhelm von Herrmann, 2009; notes 1941–1942.
    - *The Event*. Translated by Richard Rojcewicz. Bloomington: Indiana University Press, 2013.

- GA 72: *Die Stege des Anfangs*. Edited by Friedrich-Wilhelm von Hermann; notes from 1944. Forthcoming.

- GA 73: *Zum Ereignis-Denken*. Edited by Peter Trawny; 2 volumes. 2013.
    - GA 73, 1: 710–712: "Die Armut" (27 June 1945) = "Poverty," translated by Thomas Kalary and Frank Schalow. In *Heidegger, Translation and the Task of Thinking*, 3–10. New York: Springer, 2011.

- GA 74: *Zum Wesen der Sprache und Zur Frage nach der Kunst*. Edited by Thomas Regehly, 2010.

- GA 75: *Zu Hölderlin. Griechenlandreisen. Edited by* Curt Ochwadt, 2000.
    - GA 75: 213–245, "Aufenthalte" = *Sojourns: The Journey to Greece*. Translated by John-Panteleimon Manoussakis. Albany: State University of New York Press, 2005.

- GA 76: *Leitgedanken zur Entstehung der Metaphysik, der neuzeitlichen Wissenschaft und der modernen Technik*. Edited by Claudius Strube, 2009; texts from 1935–1955.

- GA 77: *Feldwege-Gespräche 1944/45*. Edited by Ingrid Schüβler, 2007; first edition 1995.
    - *Country Path Conversations*. Translated by Bret W. Davis. Bloomington: Indiana University Press, 2010.

      [GA 77: 105.18–123.25; 138.16–153.19; and 156.13–157.10 mostly correspond to GA 13: 37–74, an earlier translation of which = "Conversation on a Country Path about Thinking," translated by John M. Anderson and E. Hans Freund. In

Discourse on Thinking: A Translation of Gelassenheit, edited by John M. Anderson and E. Hans Freund. New York: Harper & Row, 1966.]

- GA 78: *Der Spruch des Anaximander*. Edited by Ingeborg Schüßler, 2010; text of a lecture course not given; presumably written in the summer 1942.

- GA 79: *Bremer and Freiburger Vorträge*. Edited by Petra Jaeger, 1994. Parts of this volume were first published in *Vorträge und Aufsätze*, 1954 (See GA 7.)
  - *Bremen and Freiburg Lectures: Insight into That Which Is and Basic Principles of Thinking*. Translated by Andrew J. Mitchell. Bloomington: Indiana University Press, 2012.
  [Earlier, from the lecture series "*Einblick in das* was ist" (1949):]
  - GA 79: 5–21 (= GA 7: 165–187), "Das Ding" = "The Thing." In *Poetry, Language, Thought*, translated by Albert Hofstadter, 165–186. New York: Harper & Row, 1971.
  - GA 79: 68–77 (= GA 11: 113–124), "Die Kehre" (1949) = "The Turning." In *The Question Concerning Technology and Other Essays*, translated by William Lovitt, 33–49. New York: Harper and Row, 1982.
  [Earlier, from the lecture series "*Grundsätze des Denkens*" (1957):]
  - GA 79: 81–96 (= GA 11: 127–140), "Grundsätze des Denkens" (1957) = "Principles of Thinking," translated by James G. Hart and John C. Maraldo. In *The Piety of Thinking*, edited by James G. Hart and John C. Maraldo, 46–58. Bloomington: Indiana University Press, 1976.
  - GA 79: 115–129 (= GA 11: 31–110), "Identität und Differenz (1957)" = "Identity and Difference." In *Identity and Difference*, translated by Joan Stambaugh, 23–41. Chicago: University of Chicago, 2002; originally New York: Harper & Row, 1969.

- GA 80: *Vorträge*. Edited by Hartmut Tietjen (forthcoming). Some of these addresses have been translated:
  - "Frage und Urteil" (10 July 1915) = "Question and Judgment," translated by Theodore Kisiel. In *Becoming Heidegger*, edited by Theodore Kisiel and Thomas Sheehan, 52–59. Evanston, IL: Northwestern University Press, 2007.
  - "Wahrsein und Dasein. Aristoteles, *Ethica Nicomachea* VI." (December 1924) = "Being-There and Being-True According to Aristotle," translated by Brian Hansford Bowles. In *Becoming Heidegger*, 216–237. (See previous.)
  - See GA 13: 9–13, "Schöpferische Landschaft: Warum bleiben wir in der Provinz? (1933)" = "Why Do I Stay in the Provinces?" translated by Thomas Sheehan. In *Heidegger: The Man and the Thinker*, edited by Thomas Sheehan, 27–30. Chicago: Precedent Publishing, 1981.
  - "Wilhelm Diltheys Forschungsarbeit und der Kampf um eine historische Weltanschauung" (Kasseler Vorträge, 16–25 April 1925) = "Wilhelm Dilthey's Research and the Current Struggle for a Historical Worldview (1925)," translated by Charles Bambach. In *Supplements*, edited by John Van Buren, 147–176. Albany: State University of New York Press, 2002.

  - "Phänomenologie und Theologie. I. Teil: Die nichtphilosophischen als positive Wissenschaften und die Philosophie als transzendentale Wissenschaft" (8 July 1927 (= GA 9: 45–78) = "Phenomenology and Theology." In *Pathmarks*, edited by William McNeill, 39–62. New York: Cambridge University Press, 1998.

- GA 81: *Gedachtes*. Edited by Paola-Ludovika Coriando, 2007; texts from 1910–1975.
  - GA 81: 325–328 (= GA 13: 221–224) = "Thoughts," translated by Keith Hoeller. *Philosophy Today* 20, no. 4 (1976): 286–290.

- GA 82: *Zu eigenen Veröffentlichungen: Anmerkungen zu "Vom Wesen des Grundes"* (1936); *Eine Auseinandersetzung mit Sein und Zeit* (1936); *Laufende Anmerkungen zu Sein und Zeit* (1936). Forthcoming.

- GA 83: *Seminare: Platon—Aristoteles—Augustinus*. Edited by Mark Michalski, 2012. Seminars from 1928–1952.

- GA 84: *Seminare: Leibniz—Kant, Teil 1: Sommersemester 1931 bis Wintersemester 1935/36*. Edited by Günther Neumann, 2013. (The first of two volumes.)

- GA 85: *Seminar. Vom Wesen der Sprache. Die Metaphysik der Sprache und die Wesung des Wortes. Zu Herders Abhandlung "Über den Ursprung der Sprache."* Edited by Ingrid Schüßler, 1999; seminar, summer 1939.
  - *On the Essence of Language: The Metaphysics of Language and the Essencing of the Word: Concerning Herder's "Treatise On the Origin of Language."* Translated by Wanda Torres Gregory and Yvonne Unna. Albany: State University of New York Press, 2004.

- GA 86: *Seminare: Hegel—Schelling*. Edited by Peter Trawny, 2011.
  - GA 86: 55–184 = *Heidegger on Hegel's "Philosophy of Right": The 1934–35 Seminar and Interpretative Essays*. Edited and translated by Peter Trawny, Marcia Sá Cavalcante Schuback, and Michael Marder. London: Bloomsbury, 2014.

- GA 87: *Nietzsche. Seminare 1937 und 1944. 1. Nietzsches metaphysische Grundstellung (Sein und Schein); 2. Skizzen zu Grundbegriffe des Denkens*. Edited by Peter von Ruckteschell, 2004; seminars, summer semesters 1937 and 1944.

- GA 88: *Seminare (Übungen) 1937/38 und 1941/2. 1. Die metaphysische Grundstellung des abendländischen Denkens. 2. Einübung in das philosophische Denken*. Edited by Alfred Denker, 2008.

IV. Indications and Sketches

- GA 89: *Zollikoner Seminare*, forthcoming. See below: "B. Heidegger's Texts from Outside the Gesamtausgabe," under *Zollikoner Seminare.*

  - *Zollikon Seminars: Protocols, Conversations, Letters*. Edited by Medard Boss. Translated by Franz Mayr and Richard Askay. Evanston, IL: Northwestern University Press, 2001.

- GA 90: *Zu Ernst Jünger*. Edited by Peter Trawny, 2004.
  - GA 90: 235–239 and 253–260 = "On Ernst Jünger (1)" and "on Ernst Jünger (2)" (1939–1940), translated by Jerome Veith. In *The Heidegger Reader*, edited by Günter Figal, 189–206. Bloomington: Indiana University Press, 2009.

- GA 91: *Ergänzungen und Denksplitter*.

- GA 92: *Ausgewählte Briefe 1*.

- GA 93: *Ausgewählte Briefe 2*.

- GA 94: *Überlegungen II–VI (Schwarze Hefte 1931–1938)*. Edited by Peter Trawny, 2014.

- GA 95: *Überlegungen VII–XI (Schwarze Hefte 1938–1939)*. Edited by Peter Trawny, 2014.

- GA 96: *Überlegungen XII–XV (Schwarze Hefte 1939–1941)*. Edited by Peter Trawny, 2014.

- GA 97: *Anmerkungen II–V.*

- GA 98: *Anmerkungen VI–IX.*

- GA 99: *Vier Hefte I—Der Feldweg. Vier Hefte II—Durch Ereignis zu Ding und Welt.*

- GA 100: *Vigilae I, II.*

- GA 101: *Winke I, II.*

- GA 102: *Vorläufiges I–IV.*

B. Texts outside the *Gesamtausgabe*

"Aufzeichnungen zur Temporalität (Aus den Jahren 1925 bis 1927)," *Heidegger Studies* 14 (1998): 11–23.

"Dasein und Wahrsein nach Aristoteles" (manuscript)

Edited translation: *Becoming Heidegger: On the Trail of His Early Occasional Writings, 1910–1927*, edited by Theodore Kisiel and Thomas Sheehan, 218–234. Evanston, IL: Northwestern University Press, 2007.

"Der Encyclopaedia Britannica Artikel: Versuch einer zweiten Bearbeitung." In Edmund Husserl, *Phänomenologische Psychologie: Vorlesungen Sommersemester 1925*. Edited by Walter Biemel. Husserliana IX: 256–263. The Hague: Nijhoff, 1968.
Edited translation: Edmund Husserl, *Psychological and Transcendental Phenomenology and the Confrontation with Heidegger (1927–1931)*, edited and translated by Thomas Sheehan and Richard E. Palmer, Collected Works 6:107–116. Dordrecht: Kluwer, 1997.
[Also in *Becoming Heidegger: On the Trail of His Early Occasional Writings, 1910–1927*, edited by Theodore Kisiel and Thomas Sheehan, 306–313. Evanston, IL: Northwestern University Press, 2007.]

"Der Weg," manuscript. Available on request: tsheehan@stanford.edu.

"Die 'Seinsfrage' in *Sein und Zeit*," *Heidegger Studies* 27 (2011): 9–12.

Die Technik und die Kehre, Pfullingen, Germany: Günther Neske, 1962.

Être et Temps. Translated by Emmanuel Martineau. Paris: Authentica, 1985. http://t.m.p.free.fr/textes/Heidegger_etre_et_temps.pdf

Existence and Being. Edited by Werner Brock. Chicago: Regnery, 1949.

"Grundbegriffe der Metaphysik," lecture course 1929–1930. Nachschrift (verbatim transcript). Edited by Simon Moser, Simon Silverman Phenomenology Center, Pennsylvania State University Archives, State College, Pennsylvania. http://www.duq.edu/about/centers-and-institutes/simon-silverman-phenomenology-center/special-collections.

"Lettre à Monsieur Beaufret (23 novembre 1945)." In Martin Heidegger, *Lettre sur l'humanisme*, edited and translated by Roger Munier, new, revised edition, 180–185. Paris: Aubier, Éditions Montaigne, 1964.

Martin Heidegger/Elisabeth Blochmann, Briefwechsel 1918–1969. Edited by Joachim W. Storck. Marbach: Deutsches Literaturarchiv, 1989.

Schellings Abhandlung: Über das Wesen der menschlichen Freiheit (1809). Edited by Hildegard Feick, Tübingen: Max Niemeyer, 1971. (See GA 42.)
English translation: Martin Heidegger, *Schelling's Treatise on the Essence of Human Freedom*. Translated by Joan Stambaugh. Athens: Ohio University Press, 1985.

Überlieferte Sprache und technische Sprache. Edited by Hermann Heidegger. St. Gallen: Ecker, 1989.

"'Über Wesen und Begriff von Natur, Geschichte und Staat': Übung aus dem Wintersemester 1933/34." In *Heidegger-Jarhbuch 4–Heidegger under der Nationalsozialismus I, Dokumente*, edited by Alfred Denker and Holger Zaborowski, 53–88. Freiburg im Breisgau: Verlag Karl Alber, 2009.
Edited translation: Martin Heidegger, *Nature, History, State*, 1933–1934. Translated and edited by Gregory Fried and Richard Polt. With essays by Robert Bernasconi, Peter E. Gordon, Marion Heinz, Theodore Kisiel, and Slavoj Žižek. London: Bloomsbury, 2013.

Übungen im Lesen, winter semesters 1950–1951 and 1951–1952. Manuscript record by Ernst Tugendhat, Stanford University, Green Library Archives.

Zollikoner Seminare: Protokolle—Gespräche—Briefe. Edited by Medard Boss. Frankfurt am Main: Klostermann, 1987. (See GA 89.)

Edited translation: *Zollikon Seminars: Protocols, Conversations, Letters*. Edited by Medard Boss. Translated by Franz Mayr and Richard Askay. Evanston, IL: Northwestern University Press, 2001.
"Zum 'Brief' über den 'Humanismus,'" *Heidegger Studies* 26, 2010, 9–16.

OTHER TEXTS CITED

Aristotle. *Aristotelis opera*. Edited by Immanuel Bekker, Christian August Brandis, and Hermann Bonitz. 4 vols. Academia Regia Borussica [The Royal Prussian Academy]. Berlin: Georg Reimer, 1831.
———. *Aristotle's Metaphysics: A Revised Text with Introduction and Commentary*. Edited and translated by William David Ross. Oxford: Clarendon Press, 1924.
———. *Aristotle's Physics*. Translated by Hippocrates G. Apostle. Bloomington: Indiana University Press, 1969.
———. *Aristotle's Physics*. Translated by Richard Hope. Lincoln: University of Nebraska Press, 1961.
———. *Aristotle's Physics: A Guided Study*. Edited and translated by Joe Sachs. New Brunswick, NJ: Rutgers University Press, 1995.
———. *Physics*. Translated by. Philip H. Wicksteed and Francis M. Cornford. 2 vols. Cambridge, MA: Harvard University Press, 1934.
———. *Physics*. Translated by R. P. Hardie and R. K. Gaye. In *The Works of Aristotle*. Vol. 2. Great Books of the Western World, edited by Mortimer J. Adler. Chicago: Encyclopedia Britannica, 1952.
———. *Der Protreptikos des Aristoteles*. Edited and translated by Ingemar Düring. Frankfurt: Klostermann, 1969.
———. *The Works of Aristotle*. Edited by John Alexander Smith and William David Ross. 11 vols. Oxford: Clarendon Press, 1908–1952.
Beekes, Robert, with Lucien van Beek. *Etymological Dictionary of Greek*. 2 vols. Leiden: Brill, 2009.
Bekker, Immanuel, ed. *Suidae Lexicon*. Berlin: Georg Reimer, 1854.
Benjamin, B. V., et al. "Neurogrid: A Mixed-Analog-Digital Multichip System for Large-Scale Neural Simulations." In "Engineering Intelligent Electronic Systems Based on Computational Neuroscience," special issue, *Proceedings, IEEE* [Institute of Electrical and Electronics Engineers] 102, no. 5 (May 2014): 699–717. https://ieeexplore.ieee.org/stamp/stamp.jsp?tp=&arnumber=6807554.
Bradey, Ian. *The Annotated Gilbert and Sullivan*. 2 vols. Harmondsworth, UK: Penguin, 1984.
Braig, Carl. *Die Grundzüge der Philosophie: Abriß der Ontologie*. Freiburg im Breisgau: Herder, 1896.
Brock, Werner. "An Account of *Being and Time*." In *Existence and Being*, by Martin Heidegger. Chicago: Regnery, 1949.
Burckhardt, Jacob. *Griechische Kulturgeschichte*. 4 vols. 1898–1902. Reprint, Basel: Benno Schwabe, 1956–1957.
———. *The Greeks and Greek Civilization*. Edited by Oswyn Murray. Translated by Sheila Stern. London: HarperCollins, 1998.

Carroll, Lewis (Dodgson, Charles). *Through the Looking Glass*. 1871. Reprint, Cincinnati: Johnson and Hardin, 1920.

Cicero. *De natura deorum*. Translated by H. Rackham. Cambridge, MA: Harvard University Press, 1956.

———. *Tusculan Disputations*. Edited and translated by J. E. King. Cambridge, MA: Harvard University Press, 1950.

Dahlstrom, Daniel. *Heidegger's Concept of Truth*. Cambridge: Cambridge University Press, 2001.

Damascius. *Dubitationes et solutiones de primis principiis, in Platonis Parmenidem*. Edited by Carolus Aemelius Ruelle. 2 vols. Paris, 1889. Reprint, Amsterdam: Adolf M. Hakkert, 1966.

———. *De Principiis* in *Traité des premièrs principles*. Edited by Leendert Gerrit Westerink. Translated by Joseph Combès. 3 vols. Paris: Les Belles Lettres, 1986–1991.

De Waelhens, Alphonse. *La philosophie de Martin Heidegger*. Louvain: Institut Supérieur de Philosophie, 1942.

Diels, Hermann, ed. *Die Fragmente der Vorsokratiker*. 9th revised ed. Edited by Walter Kranz. 3 vols. Berlin-Grunewald: Weidmann, 1960.

———. *Ancilla to The Pre-Socratic Philosophers*. Translated by Kathleen Freeman, Cambridge, MA: Harvard University Press, 1951.

Dreyfus, Hubert L., and Mark A. Wrathall, eds. *A Companion to Heidegger*. London: Blackwell, 2005.

Einstein, Albert. *Essays in Physics*. New York: Philosophical Library, 1950.

Eliot, T. S. *The Complete Poems and Plays of T.S. Eliot*. Edited by Valerie Eliot. London: Faber and Faber, 1969.

Feuerbach, Ludwig. *Grundsätze der Philosophie der Zukunft* (1843). Volume 9 of *Gesammelte Werke*. Edited by Werner Schuffenhauer, 9: 264–341. Berlin: Akademie-Verlag, 1970.

———. *Principles of the Philosophy of the Future*. Translated by Manfred H. Vogel. Indianapolis: Hackett, 1986.

Finley, John Huston. *Four Stages of Greek Thought*. Stanford: Stanford University Press, 1966.

Geyl, Pieter, Arnold Toynbee, and Pitirim A. Sorokin. *The Pattern of the Past: Can We Discern It?* Boston: Beacon, 1949.

Gibson, William Ralph Boyce. "From Husserl to Heidegger: Excerpts from a 1928 Freiburg Diary." Edited by Herbert Spiegelberg. *Journal of the British Society for Phenomenology* 2 (1971): 58–81.

Glare, P. G. W., ed. *Oxford Latin Dictionary*. Oxford: Clarendon, 1982.

Goethe, Johann Wolfgang, *Die Wahlverwandtschaften* (1809). Edited by Christoph Siegrist et al. Volume 9 of *Sämtliche Werke*, edited by Karl Richter, 286–529. Munich: Carl Hanser, 1987.

———. *Elective Affinities*. Translated by David Constantine. Oxford: Oxford University Press, 1994.

———. *Elective Affinities*. Translated by R. J. Hollingdale. Harmondsworth, UK: Penguin, 1971.

Grimm, Jacob, and Wilhelm Grimm, *Deutsches Wörterbuch*. Originally 32 vols. Leipzig: S. Hirzel, 1854–1971.

Gurwitsch, Aron. Review of *Le Cogito dans la Philosophie de Husserl*, by Gaston Berger. *Philosophy and Phenomenological Research* 7, no. 4 (1947): 649–654.

Haugland, John. "Truth and Finitude: Heidegger's Transcendental Existentialism." In *Heidegger, Authenticity and Modernity: Essays in Honor of Hubert L. Dreyfus*. Edited by Mark Wrathall and Jeff Malpas, 1: 43–77. Cambridge, MA: MIT Press, 2000.

Hegel, G. F. W. *Philosophie der Weltgeschichte* [1830–1831]. Vol. 9 of *Sämtliche Werke*. Edited by Georg Lasson. Leipzig: Felix Meiner, 1923.

———. *Wissenschaft der Logik*. Vol. 11 of *Gesammelte Werke*. Edited by Friedrich Hogemann und Walther Jaeschke. Hamburg: Felix Meiner, 1978.

———. *The Science of Logic*. Edited and translated by George di Giovanni. Cambridge: Cambridge University Press, 2010.

Herodotus. *Histories*. http://www.sacred-texts.com/cla/hh/

Hölderlin, Friedrich. *Selected Poems and Fragments* [German and English]. Translated by Michael Hamburger. Edited by Jeremy Adler. London: Penguin, 1994.

Husserl, Edmund. *Die Krisis der europäischen Wissenschaften und die transzendentale Phänomenologie*. Edited by Walter Biemel. Husserliana VI. The Hague: Martinus Nijhoff, 1954.

———. *The Crisis of European Science and Transcendental Phenomenology*. Translated by David Carr. Evanston, IL: Northwestern University Press, 1970.

Husserl, Edmund. *Ideen zu einer reinen Phänomenologie und phänomenologischen Philosophie*. Book 1. Edited by Karl Schuhmann. Husserliana III. The Hague: Martinus Nijhoff, 1976.

———. *Ideas Pertaining to a Pure Phenomenology and to a Phenomenological Philosophy: General Introduction to a Pure Phenomenology*. Translated by Fred Kersten. Collected Works, vol. 2. The Hague: Martinus Nijhoff, 1980.

Husserl, Edmund. *Ideen zu einer reinen Phänomenologie und phänomenologischen Philosophie* Book 3, *Die Phänomenologie und die Fundamente der Wissenschaften*. Edited by Marly Biemel. (Husserliana V). The Hague: Martinus Nijhoff, 1952.

———. *Ideas Pertaining to a Pure Phenomenology and to a Phenomenological Philosophy*. Book 3, *Phenomenology and the Foundations of the Sciences*. Translated by Ted E. Klein and William E. Pohl. The Hague: Martinus Nijhoff, 1980.

Husserl, Edmund. *Logische Untersuchungen*. Edited by Ursula Panzer. Husserliana XIX, Books 1 and 2. The Hague: Nijhoff, 1984.

———. *Logical Investigations*. Translated by J. N. Findlay. 2 vols. London: Routledge Kegan Paul, 1970.

Husserl, Edmund. *Phänomenologische Psychologie: Vorlesungen Sommersemester 1925*. Edited by Walter Biemel. Husserliana IX. The Hague: Nijhoff, 1968.

———. *Psychological and Transcendental Phenomenology and the Confrontation with Heidegger (1927–1931)*. Edited and translated by Thomas Sheehan and Richard E. Palmer. Collected Works, vol. 6. Dordrecht: Kluwer, 1997.

Husserl, Edmund. "Über psychologische Begründung der Logik." *Zeitschrift für philosophische Forschung*, 13 (1959): 346–348.

———. "On the Psychological Grounding of Logic." Translated by Thomas Sheehan. In *Husserl: Shorter Writings*, edited by Peter McCormick and Fredrick Elliston, 146–147. Notre Dame, IN: Notre Dame University Press, 1981.

Jaeger, Werner, *Humanism and Theology*. Milwaukee, WI: Marquette University Press, 1943.

———. *Paideia: The Ideals of Greek Culture*. 3 vols. 2nd ed. New York: Oxford University Press, 1943–1945.

Jaran, François, and Christophe Perrin. *The Heidegger Concordance*. London: Bloomsbury, 2013.

Jaspers, Karl. *Notizien zu Martin Heidegger*. Edited by Hans Saner. Munich: R. Piper & Co., 1978.

———. *Philosophische Autobiographie*. Expanded ed. Munich: R. Piper & Co., 1977.

Joyce, James. *Ulysses*. New York: Modern Library, 1961.

Kant, Immanuel. *Critique of Pure Reason*. Edited and translated by Paul Guyer and Alan Wood. Cambridge: Cambridge University Press, 1998.

Kisiel, Theodore. "The Demise of *Being and Time*: 1927–1930." In *Heidegger's Being and Time*, edited by Richard Polt, 189–214. Lanham, MD: Rowman and Littlefield, 2005.

Kluge, Friedrich. *Etymologisches Wörterbuch der deutschen Sprache*. Edited by Walther Mitzka. 1883. Reprint, 18th edition, Berlin: Walter de Gruyter & Co., 1960.

Langan, Thomas. *The Meaning of Heidegger*. New York: Columbia University Press, 1959.

Locke, John. *Two Treatises of Government and a Letter Concerning Toleration*. Edited by Ian Shipiro. New Haven, CT: Yale University Press, 2003.

Luther, Wilhelm. *"Wahrheit" und "Lüge" im ältesten Griechentum*. Borna-Leipzig: Noske, 1935.

McDougall, Walter A."'*C'est magnifique, mais ce n'est pas l'histoire!*': Some Thoughts on Toynbee, McNeill, and the Rest of Us." *Journal of Modern History* 58, no. 1 (March 1986): 19–42.

Mao Zedong. "On the Correct Handling of Contradictions Among the People." *People's Daily* (Beijing), 19 June 1957, p. 1. http://www.marxists.org/reference/archive/mao/selected-works/volume-5/mswv5_58.htm.

Marx, Karl. *Capital: A Critique of Political Economy*. Vol. 1. Edited by Frederick Engels. Translated by Samuel Moore and Edward Aveling. New York: International Publishers, 1967.

———. *Capital: A Critique of Political Economy*. Vol. 1. Translated by Ben Fowkes. New York: Vintage/Random House, 1976.

———. *Das Kapital: Kritik der Politischen Ökonomie, Erster Band* (Hamburg, 1867). In *Marx-Engels Gesamtausgabe* (MEGA), 2, 5 [= Zweite Abteilung, Band 5]. Berlin: Dietz, 1983.

Marx, Karl, and Friedrich Engels. *Marx Engels Gesamtausgabe* (MEGA). Berlin: Dietz, 1975–.

———. *Die deutsche Ideologie: Kritik der neuesten deutschen Philosophie in ihren Repräsentanten, Feuerbach, B. Bauer und Stirner, und des deutschen Sozialismus in seinen verschiedenen Propheten, 1845–1846*. Edited by V. Adortskij. Vienna: Vergag für Literatur und Politik, 1932.

Milton, John. "Paradise Lost." http://www.literature.org/authors/milton-john/paradise-lost/.

Müller, Max. *Existenzphilosophie im geistigen Leben der Gegenwart*. Heidelberg: Kerle, 1949.

Neske, Günther, ed. *Erinnerung an Martin Heidegger*. Pfullingen, Germany: Neske, 1977.

Neske, Günther, and Emil Kettering, eds. *Martin Heidegger and National Socialism: Questions and Answers*. Translated by Lisa Harries. New York: Paragon House, 1990.

Nietzsche, Friedrich. *Sämtliche Werke: Kritische Studienausgabe*. Edited by Giorgio Colli and Mazzino Montinari. Berlin: de Gruyter, 1980.

———. *The Will to Power*. Translated by Walter Kaufmann. New York: Random House, 1967.

Oxford English Dictionary, The Compact Edition. 2 vols. Glasgow: Oxford University Press, 1971.

Patrologia Graeca. http://graeca.patristica.net.

Patrologia Latina. http://latina.patristica.net.

Petzet, Heinrich Wiegand. *Auf einen Stern zugehen*. Frankfurt: Societät, 1983.

———. *Encounters and Dialogues with Martin Heidegger, 1929–1976*. Translated by Parvis Emad and Kenneth Maly. Chicago: University of Chicago Press, 1993.

Philoponus, Johannes. *In Aristotelis de anima.* Volume 15 of *Commentaria in Aristotelem Graeca*, edited by Michael Hayduck. Berlin: Reimer, 1897.

Pindar of Thebes. *The Works of Pindar*. Edited by Lewis Richard Farnell. 3 vols. London: Macmillan, 1932.

Plato. *Platonis opera*. Edited by John Burnet. 5 vols. Oxford: Clarendon, 1899–1906.

Plotinus. *Plotini opera*. Edited by Paul Henry and Hans-Rudolf Schwyzer. 3 vols. Paris: Desclée de Brouwer, and Brussels: L'Édition universelle, 1951.

———. *Enneads*. Translated by A. H. Armstrong. 7 vols. Cambridge, MA: Harvard University Press, 1966–1988, revised and corrected ed., 1989 and 1993.

Pöggeler, Otto. *Der Denkweg Martin Heideggers*. Pfullingen, Germany: Neske, 1963.

———. *Martin Heidegger's Path of Thinking*. Translated by Daniel Magurshak and Sigmund Barber, Atlantic Highlands, NJ: Humanities Press International, 1987.

Proclus. *The Elements of Theology: A Revised Text* (Greek and English). Edited and translated by E. R. Dodd. Oxford: Clarendon Press, 1933.

Prufer, Thomas. "A Protreptric: What Is Philosophy?" In *Studies in Philosophy and the History of Philosophy*, edited by John K. Ryan, 2:1–19. Washington, DC: The Catholic University of America Press, 1963.

Richardson, William J. *Heidegger: Through Phenomenology to Thought*. The Hague: Nijhoff, 1963.

Rorty, Richard. *The Consequences of Pragmatism: Essays, 1972–1980*. Minneapolis: University of Minnesota Press, 1982.

Ross, W. D. *Aristotle*. London: Methuen, 1923.

Rousselot, Pierre. *L'Intellectualisme de St. Thomas*. 2nd ed. Paris: Beauchesne, 1924.

———. *The Intellectualism of St. Thomas.* Translated by James E. O'Maloney. New York: Sheed and Ward, 1935.

Sartre Jean-Paul. *La nausée*. Paris: Gallimard, 1938.
———. *Nausea*. Translated by Lloyd Alexander. New York: New Directions, 1959.
Saffrey, Henri-Domenique. "Ἀγεωμέτρητος μηδεὶς εἰσίτω. Une inscription légendaire." *Revue des Études Grecques* 81 (1968): 67–87.
Schapiro, Meyer. "Nature of Abstract Art." *Marxist Quarterly* 1 (1937): 77–98.
———. "Abstract Art." In Meyer Schapiro, *Modern Art: 19th and 20th Centuries*, 185–232. New York: G. Braziller, 1978.
Sheehan, Thomas. "'Everyone Has to Tell the Truth': Heidegger and the Jews." *Continuum* 1, no. 1 (Autumn, 1990): 30 44.
———. "Heidegger and the Nazis." *New York Review of Books* 35, no. 10 (June 16, 1988): 38–47.
Specht, Friedrich. "Beiträge zur griechischen Grammatik." In *Zeitschrift für vergleichende Sprachforschung* (Vandenhoeck & Ruprecht), 59 1./2. (1931): 31–131.
Suárez, Francisco. Disputationes Metaphysicae. http://homepage.ruhr-uni-bochum.de/michael.renemann/suarez/index.html.
Textor, Mark. "States of Affairs." In *The Stanford Encyclopedia of Philosophy* (Summer 2012 ed.). Edited by Edward N. Zalta. http://plato.stanford.edu/entries/states-of-affairs/.
Thomas Aquinas. *Omnia Opera*. http://www.corpusthomisticum.org/iopera.html and http://www.dhspriory.org/thomas/.
Virgil. *P. Vergili Maronis Aeneidos*. http://www.thelatinlibrary.com/vergil/aen1.shtml.
———. *The Aeneid*. Translated by Robert Fagles. New York: Viking Penguin, 2006.
———. *Virgil, with an English Translation*. 2 vols. I: Eclogues, Georgics, Aeneid I–VI. Cambridge, MA: Harvard University Press, 1956.
Weekley, Ernest. *An Etymological Dictionary of Modern English*. 2 vols. 1921. Reprint, New York: Dover, 1967.
Whitman, Walt, *Leaves of Grass*. Edited by Malcolm Cowley. New York: Penguin, 1986.
Young-Bruehl, Elisabeth. *Hannah Arendt: For Love of the World*. New Haven, CT: Yale University Press, 1982.

Index of German, English, and Latin Terms

Index of Greek Terms